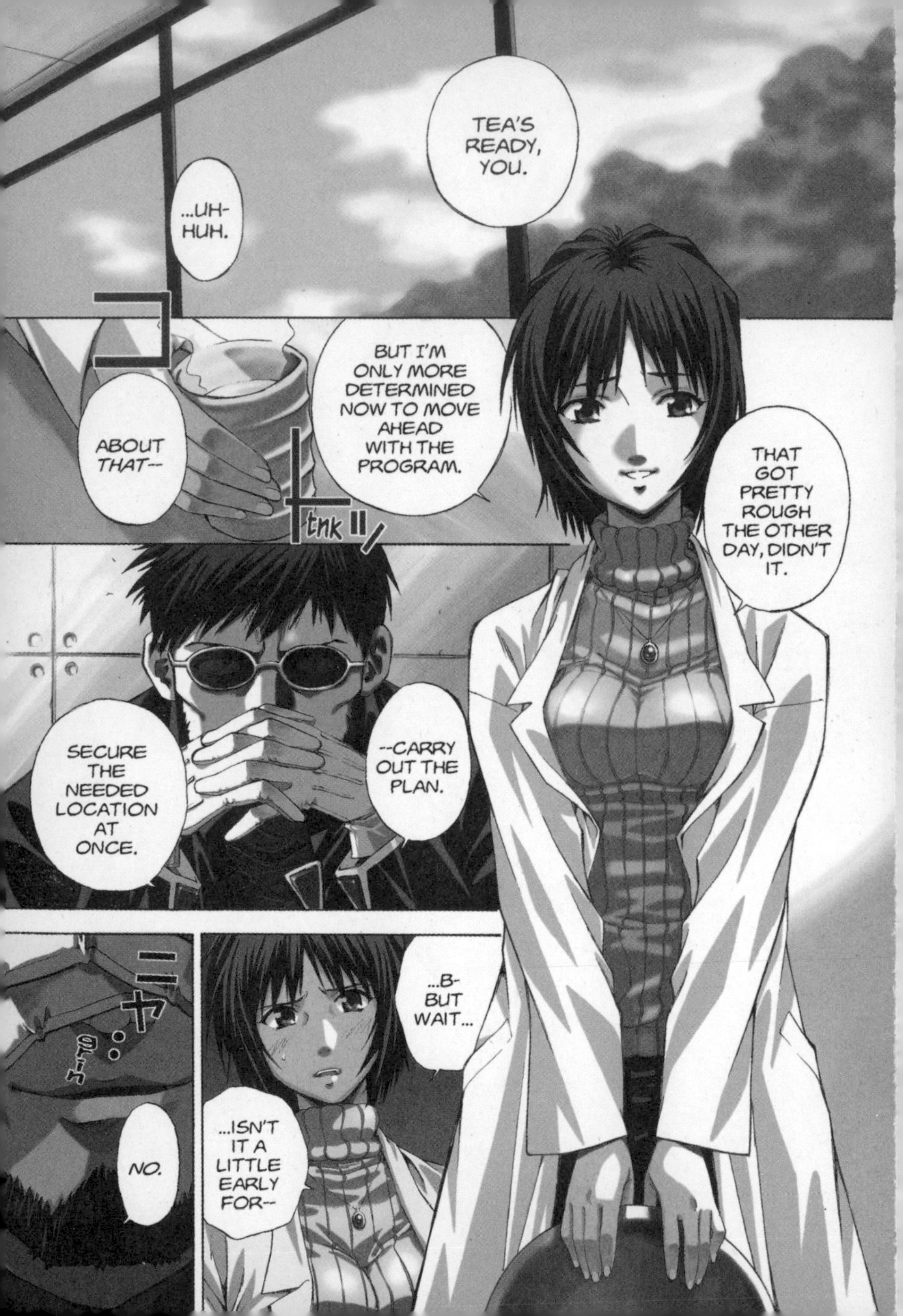
TEA'S READY, YOU.
...UH-HUH.
THAT GOT PRETTY ROUGH THE OTHER DAY, DIDN'T IT.
コト
tnk
ABOUT THAT--
BUT I'M ONLY MORE DETERMINED NOW TO MOVE AHEAD WITH THE PROGRAM.
--CARRY OUT THE PLAN.
SECURE THE NEEDED LOCATION AT ONCE.
...B-BUT WAIT...
...ISN'T IT A LITTLE EARLY FOR--
ニヤ..
grin
NO.

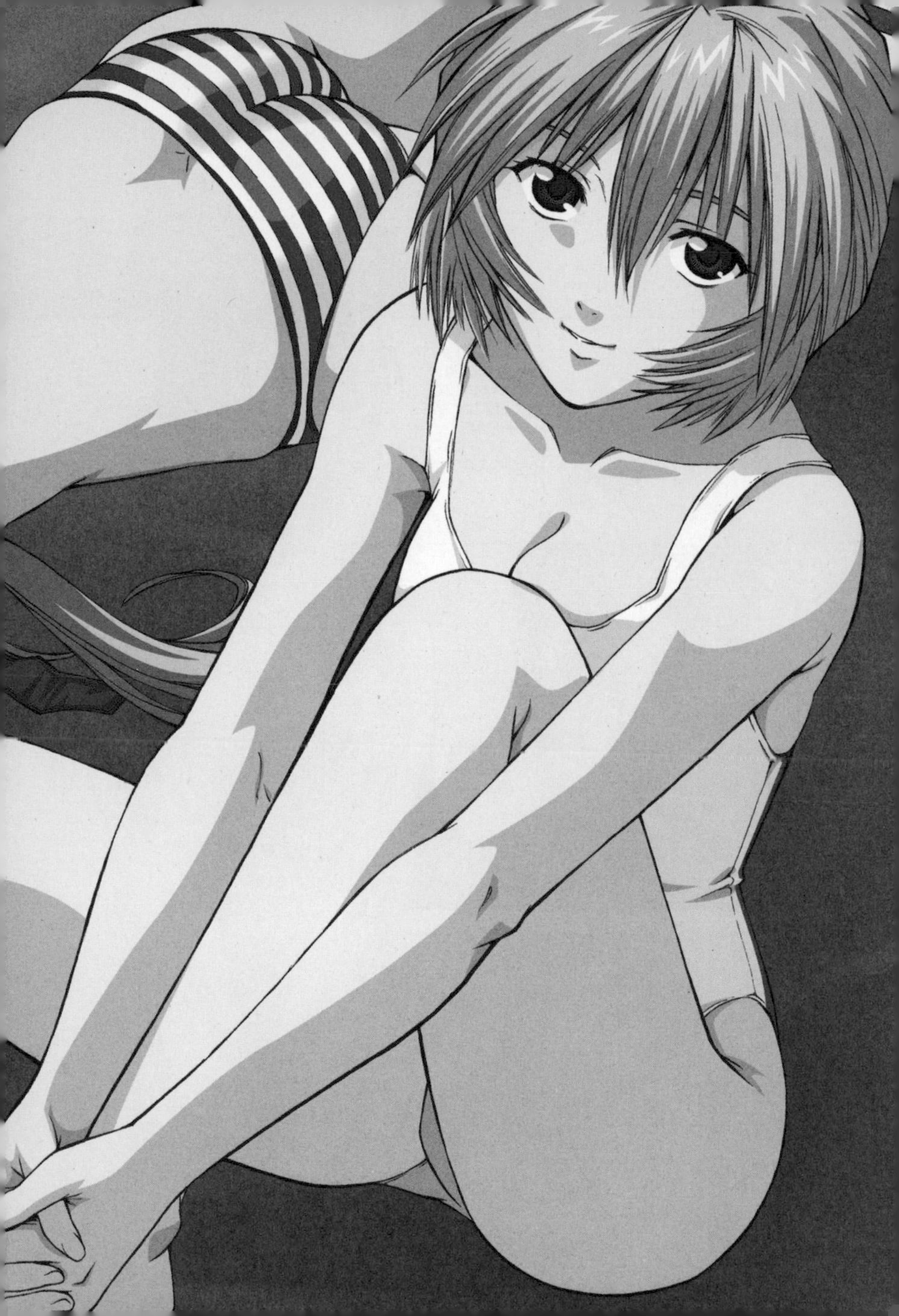

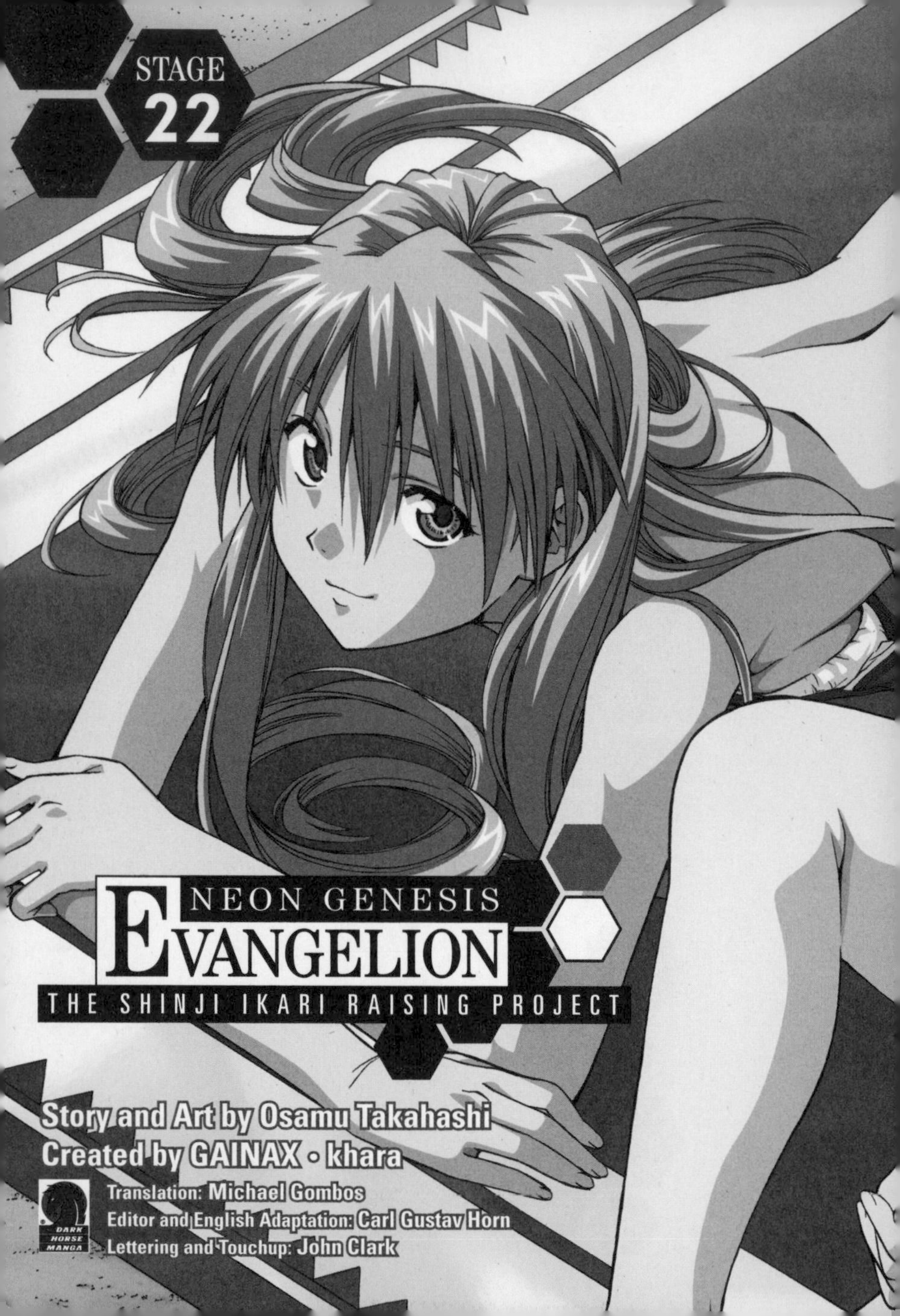
STAGE 22
NEON GENESIS EVANGELION
THE SHINJI IKARI RAISING PROJECT
Story and Art by Osamu Takahashi
Created by GAINAX • khara
Translation: Michael Gombos
Editor and English Adaptation: Carl Gustav Horn
Lettering and Touchup: John Clark
DARK HORSE MANGA

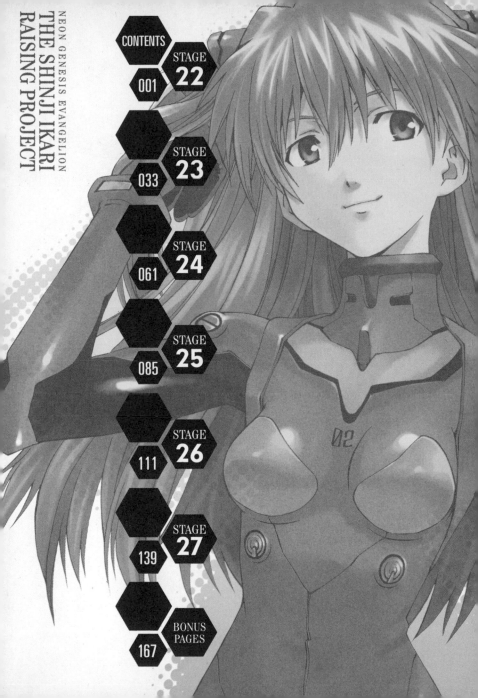

NEON GENESIS EVANGELION
THE SHINJI IKARI
RAISING PROJECT

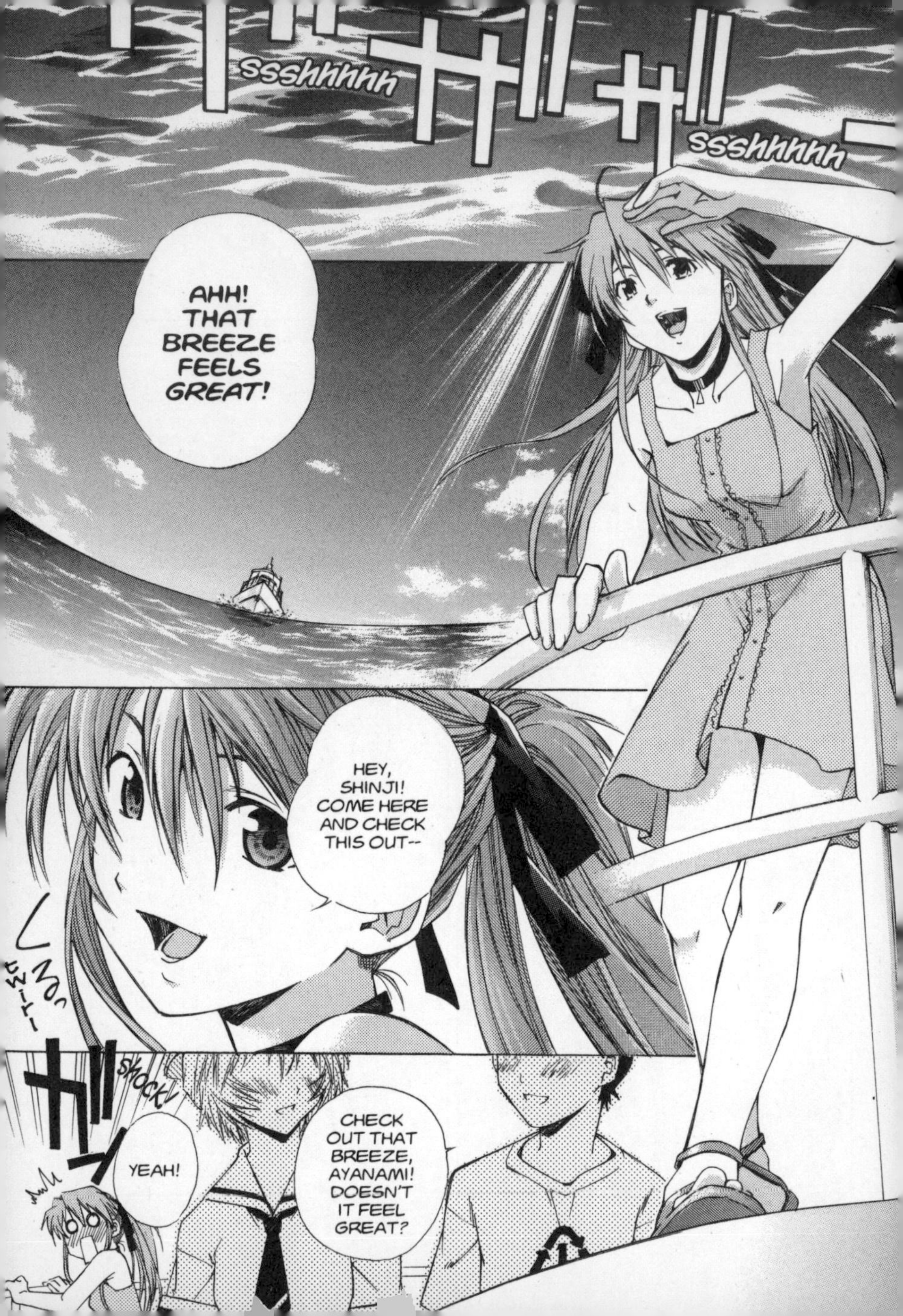
SSSHHHHH
SSSHHHHH
AHH! THAT BREEZE FEELS GREAT!
HEY, SHINJI! COME HERE AND CHECK THIS OUT--
TWIRL
CHECK OUT THAT BREEZE, AYANAMI! DOESN'T IT FEEL GREAT?
SHOCK!
YEAH!

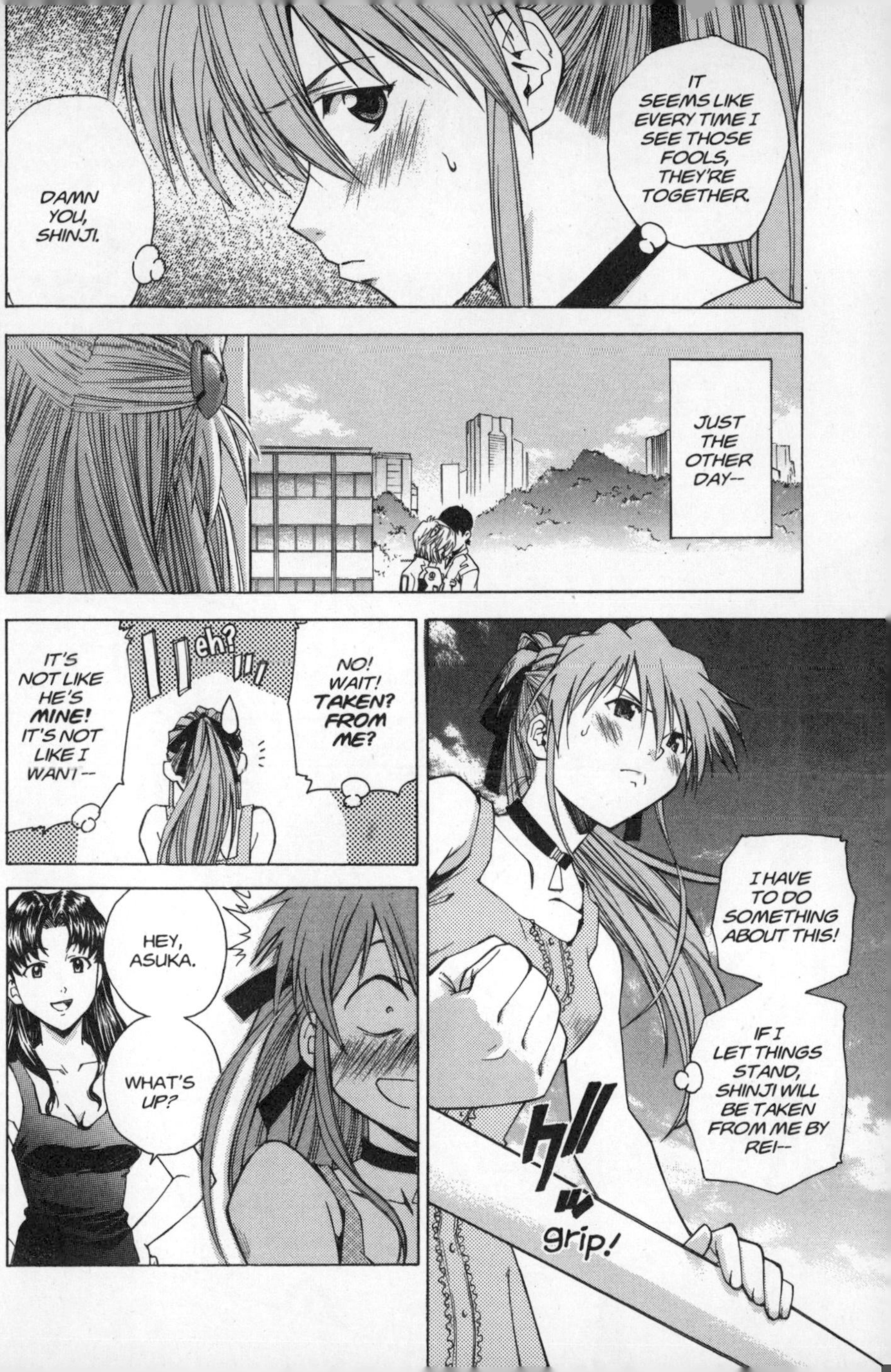
IT SEEMS LIKE EVERY TIME I SEE THOSE FOOLS, THEY'RE TOGETHER.
DAMN YOU, SHINJI.
JUST THE OTHER DAY--
I HAVE TO DO SOMETHING ABOUT THIS!
IF I LET THINGS STAND, SHINJI WILL BE TAKEN FROM ME BY REI--
grip!
NO! WAIT! TAKEN? FROM ME?
eh?
IT'S NOT LIKE HE'S MINE! IT'S NOT LIKE I WANT--
HEY, ASUKA.
WHAT'S UP?

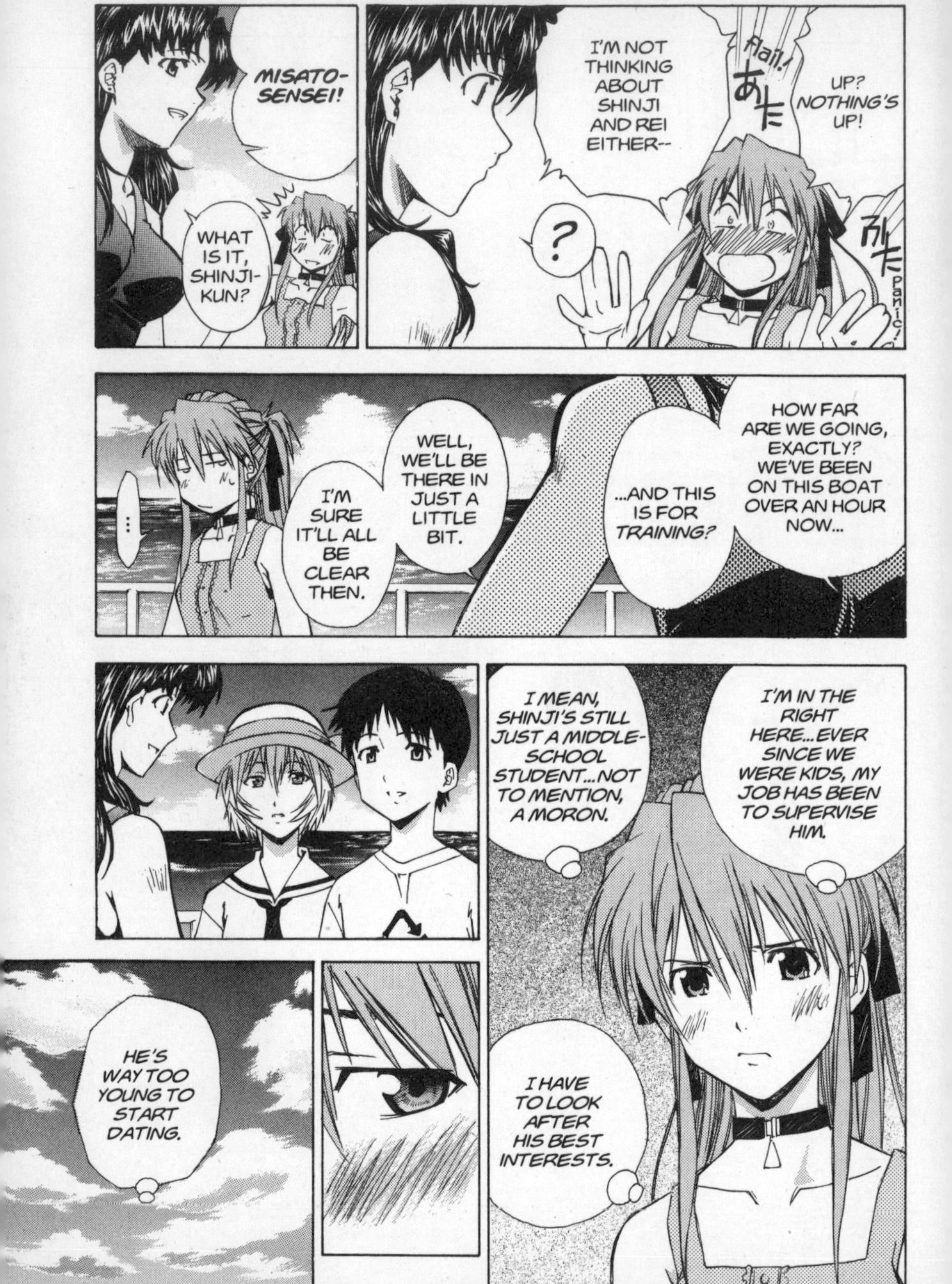
flail!
UP? NOTHING'S UP!
I'M NOT THINKING ABOUT SHINJI AND REI EITHER--
?
panic!
MISATO-SENSEI!
WHAT IS IT, SHINJI-KUN?
HOW FAR ARE WE GOING, EXACTLY? WE'VE BEEN ON THIS BOAT OVER AN HOUR NOW...
...AND THIS IS FOR TRAINING?
WELL, WE'LL BE THERE IN JUST A LITTLE BIT.
I'M SURE IT'LL ALL BE CLEAR THEN.
...
I'M IN THE RIGHT HERE... EVER SINCE WE WERE KIDS, MY JOB HAS BEEN TO SUPERVISE HIM.
I MEAN, SHINJI'S STILL JUST A MIDDLE-SCHOOL STUDENT... NOT TO MENTION, A MORON.
I HAVE TO LOOK AFTER HIS BEST INTERESTS.
HE'S WAY TOO YOUNG TO START DATING.

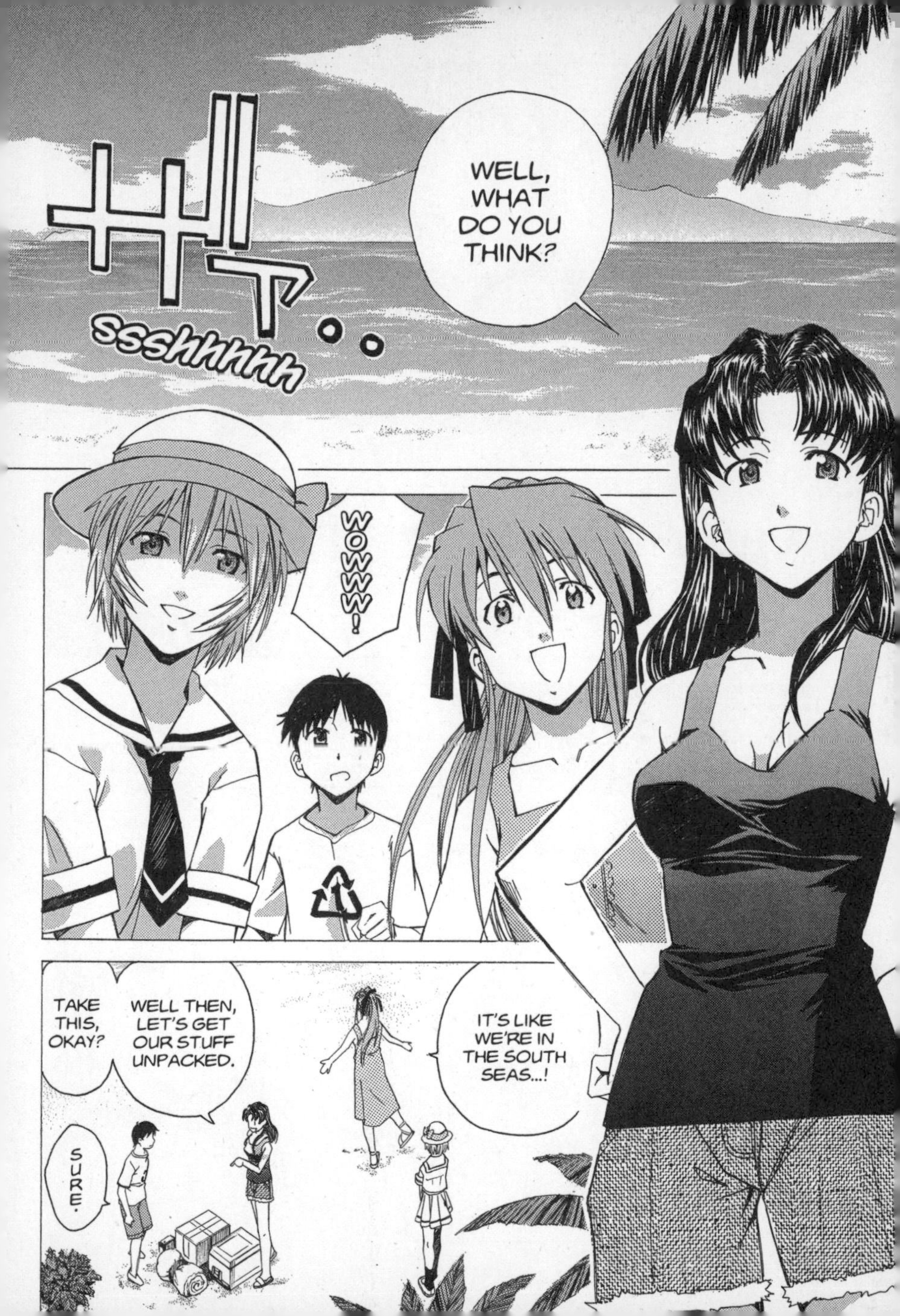
WELL, WHAT DO YOU THINK?
ssshhhhh
WOWWW!
IT'S LIKE WE'RE IN THE SOUTH SEAS...!
WELL THEN, LET'S GET OUR STUFF UNPACKED.
TAKE THIS, OKAY?
SURE.

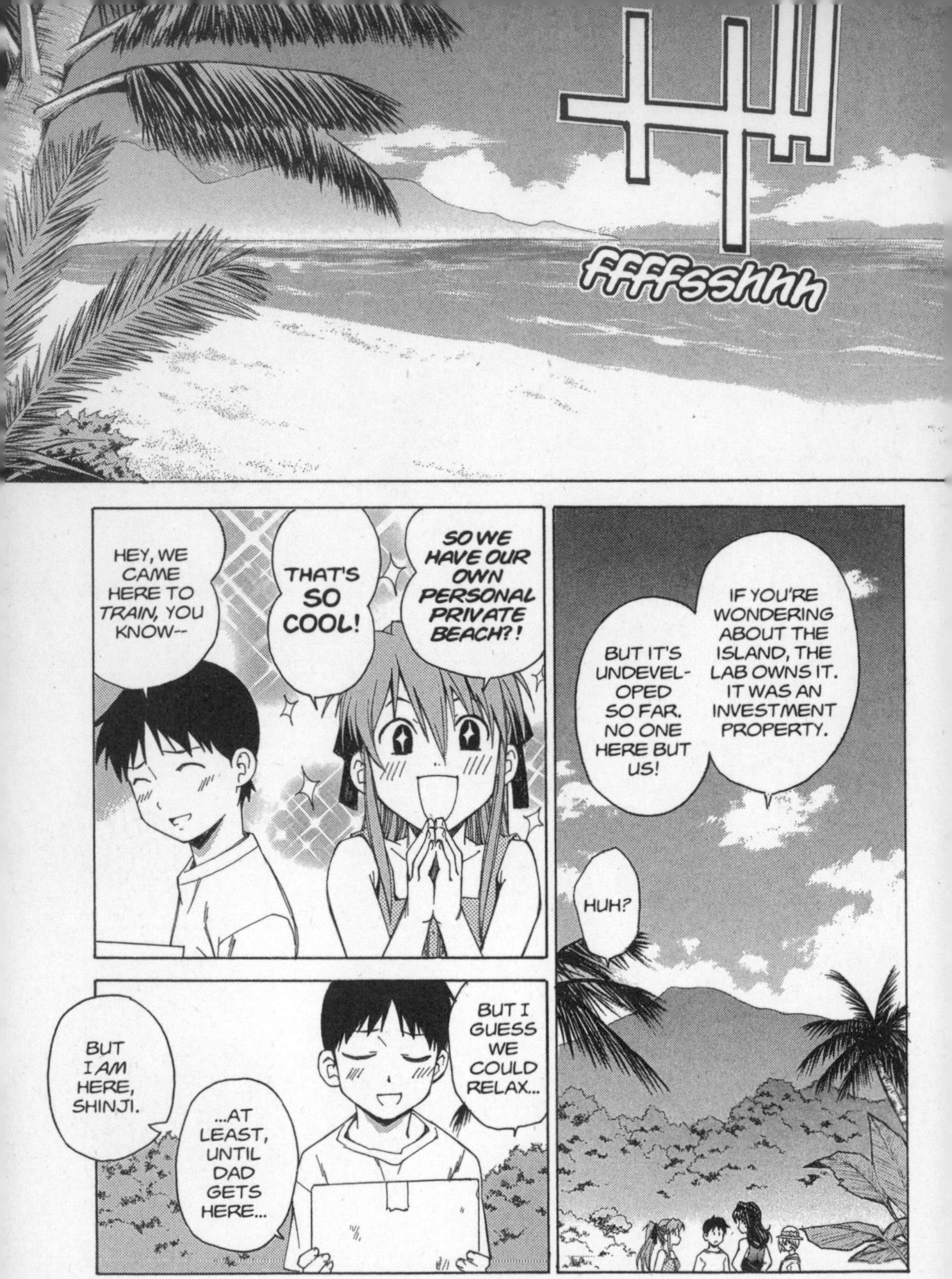
ffffsshhh
IF YOU'RE WONDERING ABOUT THE ISLAND, THE LAB OWNS IT. IT WAS AN INVESTMENT PROPERTY.
BUT IT'S UNDEVEL-OPED SO FAR. NO ONE HERE BUT US!
HUH?
SO WE HAVE OUR OWN PERSONAL PRIVATE BEACH?!
THAT'S SO COOL!
HEY, WE CAME HERE TO TRAIN, YOU KNOW--
BUT I GUESS WE COULD RELAX...
...AT LEAST, UNTIL DAD GETS HERE...
BUT I AM HERE, SHINJI.

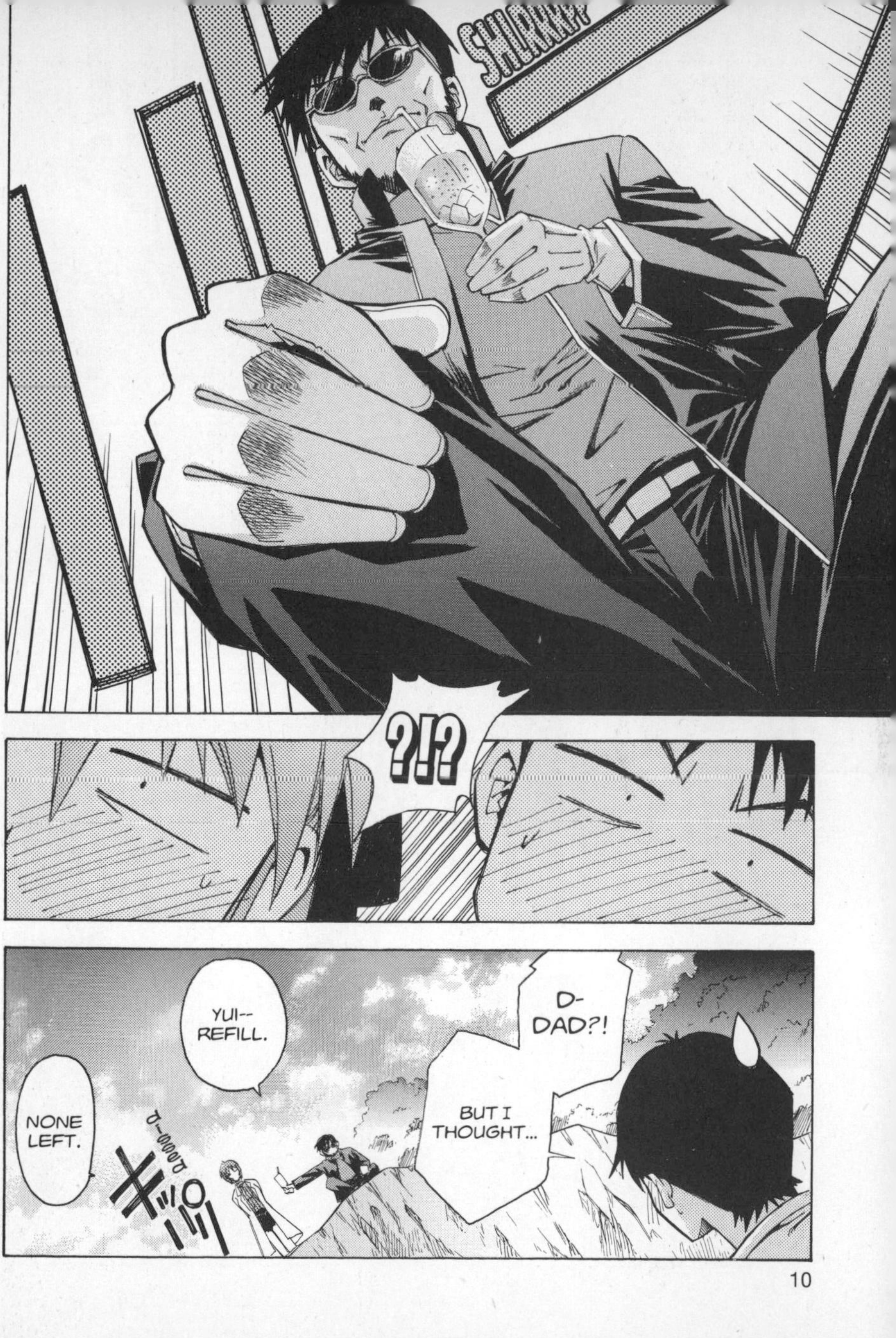
SHLRRRP
?!?
D-DAD?!
BUT I THOUGHT...
YUI-- REFILL.
NONE LEFT.

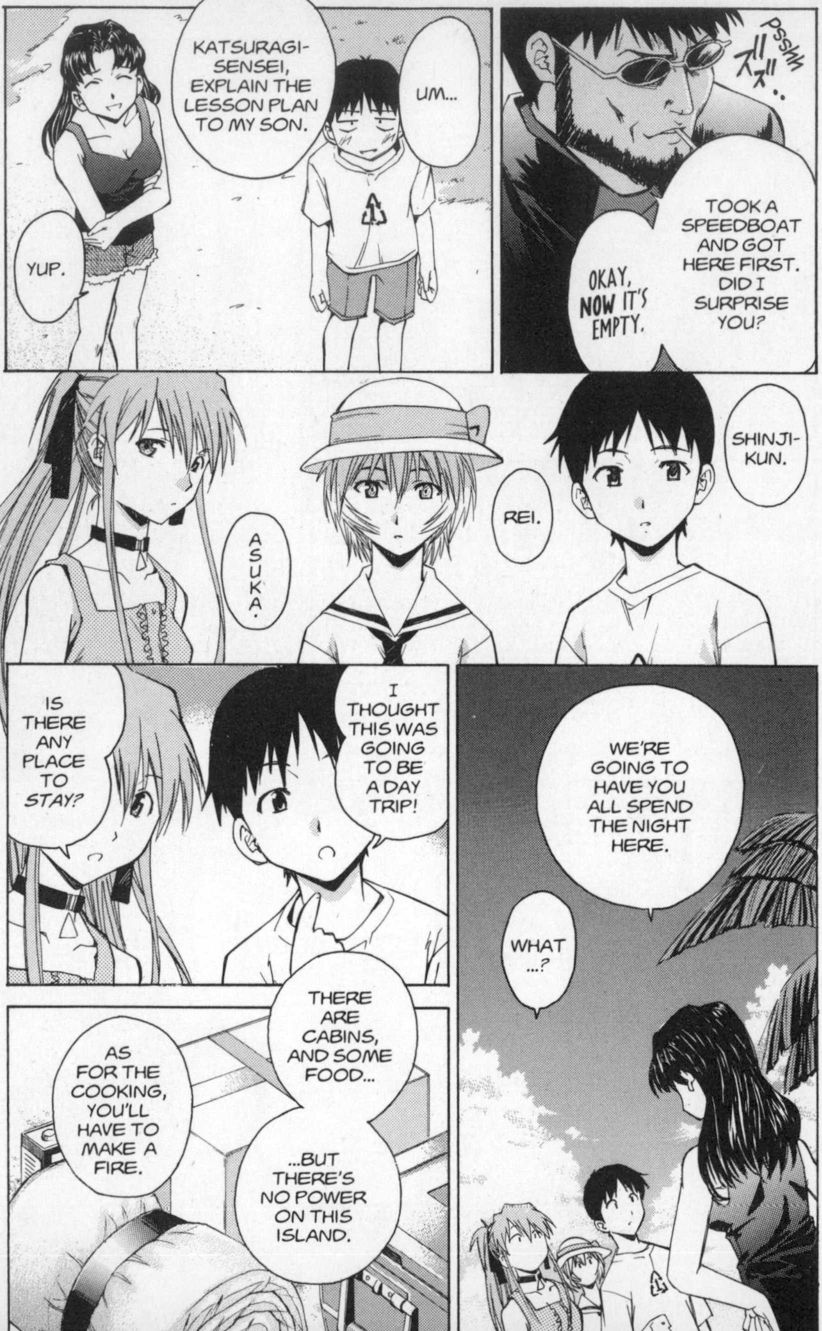
Psshh
ズズ..
TOOK A SPEEDBOAT AND GOT HERE FIRST. DID I SURPRISE YOU?
OKAY, NOW IT'S EMPTY.
KATSURAGI-SENSEI, EXPLAIN THE LESSON PLAN TO MY SON.
UM...
YUP.
SHINJI-KUN.
REI.
ASUKA.
WE'RE GOING TO HAVE YOU ALL SPEND THE NIGHT HERE.
WHAT ...?
I THOUGHT THIS WAS GOING TO BE A DAY TRIP!
IS THERE ANY PLACE TO STAY?
THERE ARE CABINS, AND SOME FOOD...
...BUT THERE'S NO POWER ON THIS ISLAND.
AS FOR THE COOKING, YOU'LL HAVE TO MAKE A FIRE.

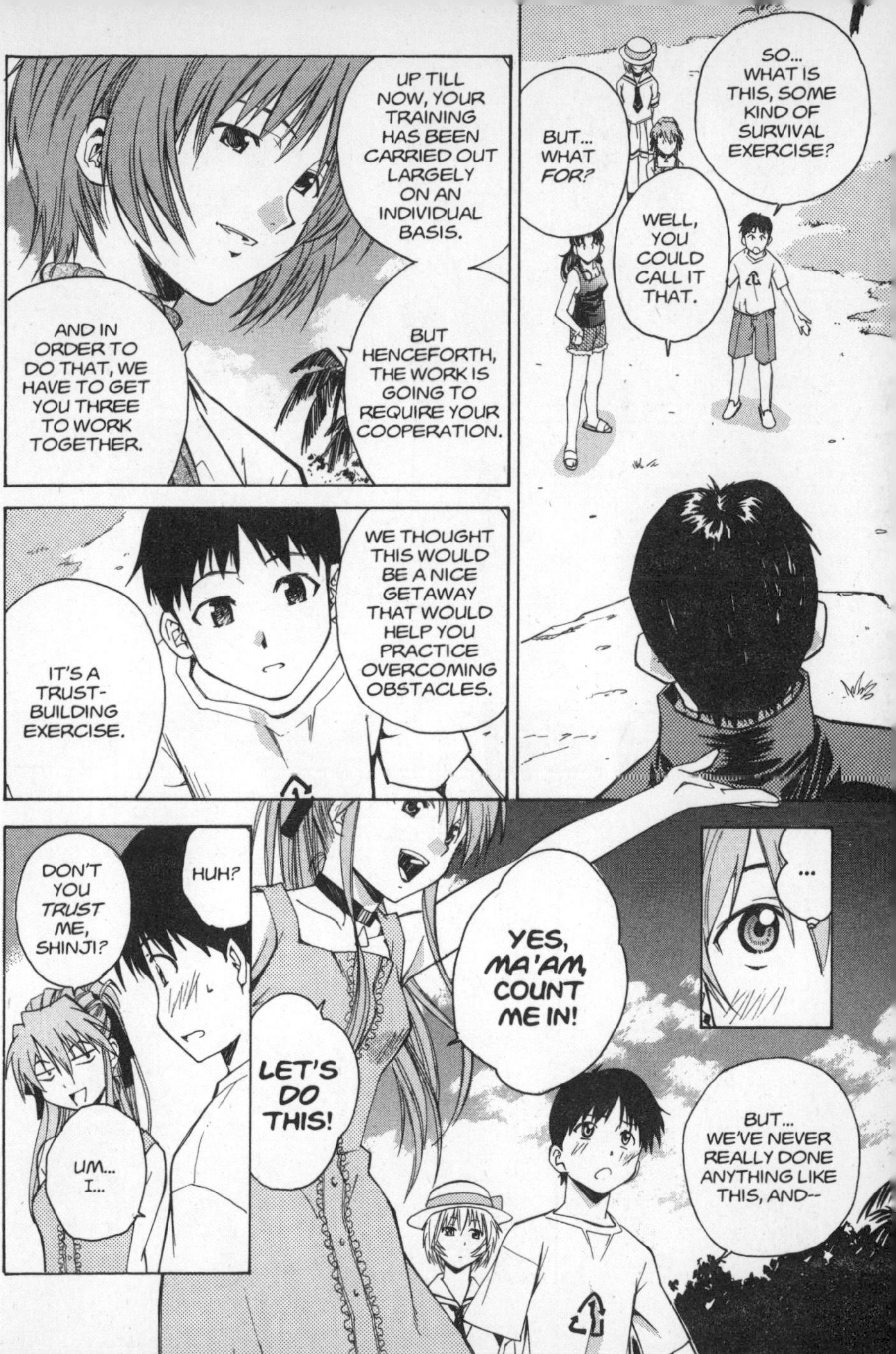

SO... WHAT IS THIS, SOME KIND OF SURVIVAL EXERCISE?
WELL, YOU COULD CALL IT THAT.
BUT... WHAT FOR?
UP TILL NOW, YOUR TRAINING HAS BEEN CARRIED OUT LARGELY ON AN INDIVIDUAL BASIS.
BUT HENCEFORTH, THE WORK IS GOING TO REQUIRE YOUR COOPERATION.
AND IN ORDER TO DO THAT, WE HAVE TO GET YOU THREE TO WORK TOGETHER.
WE THOUGHT THIS WOULD BE A NICE GETAWAY THAT WOULD HELP YOU PRACTICE OVERCOMING OBSTACLES.
IT'S A TRUST-BUILDING EXERCISE.
...
BUT... WE'VE NEVER REALLY DONE ANYTHING LIKE THIS, AND--
YES, MA'AM, COUNT ME IN!
LET'S DO THIS!
HUH?
DON'T YOU TRUST ME, SHINJI?
UM... I...

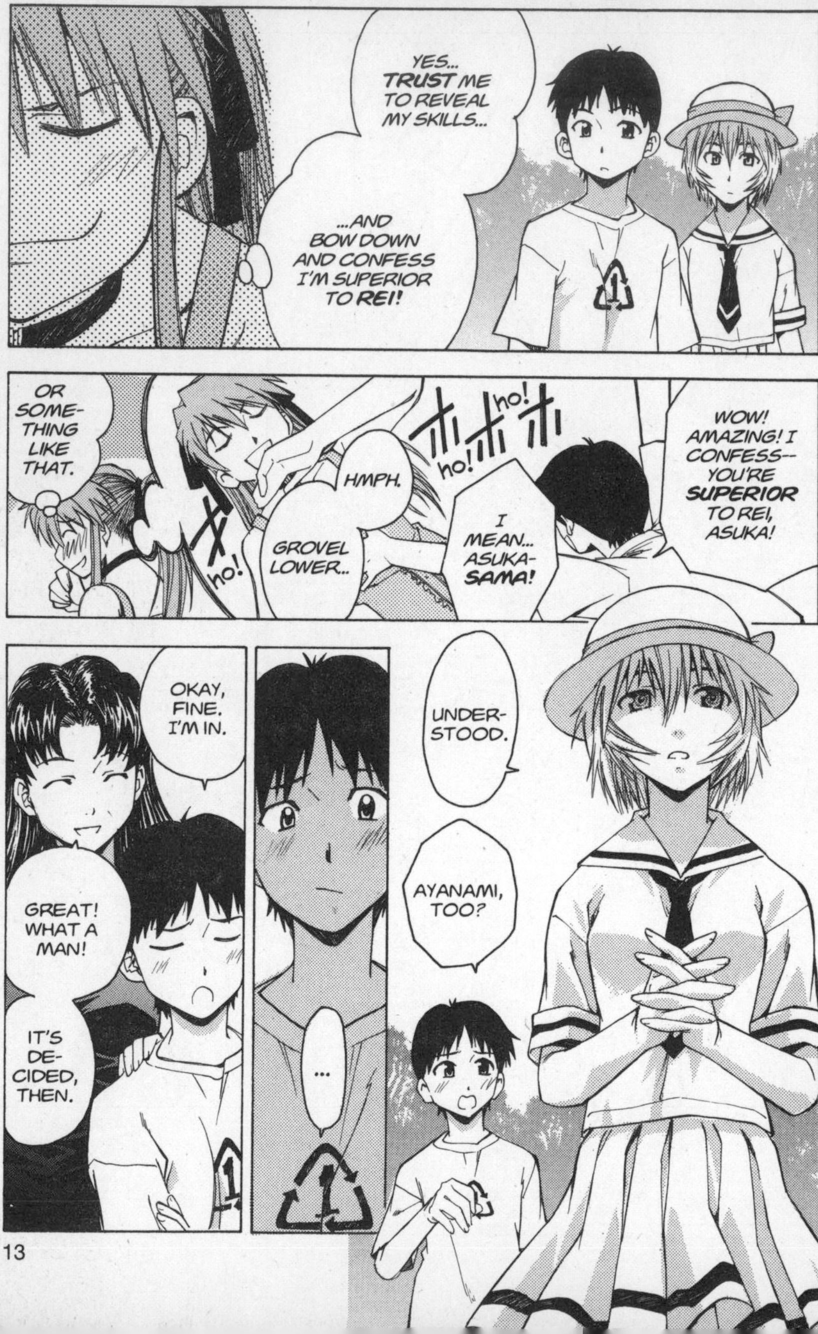
YES... TRUST ME TO REVEAL MY SKILLS...
...AND BOW DOWN AND CONFESS I'M SUPERIOR TO REI!
WOW! AMAZING! I CONFESS-- YOU'RE SUPERIOR TO REI, ASUKA!
I MEAN... ASUKA-SAMA!
ho!
ho!
ho!
HMPH.
GROVEL LOWER...
OR SOMETHING LIKE THAT.
UNDERSTOOD.
AYANAMI, TOO?
OKAY, FINE. I'M IN.
...
GREAT! WHAT A MAN!
IT'S DECIDED, THEN.

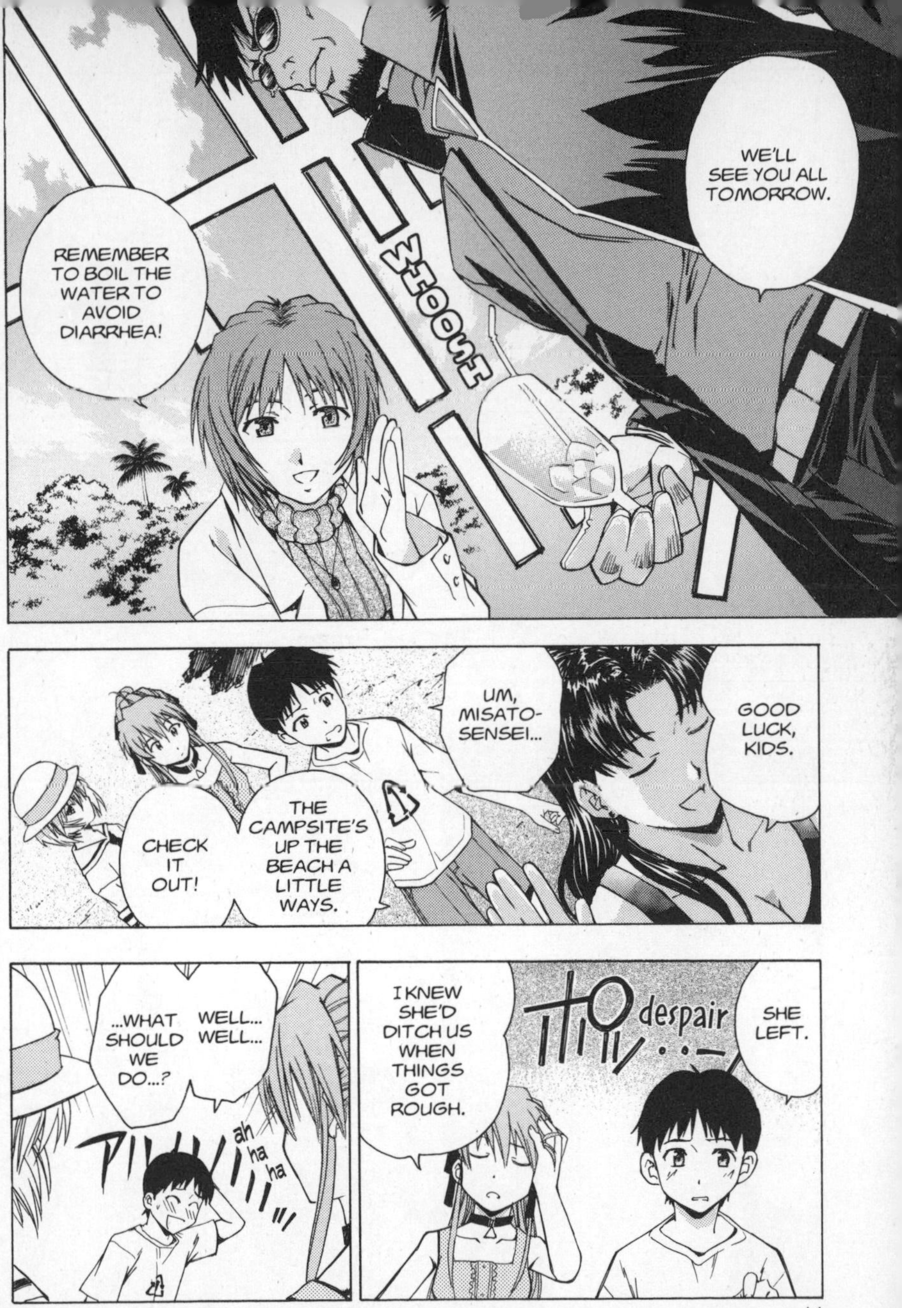
WE'LL SEE YOU ALL TOMORROW.
WHOOSH
REMEMBER TO BOIL THE WATER TO AVOID DIARRHEA!
GOOD LUCK, KIDS.
UM, MISATO-SENSEI...
THE CAMPSITE'S UP THE BEACH A LITTLE WAYS.
CHECK IT OUT!
SHE LEFT.
despair
I KNEW SHE'D DITCH US WHEN THINGS GOT ROUGH.
WELL... WELL...
...WHAT SHOULD WE DO...?
ah ha ha

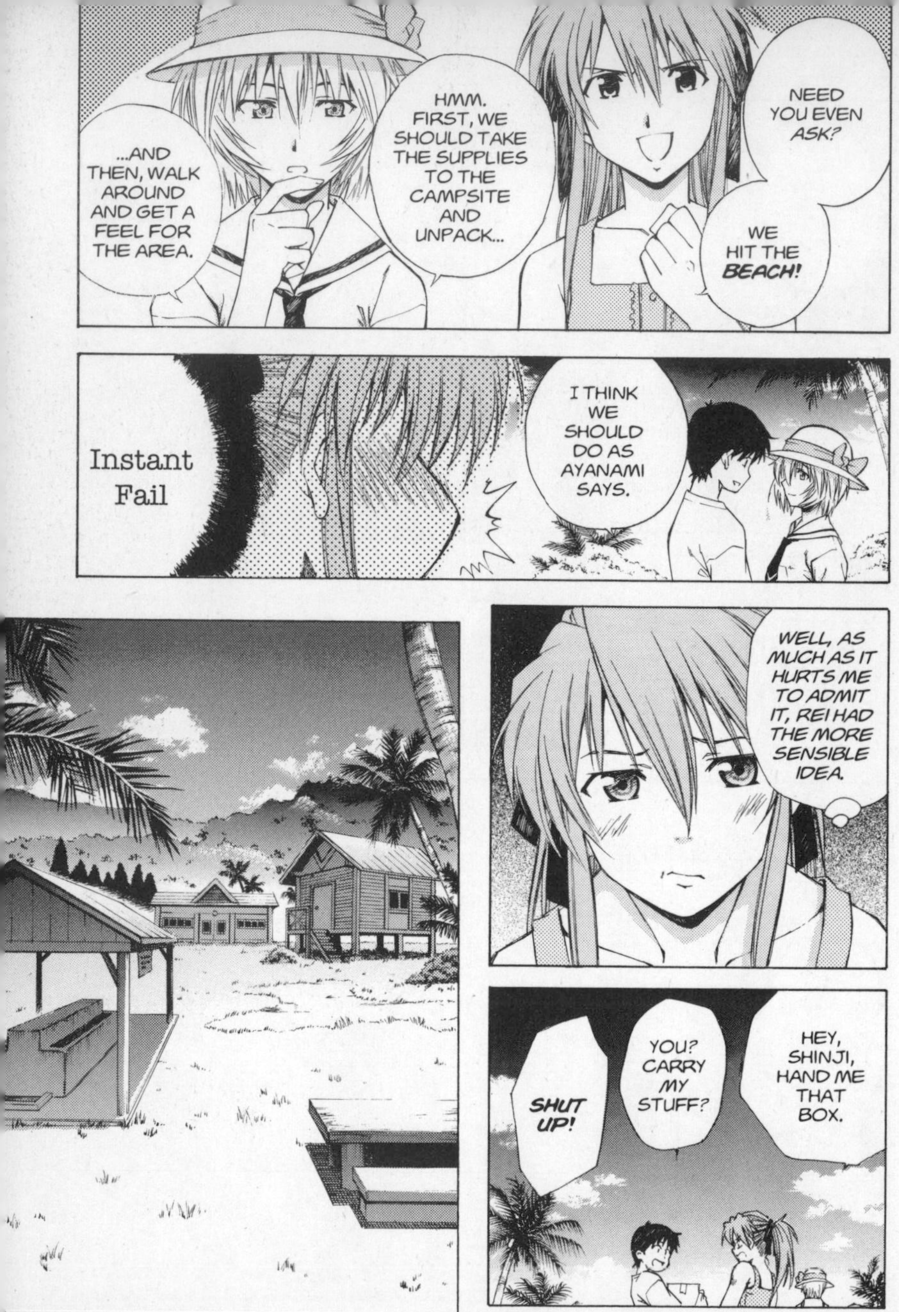
NEED YOU EVEN ASK?
WE HIT THE BEACH!
HMM. FIRST, WE SHOULD TAKE THE SUPPLIES TO THE CAMPSITE AND UNPACK...
...AND THEN, WALK AROUND AND GET A FEEL FOR THE AREA.
I THINK WE SHOULD DO AS AYANAMI SAYS.
Instant Fail
WELL, AS MUCH AS IT HURTS ME TO ADMIT IT, REI HAD THE MORE SENSIBLE IDEA.
HEY, SHINJI, HAND ME THAT BOX.
YOU? CARRY MY STUFF?
SHUT UP!

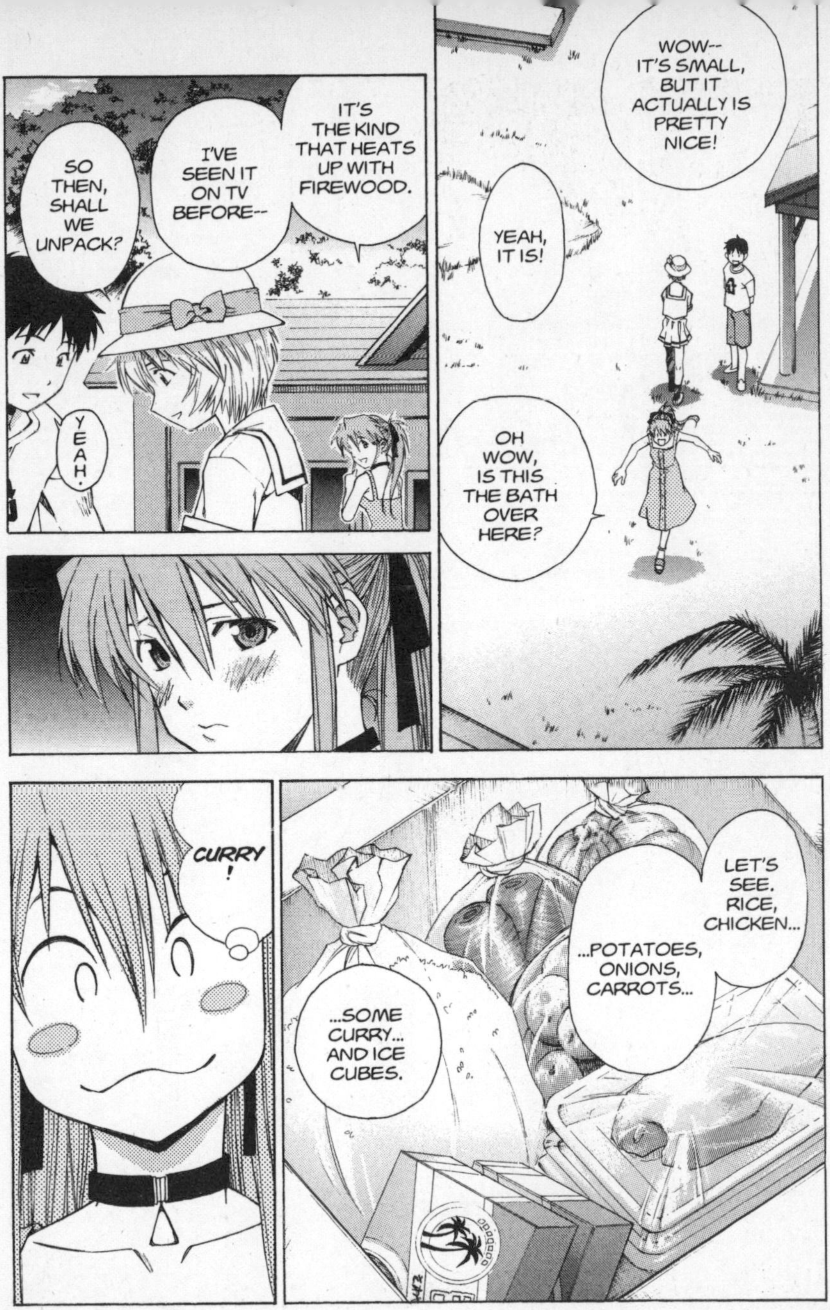
WOW-- IT'S SMALL, BUT IT ACTUALLY IS PRETTY NICE!
YEAH, IT IS!
OH WOW, IS THIS THE BATH OVER HERE?
IT'S THE KIND THAT HEATS UP WITH FIREWOOD.
I'VE SEEN IT ON TV BEFORE--
SO THEN, SHALL WE UNPACK?
YEAH.
LET'S SEE. RICE, CHICKEN...
...POTATOES, ONIONS, CARROTS...
...SOME CURRY... AND ICE CUBES.
CURRY!

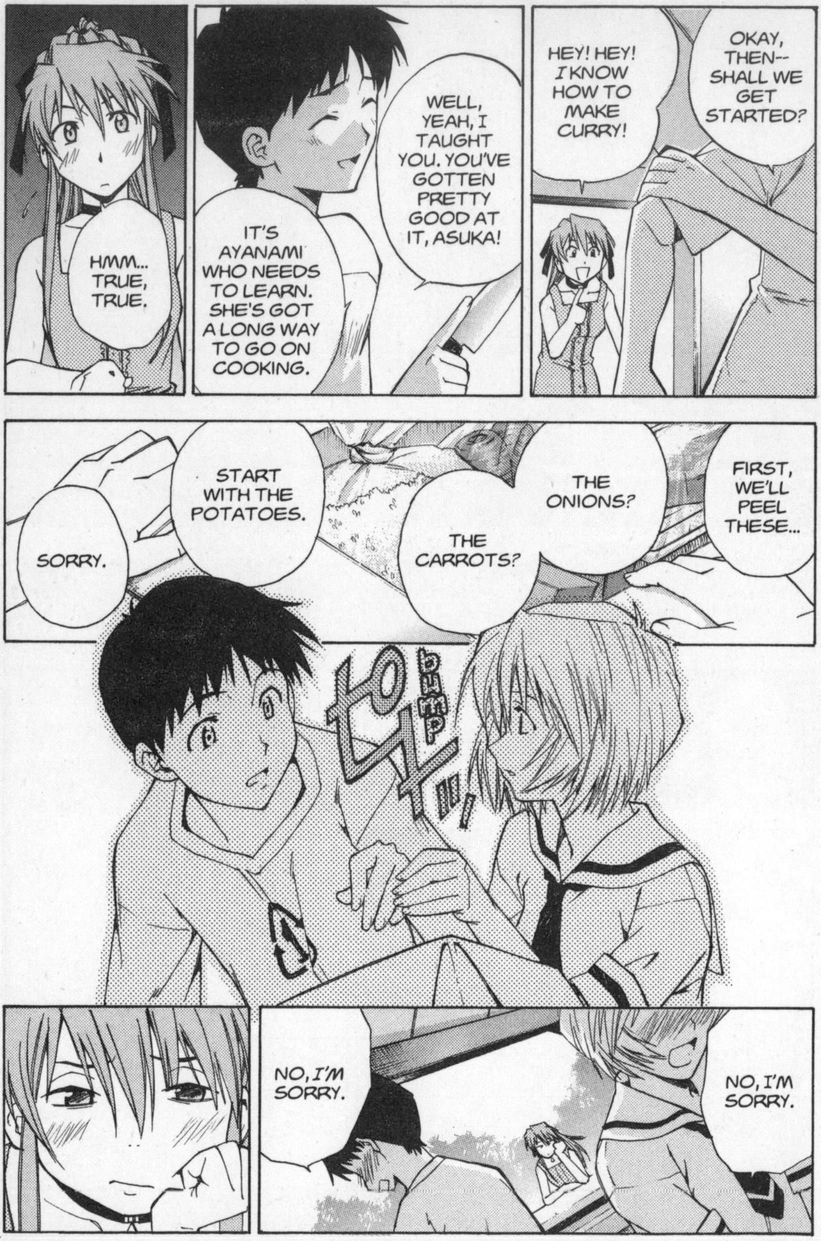
OKAY, THEN-- SHALL WE GET STARTED?
HEY! HEY! I KNOW HOW TO MAKE CURRY!
WELL, YEAH, I TAUGHT YOU. YOU'VE GOTTEN PRETTY GOOD AT IT, ASUKA!
IT'S AYANAMI WHO NEEDS TO LEARN. SHE'S GOT A LONG WAY TO GO ON COOKING.
HMM... TRUE, TRUE.
FIRST, WE'LL PEEL THESE...
THE ONIONS?
THE CARROTS?
START WITH THE POTATOES.
SORRY.
BUMP
NO, I'M SORRY.
NO, I'M SORRY.

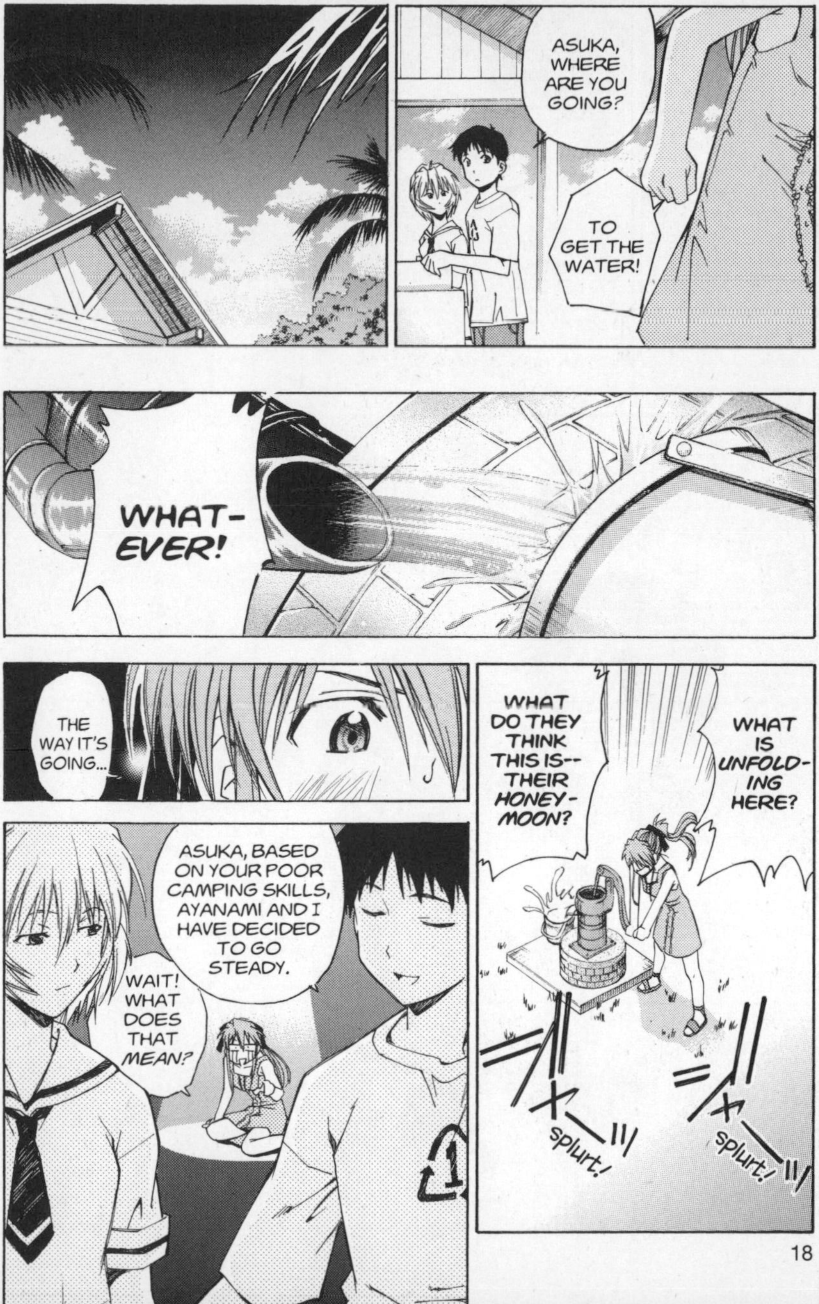
ASUKA, WHERE ARE YOU GOING?
TO GET THE WATER!
WHAT-EVER!
WHAT IS UNFOLDING HERE?
WHAT DO THEY THINK THIS IS-- THEIR HONEY-MOON?
splurt!
splurt!
THE WAY IT'S GOING...
ASUKA, BASED ON YOUR POOR CAMPING SKILLS, AYANAMI AND I HAVE DECIDED TO GO STEADY.
WAIT! WHAT DOES THAT MEAN?

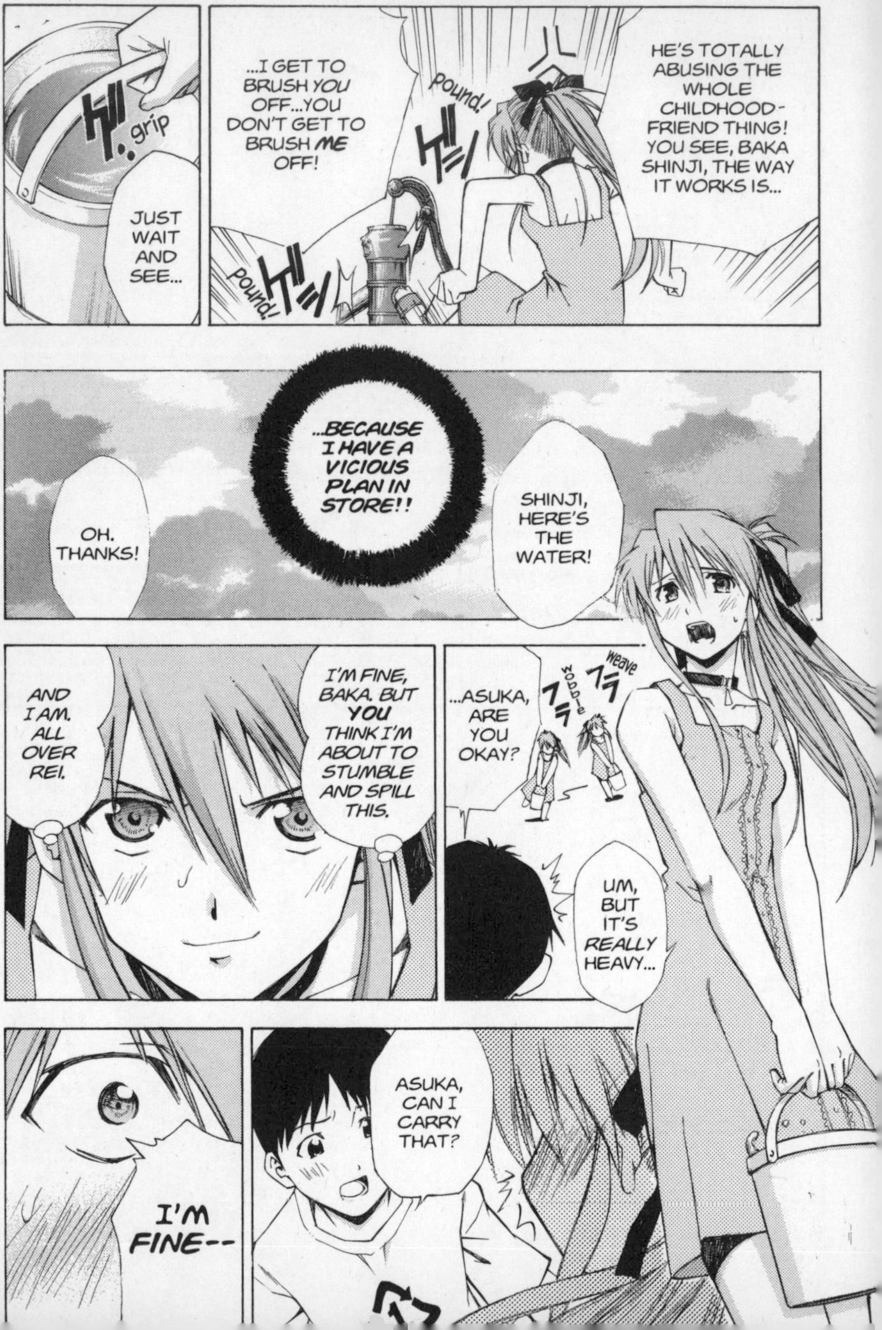
HE'S TOTALLY ABUSING THE WHOLE CHILDHOOD-FRIEND THING! YOU SEE, BAKA SHINJI, THE WAY IT WORKS IS...
Pound!
...I GET TO BRUSH YOU OFF...YOU DON'T GET TO BRUSH ME OFF!
Pound!
grip
JUST WAIT AND SEE...
...BECAUSE I HAVE A VICIOUS PLAN IN STORE!!
SHINJI, HERE'S THE WATER!
OH. THANKS!
weave
wobble
...ASUKA, ARE YOU OKAY?
UM, BUT IT'S REALLY HEAVY...
I'M FINE, BAKA. BUT YOU THINK I'M ABOUT TO STUMBLE AND SPILL THIS.
AND I AM. ALL OVER REI.
ASUKA, CAN I CARRY THAT?
I'M FINE--

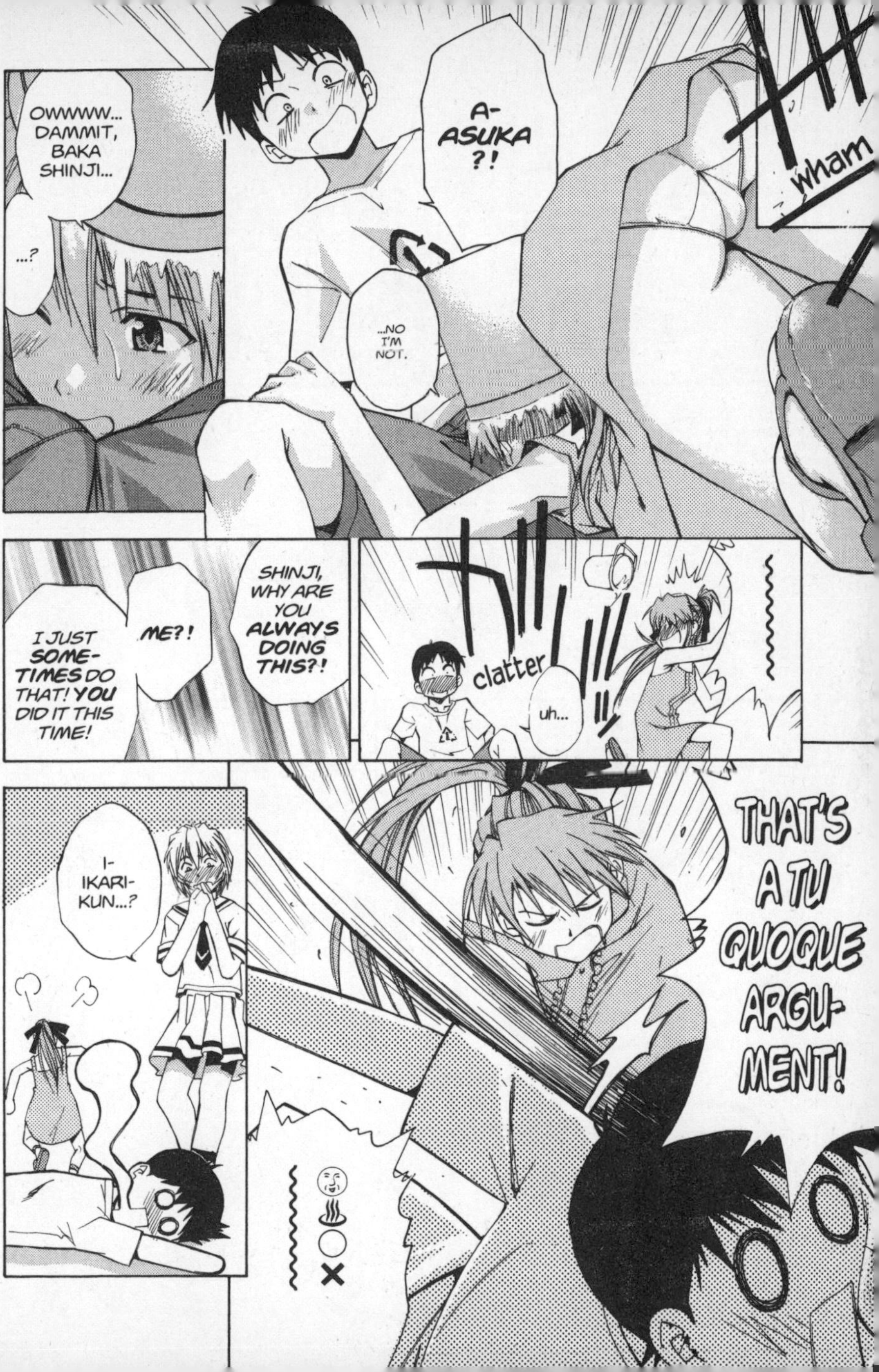
wham
A-ASUKA?!
...NO I'M NOT.
OWWWW... DAMMIT, BAKA SHINJI...
...?
clatter
uh...
SHINJI, WHY ARE YOU ALWAYS DOING THIS?!
ME?!
I JUST SOMETIMES DO THAT! YOU DID IT THIS TIME!
THAT'S A TU QUOQUE ARGUMENT!
I-IKARI-KUN...?

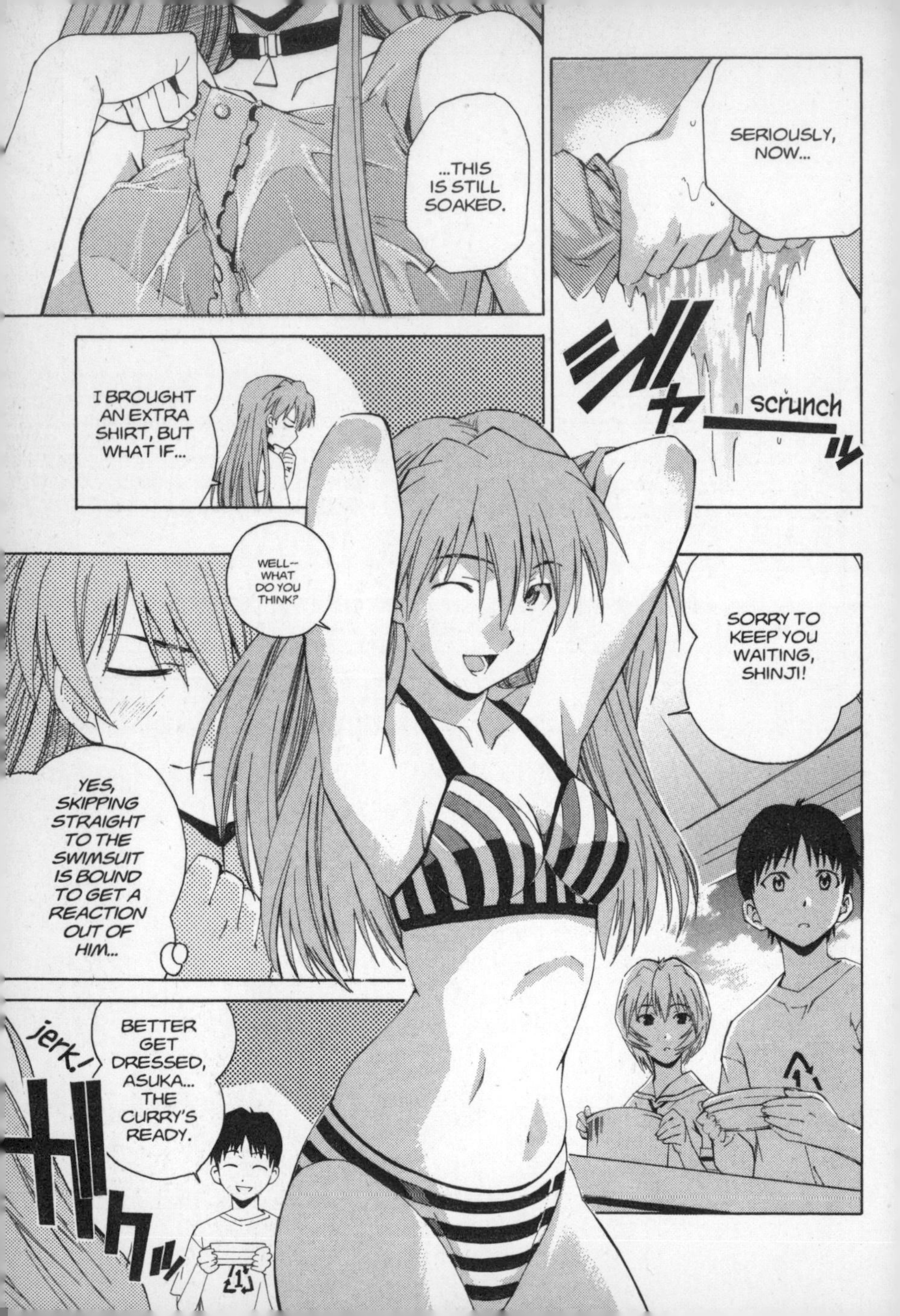
SERIOUSLY, NOW...
...THIS IS STILL SOAKED.
シャーッ
scrunch
I BROUGHT AN EXTRA SHIRT, BUT WHAT IF...
SORRY TO KEEP YOU WAITING, SHINJI!
WELL-- WHAT DO YOU THINK?
YES, SKIPPING STRAIGHT TO THE SWIMSUIT IS BOUND TO GET A REACTION OUT OF HIM...
BETTER GET DRESSED, ASUKA... THE CURRY'S READY.
jerk!
ガクッ

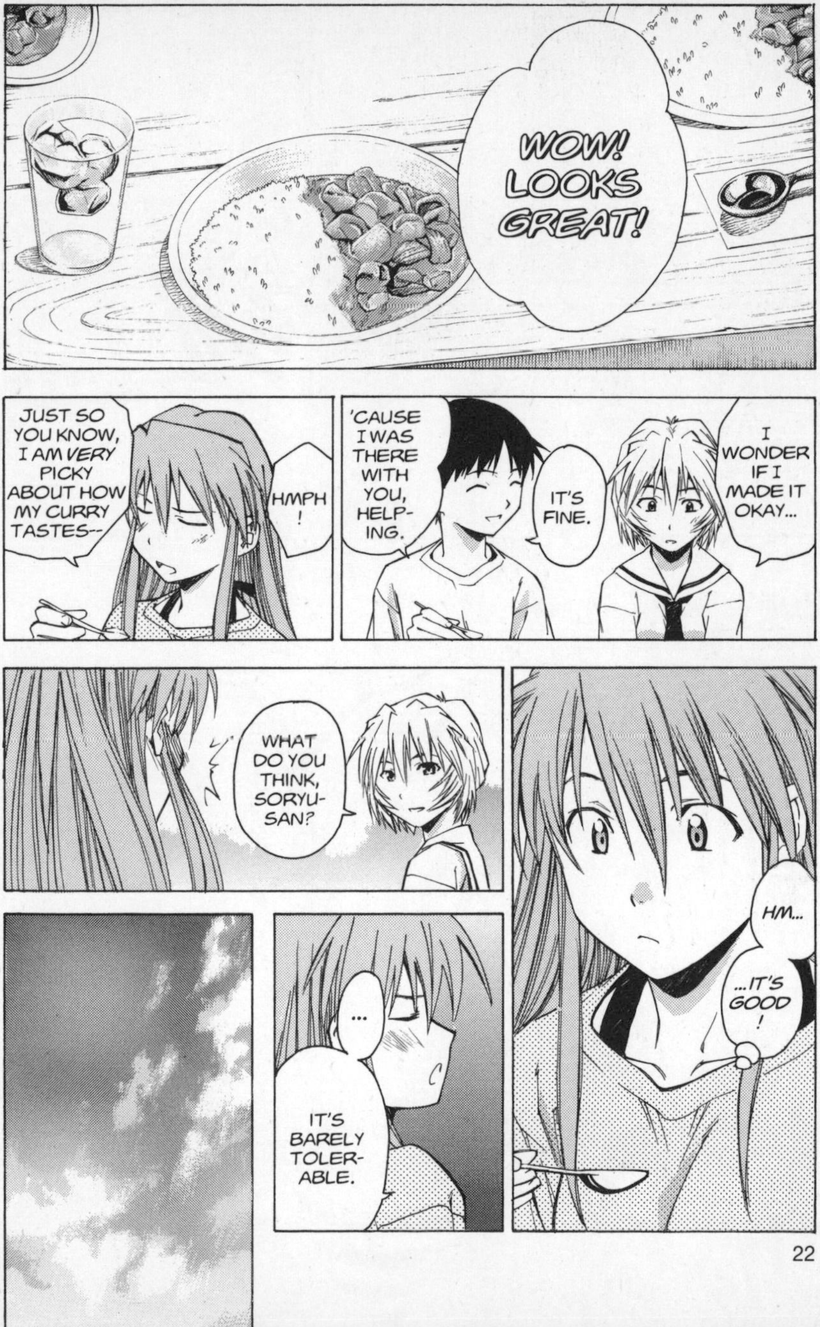
WOW! LOOKS GREAT!
I WONDER IF I MADE IT OKAY...
IT'S FINE.
'CAUSE I WAS THERE WITH YOU, HELPING.
HMPH!
JUST SO YOU KNOW, I AM VERY PICKY ABOUT HOW MY CURRY TASTES--
HM...
...IT'S GOOD!
WHAT DO YOU THINK, SORYU-SAN?
...
IT'S BARELY TOLERABLE.

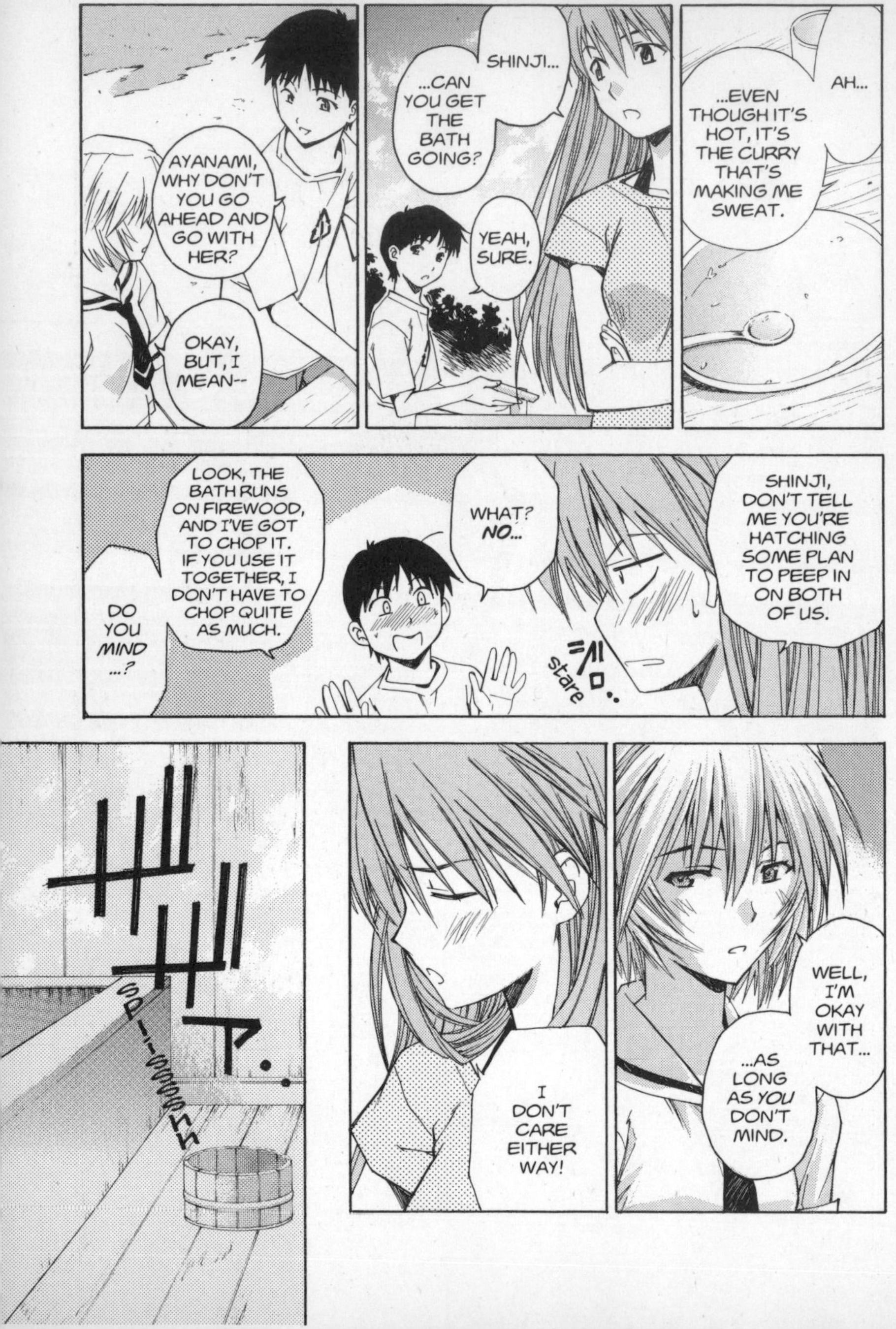
AH...
...EVEN THOUGH IT'S HOT, IT'S THE CURRY THAT'S MAKING ME SWEAT.
SHINJI...
...CAN YOU GET THE BATH GOING?
YEAH, SURE.
AYANAMI, WHY DON'T YOU GO AHEAD AND GO WITH HER?
OKAY, BUT, I MEAN--
SHINJI, DON'T TELL ME YOU'RE HATCHING SOME PLAN TO PEEP IN ON BOTH OF US.
stare
WHAT? *NO*...
LOOK, THE BATH RUNS ON FIREWOOD, AND I'VE GOT TO CHOP IT. IF YOU USE IT TOGETHER, I DON'T HAVE TO CHOP QUITE AS MUCH.
DO YOU *MIND* ...?
WELL, I'M OKAY WITH THAT...
...AS LONG AS *YOU* DON'T MIND.
I DON'T CARE EITHER WAY!
SPIISSSSSHH

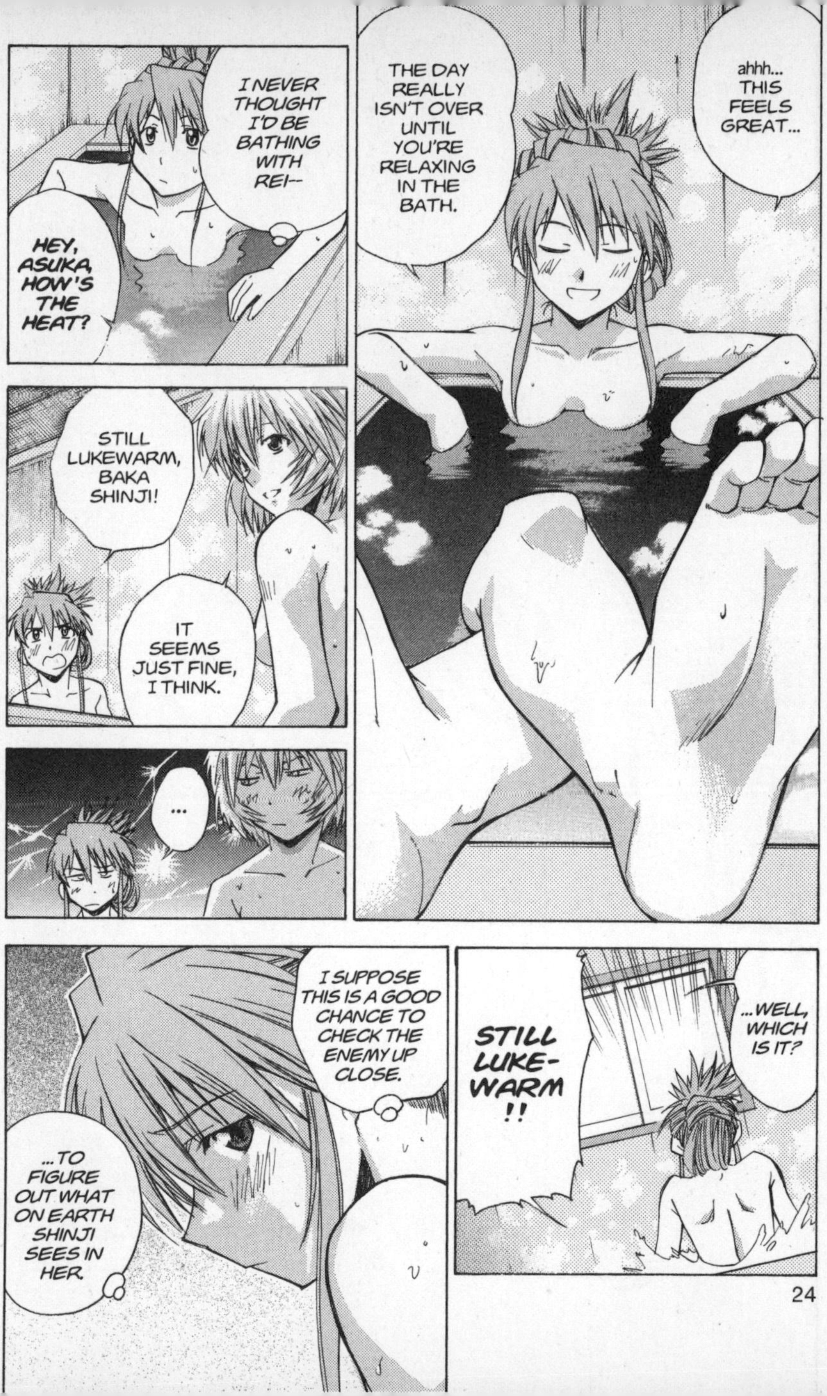
ahhh... THIS FEELS GREAT...
THE DAY REALLY ISN'T OVER UNTIL YOU'RE RELAXING IN THE BATH.
I NEVER THOUGHT I'D BE BATHING WITH REI--
HEY, ASUKA, HOW'S THE HEAT?
STILL LUKEWARM, BAKA SHINJI!
IT SEEMS JUST FINE, I THINK.
...
...WELL, WHICH IS IT?
STILL LUKE-WARM!!
I SUPPOSE THIS IS A GOOD CHANCE TO CHECK THE ENEMY UP CLOSE.
...TO FIGURE OUT WHAT ON EARTH SHINJI SEES IN HER.

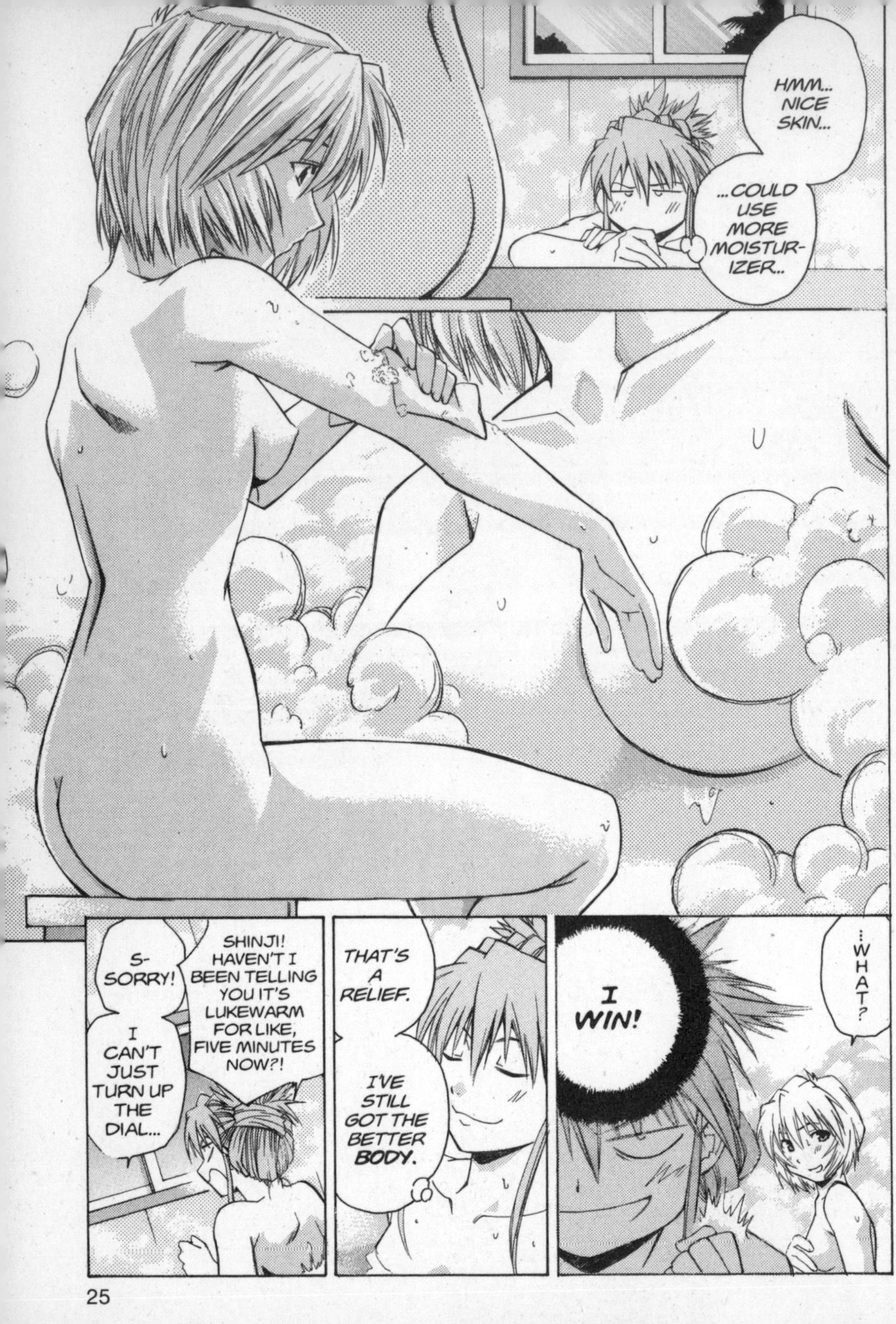
HMM... NICE SKIN...
...COULD USE MORE MOISTUR-IZER...
...WHAT?
I WIN!
THAT'S A RELIEF.
I'VE STILL GOT THE BETTER BODY.
SHINJI! HAVEN'T I BEEN TELLING YOU IT'S LUKEWARM FOR LIKE, FIVE MINUTES NOW?!
S-SORRY!
I CAN'T JUST TURN UP THE DIAL...

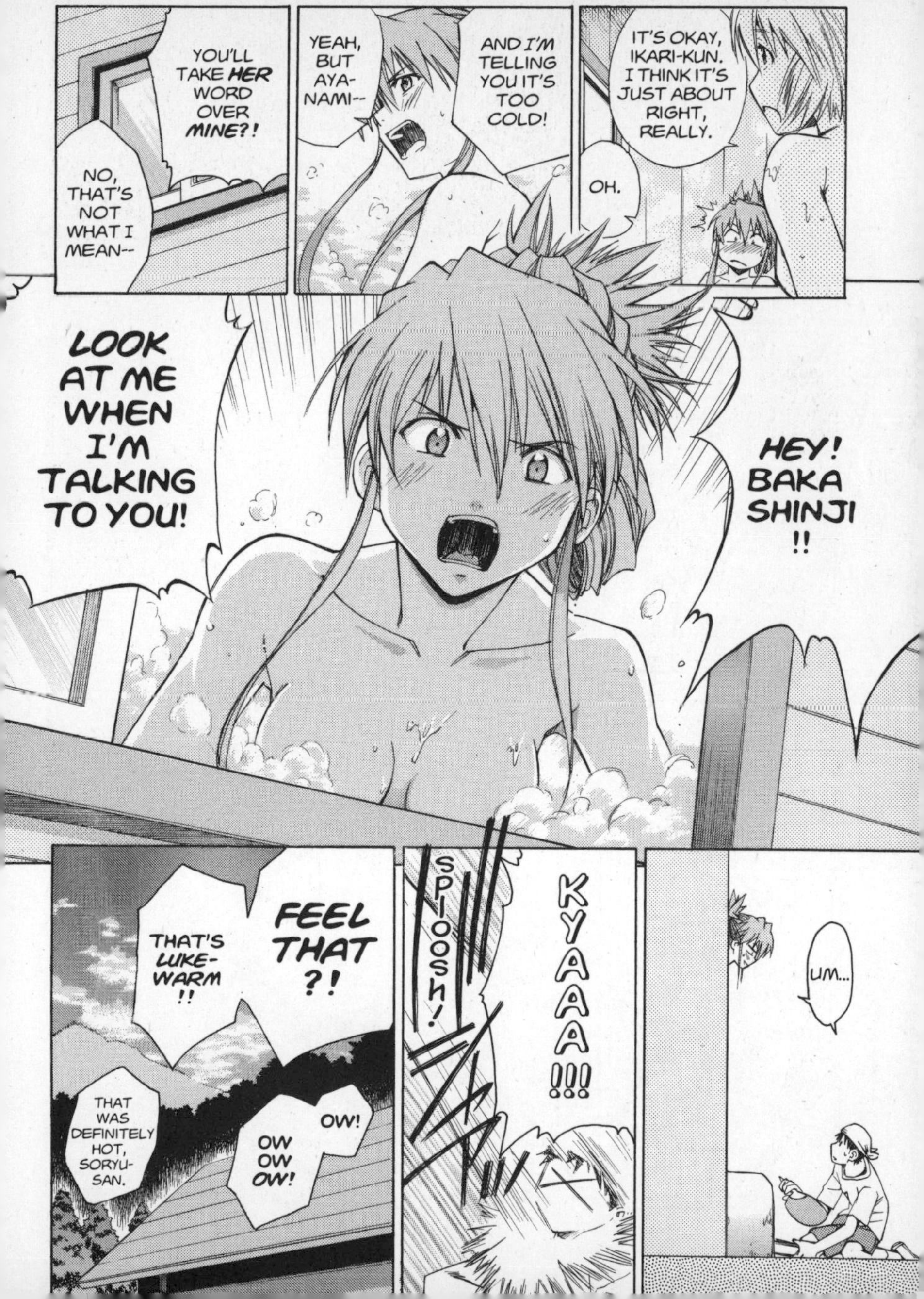
IT'S OKAY, IKARI-KUN. I THINK IT'S JUST ABOUT RIGHT, REALLY.
OH.
AND I'M TELLING YOU IT'S TOO COLD!
YEAH, BUT AYA-NAMI--
YOU'LL TAKE HER WORD OVER MINE?!
NO, THAT'S NOT WHAT I MEAN--
HEY! BAKA SHINJI!!
LOOK AT ME WHEN I'M TALKING TO YOU!
UM...
KYAAAA!!!
SPLOOSH!
FEEL THAT?!
THAT'S LUKE-WARM!!
OW! OW OW OW!
THAT WAS DEFINITELY HOT, SORYU-SAN.

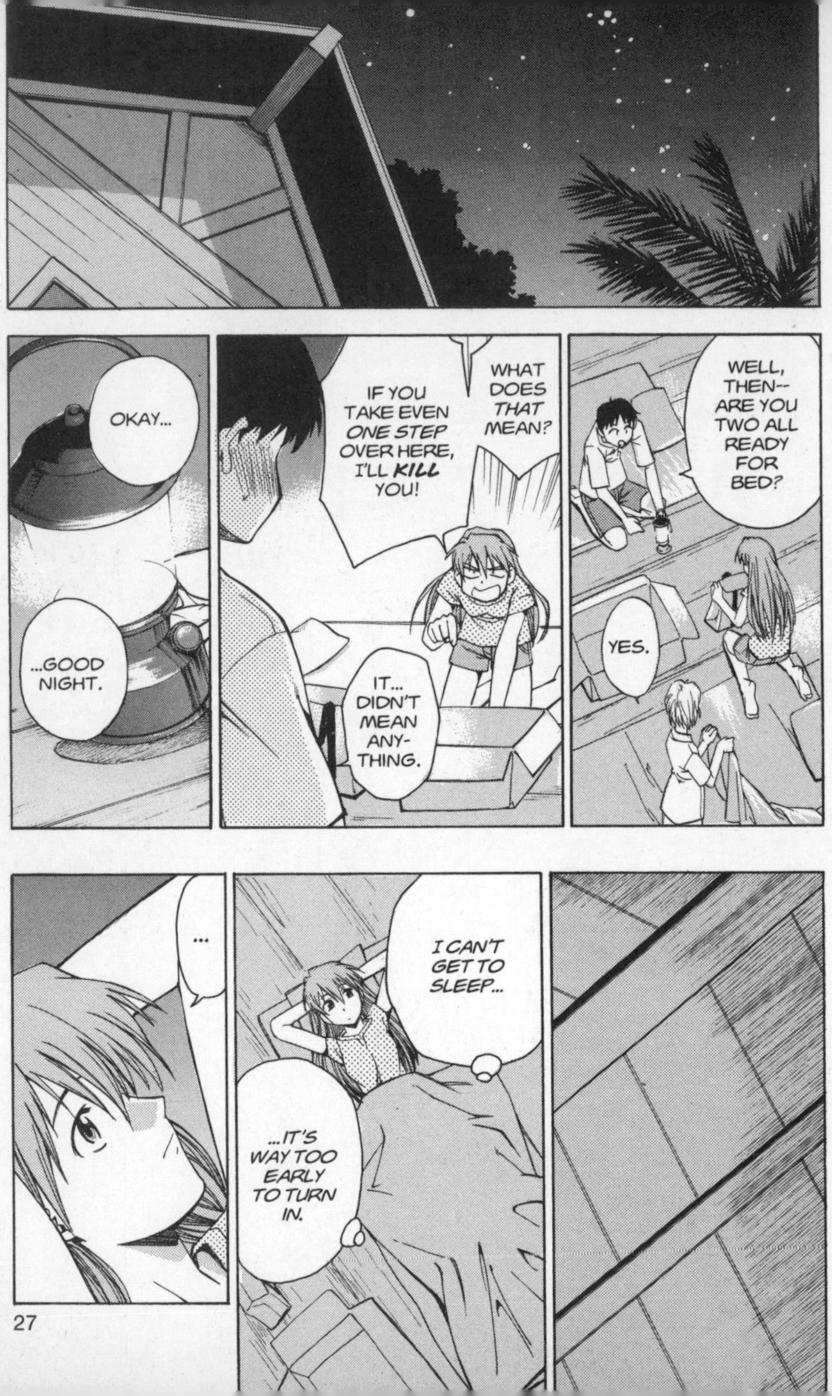
WELL, THEN-- ARE YOU TWO ALL READY FOR BED?
YES.
WHAT DOES THAT MEAN?
IF YOU TAKE EVEN ONE STEP OVER HERE, I'LL KILL YOU!
IT... DIDN'T MEAN ANY-THING.
OKAY...
...GOOD NIGHT.
I CAN'T GET TO SLEEP...
...IT'S WAY TOO EARLY TO TURN IN.
...

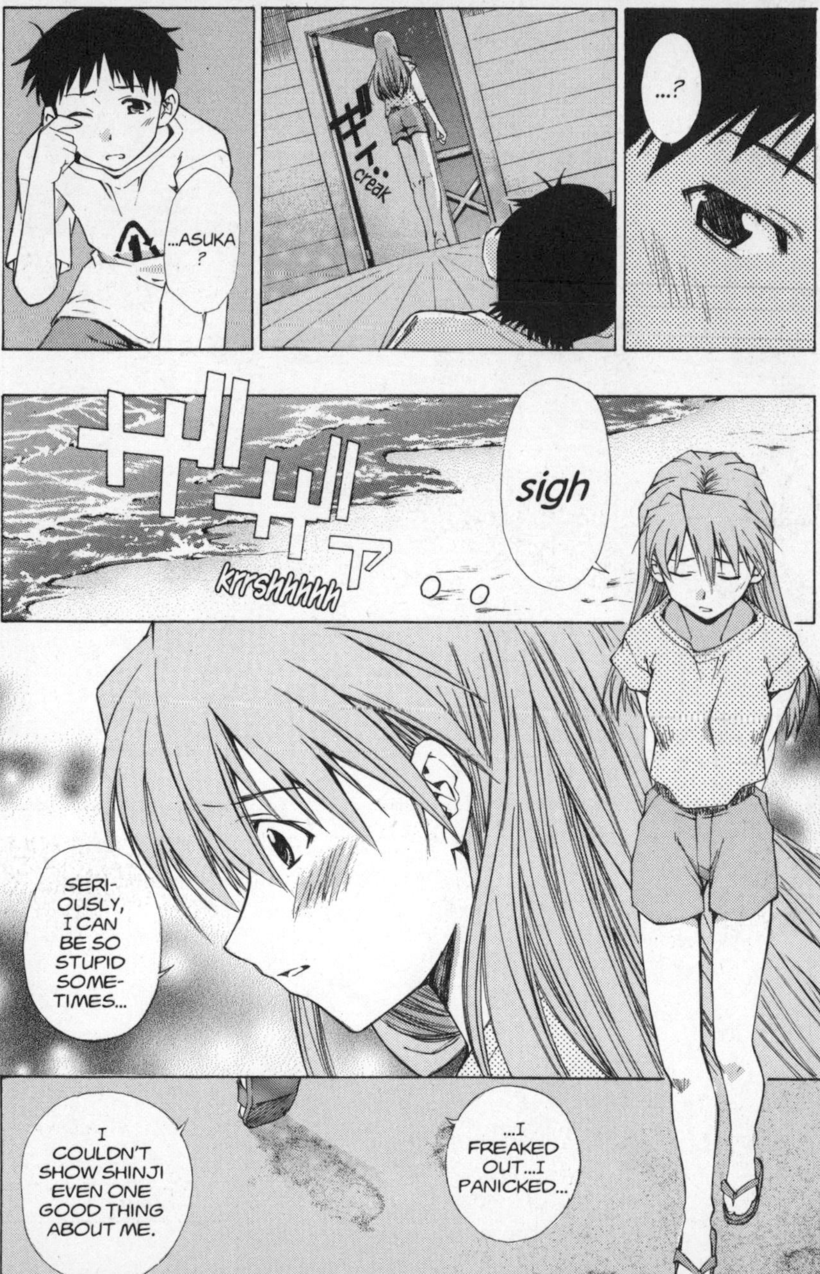

...?
ギイ...
creak
...ASUKA ?
sigh
ザザザァ
krrshhhhh
SERIOUSLY, I CAN BE SO STUPID SOMETIMES...
...I FREAKED OUT...I PANICKED...
I COULDN'T SHOW SHINJI EVEN ONE GOOD THING ABOUT ME.

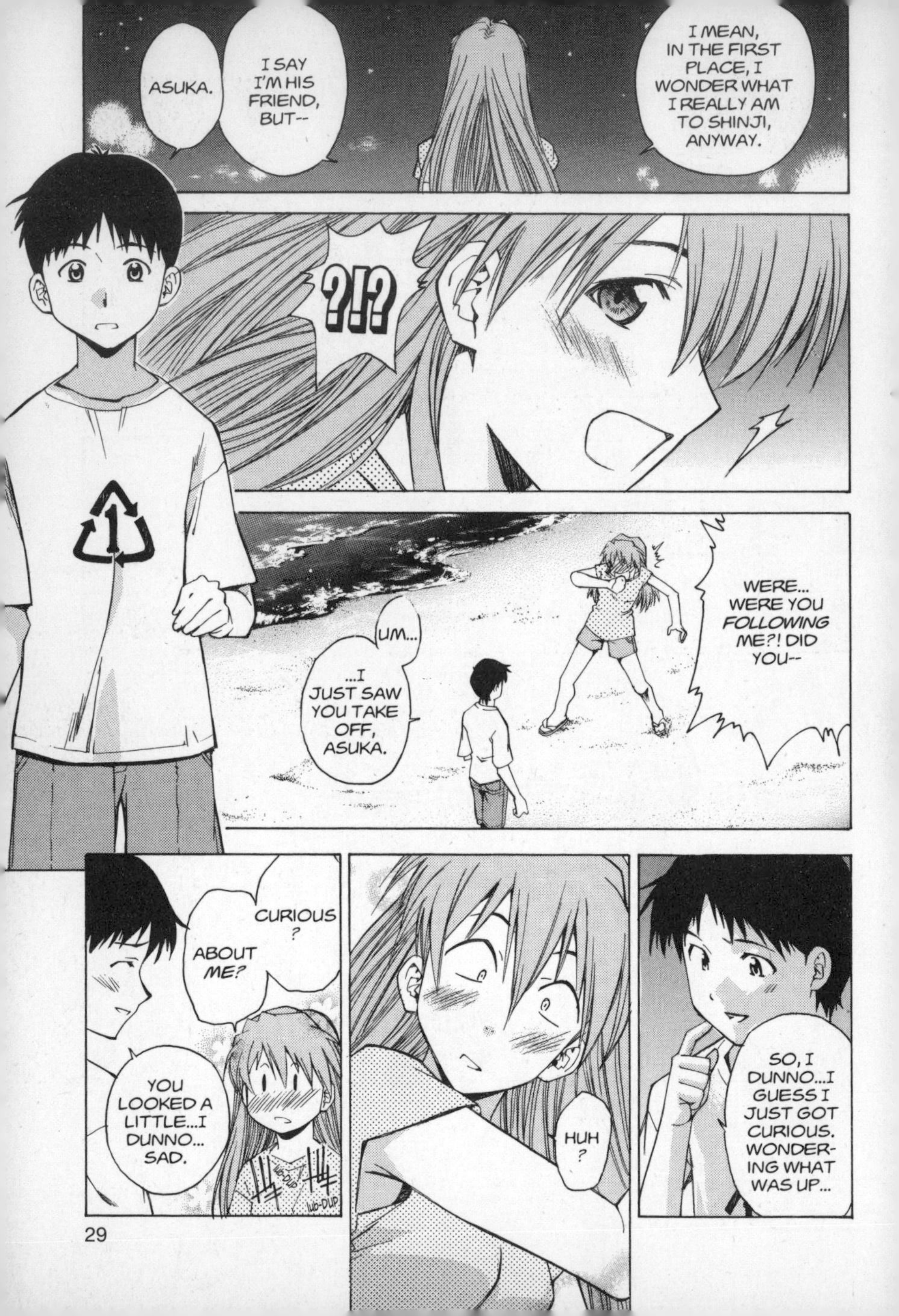
I MEAN, IN THE FIRST PLACE, I WONDER WHAT I REALLY AM TO SHINJI, ANYWAY.
I SAY I'M HIS FRIEND, BUT--
ASUKA.
?!?
WERE... WERE YOU FOLLOWING ME?! DID YOU--
UM...
...I JUST SAW YOU TAKE OFF, ASUKA.
SO, I DUNNO...I GUESS I JUST GOT CURIOUS. WONDERING WHAT WAS UP...
HUH?
CURIOUS?
ABOUT ME?
YOU LOOKED A LITTLE...I DUNNO... SAD.
lub-DUP
lub-DUP

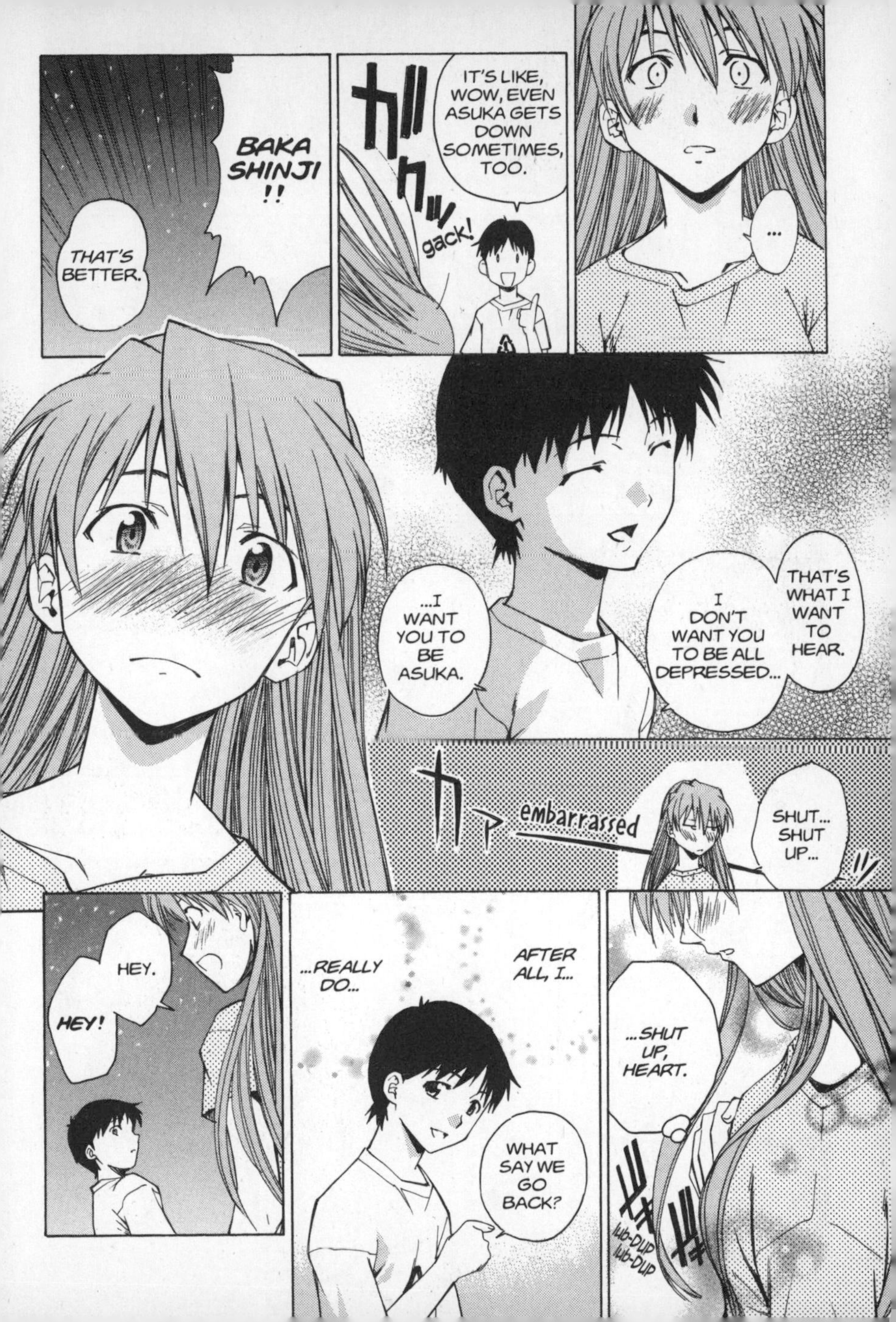
...
IT'S LIKE, WOW, EVEN ASUKA GETS DOWN SOMETIMES, TOO.
gack!
BAKA SHINJI !!
THAT'S BETTER.
THAT'S WHAT I WANT TO HEAR.
I DON'T WANT YOU TO BE ALL DEPRESSED...
...I WANT YOU TO BE ASUKA.
SHUT... SHUT UP...
embarrassed
...SHUT UP, HEART.
lub-DUP lub-DUP
AFTER ALL, I...
...REALLY DO...
WHAT SAY WE GO BACK?
HEY.
HEY!

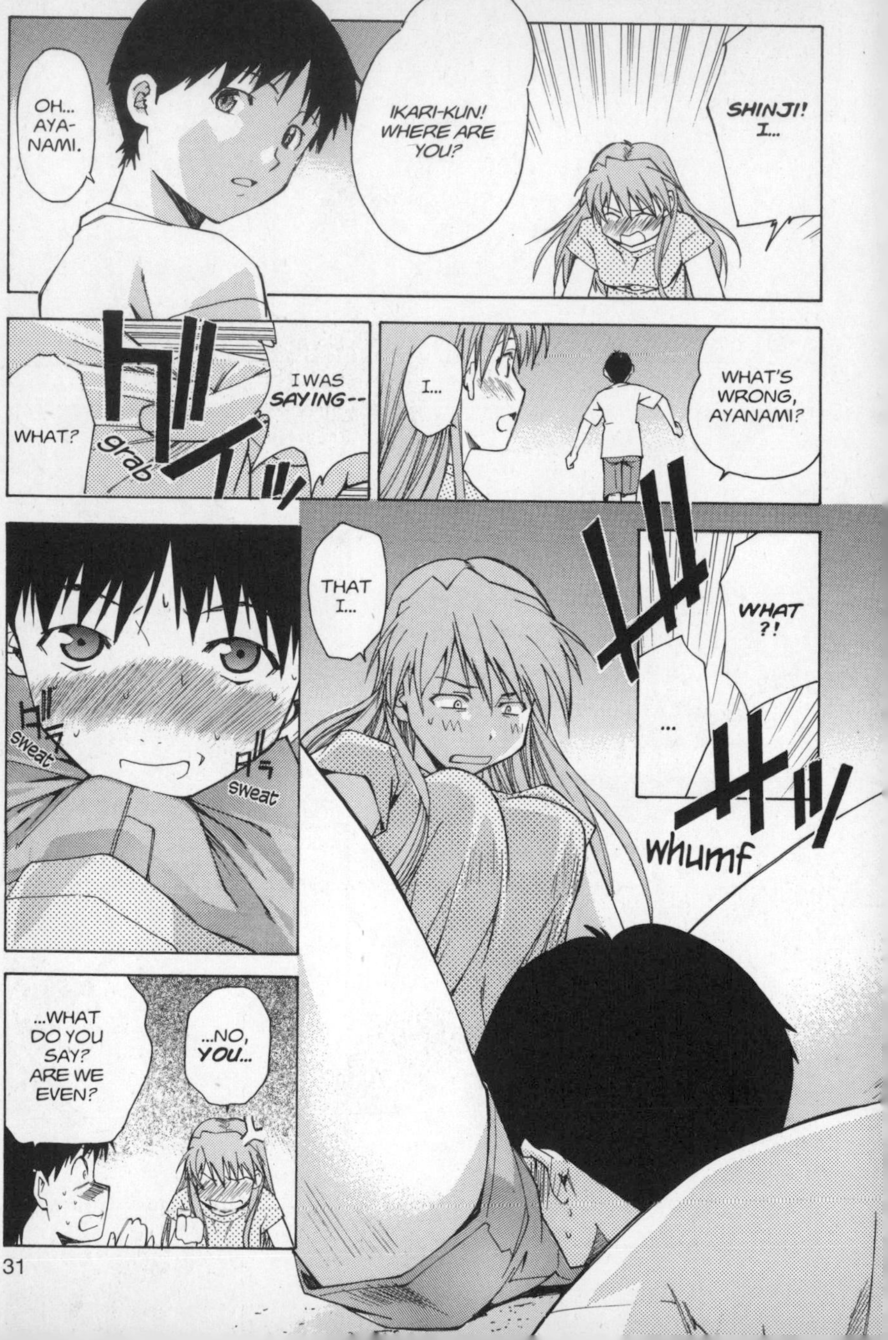
SHINJI! I...
IKARI-KUN! WHERE ARE YOU?
OH... AYA-NAMI.
WHAT'S WRONG, AYANAMI?
I...
I WAS SAYING--
grab
WHAT?
THAT I...
WHAT ?!
...
whumf
sweat
sweat
...NO, YOU...
...WHAT DO YOU SAY? ARE WE EVEN?

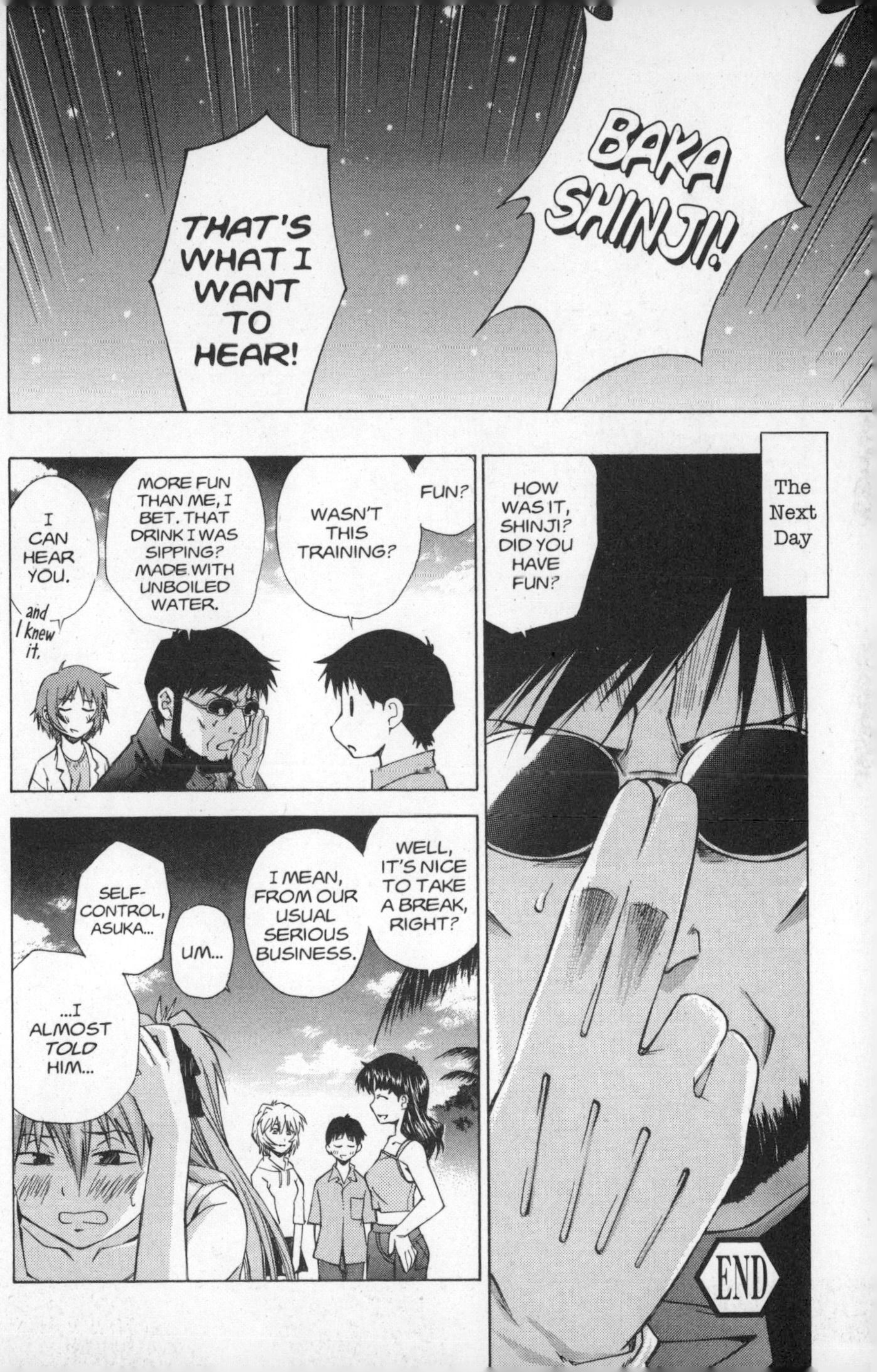
BAKA SHINJI!
THAT'S WHAT I WANT TO HEAR!
The Next Day
HOW WAS IT, SHINJI? DID YOU HAVE FUN?
END
FUN?
WASN'T THIS TRAINING?
MORE FUN THAN ME, I BET. THAT DRINK I WAS SIPPING? MADE WITH UNBOILED WATER.
I CAN HEAR YOU.
and I knew it.
WELL, IT'S NICE TO TAKE A BREAK, RIGHT?
I MEAN, FROM OUR USUAL SERIOUS BUSINESS.
UM...
SELF-CONTROL, ASUKA...
...I ALMOST TOLD HIM...

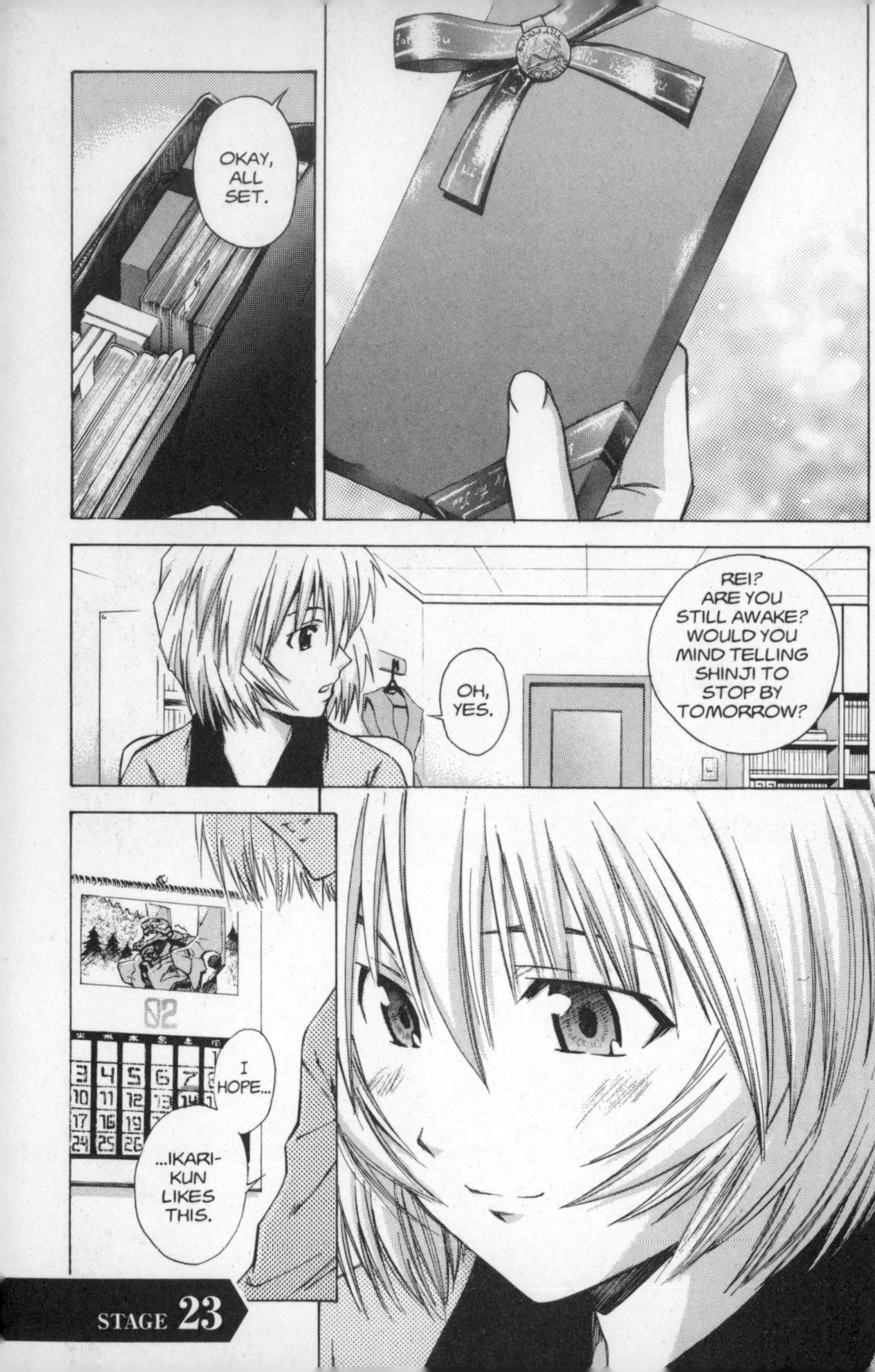
OKAY, ALL SET.
REI? ARE YOU STILL AWAKE? WOULD YOU MIND TELLING SHINJI TO STOP BY TOMORROW?
OH, YES.
I HOPE...
...IKARI-KUN LIKES THIS.
STAGE 23

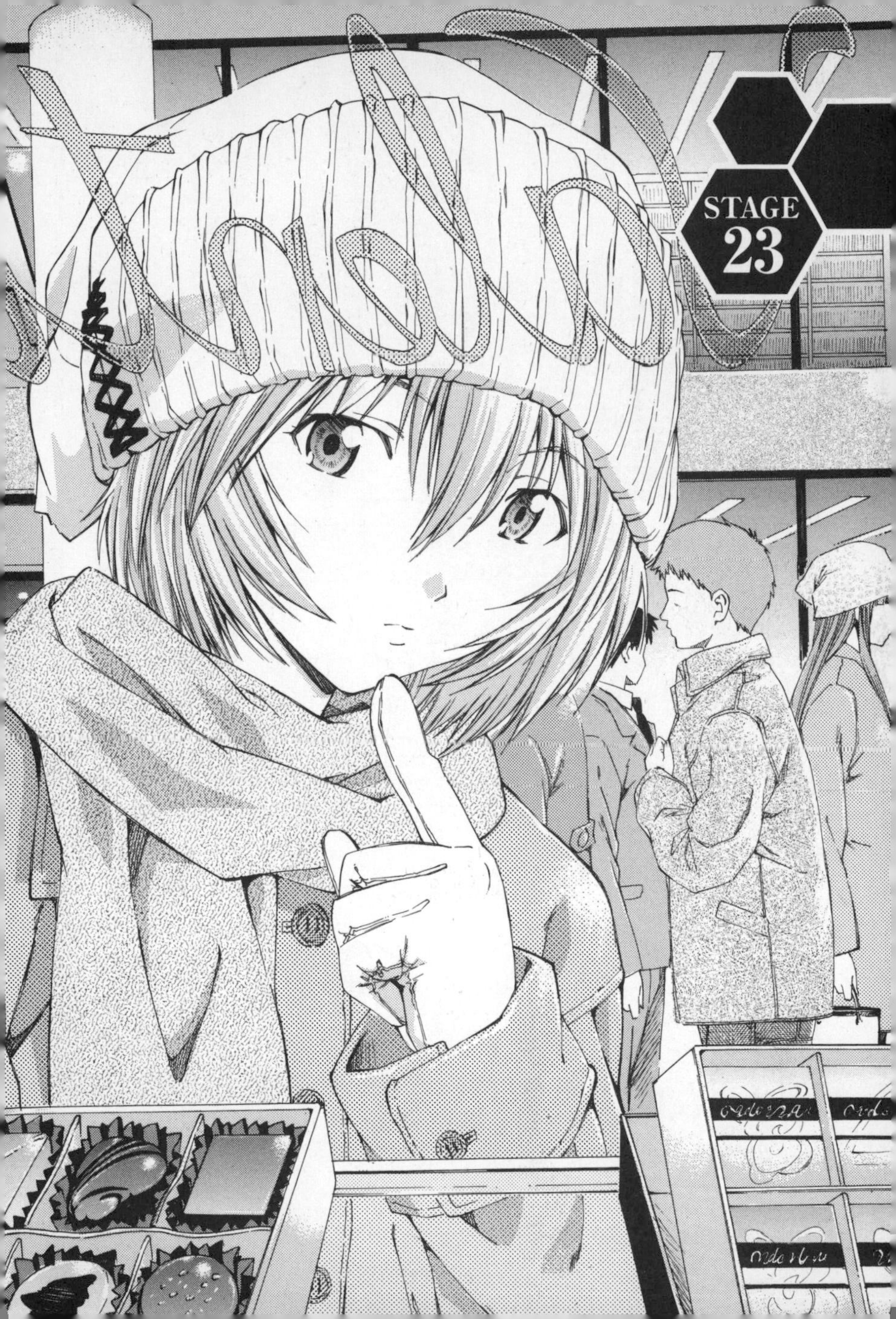
STAGE
23

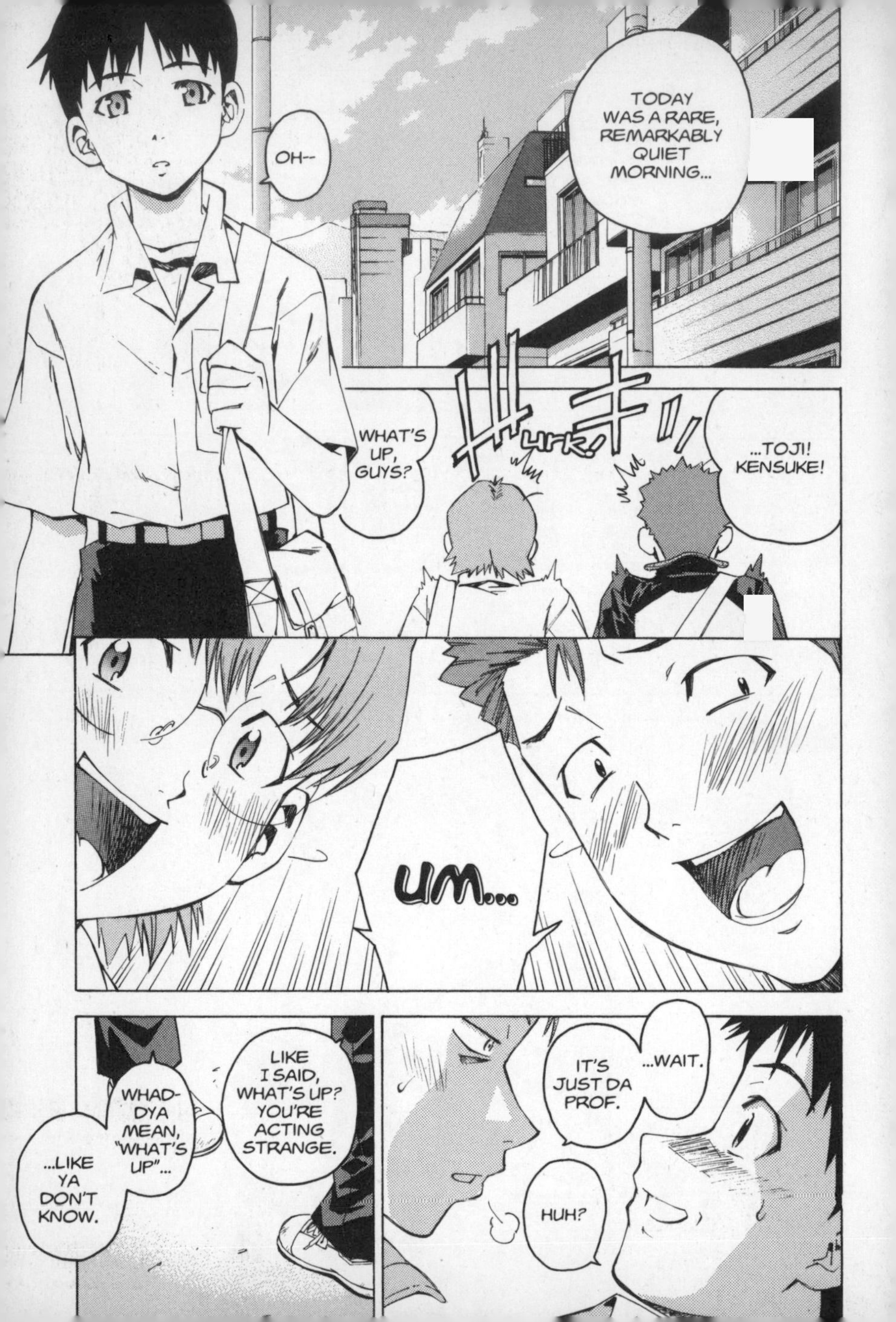
TODAY WAS A RARE, REMARKABLY QUIET MORNING...
...TOJI! KENSUKE!
Hurk!
WHAT'S UP, GUYS?
OH--
UM...
...WAIT.
IT'S JUST DA PROF.
HUH?
LIKE I SAID, WHAT'S UP? YOU'RE ACTING STRANGE.
WHAD-DYA MEAN, "WHAT'S UP"...
...LIKE YA DON'T KNOW.

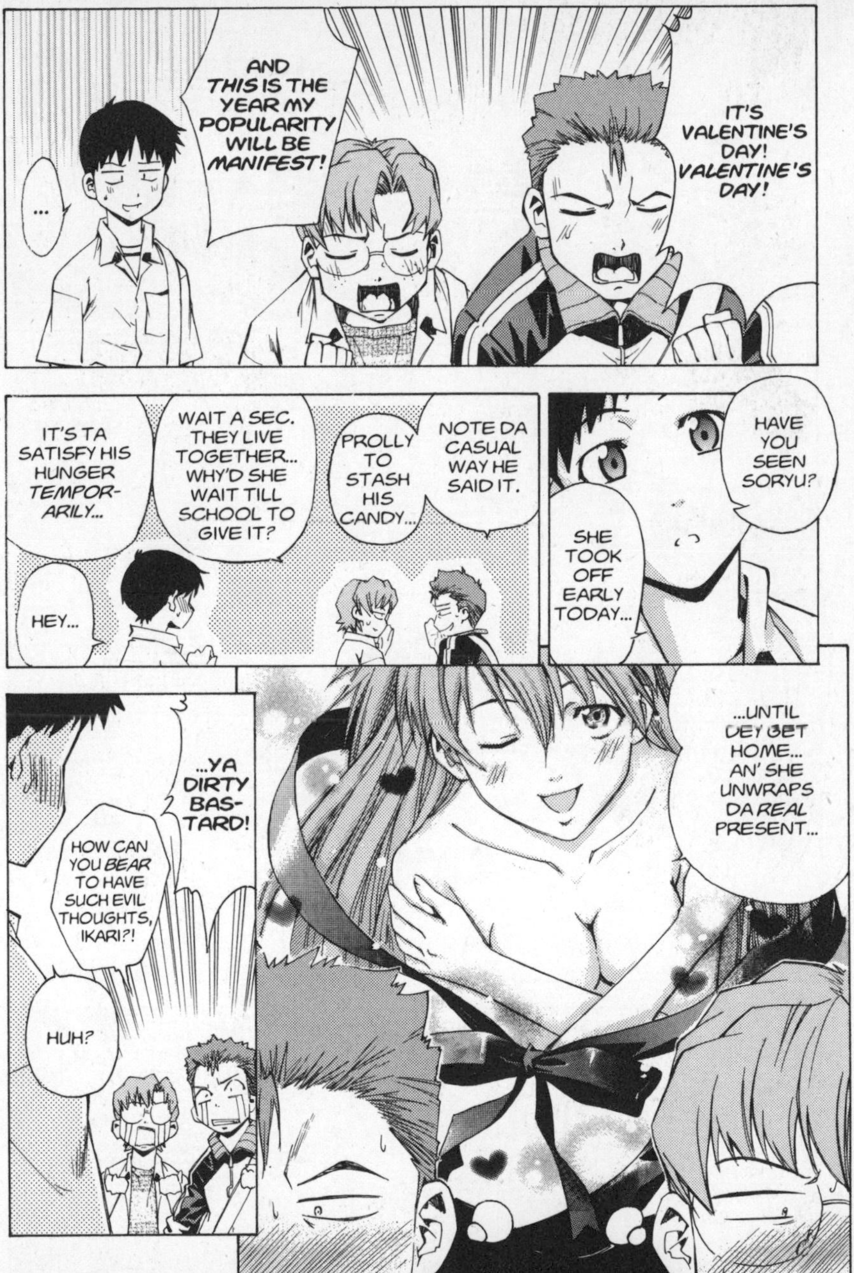
IT'S VALENTINE'S DAY! VALENTINE'S DAY!
AND THIS IS THE YEAR MY POPULARITY WILL BE MANIFEST!
...
HAVE YOU SEEN SORYU?
SHE TOOK OFF EARLY TODAY...
NOTE DA CASUAL WAY HE SAID IT.
PROLLY TO STASH HIS CANDY...
WAIT A SEC. THEY LIVE TOGETHER... WHY'D SHE WAIT TILL SCHOOL TO GIVE IT?
IT'S TA SATISFY HIS HUNGER TEMPORARILY...
HEY...
...UNTIL DEY GET HOME... AN' SHE UNWRAPS DA REAL PRESENT...
...YA DIRTY BASTARD!
HOW CAN YOU BEAR TO HAVE SUCH EVIL THOUGHTS, IKARI?!
HUH?

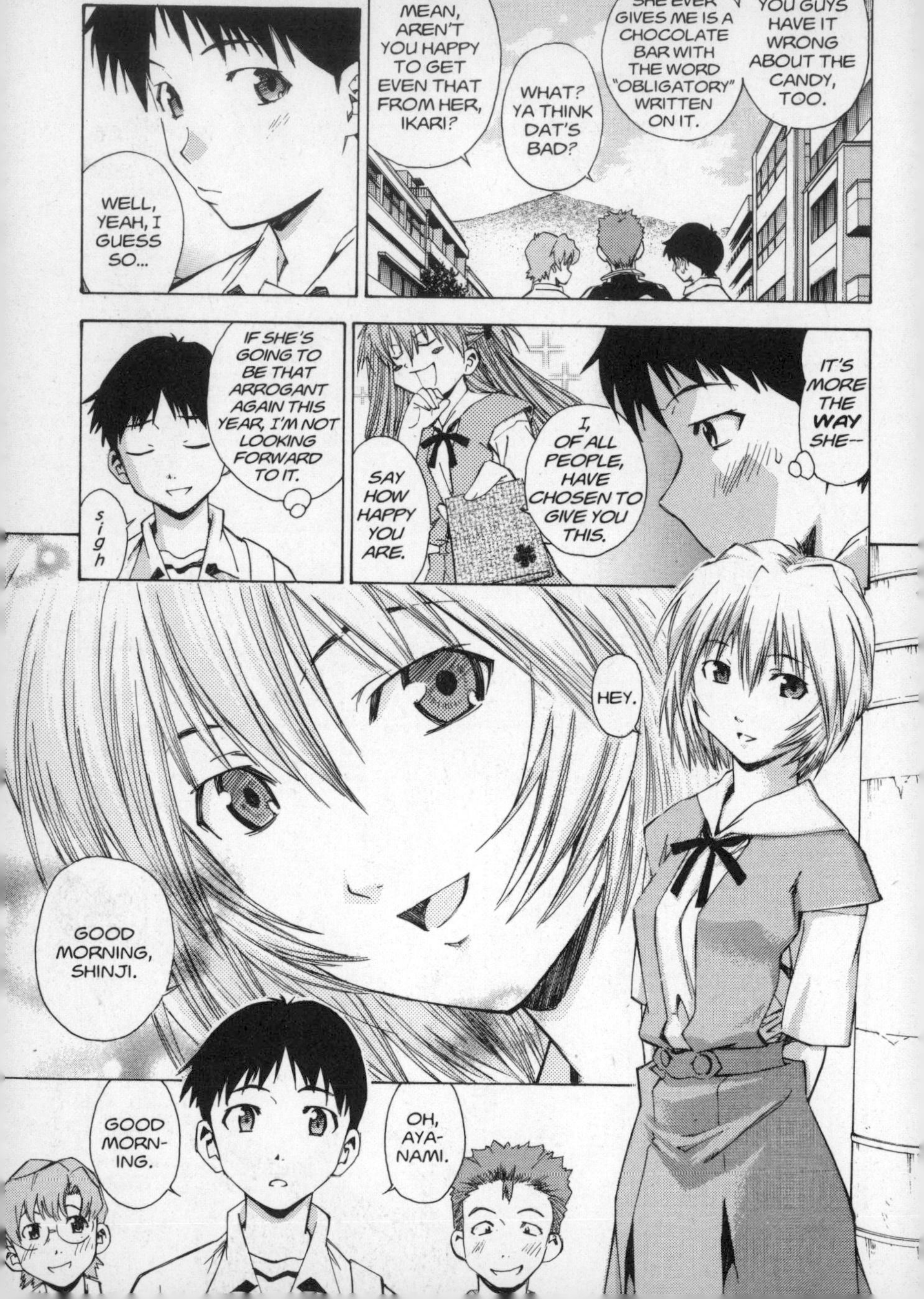
ANYWAY, YOU GUYS HAVE IT WRONG ABOUT THE CANDY, TOO.
ALL SHE EVER GIVES ME IS A CHOCOLATE BAR WITH THE WORD "OBLIGATORY" WRITTEN ON IT.
WHAT? YA THINK DAT'S BAD?
I MEAN, AREN'T YOU HAPPY TO GET EVEN THAT FROM HER, IKARI?
WELL, YEAH, I GUESS SO...
IT'S MORE THE **WAY** SHE--
I, OF ALL PEOPLE, HAVE CHOSEN TO GIVE YOU THIS.
SAY HOW HAPPY YOU ARE.
IF SHE'S GOING TO BE THAT ARROGANT AGAIN THIS YEAR, I'M NOT LOOKING FORWARD TO IT.
sigh
HEY.
GOOD MORNING, SHINJI.
OH, AYA-NAMI.
GOOD MORN-ING.

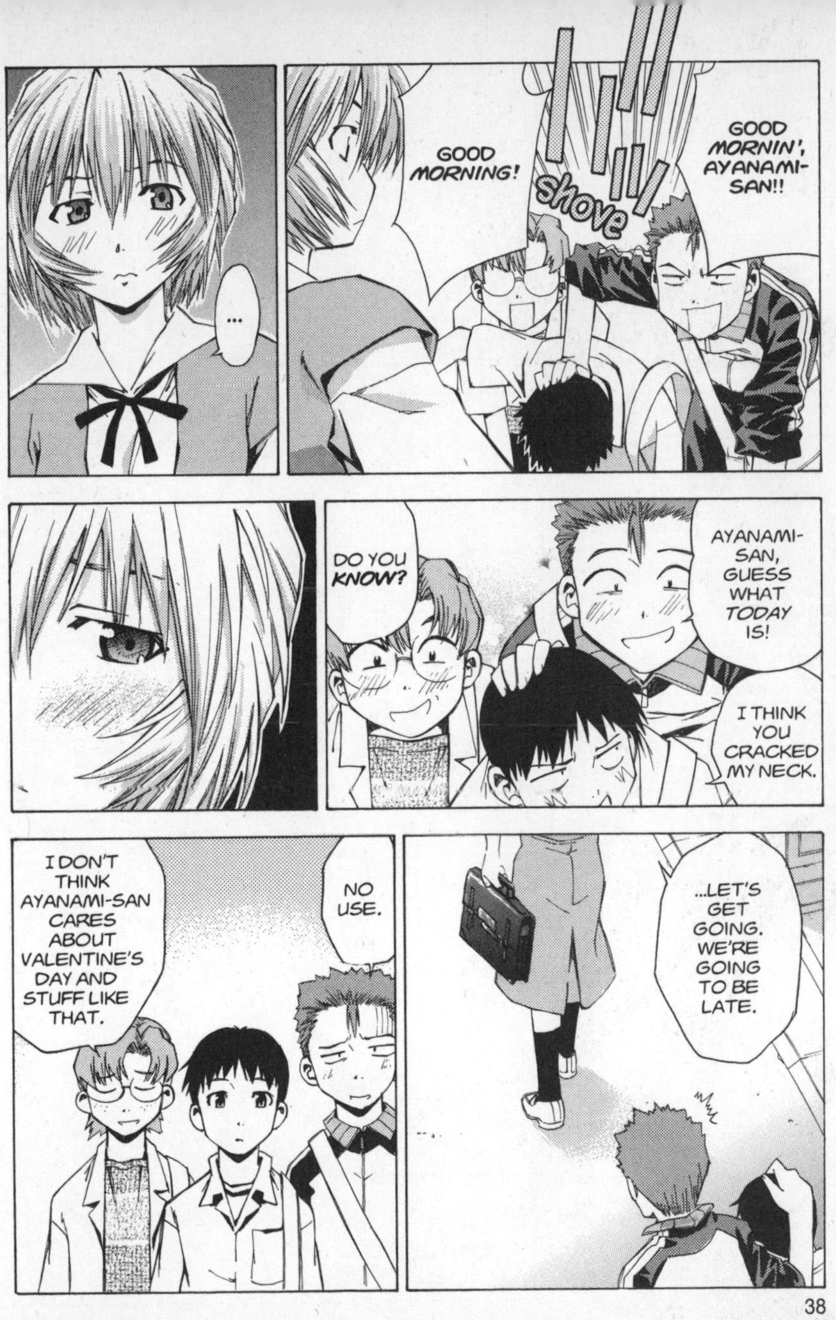
GOOD MORNIN', AYANAMI-SAN!!
shove
GOOD MORNING!
...
AYANAMI-SAN, GUESS WHAT TODAY IS!
DO YOU KNOW?
I THINK YOU CRACKED MY NECK.
...LET'S GET GOING. WE'RE GOING TO BE LATE.
NO USE.
I DON'T THINK AYANAMI-SAN CARES ABOUT VALENTINE'S DAY AND STUFF LIKE THAT.

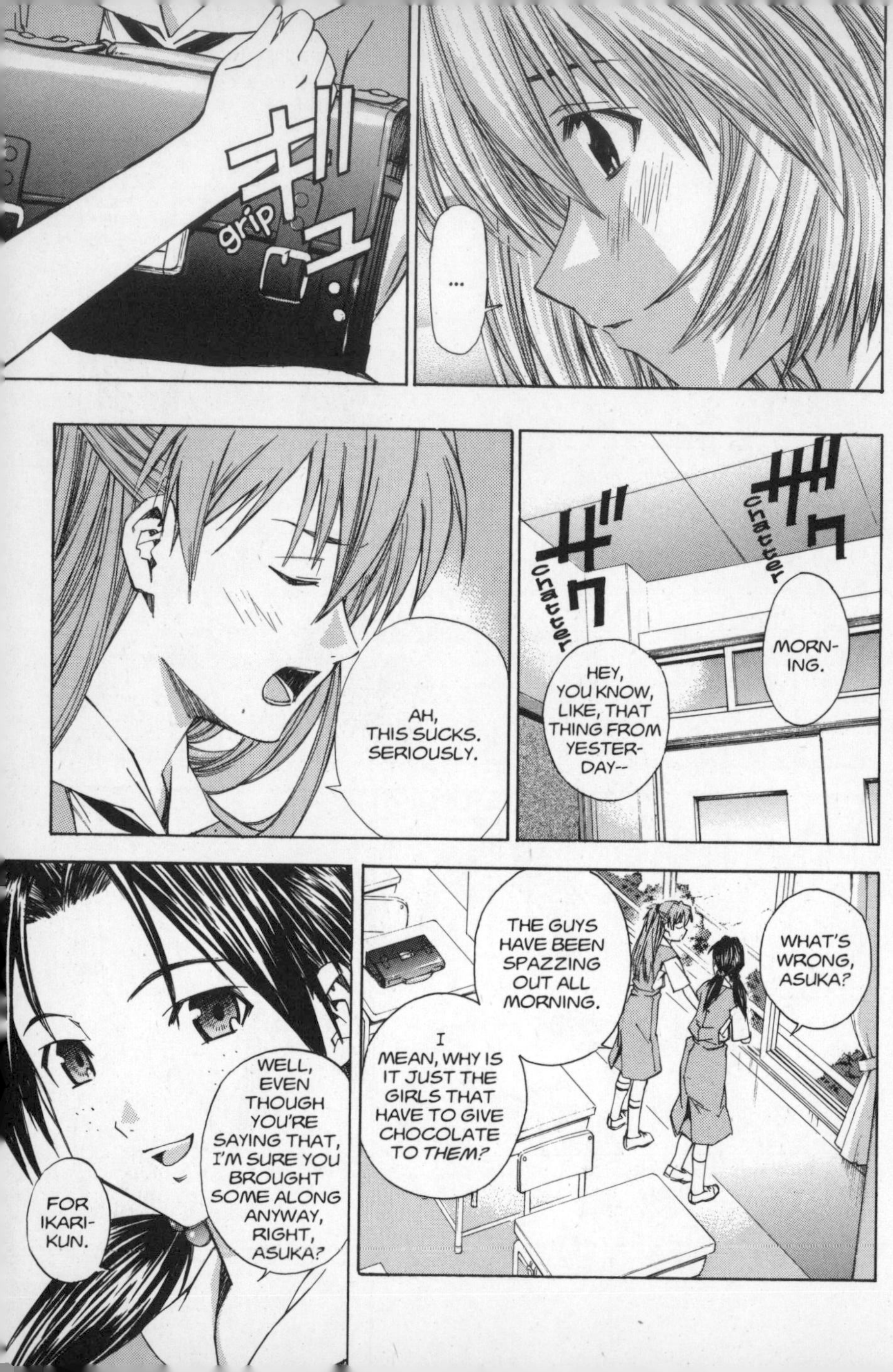
...
grip
chatter
chatter
MORNING.
HEY, YOU KNOW, LIKE, THAT THING FROM YESTERDAY--
AH, THIS SUCKS. SERIOUSLY.
WHAT'S WRONG, ASUKA?
THE GUYS HAVE BEEN SPAZZING OUT ALL MORNING.
I MEAN, WHY IS IT JUST THE GIRLS THAT HAVE TO GIVE CHOCOLATE TO *THEM*?
WELL, EVEN THOUGH YOU'RE SAYING THAT, I'M SURE YOU BROUGHT SOME ALONG ANYWAY, RIGHT, ASUKA?
FOR IKARI-KUN.

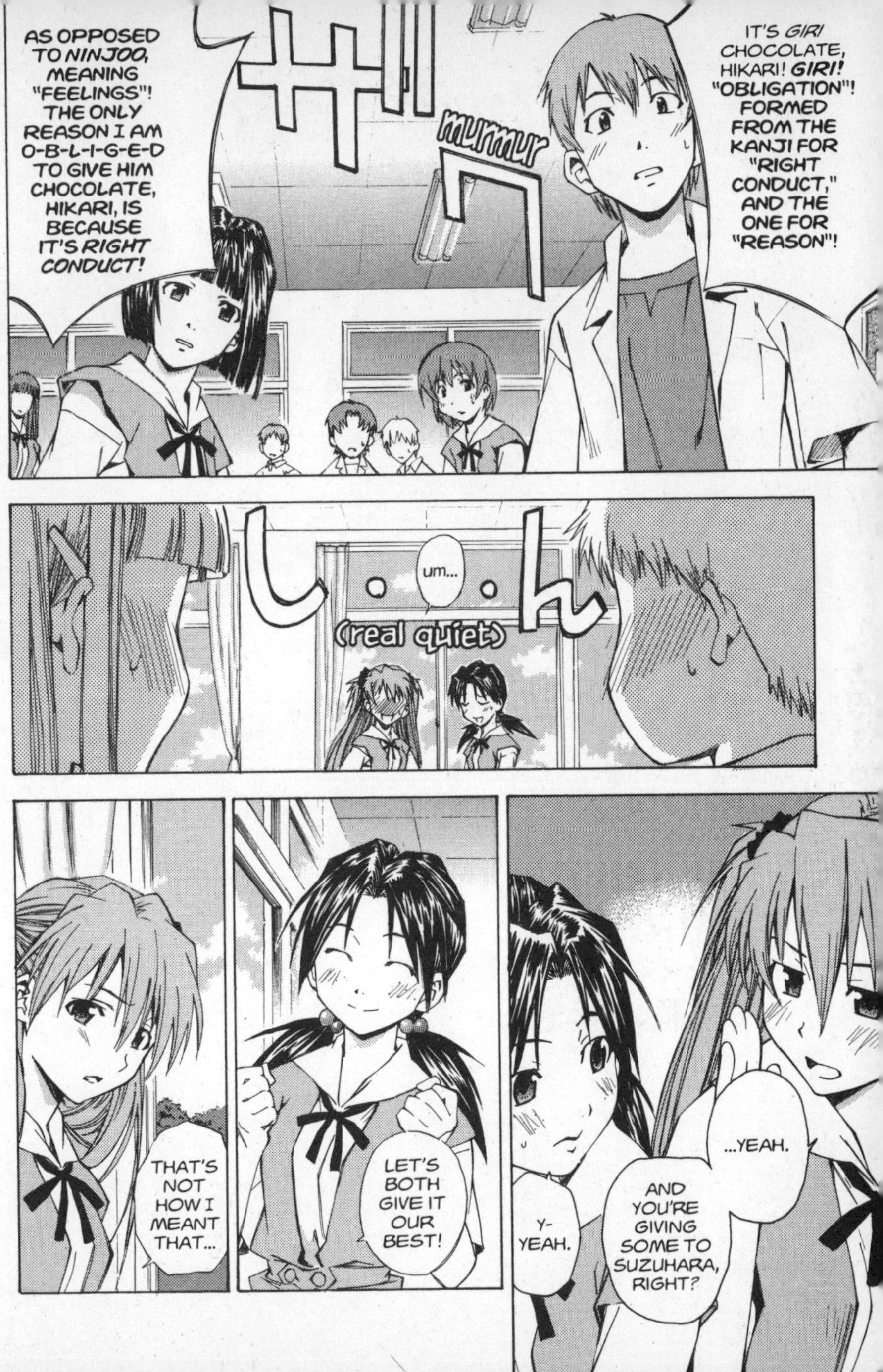
IT'S GIRI CHOCOLATE, HIKARI! GIRI! "OBLIGATION"! FORMED FROM THE KANJI FOR "RIGHT CONDUCT," AND THE ONE FOR "REASON"!
murmur
AS OPPOSED TO NINJOO, MEANING "FEELINGS"! THE ONLY REASON I AM O-B-L-I-G-E-D TO GIVE HIM CHOCOLATE, HIKARI, IS BECAUSE IT'S RIGHT CONDUCT!
し・・ん
um...
(real quiet)
...YEAH.
AND YOU'RE GIVING SOME TO SUZUHARA, RIGHT?
Y-YEAH.
LET'S BOTH GIVE IT OUR BEST!
THAT'S NOT HOW I MEANT THAT...

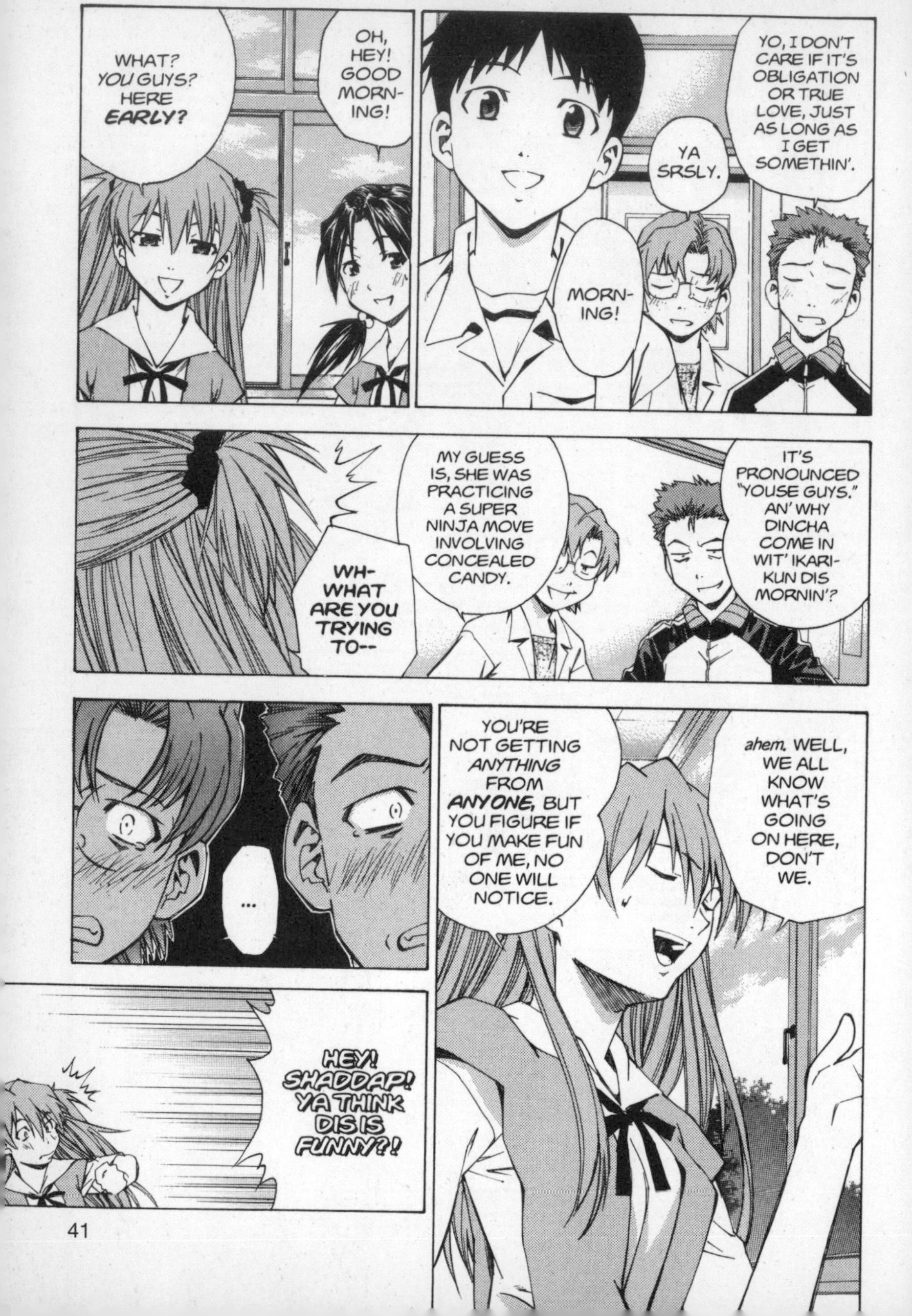
YO, I DON'T CARE IF IT'S OBLIGATION OR TRUE LOVE, JUST AS LONG AS I GET SOMETHIN'.
YA SRSLY.
MORNING!
OH, HEY! GOOD MORNING!
WHAT? YOU GUYS? HERE EARLY?
IT'S PRONOUNCED "YOUSE GUYS." AN' WHY DINCHA COME IN WIT' IKARI-KUN DIS MORNIN'?
MY GUESS IS, SHE WAS PRACTICING A SUPER NINJA MOVE INVOLVING CONCEALED CANDY.
WH- WHAT ARE YOU TRYING TO--
ahem. WELL, WE ALL KNOW WHAT'S GOING ON HERE, DON'T WE.
YOU'RE NOT GETTING ANYTHING FROM ANYONE, BUT YOU FIGURE IF YOU MAKE FUN OF ME, NO ONE WILL NOTICE.
...
HEY! SHADDAP! YA THINK DIS IS FUNNY?!

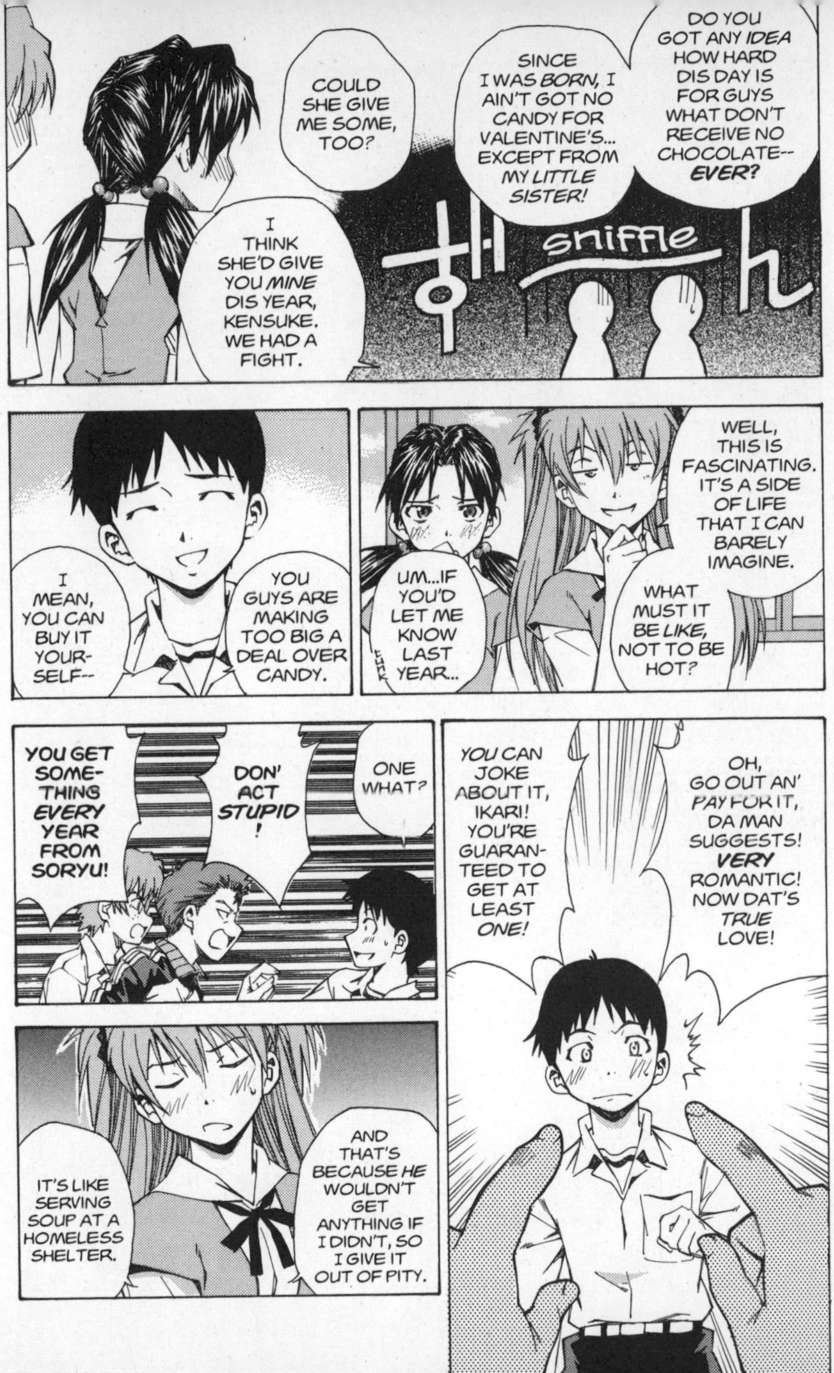
DO YOU GOT ANY IDEA HOW HARD DIS DAY IS FOR GUYS WHAT DON'T RECEIVE NO CHOCOLATE-- EVER?
SINCE I WAS BORN, I AIN'T GOT NO CANDY FOR VALENTINE'S... EXCEPT FROM MY LITTLE SISTER!
COULD SHE GIVE ME SOME, TOO?
sniffle
I THINK SHE'D GIVE YOU MINE DIS YEAR, KENSUKE. WE HAD A FIGHT.
WELL, THIS IS FASCINATING. IT'S A SIDE OF LIFE THAT I CAN BARELY IMAGINE.
WHAT MUST IT BE LIKE, NOT TO BE HOT?
UM...IF YOU'D LET ME KNOW LAST YEAR...
YOU GUYS ARE MAKING TOO BIG A DEAL OVER CANDY.
I MEAN, YOU CAN BUY IT YOURSELF--
OH, GO OUT AN' PAY FOR IT, DA MAN SUGGESTS! VERY ROMANTIC! NOW DAT'S TRUE LOVE!
YOU CAN JOKE ABOUT IT, IKARI! YOU'RE GUARANTEED TO GET AT LEAST ONE!
ONE WHAT?
DON' ACT STUPID!
YOU GET SOMETHING EVERY YEAR FROM SORYU!
AND THAT'S BECAUSE HE WOULDN'T GET ANYTHING IF I DIDN'T, SO I GIVE IT OUT OF PITY.
IT'S LIKE SERVING SOUP AT A HOMELESS SHELTER.

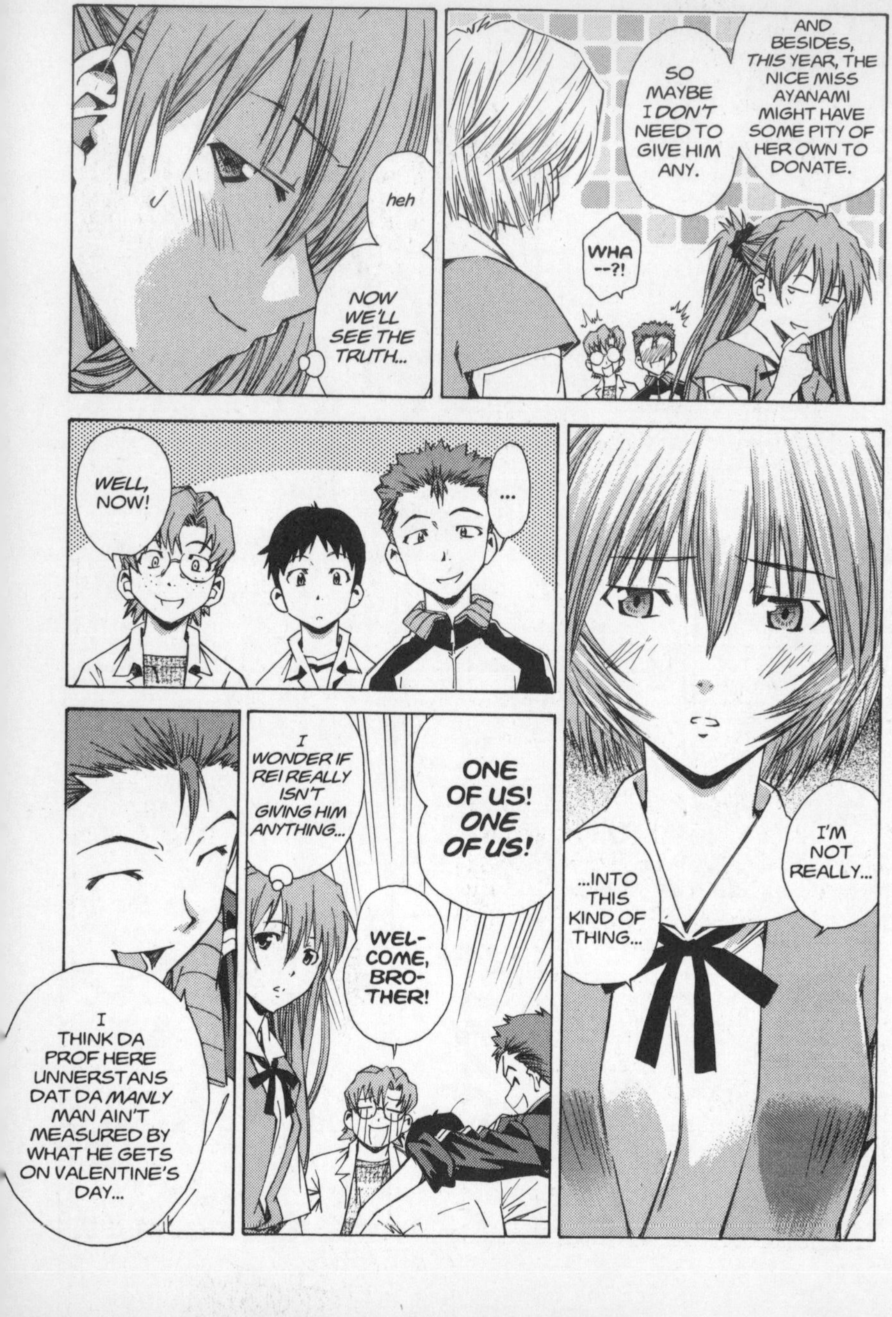
AND BESIDES, THIS YEAR, THE NICE MISS AYANAMI MIGHT HAVE SOME PITY OF HER OWN TO DONATE.
SO MAYBE I DON'T NEED TO GIVE HIM ANY.
WHA --?!
heh
NOW WE'LL SEE THE TRUTH...
I'M NOT REALLY...
...INTO THIS KIND OF THING...
...
WELL, NOW!
ONE OF US! ONE OF US!
I WONDER IF REI REALLY ISN'T GIVING HIM ANYTHING...
WEL-COME, BRO-THER!
I THINK DA PROF HERE UNNERSTANS DAT DA MANLY MAN AIN'T MEASURED BY WHAT HE GETS ON VALENTINE'S DAY...

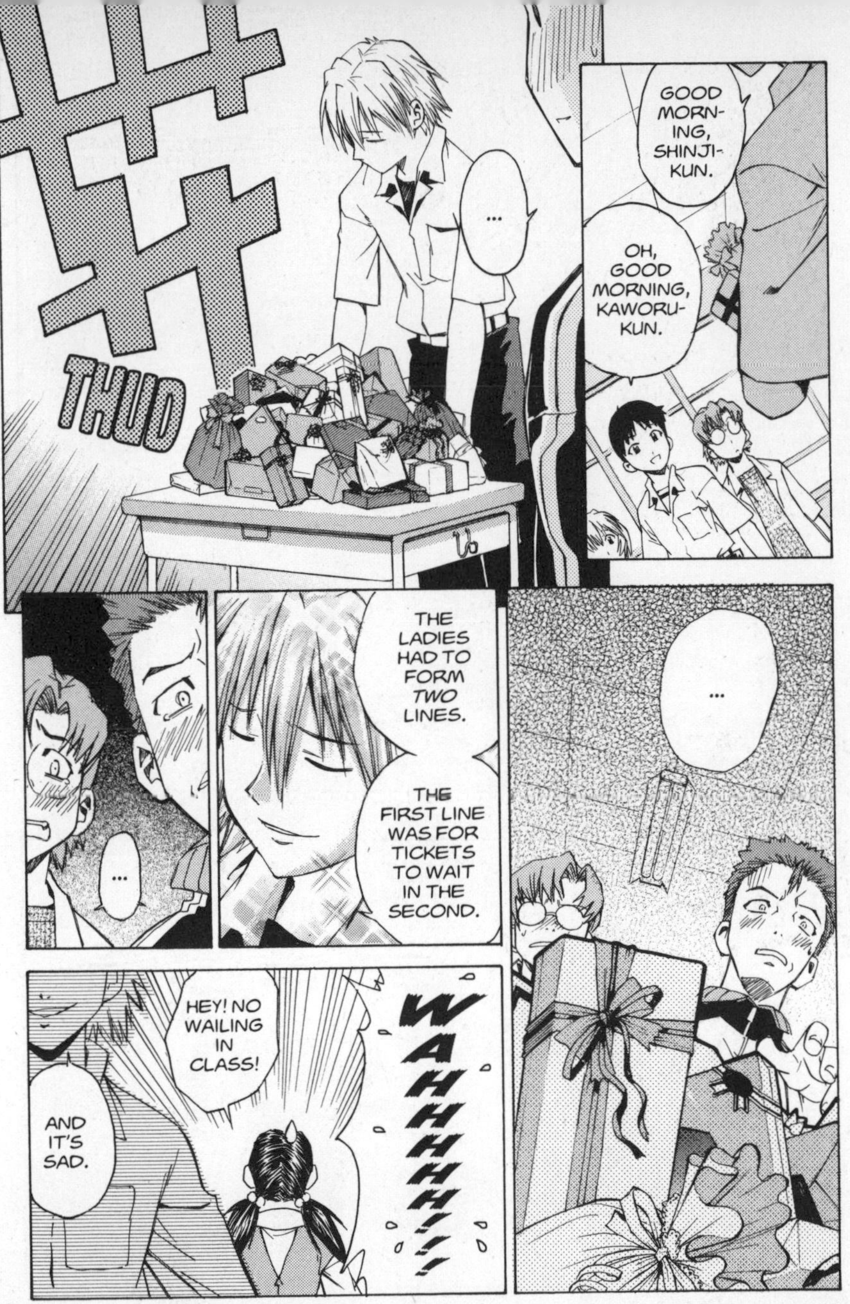
GOOD MORNING, SHINJI-KUN.
OH, GOOD MORNING, KAWORU-KUN.
...
THUD
...
THE LADIES HAD TO FORM *TWO* LINES.
THE FIRST LINE WAS FOR TICKETS TO WAIT IN THE SECOND.
...
WAHHHHHH!!!
HEY! NO WAILING IN CLASS!
AND IT'S SAD.

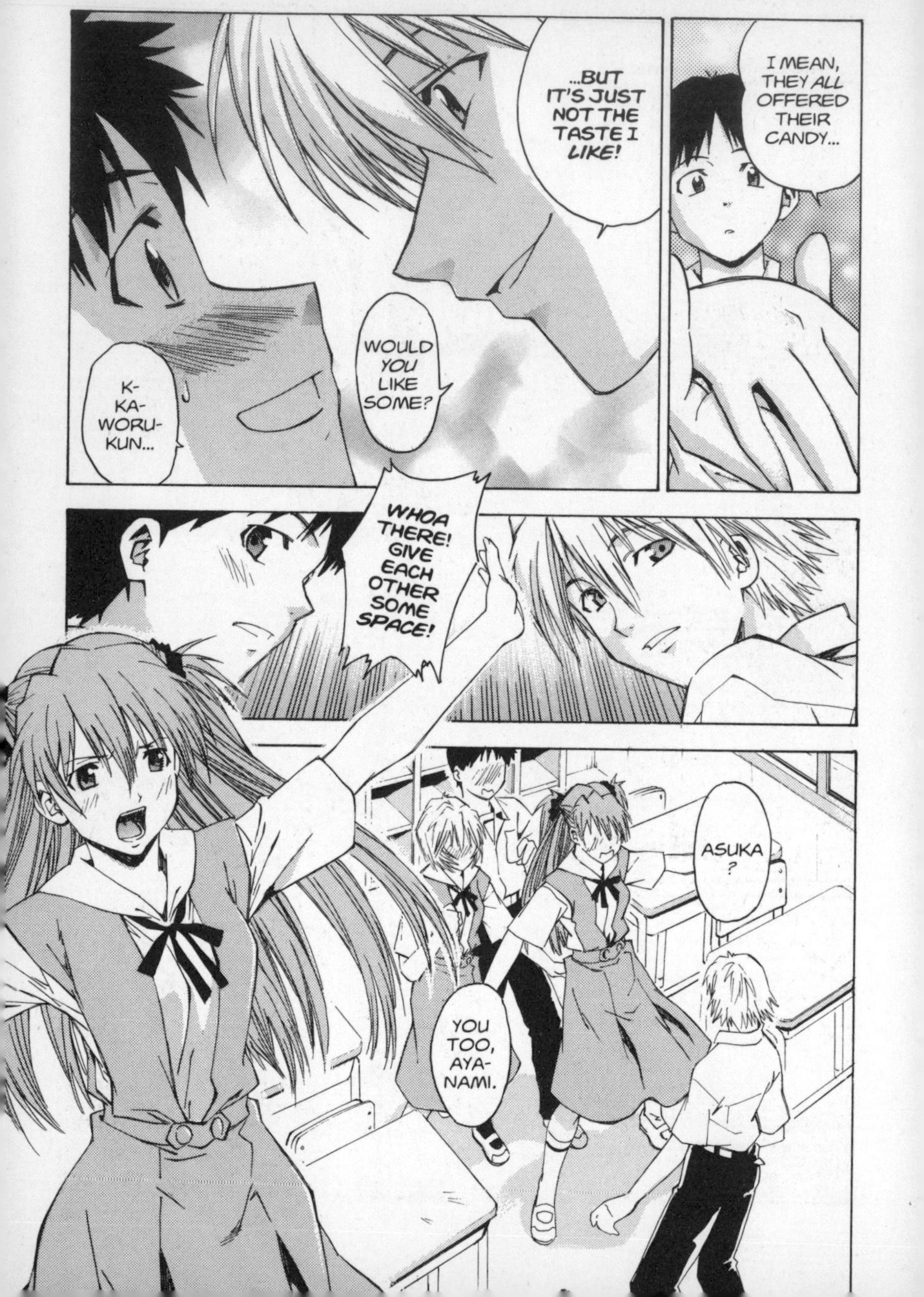
I MEAN, THEY ALL OFFERED THEIR CANDY...
...BUT IT'S JUST NOT THE TASTE I LIKE!
WOULD YOU LIKE SOME?
K-KA-WORU-KUN...
WHOA THERE! GIVE EACH OTHER SOME SPACE!
ASUKA?
YOU TOO, AYA-NAMI.

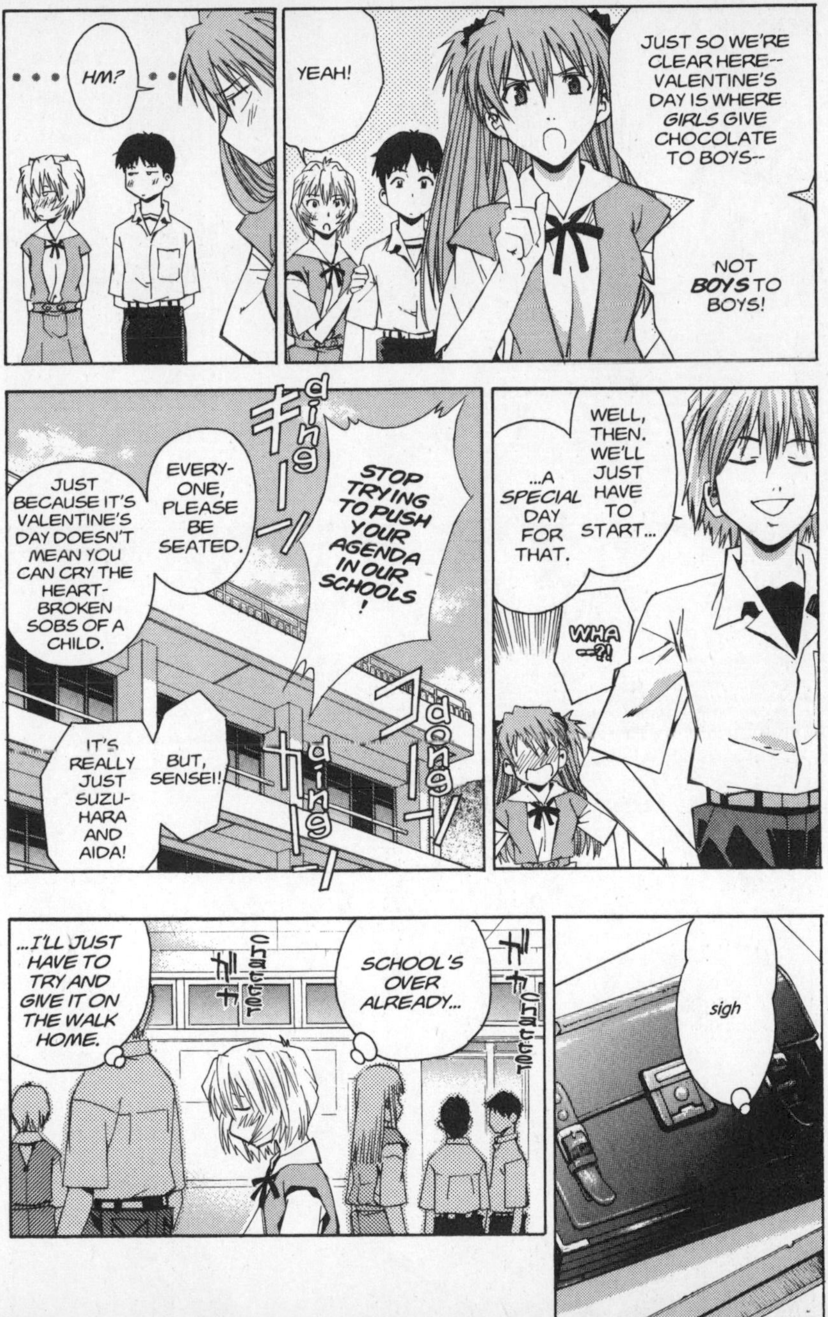
JUST SO WE'RE CLEAR HERE-- VALENTINE'S DAY IS WHERE GIRLS GIVE CHOCOLATE TO BOYS--
YEAH!
NOT BOYS TO BOYS!
... HM? ..
WELL, THEN. WE'LL JUST HAVE TO START...
...A SPECIAL DAY FOR THAT.
WHA--?!
ding dong ding
STOP TRYING TO PUSH YOUR AGENDA IN OUR SCHOOLS!
EVERY-ONE, PLEASE BE SEATED.
JUST BECAUSE IT'S VALENTINE'S DAY DOESN'T MEAN YOU CAN CRY THE HEART-BROKEN SOBS OF A CHILD.
BUT, SENSEI!
IT'S REALLY JUST SUZU-HARA AND AIDA!
sigh
chatter
SCHOOL'S OVER ALREADY...
chatter
...I'LL JUST HAVE TO TRY AND GIVE IT ON THE WALK HOME.

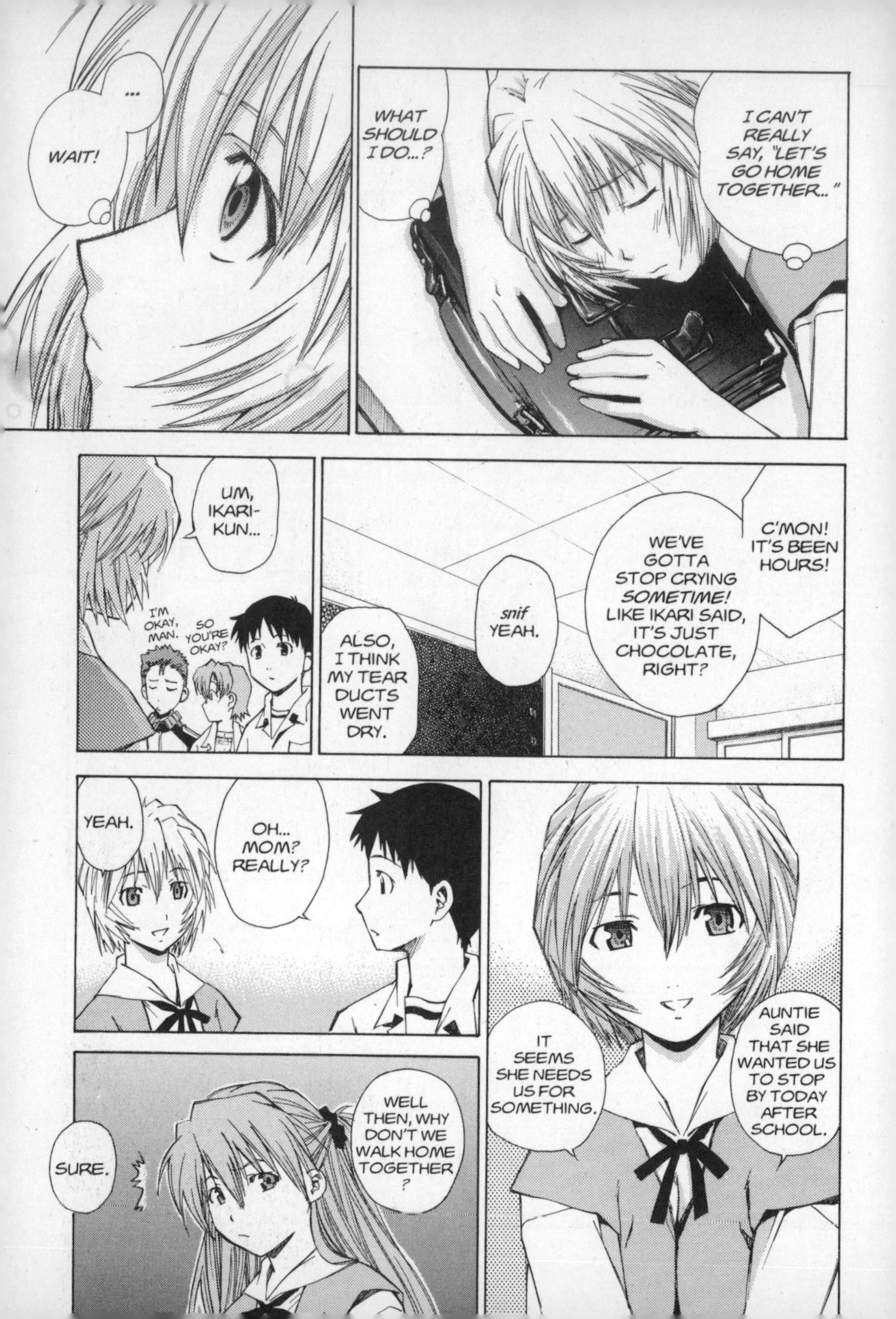
I CAN'T REALLY SAY, "LET'S GO HOME TOGETHER.."
WHAT SHOULD I DO...?
...
WAIT!
C'MON! IT'S BEEN HOURS!
WE'VE GOTTA STOP CRYING SOMETIME! LIKE IKARI SAID, IT'S JUST CHOCOLATE, RIGHT?
snif YEAH.
ALSO, I THINK MY TEAR DUCTS WENT DRY.
UM, IKARI-KUN...
SO YOU'RE OKAY?
I'M OKAY, MAN.
AUNTIE SAID THAT SHE WANTED US TO STOP BY TODAY AFTER SCHOOL.
IT SEEMS SHE NEEDS US FOR SOMETHING.
OH... MOM? REALLY?
YEAH.
WELL THEN, WHY DON'T WE WALK HOME TOGETHER?
SURE.

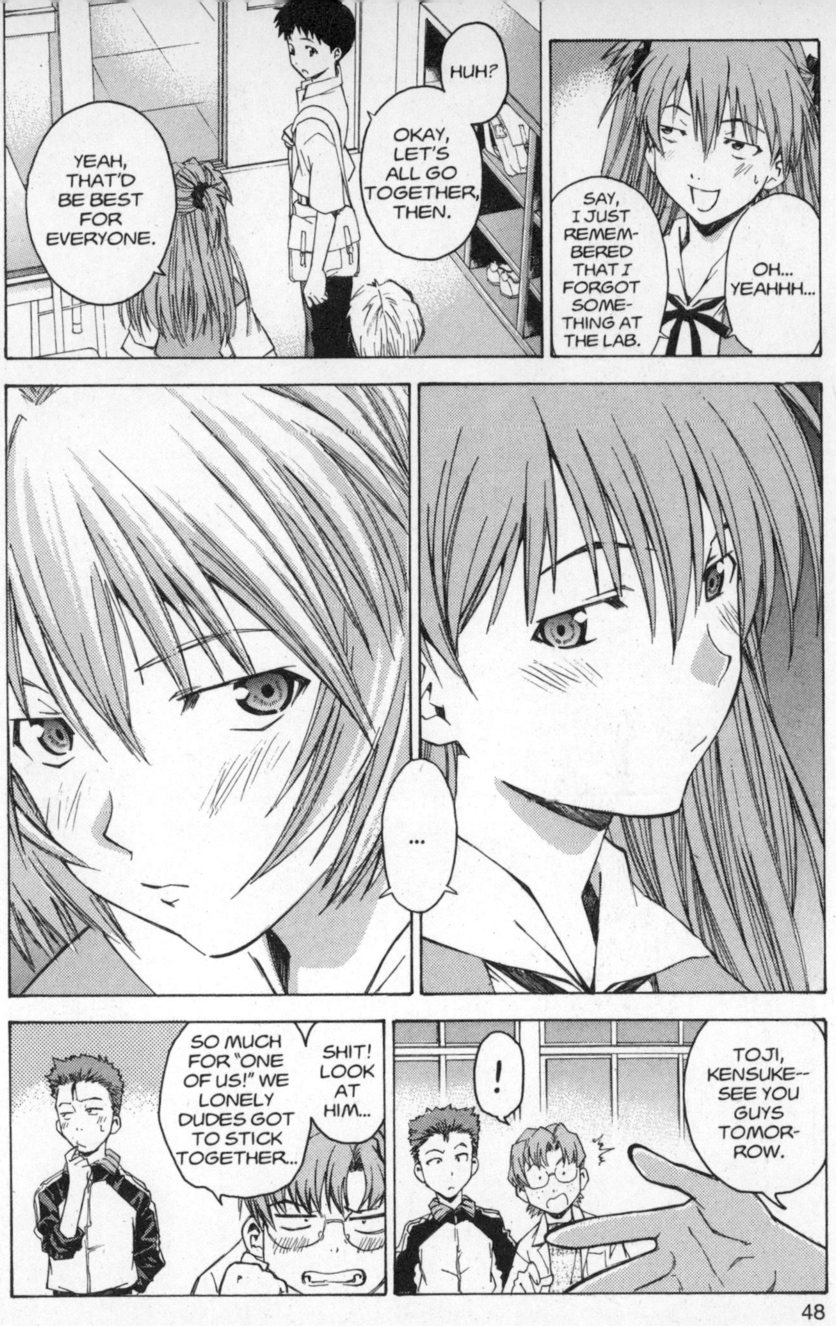
SAY, I JUST REMEMBERED THAT I FORGOT SOMETHING AT THE LAB.
OH... YEAHHH...
HUH?
OKAY, LET'S ALL GO TOGETHER, THEN.
YEAH, THAT'D BE BEST FOR EVERYONE.
...
TOJI, KENSUKE-- SEE YOU GUYS TOMORROW.
!
SHIT! LOOK AT HIM...
SO MUCH FOR "ONE OF US!" WE LONELY DUDES GOT TO STICK TOGETHER...

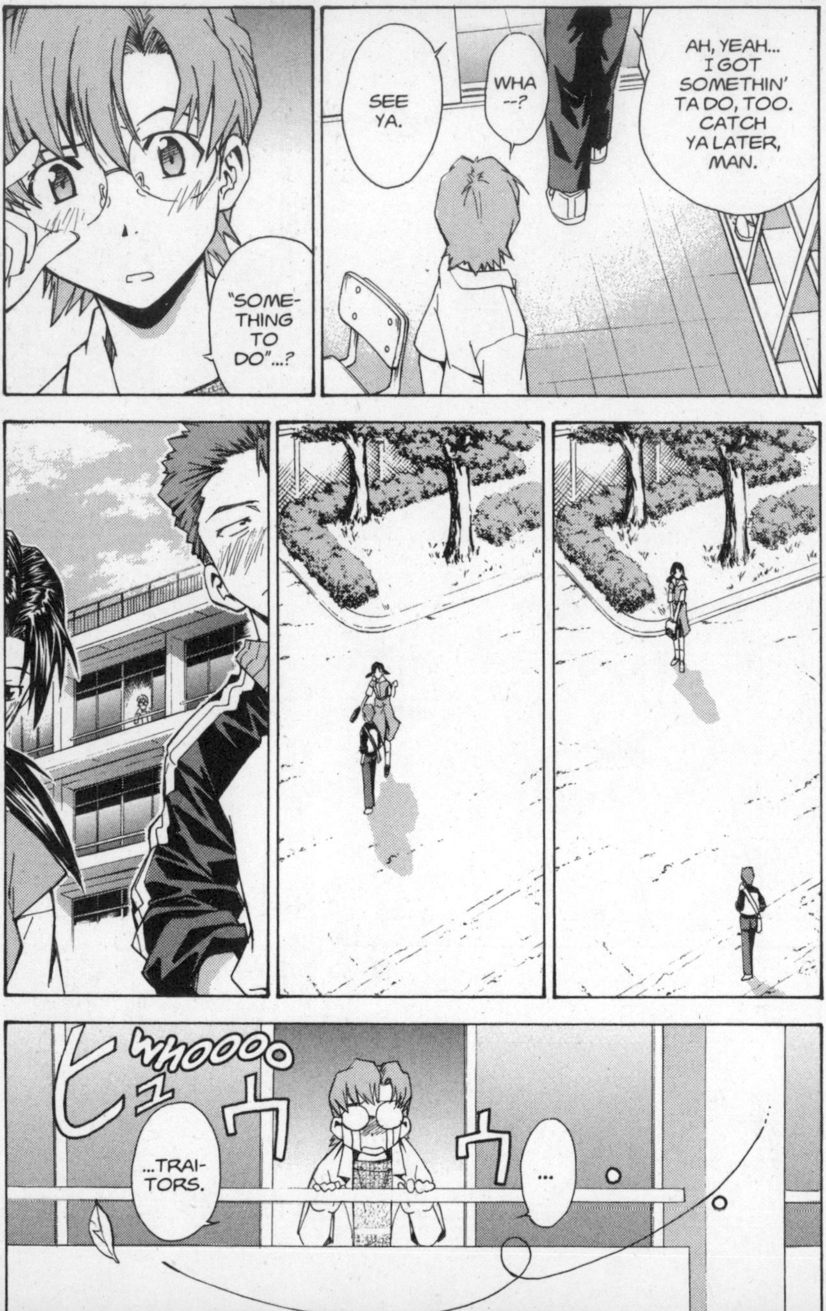
AH, YEAH... I GOT SOMETHIN' TA DO, TOO. CATCH YA LATER, MAN.
WHA --?
SEE YA.
"SOME-THING TO DO"...?
ヒュウウ
WHOOOO
...
...TRAI-TORS.

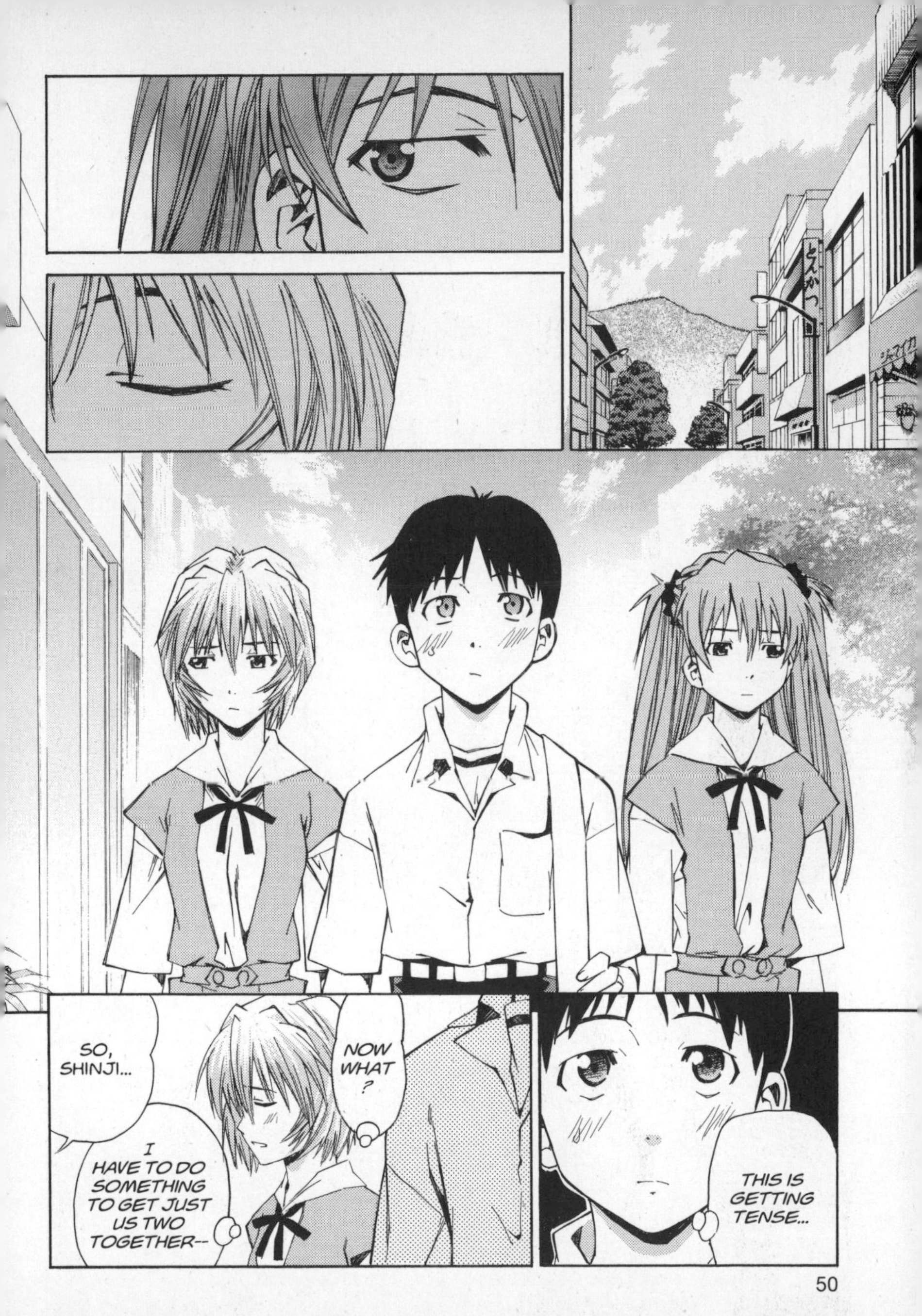
THIS IS GETTING TENSE...
NOW WHAT?
SO, SHINJI...
I HAVE TO DO SOMETHING TO GET JUST US TWO TOGETHER--

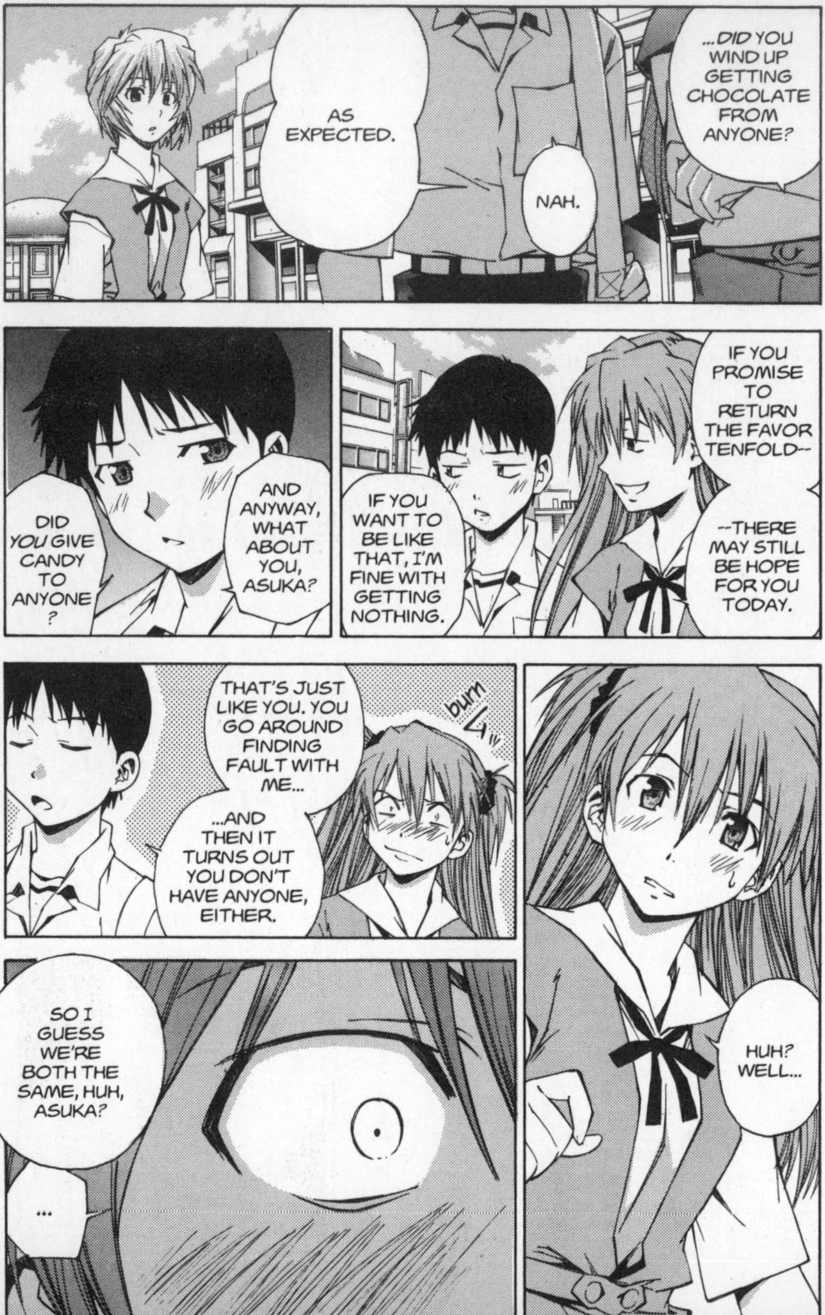
...DID YOU WIND UP GETTING CHOCOLATE FROM ANYONE?
NAH.
AS EXPECTED.
IF YOU PROMISE TO RETURN THE FAVOR TENFOLD--
--THERE MAY STILL BE HOPE FOR YOU TODAY.
IF YOU WANT TO BE LIKE THAT, I'M FINE WITH GETTING NOTHING.
AND ANYWAY, WHAT ABOUT YOU, ASUKA?
DID *YOU* GIVE CANDY TO ANYONE?
HUH? WELL...
burn
THAT'S JUST LIKE YOU. YOU GO AROUND FINDING FAULT WITH ME...
...AND THEN IT TURNS OUT YOU DON'T HAVE ANYONE, EITHER.
SO I GUESS WE'RE BOTH THE SAME, HUH, ASUKA?
...

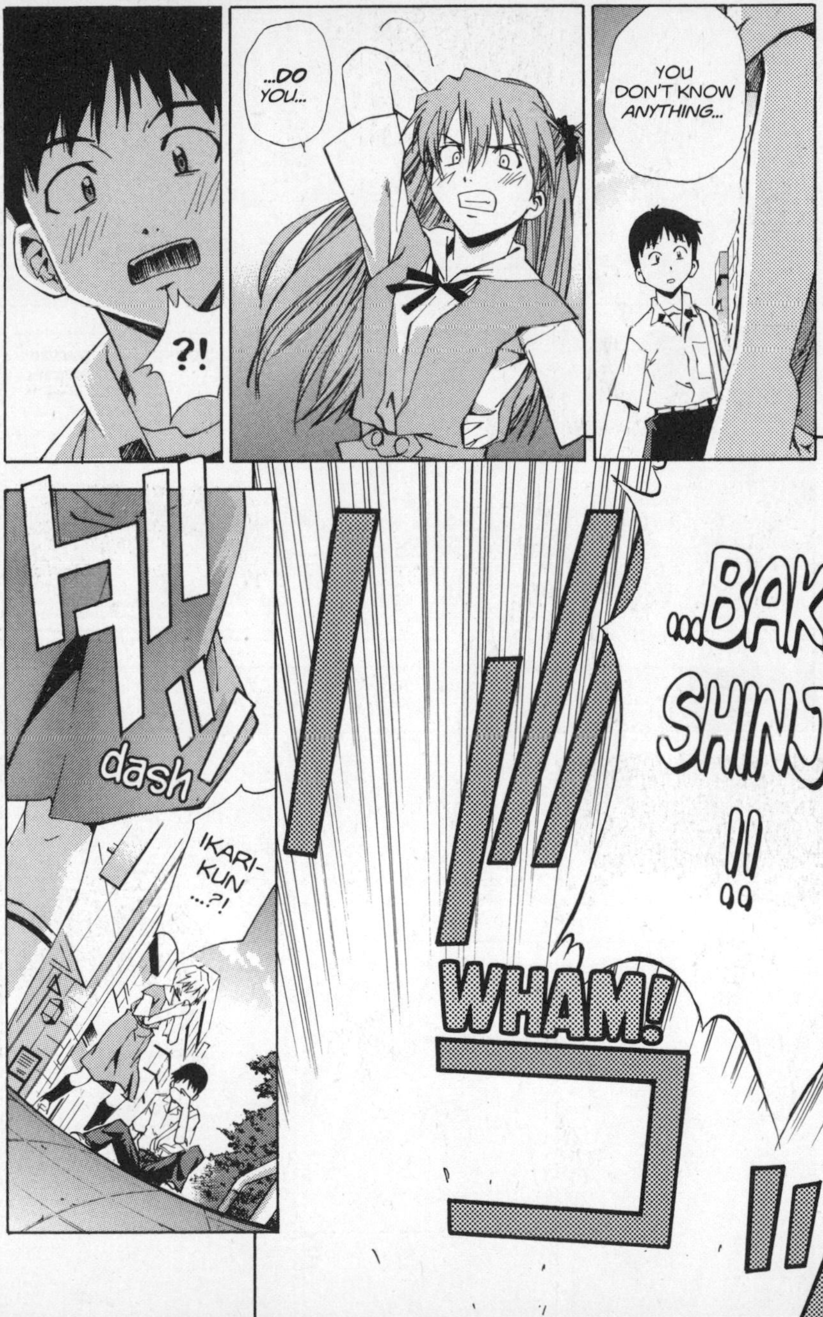
YOU DON'T KNOW ANYTHING...
...DO YOU...
?!
...BAKA SHINJI!!
WHAM!
dash
IKARI-KUN ...?!

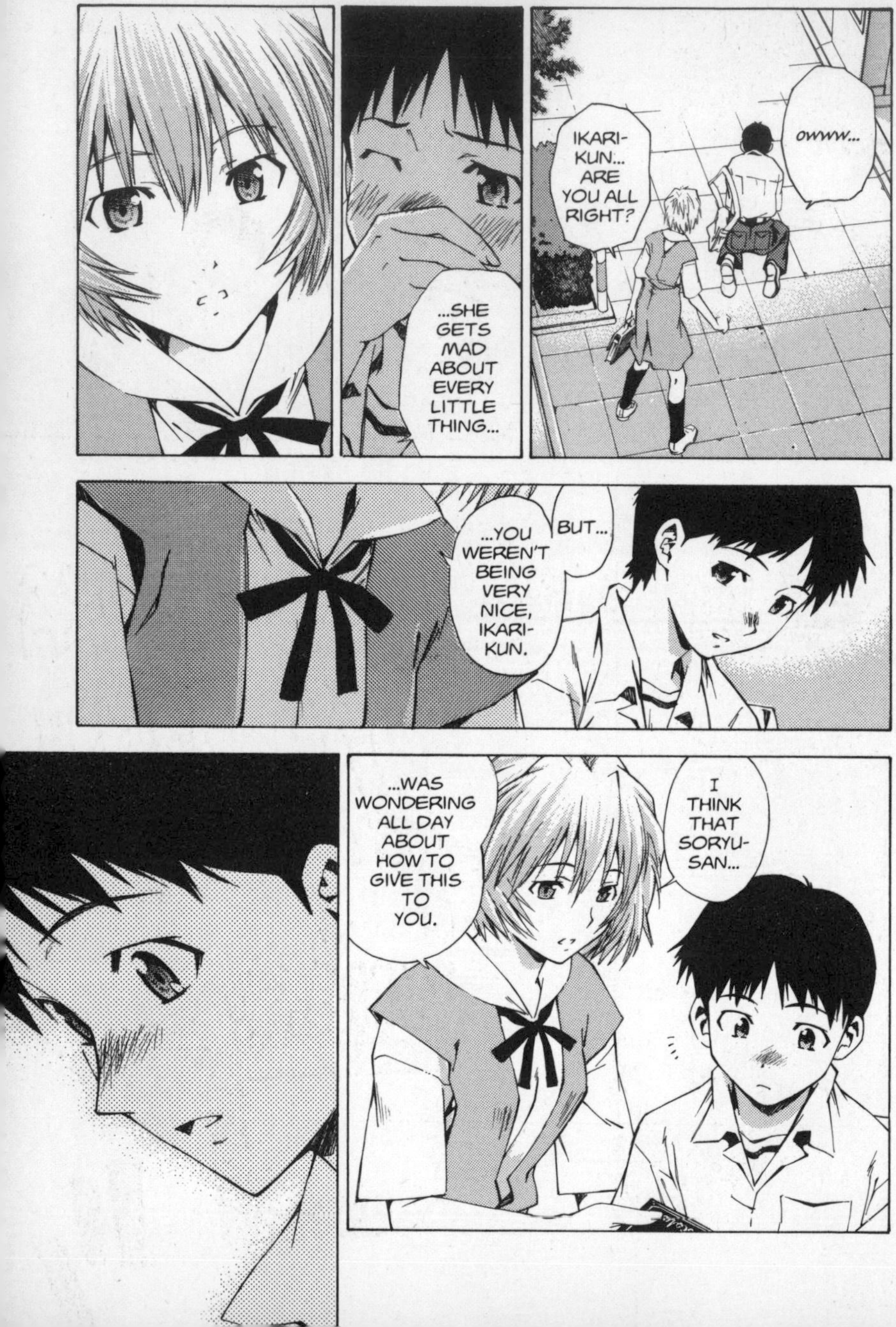
OWWW...
IKARI-KUN... ARE YOU ALL RIGHT?
...SHE GETS MAD ABOUT EVERY LITTLE THING...
BUT...
...YOU WEREN'T BEING VERY NICE, IKARI-KUN.
I THINK THAT SORYU-SAN...
...WAS WONDERING ALL DAY ABOUT HOW TO GIVE THIS TO YOU.

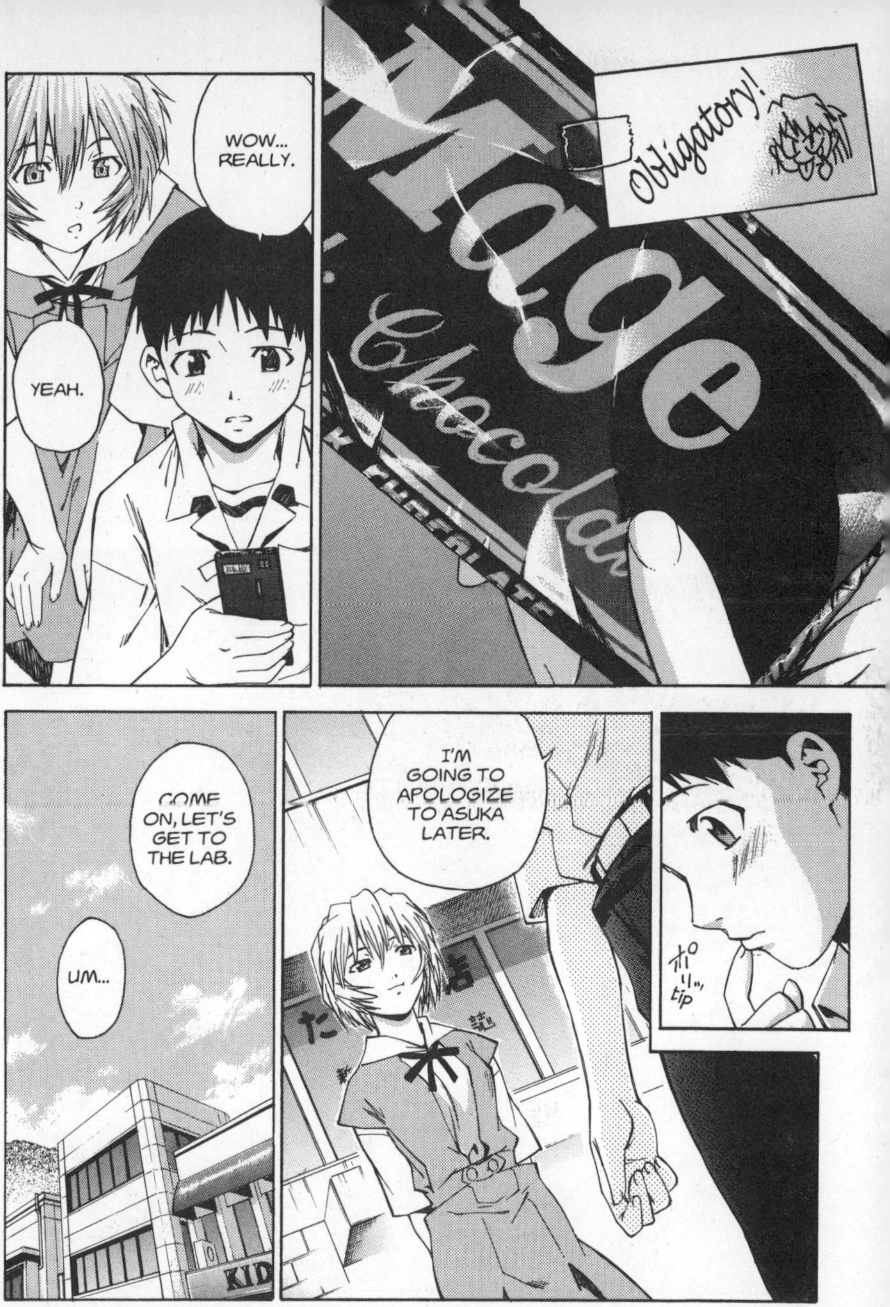
Obligatory!
WOW... REALLY.
YEAH.
ポリッ
tip
I'M GOING TO APOLOGIZE TO ASUKA LATER.
COME ON, LET'S GET TO THE LAB.
UM...

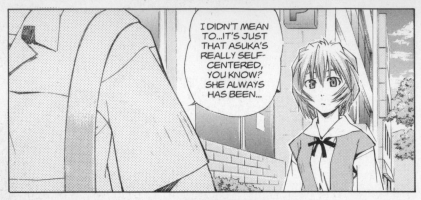

I DIDN'T MEAN TO...IT'S JUST THAT ASUKA'S REALLY SELF-CENTERED, YOU KNOW? SHE ALWAYS HAS BEEN...

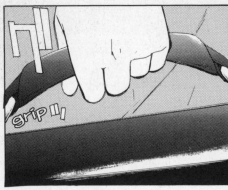

grip‖‖

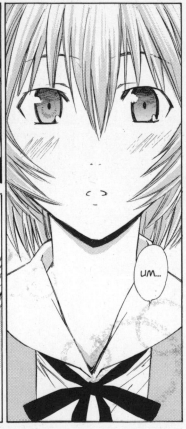

UM...

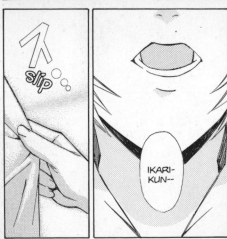

slip

IKARI-KUN--

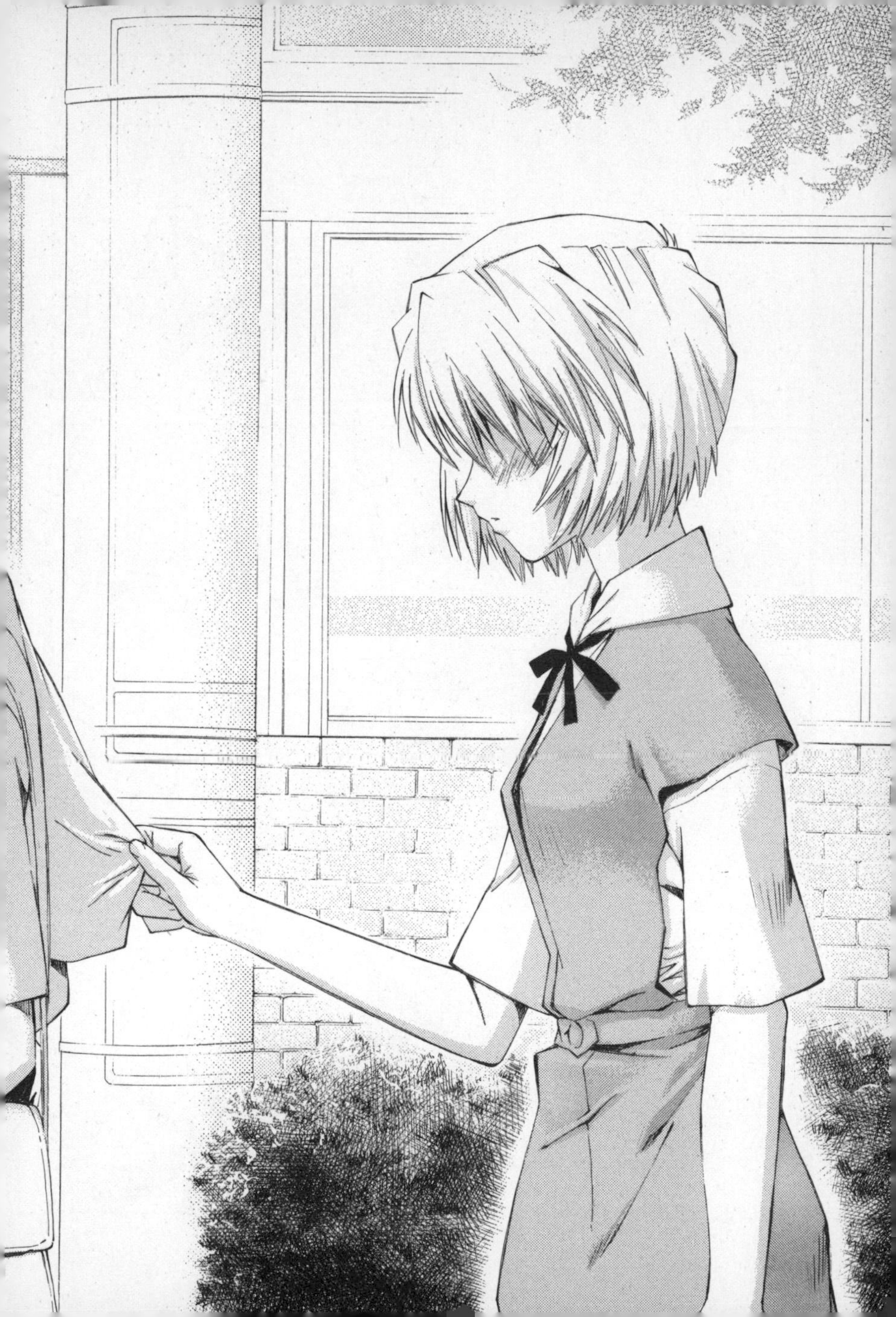

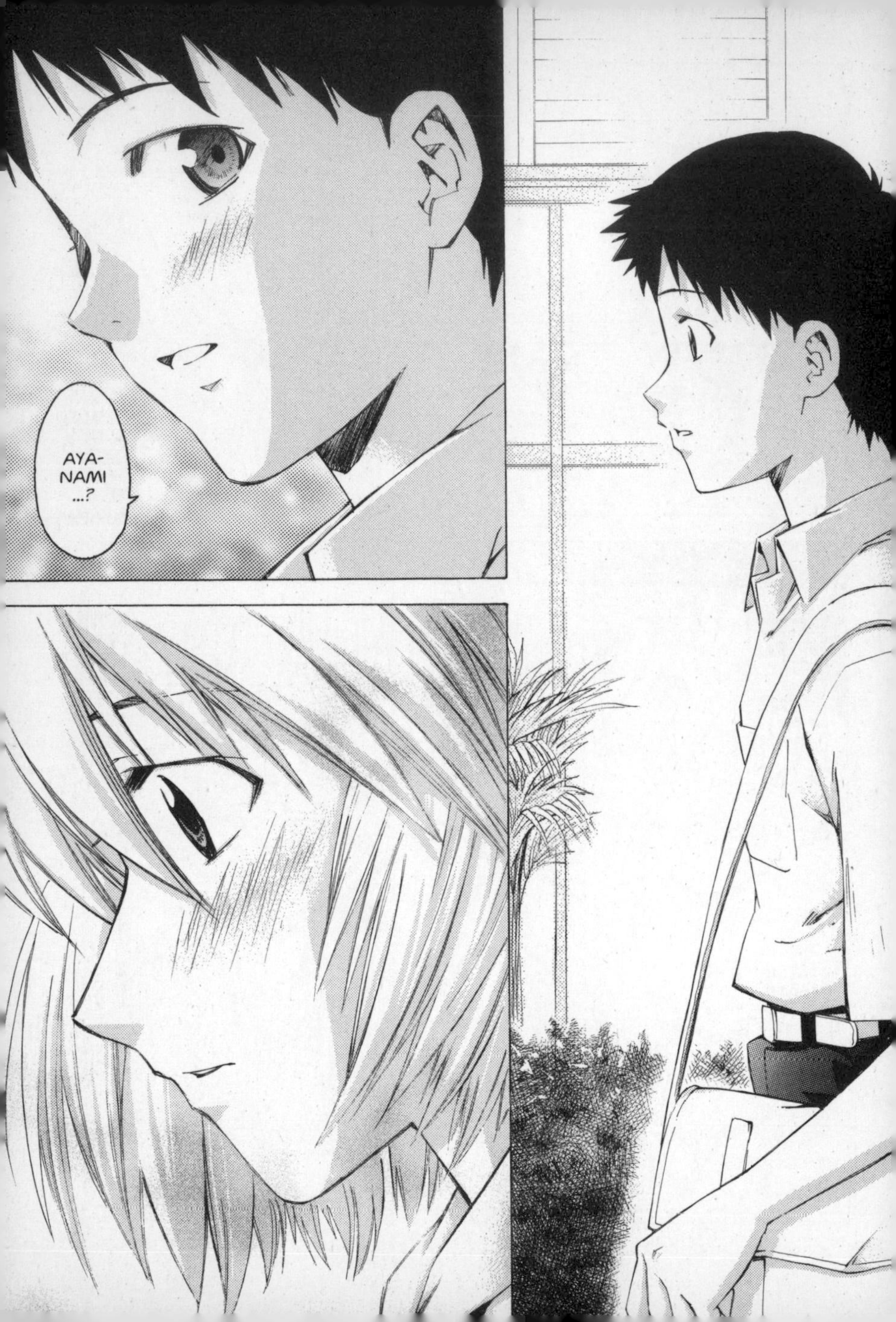
AYA-
NAMI
...?

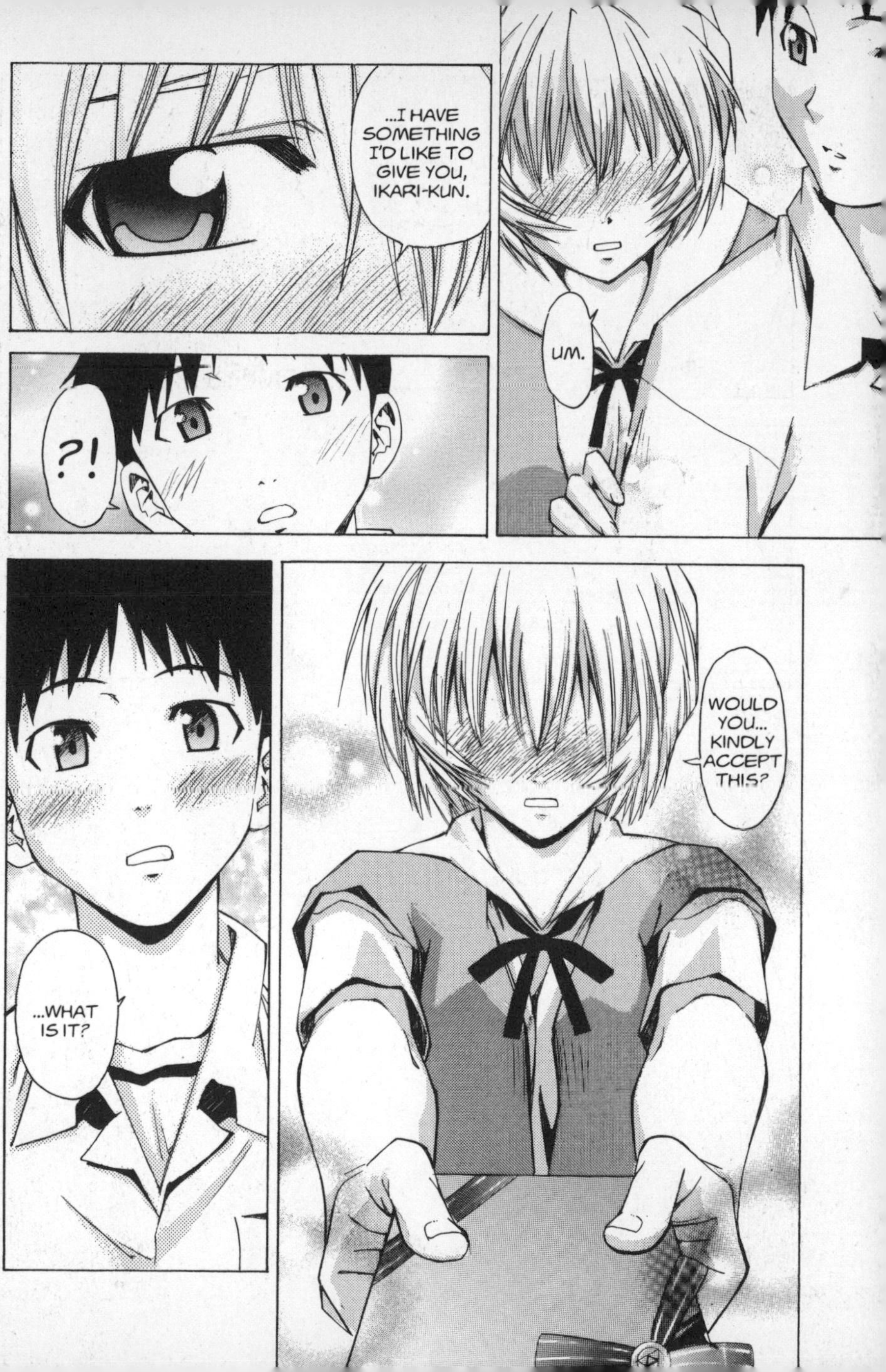
UM.
...I HAVE SOMETHING I'D LIKE TO GIVE YOU, IKARI-KUN.
?!
WOULD YOU... KINDLY ACCEPT THIS?
...WHAT IS IT?

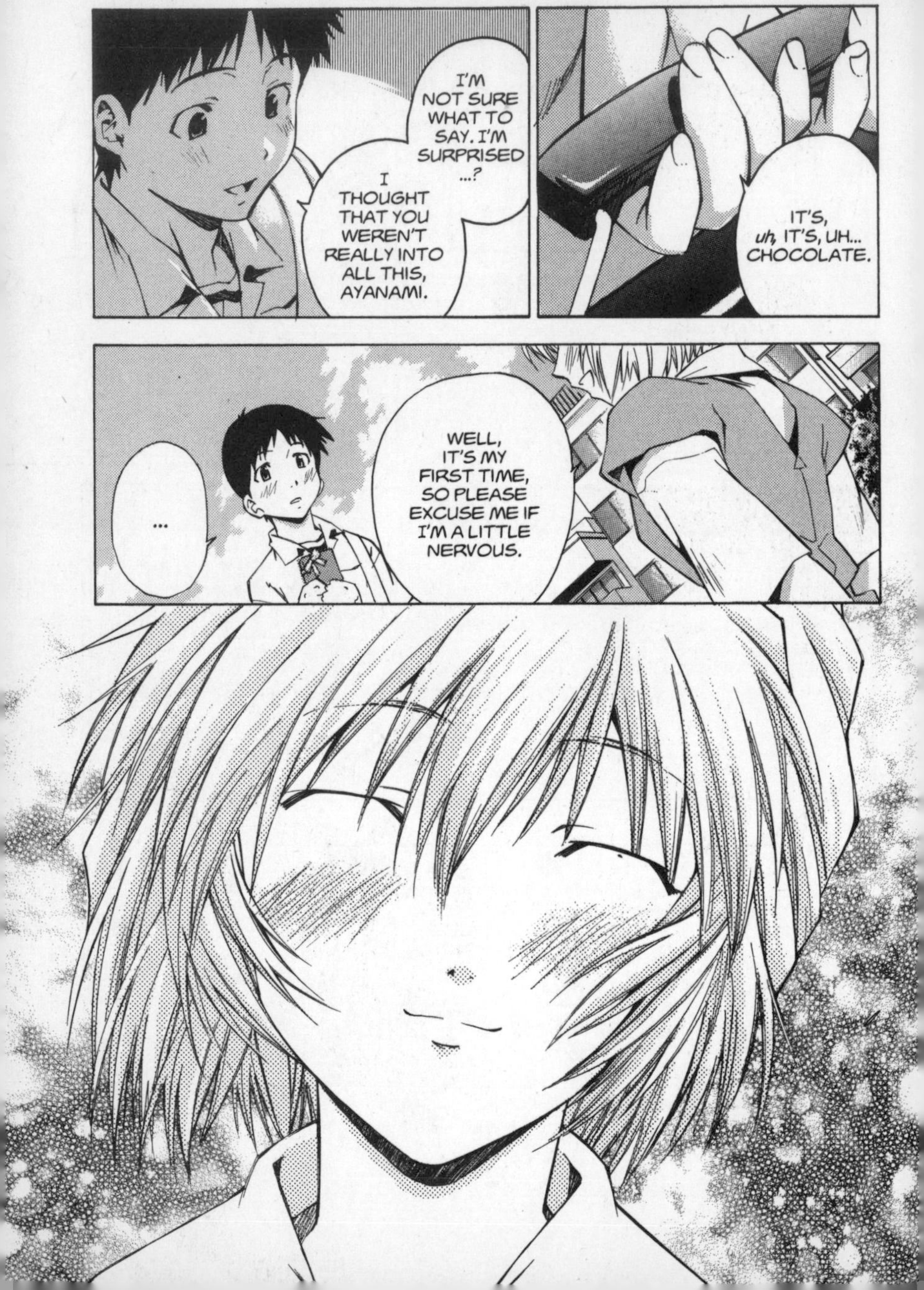
IT'S, *uh,* IT'S, UH... CHOCOLATE.
I'M NOT SURE WHAT TO SAY. I'M SURPRISED ...?
I THOUGHT THAT YOU WEREN'T REALLY INTO ALL THIS, AYANAMI.
WELL, IT'S MY FIRST TIME, SO PLEASE EXCUSE ME IF I'M A LITTLE NERVOUS.
...

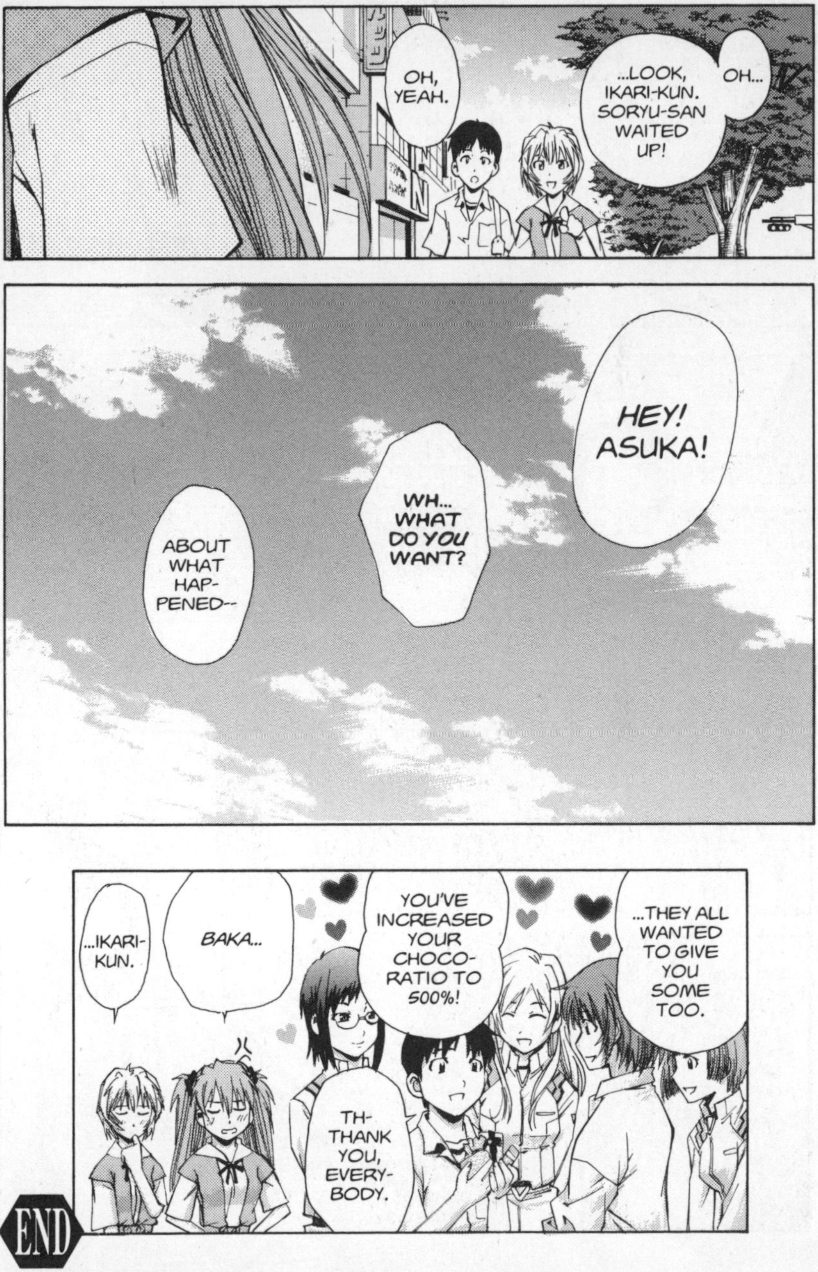
OH...
...LOOK, IKARI-KUN. SORYU-SAN WAITED UP!
OH, YEAH.
HEY! ASUKA!
WH... WHAT DO YOU WANT?
ABOUT WHAT HAP-PENED--
...THEY ALL WANTED TO GIVE YOU SOME TOO.
YOU'VE INCREASED YOUR CHOCO-RATIO TO 500%!
TH-THANK YOU, EVERYBODY.
BAKA...
...IKARI-KUN.
END

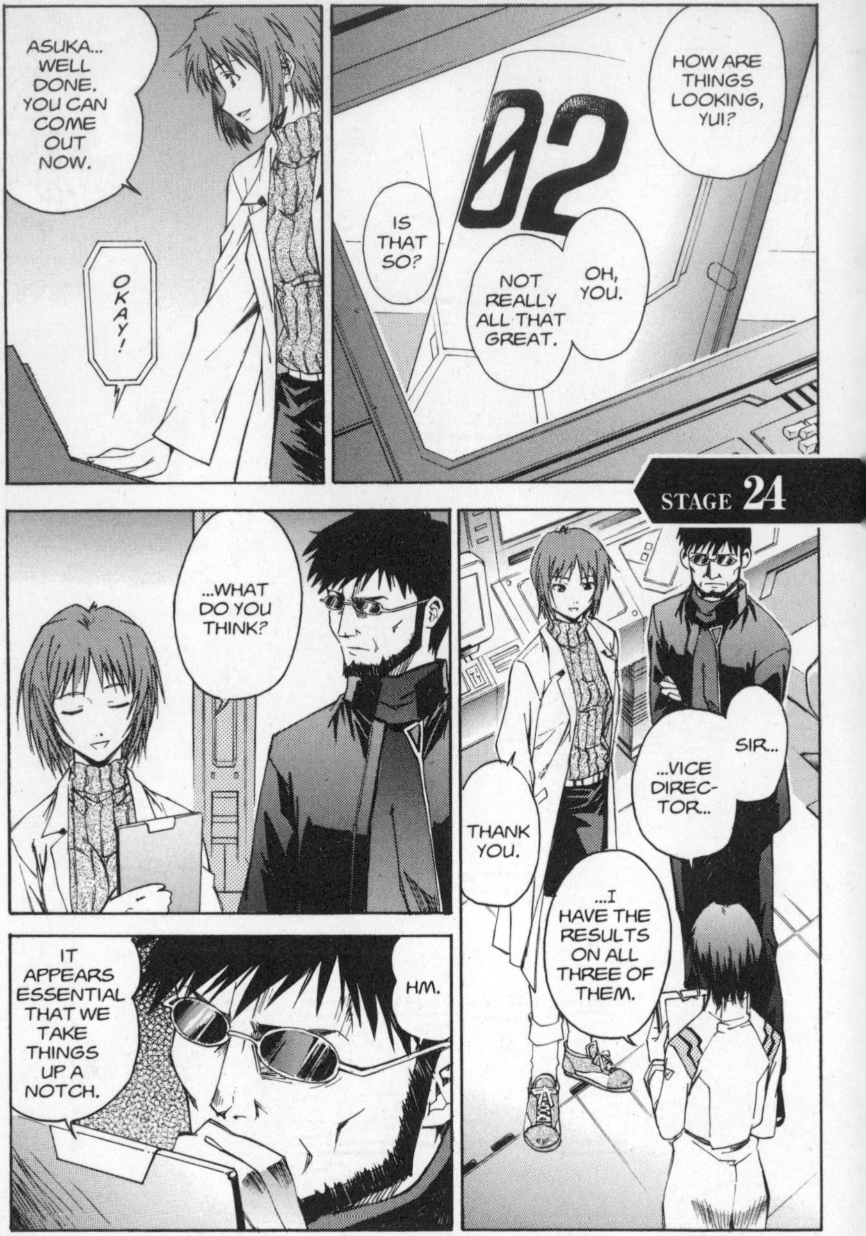
HOW ARE THINGS LOOKING, YUI?
OH, YOU.
NOT REALLY ALL THAT GREAT.
IS THAT SO?
ASUKA... WELL DONE. YOU CAN COME OUT NOW.
OKAY!
STAGE 24
SIR...
...VICE DIRECTOR...
THANK YOU.
...I HAVE THE RESULTS ON ALL THREE OF THEM.
...WHAT DO YOU THINK?
HM.
IT APPEARS ESSENTIAL THAT WE TAKE THINGS UP A NOTCH.

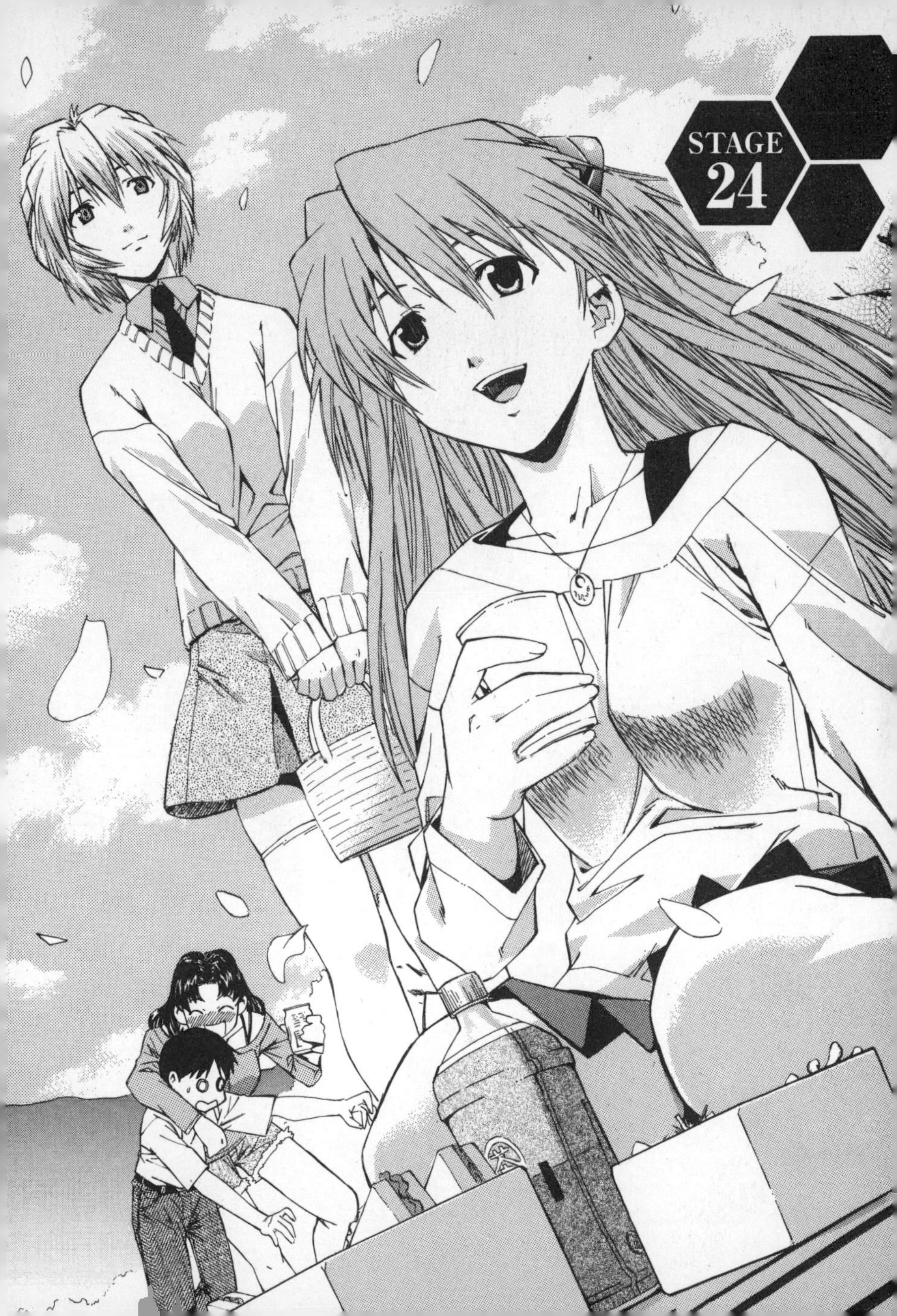
STAGE
24

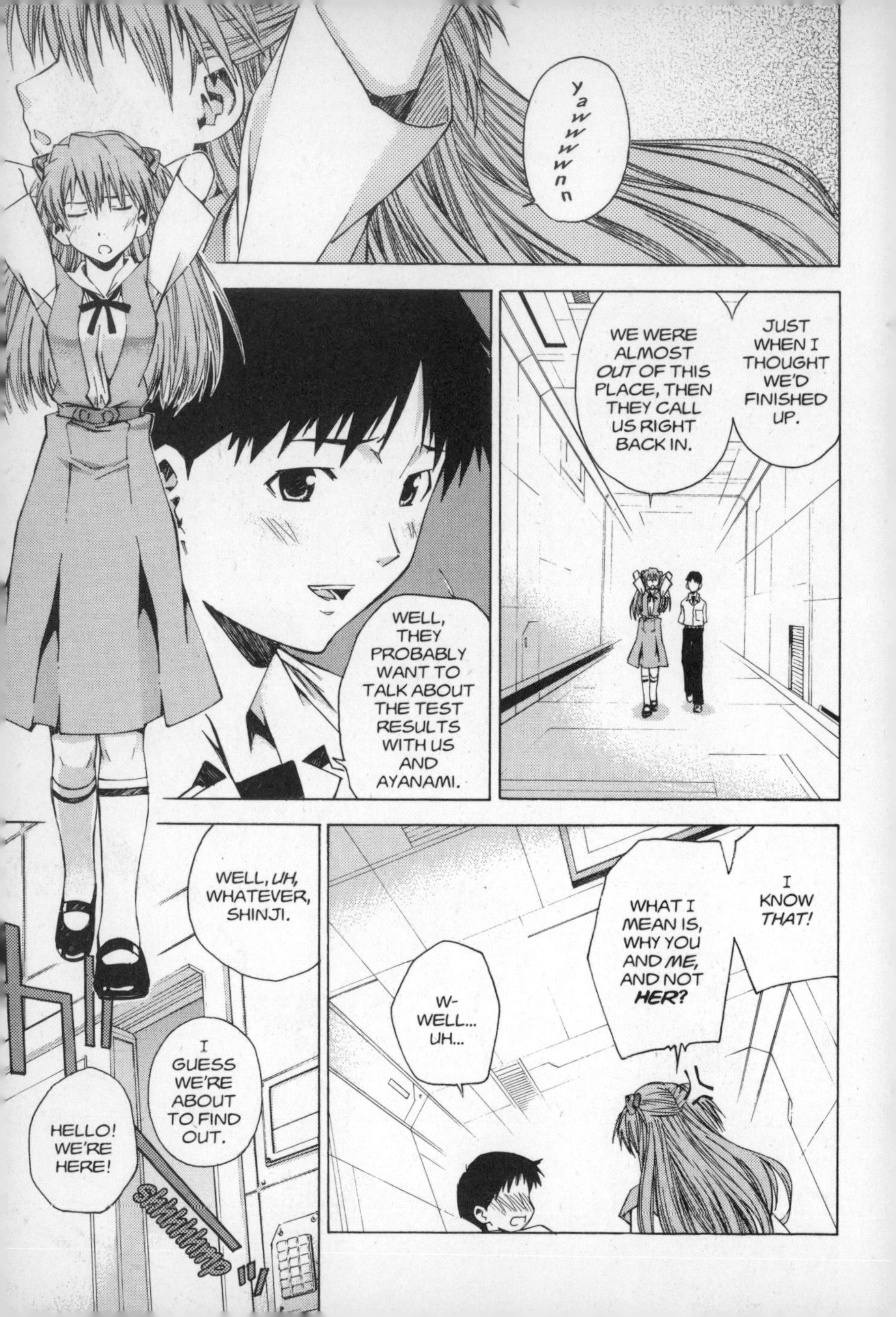
yawwwwnn
JUST WHEN I THOUGHT WE'D FINISHED UP.
WE WERE ALMOST *OUT* OF THIS PLACE, THEN THEY CALL US RIGHT BACK IN.
WELL, THEY PROBABLY WANT TO TALK ABOUT THE TEST RESULTS WITH US AND AYANAMI.
I KNOW *THAT!*
WHAT I MEAN IS, WHY YOU AND *ME*, AND NOT ***HER?***
W-WELL... UH...
WELL, *UH*, WHATEVER, SHINJI.
I GUESS WE'RE ABOUT TO FIND OUT.
HELLO! WE'RE HERE!
shhhhhmp

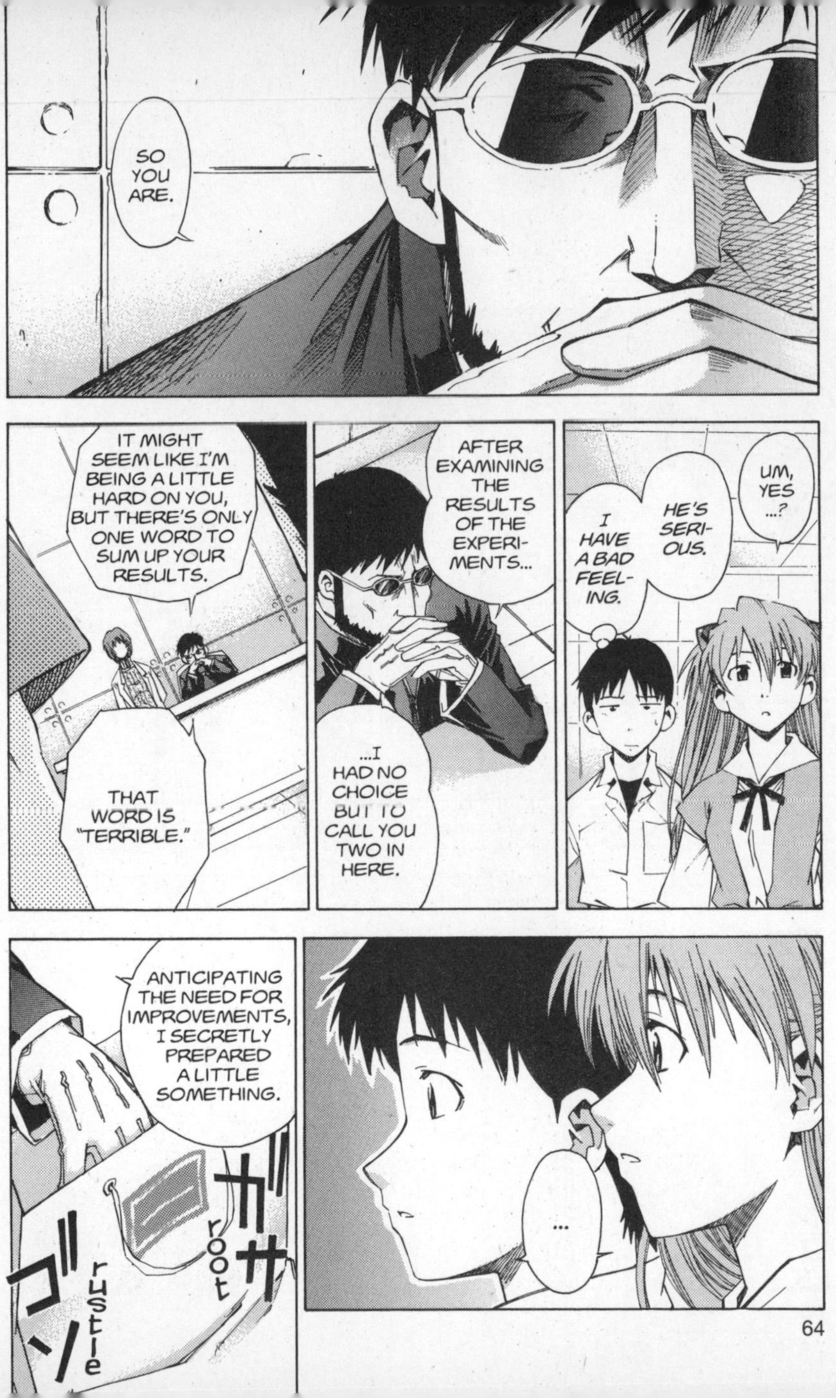
SO YOU ARE.
UM, YES ...?
HE'S SERIOUS.
I HAVE A BAD FEELING.
AFTER EXAMINING THE RESULTS OF THE EXPERIMENTS...
...I HAD NO CHOICE BUT TO CALL YOU TWO IN HERE.
IT MIGHT SEEM LIKE I'M BEING A LITTLE HARD ON YOU, BUT THERE'S ONLY ONE WORD TO SUM UP YOUR RESULTS.
THAT WORD IS "TERRIBLE."
...
ANTICIPATING THE NEED FOR IMPROVEMENTS, I SECRETLY PREPARED A LITTLE SOMETHING.
ガサ root
ゴソ rustle

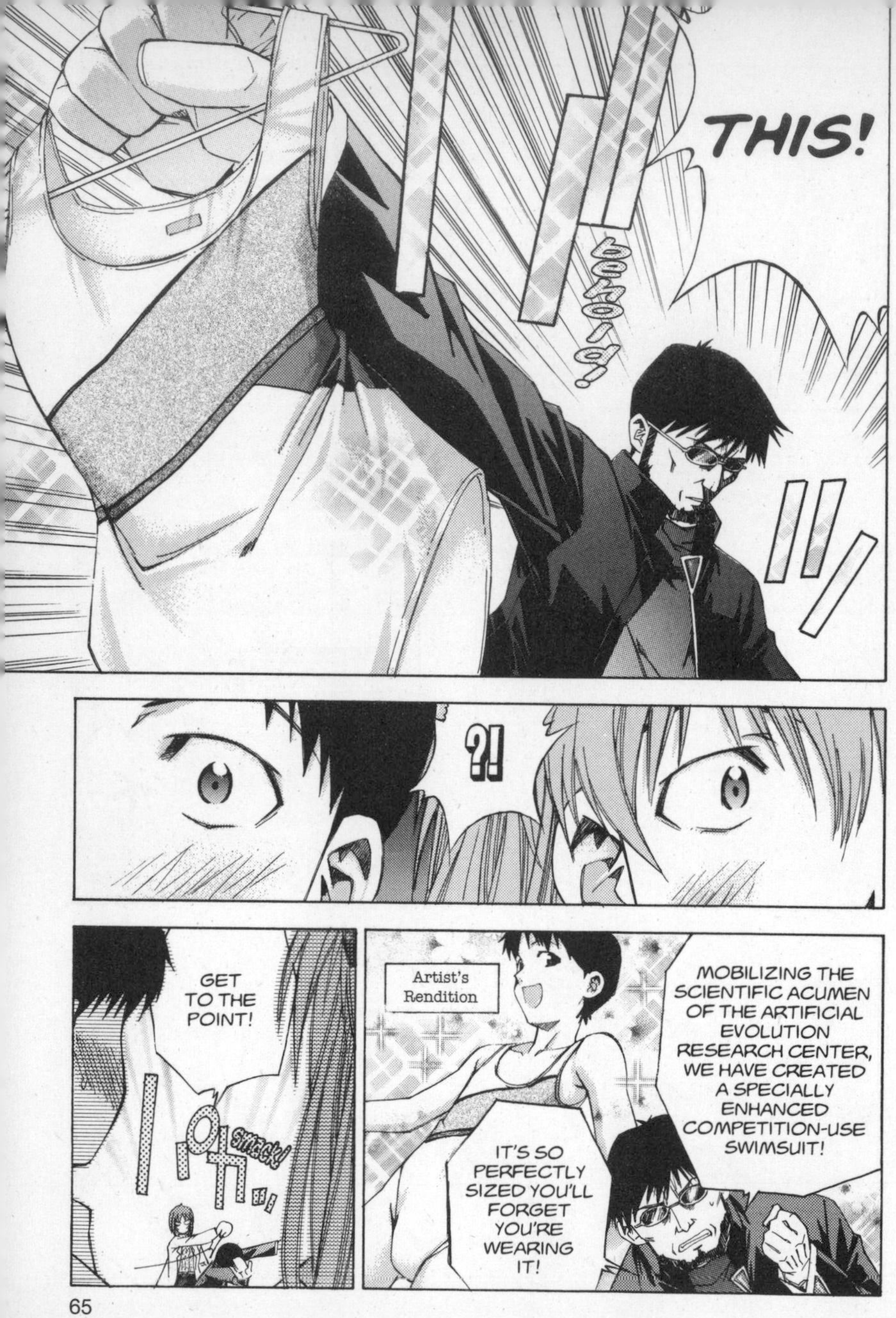
THIS!
?!
MOBILIZING THE SCIENTIFIC ACUMEN OF THE ARTIFICIAL EVOLUTION RESEARCH CENTER, WE HAVE CREATED A SPECIALLY ENHANCED COMPETITION-USE SWIMSUIT!
Artist's Rendition
IT'S SO PERFECTLY SIZED YOU'LL FORGET YOU'RE WEARING IT!
GET TO THE POINT!
SMACK!

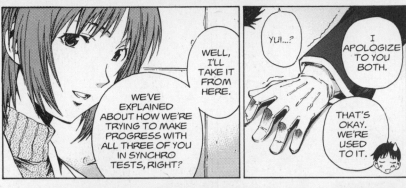

YUI...?
I APOLOGIZE TO YOU BOTH.
THAT'S OKAY. WE'RE USED TO IT.
WELL, I'LL TAKE IT FROM HERE.
WE'VE EXPLAINED ABOUT HOW WE'RE TRYING TO MAKE PROGRESS WITH ALL THREE OF YOU IN SYNCHRO TESTS, RIGHT?
THE EFFORT INCLUDES SUCH THINGS AS BREATHING TOGETHER IN UNISON, AND EQUALIZING YOUR HEART RATES.
SHINJI AND ASUKA, THINGS AREN'T FUNCTIONING QUITE AS WELL AS THEY SHOULD BE BETWEEN YOU TWO.
AND THAT'S HOLDING UP THE PROJECT AS A WHOLE. SIMPLY PUT, WE NEED TO HAVE YOU MEET YOUR SYNCH TARGETS.
IF YOU DON'T MIND MY SAYING SO, THE CONCEPT OF SHINJI'S AND MY HEARTS BEATING AS ONE IS A NON-STARTER.
HEY-- THOSE ARE MY LINES.
THAT ATTITUDE IS UNACCEPT-ABLE.
WE'RE SHORT ON TIME HERE.

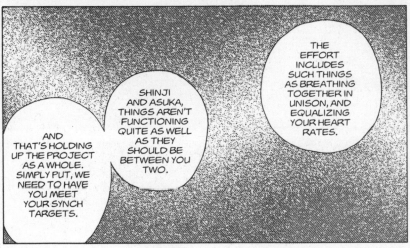

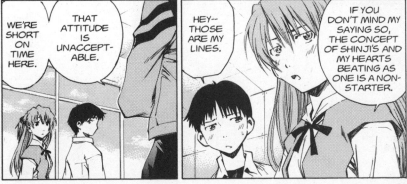

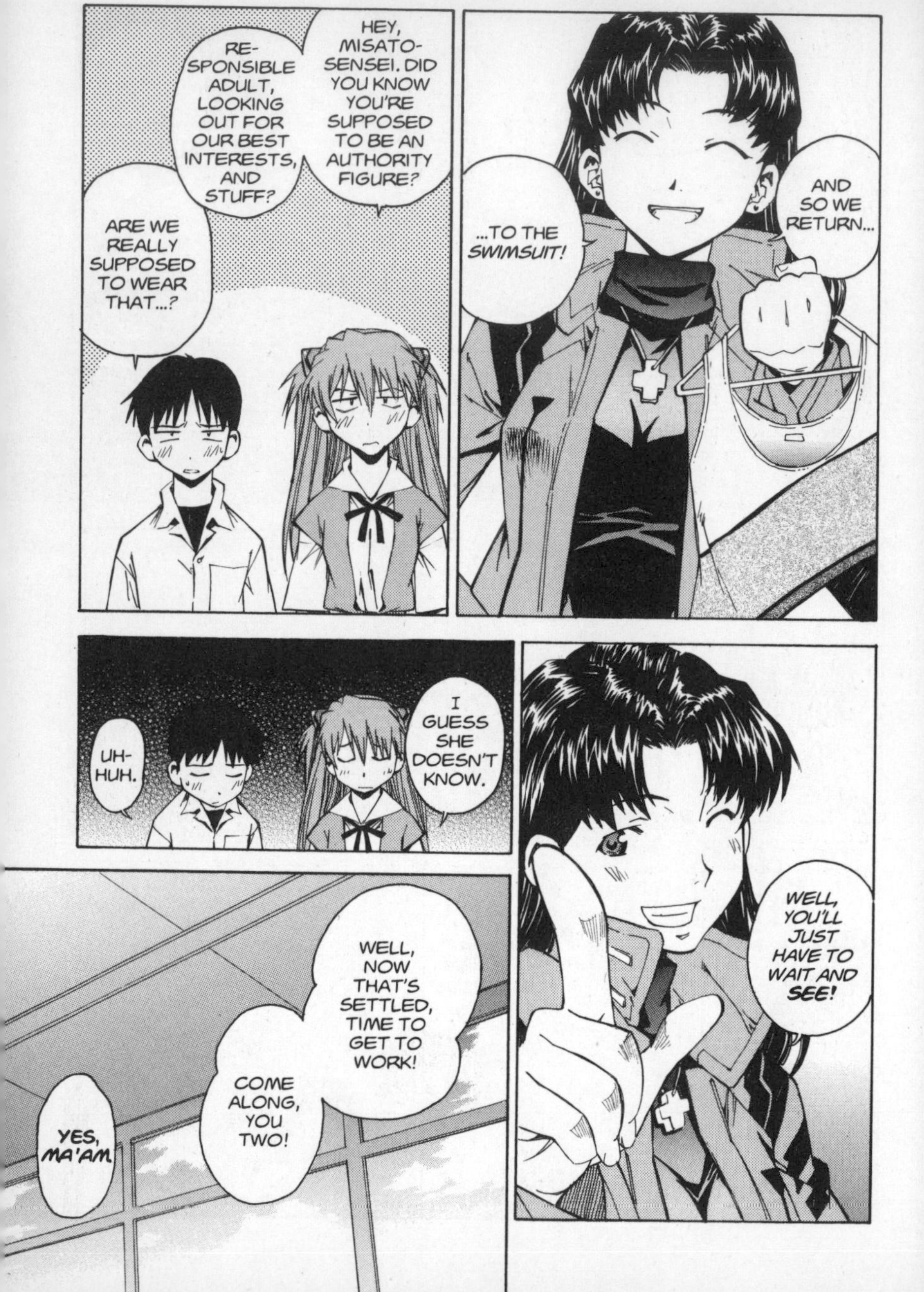
AND SO WE RETURN...
...TO THE SWIMSUIT!
HEY, MISATO-SENSEI. DID YOU KNOW YOU'RE SUPPOSED TO BE AN AUTHORITY FIGURE?
RE-SPONSIBLE ADULT, LOOKING OUT FOR OUR BEST INTERESTS, AND STUFF?
ARE WE REALLY SUPPOSED TO WEAR THAT...?
WELL, YOU'LL JUST HAVE TO WAIT AND SEE!
I GUESS SHE DOESN'T KNOW.
UH-HUH.
WELL, NOW THAT'S SETTLED, TIME TO GET TO WORK!
COME ALONG, YOU TWO!
YES, MA'AM.

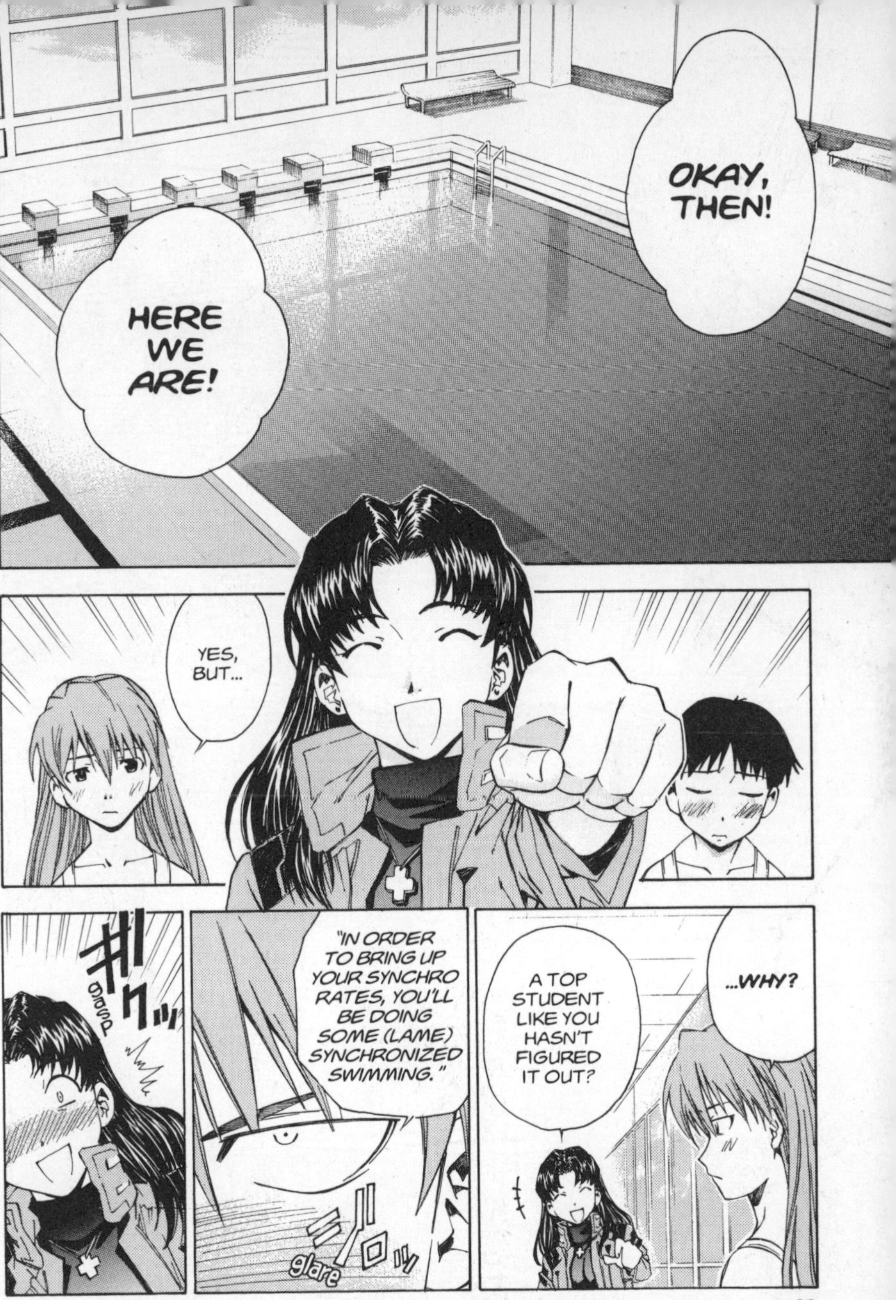
OKAY, THEN!
HERE WE ARE!
YES, BUT...
...WHY?
A TOP STUDENT LIKE YOU HASN'T FIGURED IT OUT?
"IN ORDER TO BRING UP YOUR SYNCHRO RATES, YOU'LL BE DOING SOME (LAME) SYNCHRONIZED SWIMMING."
glare
gasp

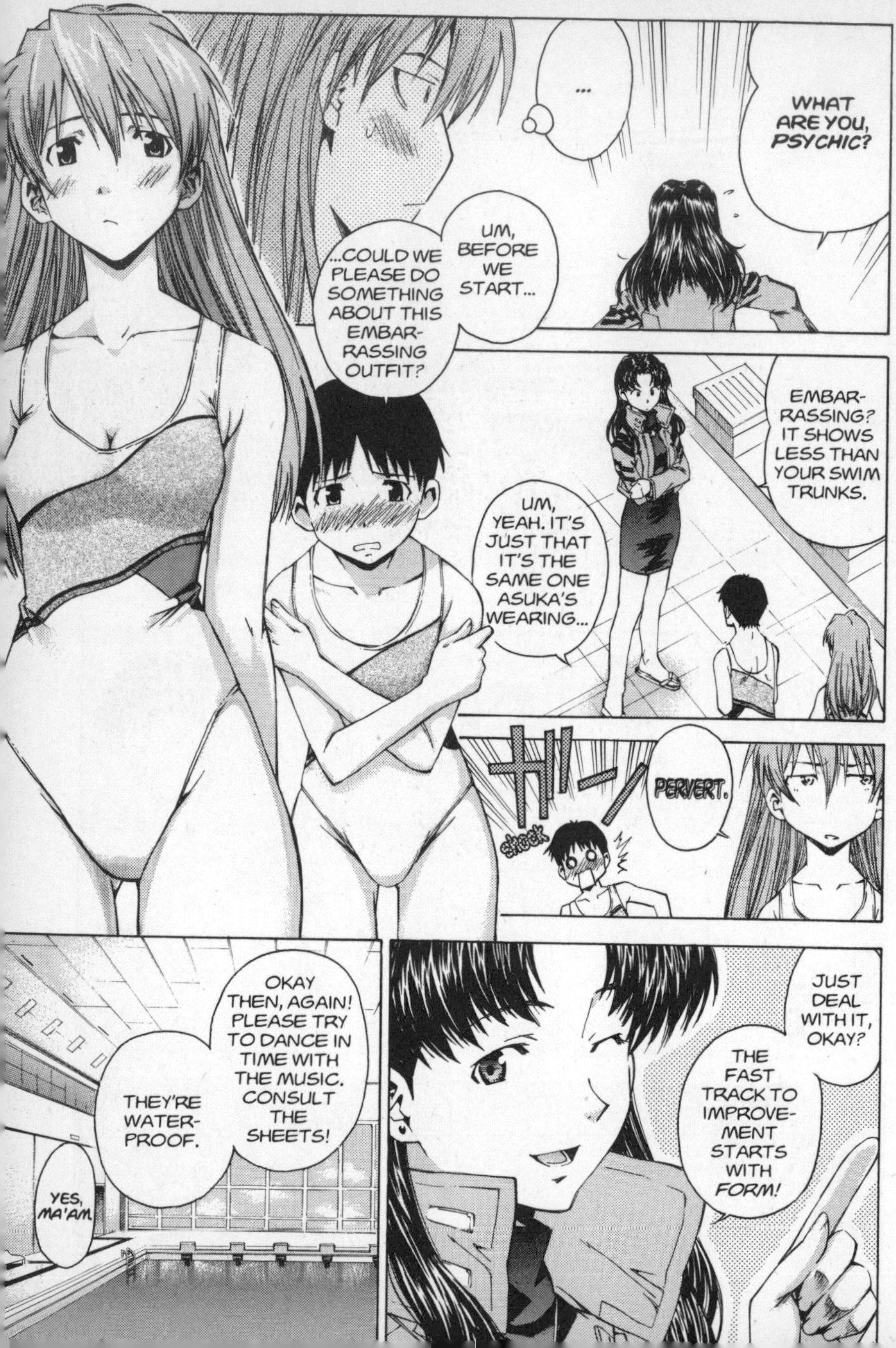
WHAT ARE YOU, PSYCHIC?
...
UM, BEFORE WE START...
...COULD WE PLEASE DO SOMETHING ABOUT THIS EMBAR-RASSING OUTFIT?
EMBAR-RASSING? IT SHOWS LESS THAN YOUR SWIM TRUNKS.
UM, YEAH. IT'S JUST THAT IT'S THE SAME ONE ASUKA'S WEARING...
PERVERT.
shock
JUST DEAL WITH IT, OKAY?
THE FAST TRACK TO IMPROVE-MENT STARTS WITH FORM!
OKAY THEN, AGAIN! PLEASE TRY TO DANCE IN TIME WITH THE MUSIC. CONSULT THE SHEETS!
THEY'RE WATER-PROOF.
YES, MA'AM.

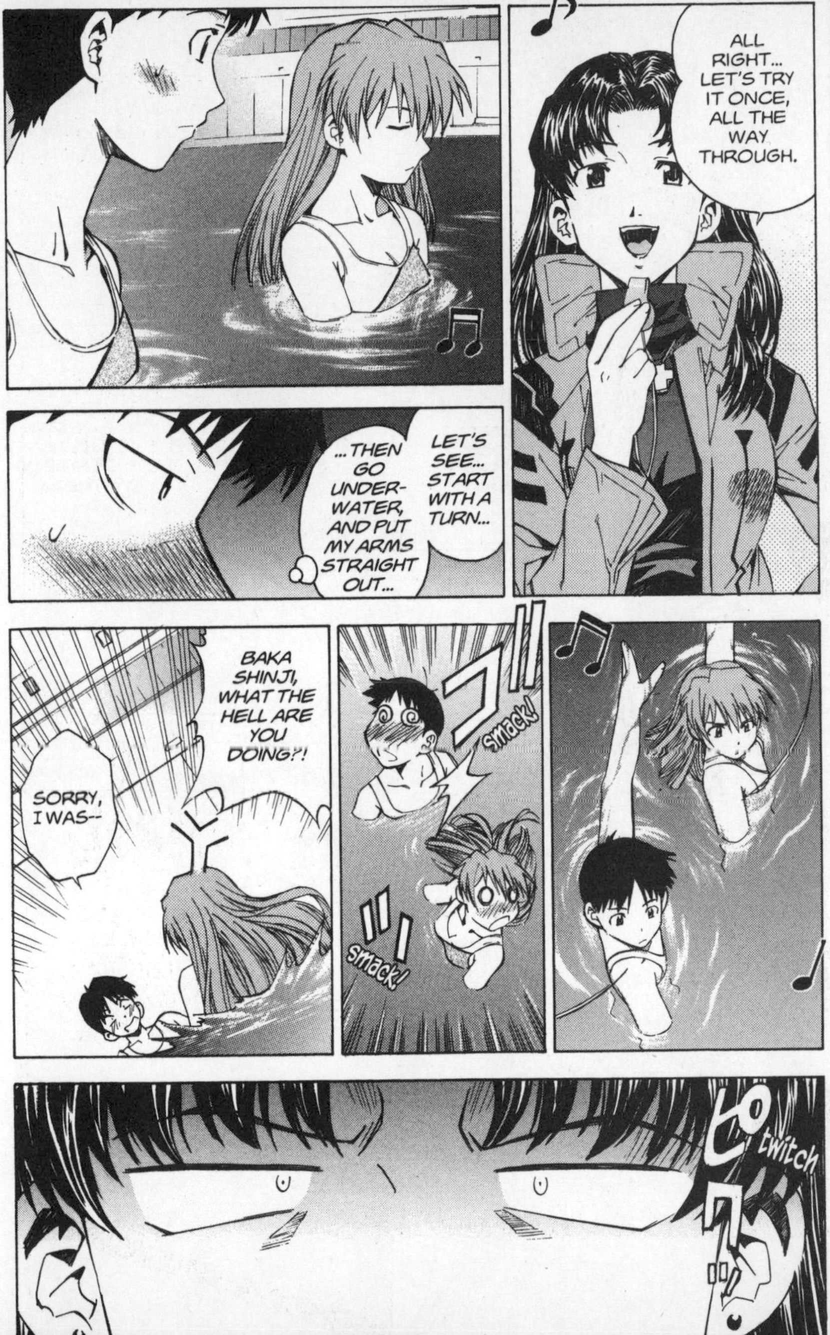
ALL RIGHT... LET'S TRY IT ONCE, ALL THE WAY THROUGH.
LET'S SEE... START WITH A TURN...
...THEN GO UNDER-WATER, AND PUT MY ARMS STRAIGHT OUT...
smack!
smack!
BAKA SHINJI, WHAT THE HELL ARE YOU DOING?!
SORRY, I WAS--
twitch

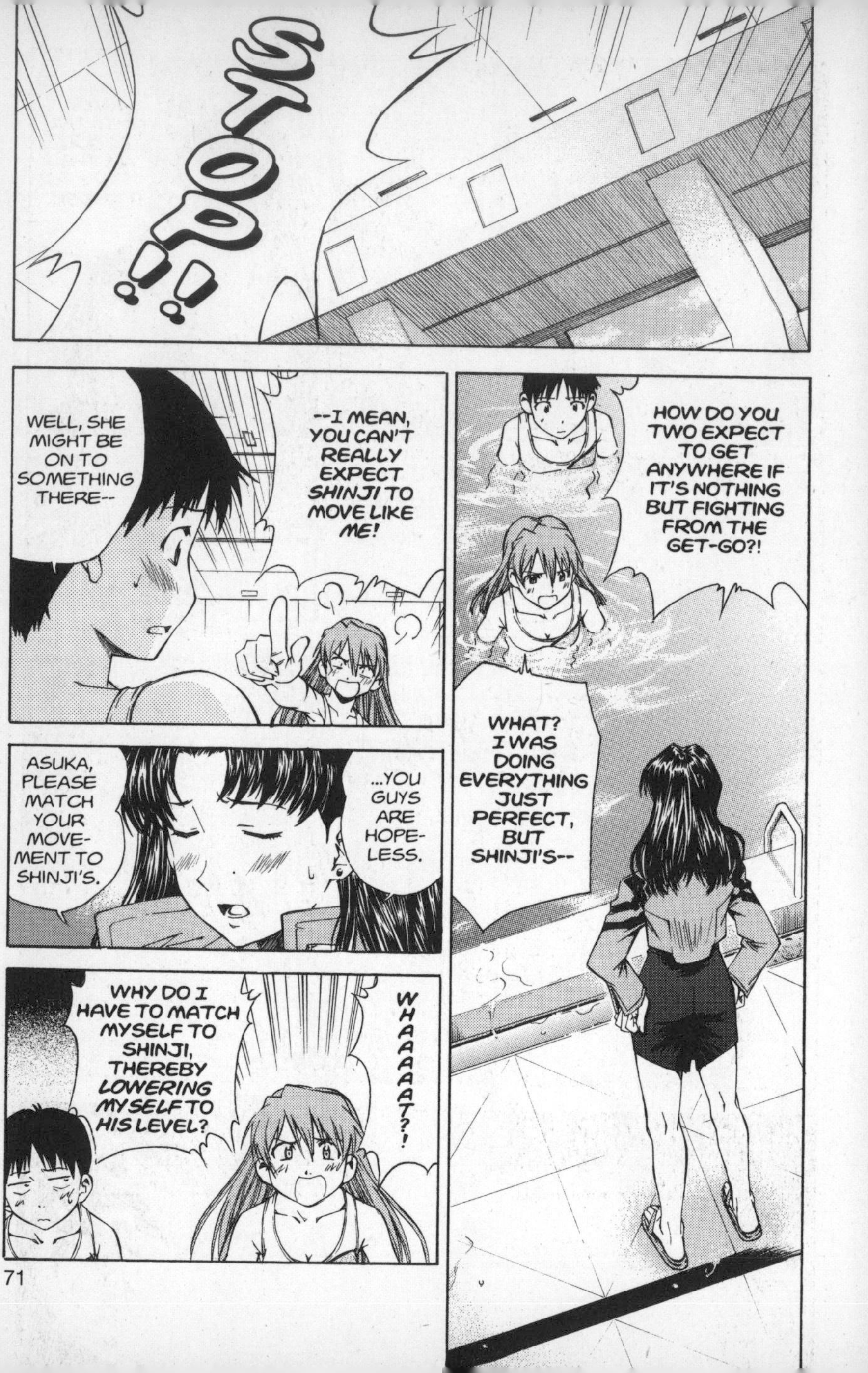
STOP!!
HOW DO YOU TWO EXPECT TO GET ANYWHERE IF IT'S NOTHING BUT FIGHTING FROM THE GET-GO?!
WHAT? I WAS DOING EVERYTHING JUST PERFECT, BUT SHINJI'S--
--I MEAN, YOU CAN'T REALLY EXPECT SHINJI TO MOVE LIKE ME!
WELL, SHE MIGHT BE ON TO SOMETHING THERE--
...YOU GUYS ARE HOPELESS.
ASUKA, PLEASE MATCH YOUR MOVEMENT TO SHINJI'S.
WHAAAAAAT?!
WHY DO I HAVE TO MATCH MYSELF TO SHINJI, THEREBY LOWERING MYSELF TO HIS LEVEL?

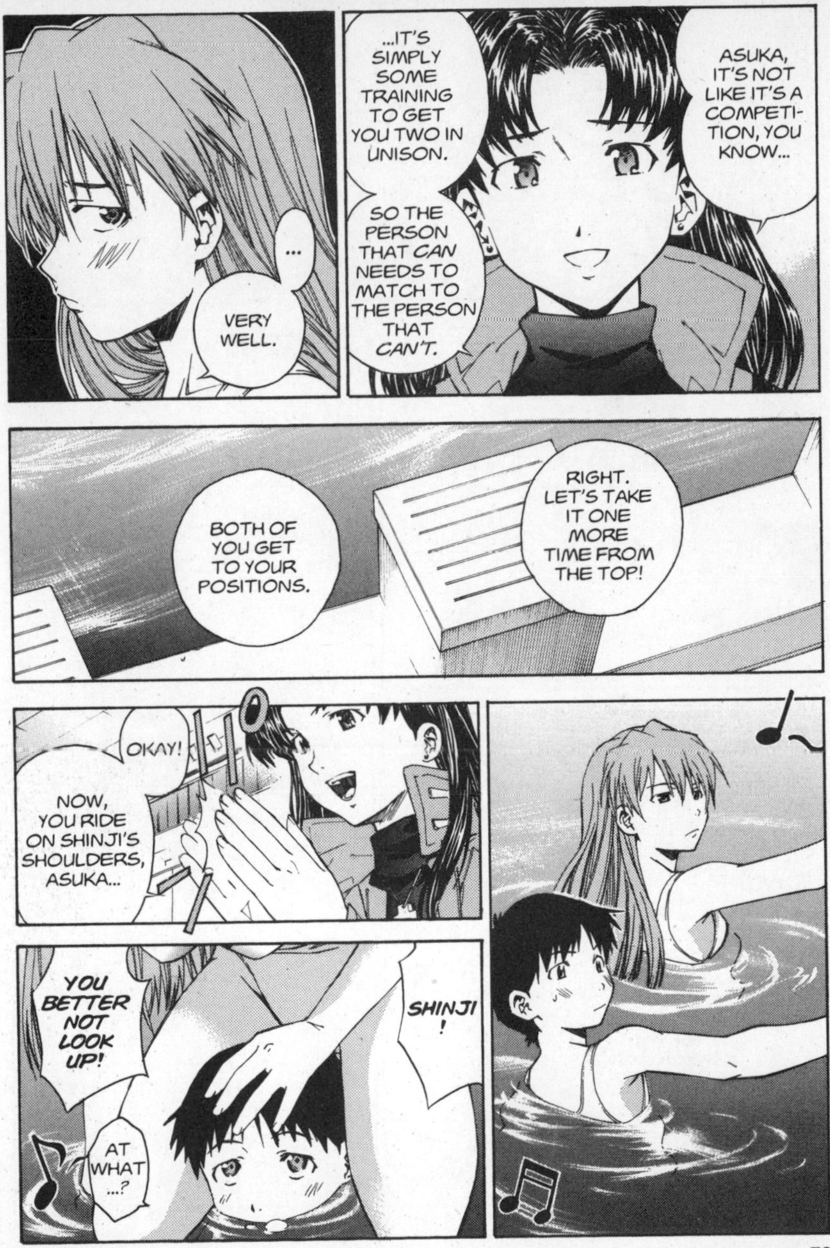
ASUKA, IT'S NOT LIKE IT'S A COMPETITION, YOU KNOW...
...IT'S SIMPLY SOME TRAINING TO GET YOU TWO IN UNISON.
SO THE PERSON THAT *CAN* NEEDS TO MATCH TO THE PERSON THAT *CAN'T*.
...
VERY WELL.
RIGHT. LET'S TAKE IT ONE MORE TIME FROM THE TOP!
BOTH OF YOU GET TO YOUR POSITIONS.
OKAY!
NOW, YOU RIDE ON SHINJI'S SHOULDERS, ASUKA...
SHINJI!
YOU BETTER NOT LOOK UP!
AT WHAT...?

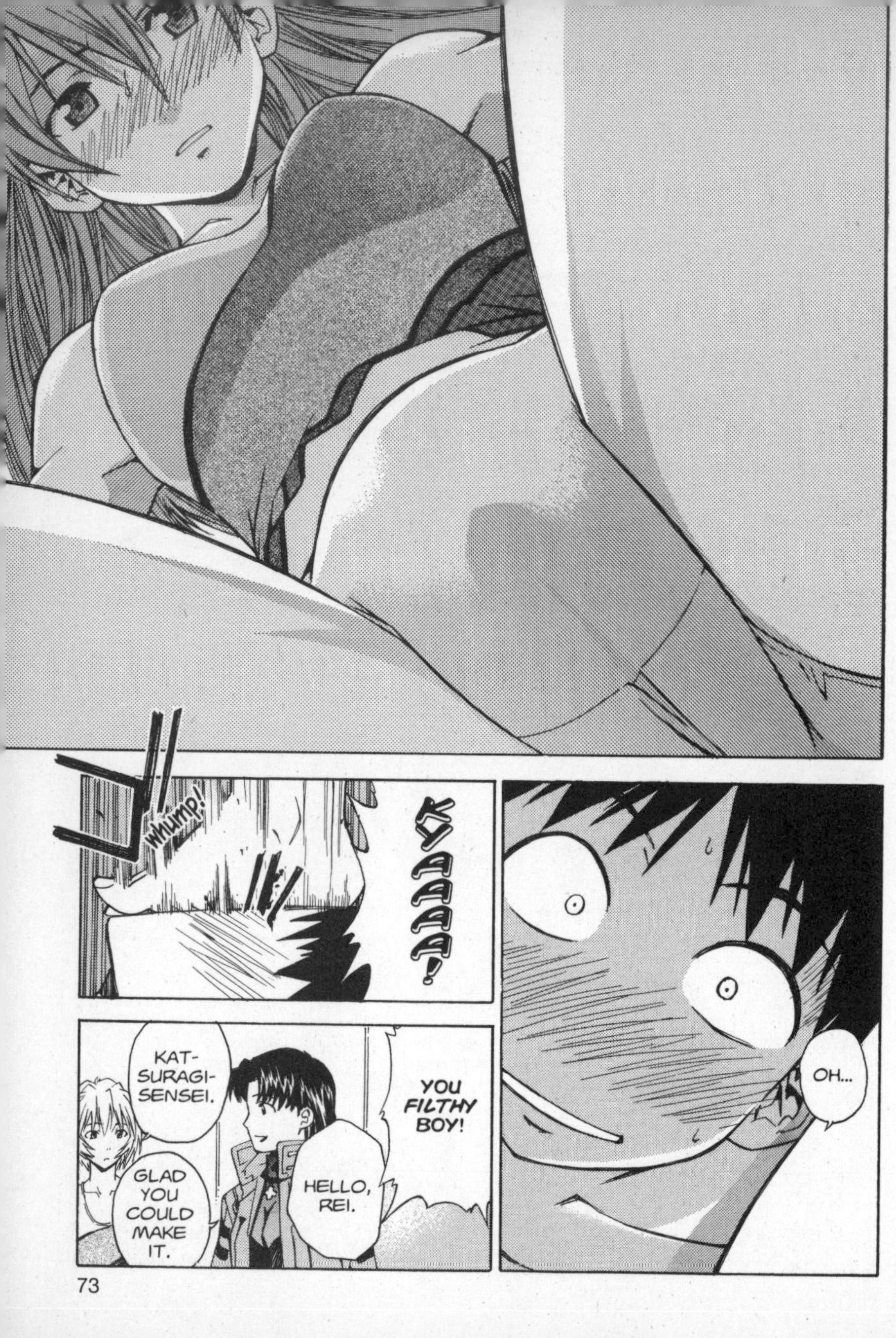
OH...
whump!
KYAAAAAA!
YOU FILTHY BOY!
KAT-SURAGI-SENSEI.
HELLO, REI.
GLAD YOU COULD MAKE IT.

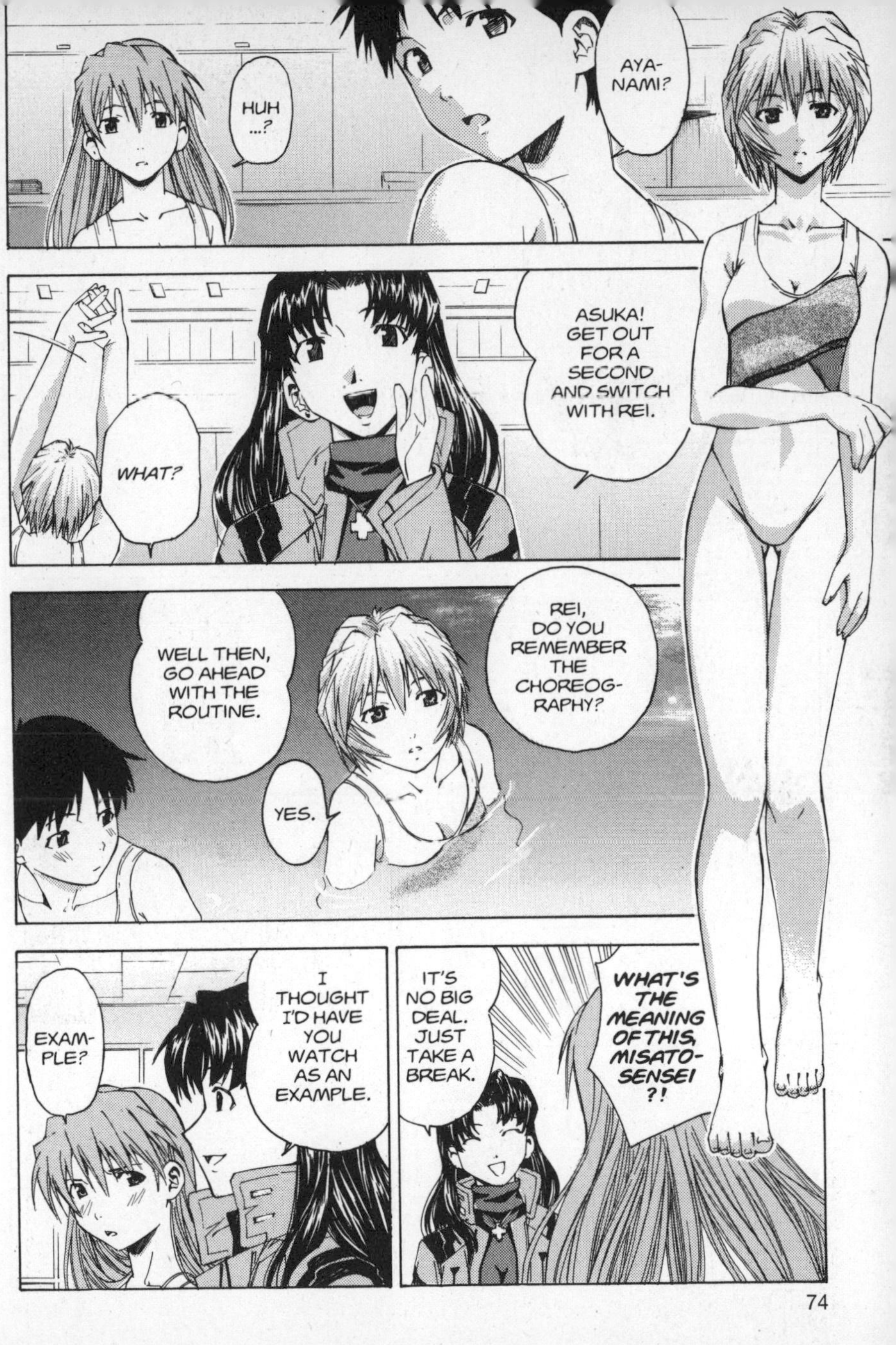
AYA-NAMI?
HUH ...?
ASUKA! GET OUT FOR A SECOND AND SWITCH WITH REI.
WHAT?
REI, DO YOU REMEMBER THE CHOREOG-RAPHY?
YES.
WELL THEN, GO AHEAD WITH THE ROUTINE.
WHAT'S THE MEANING OF THIS, MISATO-SENSEI ?!
IT'S NO BIG DEAL. JUST TAKE A BREAK.
I THOUGHT I'D HAVE YOU WATCH AS AN EXAMPLE.
EXAM-PLE?

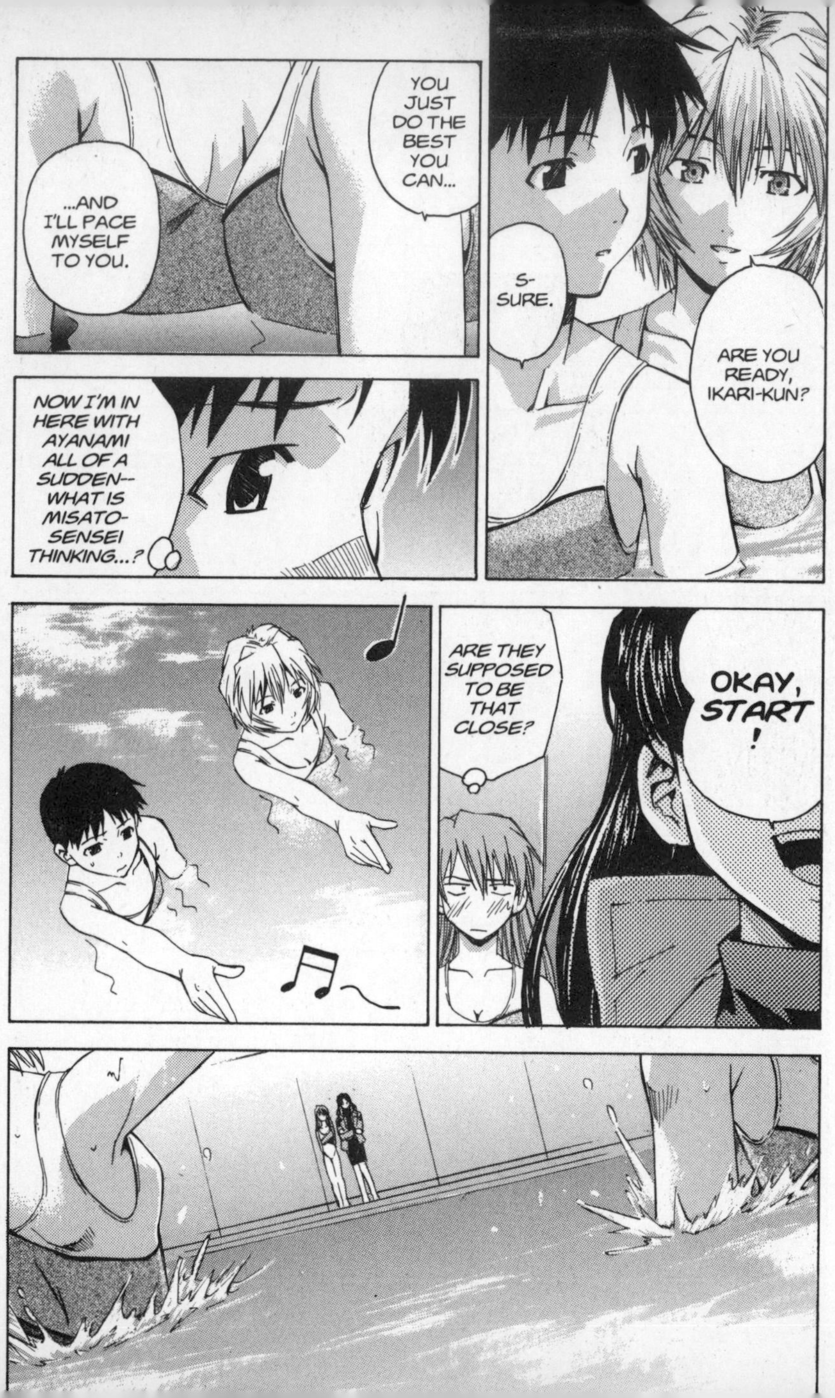
ARE YOU READY, IKARI-KUN?
S- SURE.
YOU JUST DO THE BEST YOU CAN...
...AND I'LL PACE MYSELF TO YOU.
NOW I'M IN HERE WITH AYANAMI ALL OF A SUDDEN-- WHAT IS MISATO-SENSEI THINKING...?
OKAY, START!
ARE THEY SUPPOSED TO BE THAT CLOSE?

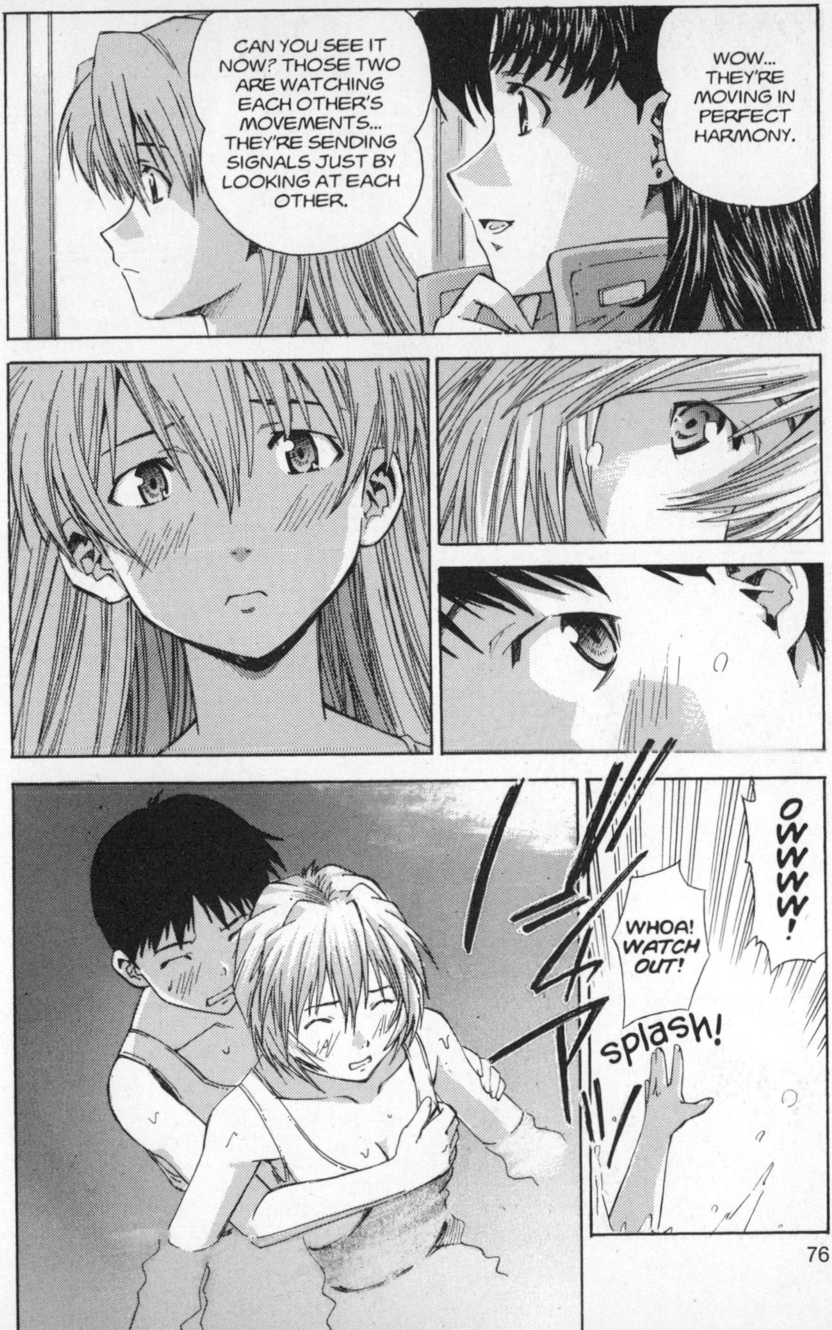
WOW... THEY'RE MOVING IN PERFECT HARMONY.
CAN YOU SEE IT NOW? THOSE TWO ARE WATCHING EACH OTHER'S MOVEMENTS... THEY'RE SENDING SIGNALS JUST BY LOOKING AT EACH OTHER.
OWWWW!
WHOA! WATCH OUT!
splash!

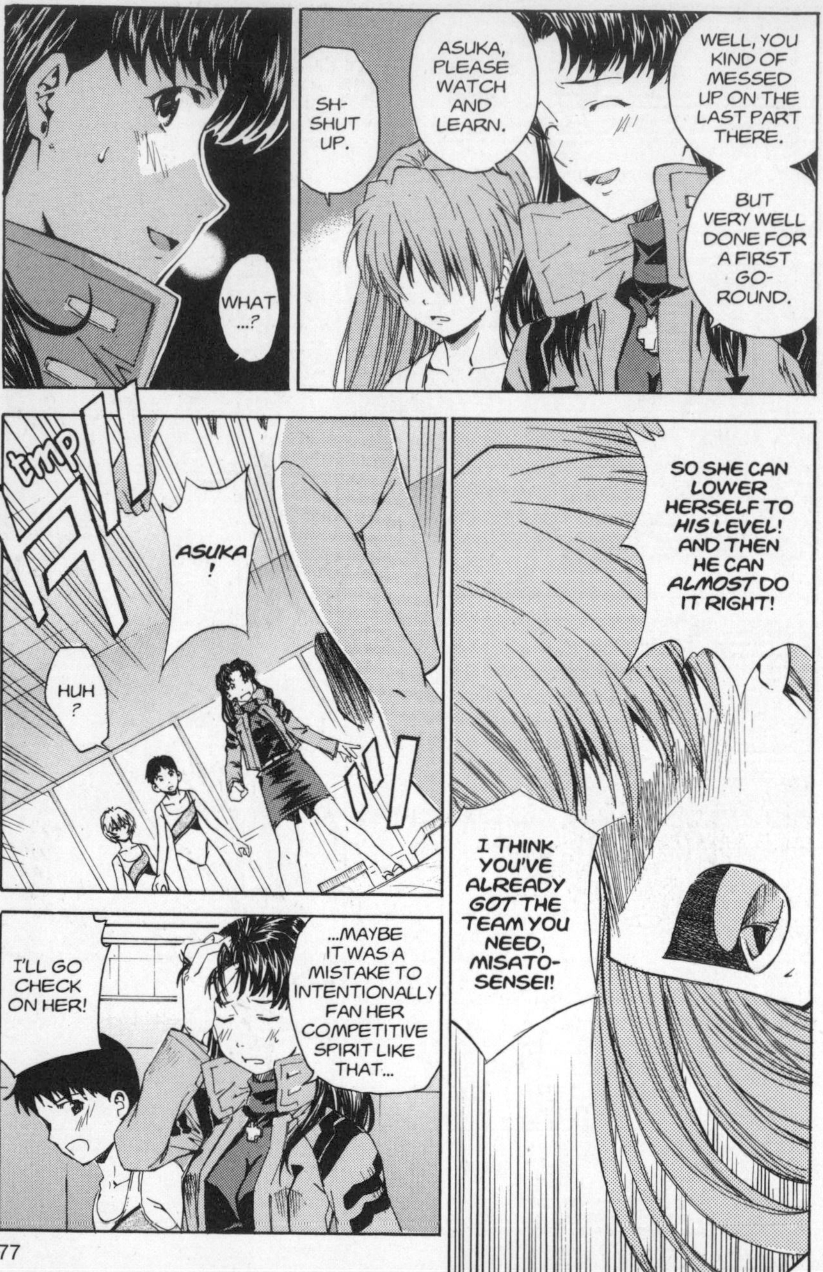
WELL, YOU KIND OF MESSED UP ON THE LAST PART THERE.
BUT VERY WELL DONE FOR A FIRST GO-ROUND.
ASUKA, PLEASE WATCH AND LEARN.
SH-SHUT UP.
WHAT ...?
SO SHE CAN LOWER HERSELF TO *HIS LEVEL*! AND THEN HE CAN *ALMOST* DO IT RIGHT!
I THINK YOU'VE ALREADY *GOT* THE TEAM YOU NEED, MISATO-SENSEI!
tmp
ASUKA!
HUH?
...MAYBE IT WAS A MISTAKE TO INTENTIONALLY FAN HER COMPETITIVE SPIRIT LIKE THAT...
I'LL GO CHECK ON HER!

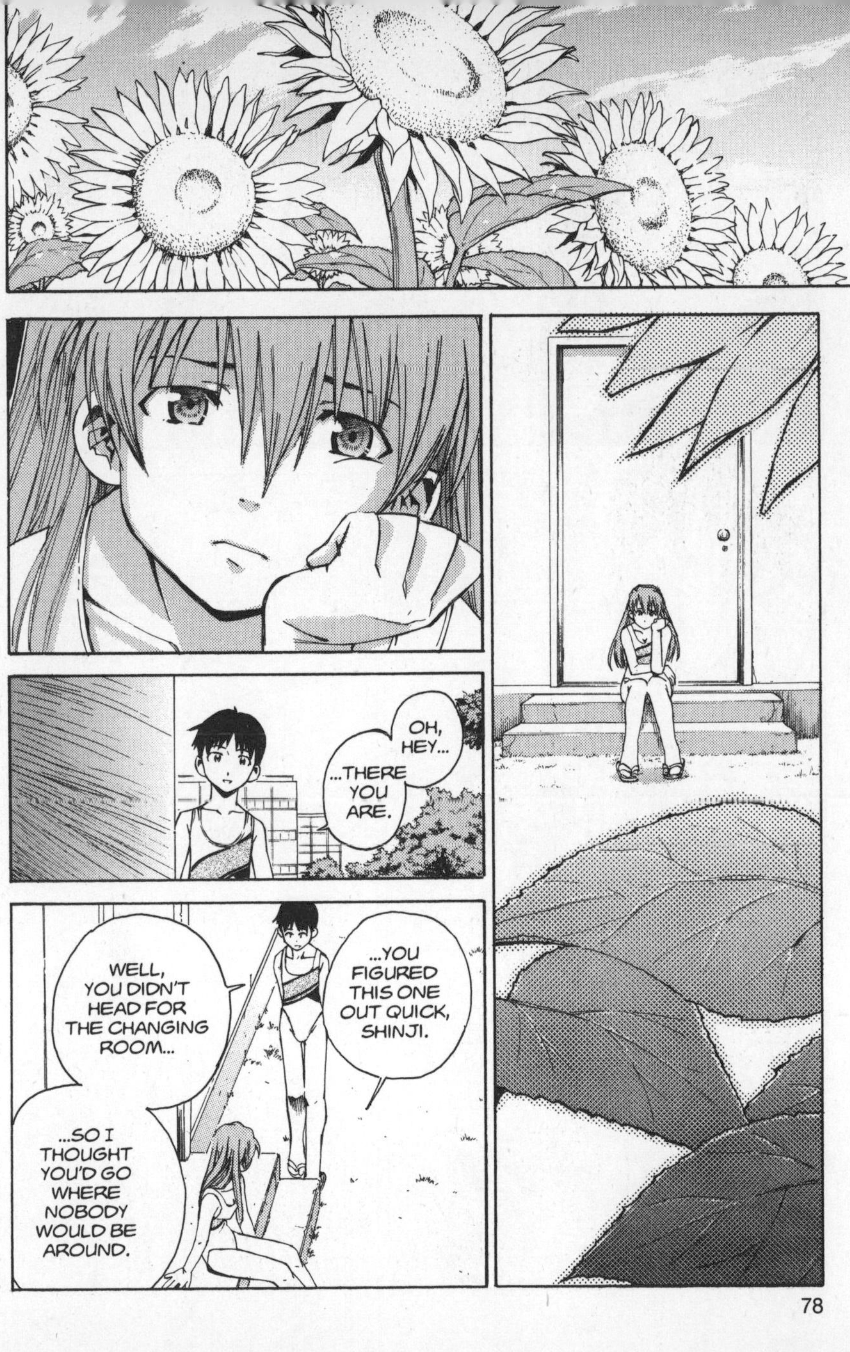
OH, HEY...
...THERE YOU ARE.
...YOU FIGURED THIS ONE OUT QUICK, SHINJI.
WELL, YOU DIDN'T HEAD FOR THE CHANGING ROOM...
...SO I THOUGHT YOU'D GO WHERE NOBODY WOULD BE AROUND.

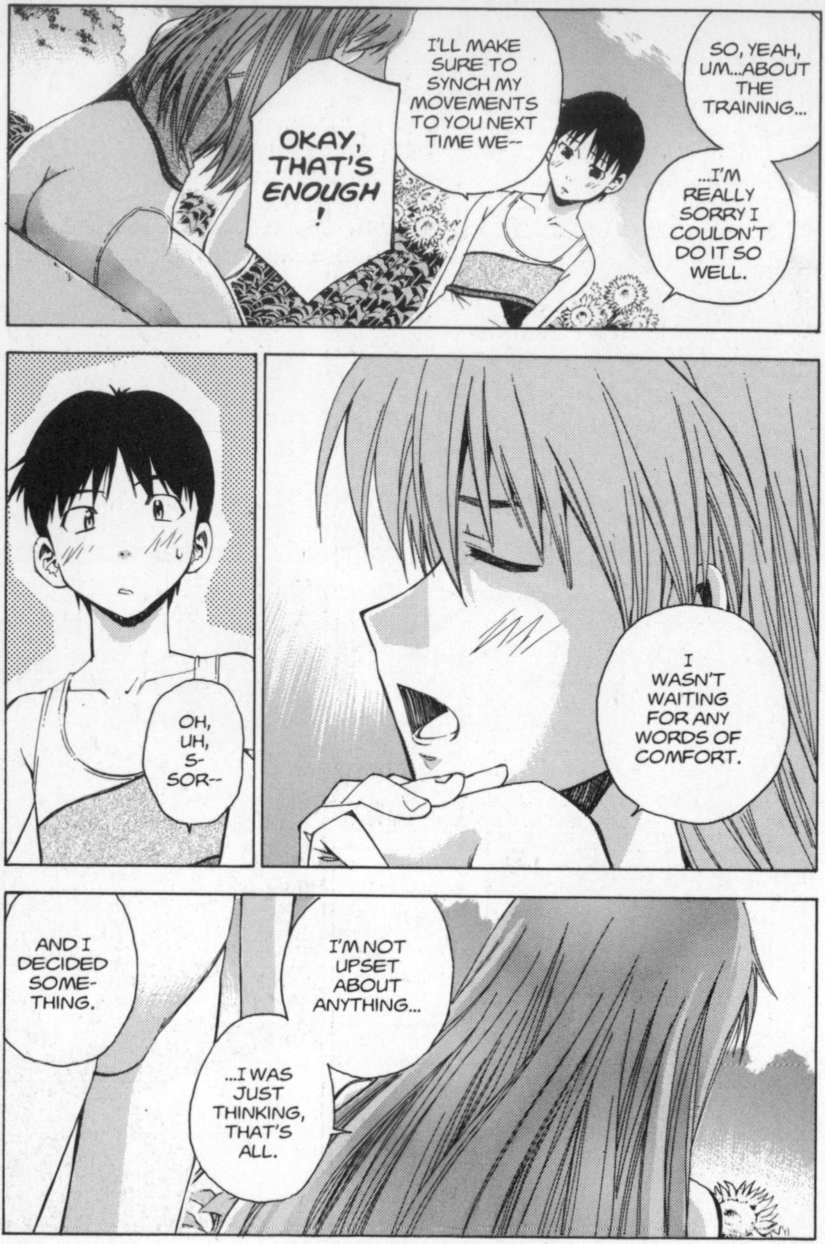
SO, YEAH, UM...ABOUT THE TRAINING...
...I'M REALLY SORRY I COULDN'T DO IT SO WELL.
I'LL MAKE SURE TO SYNCH MY MOVEMENTS TO YOU NEXT TIME WE--
OKAY, THAT'S ENOUGH!
I WASN'T WAITING FOR ANY WORDS OF COMFORT.
OH, UH, S-SOR--
I'M NOT UPSET ABOUT ANYTHING...
...I WAS JUST THINKING, THAT'S ALL.
AND I DECIDED SOME-THING.

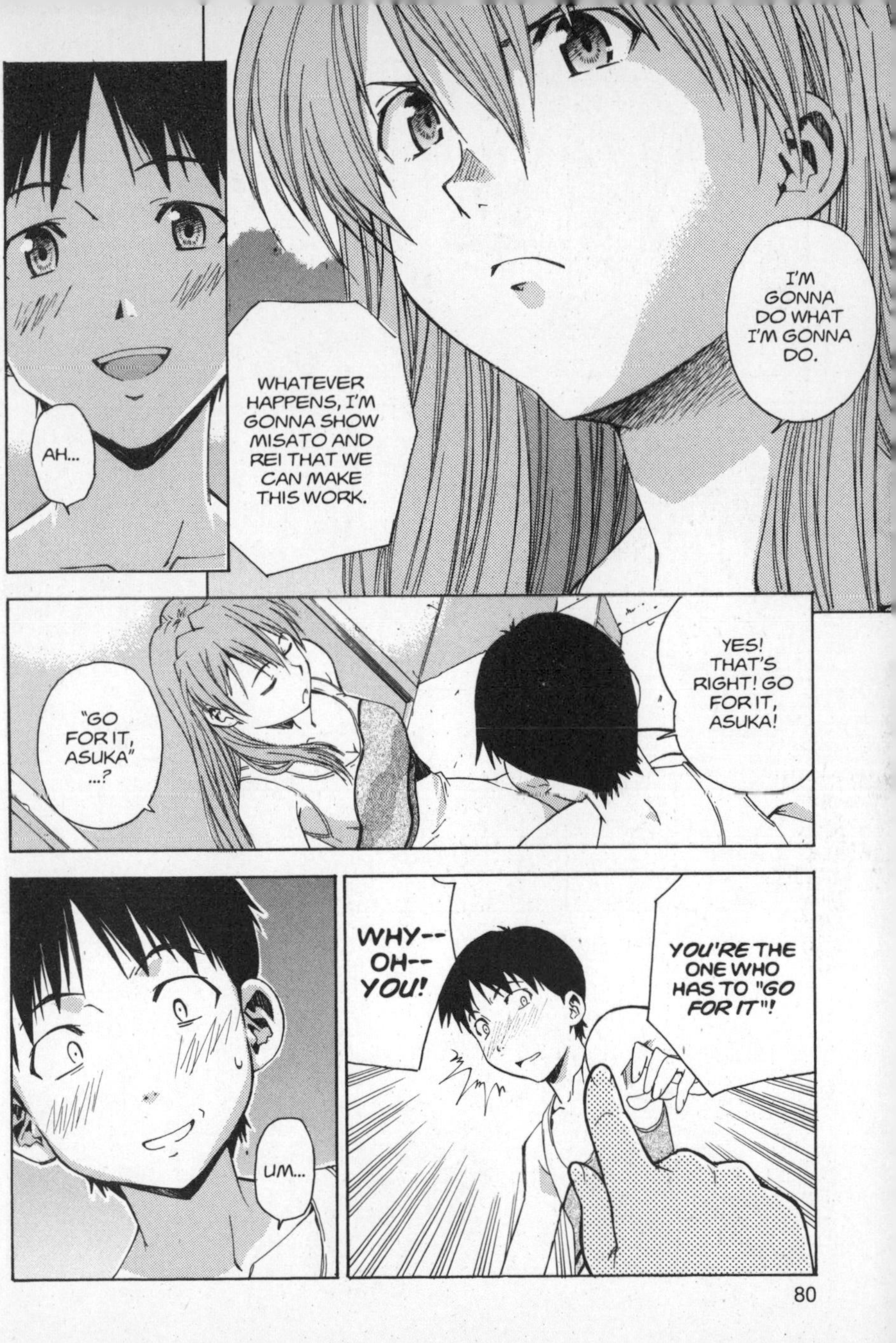
I'M GONNA DO WHAT I'M GONNA DO.
WHATEVER HAPPENS, I'M GONNA SHOW MISATO AND REI THAT WE CAN MAKE THIS WORK.
AH...
YES! THAT'S RIGHT! GO FOR IT, ASUKA!
"GO FOR IT, ASUKA" ...?
YOU'RE THE ONE WHO HAS TO "GO FOR IT"!
WHY-- OH-- YOU!
UM...

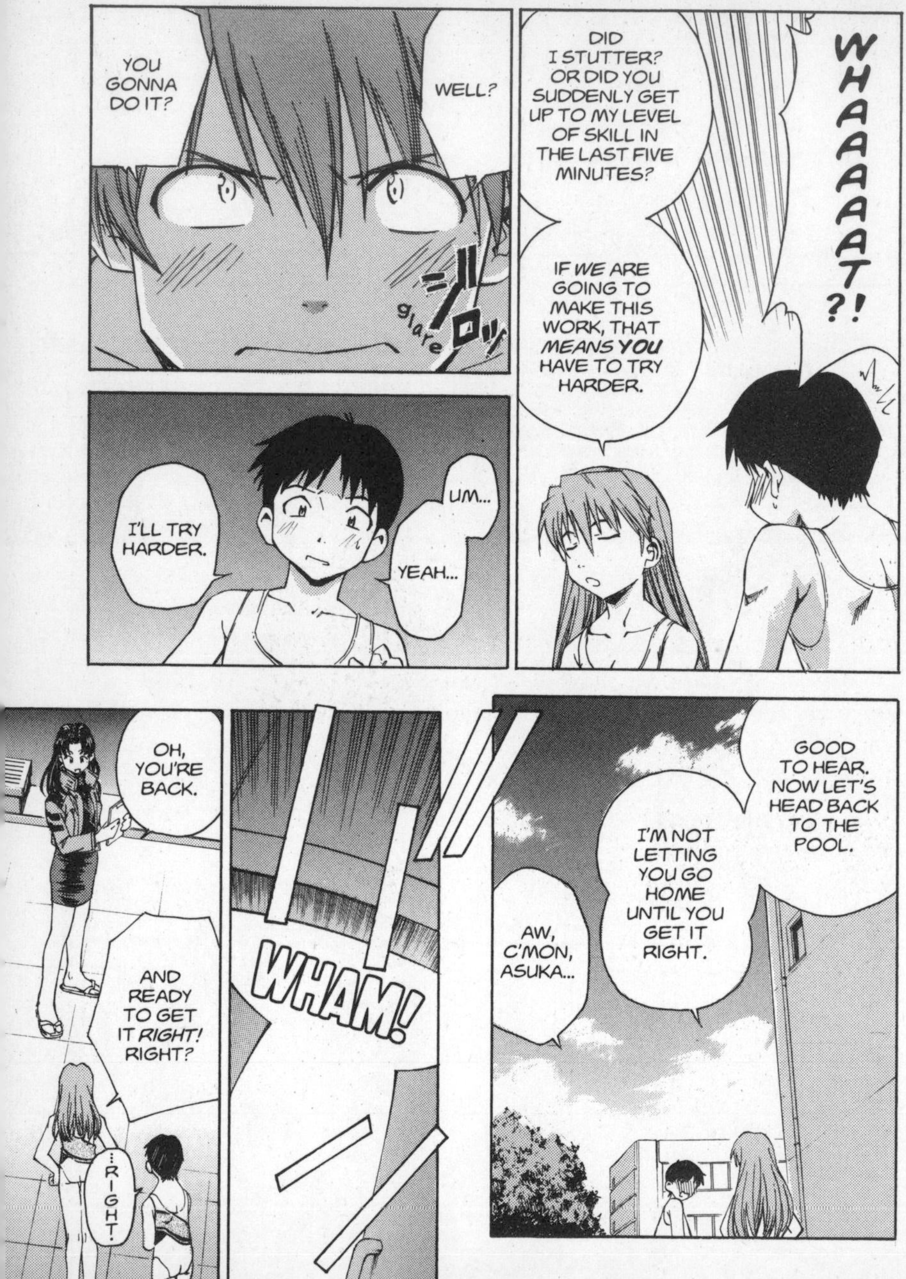
WHAAAAAT?!
DID I STUTTER? OR DID YOU SUDDENLY GET UP TO MY LEVEL OF SKILL IN THE LAST FIVE MINUTES?
IF WE ARE GOING TO MAKE THIS WORK, THAT MEANS YOU HAVE TO TRY HARDER.
WELL?
YOU GONNA DO IT?
glare
UM...
YEAH...
I'LL TRY HARDER.
GOOD TO HEAR. NOW LET'S HEAD BACK TO THE POOL.
I'M NOT LETTING YOU GO HOME UNTIL YOU GET IT RIGHT.
AW, C'MON, ASUKA...
WHAM!
OH, YOU'RE BACK.
AND READY TO GET IT RIGHT! RIGHT?
...RIGHT.

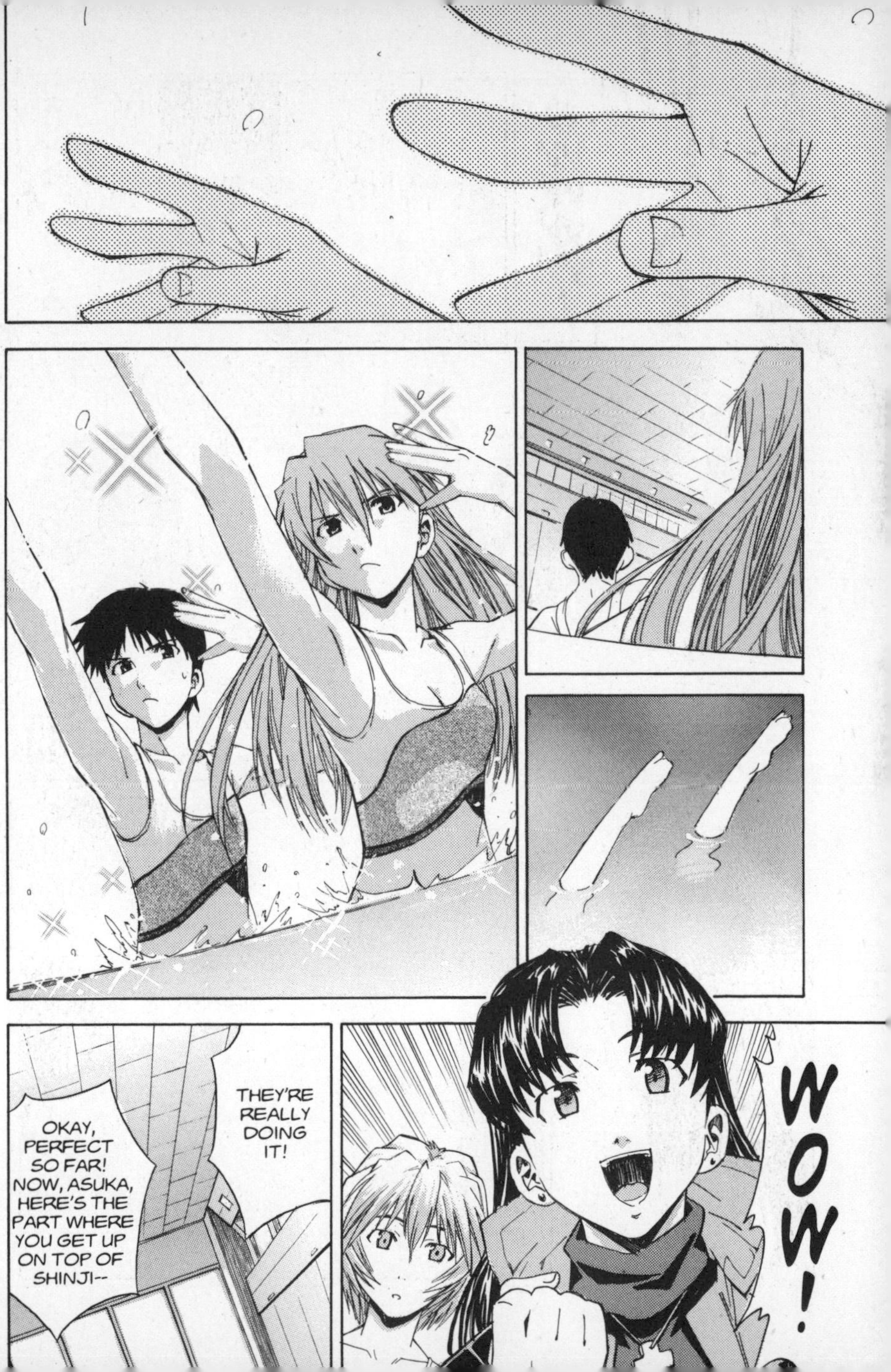
WOW!
THEY'RE REALLY DOING IT!
OKAY, PERFECT SO FAR! NOW, ASUKA, HERE'S THE PART WHERE YOU GET UP ON TOP OF SHINJI--

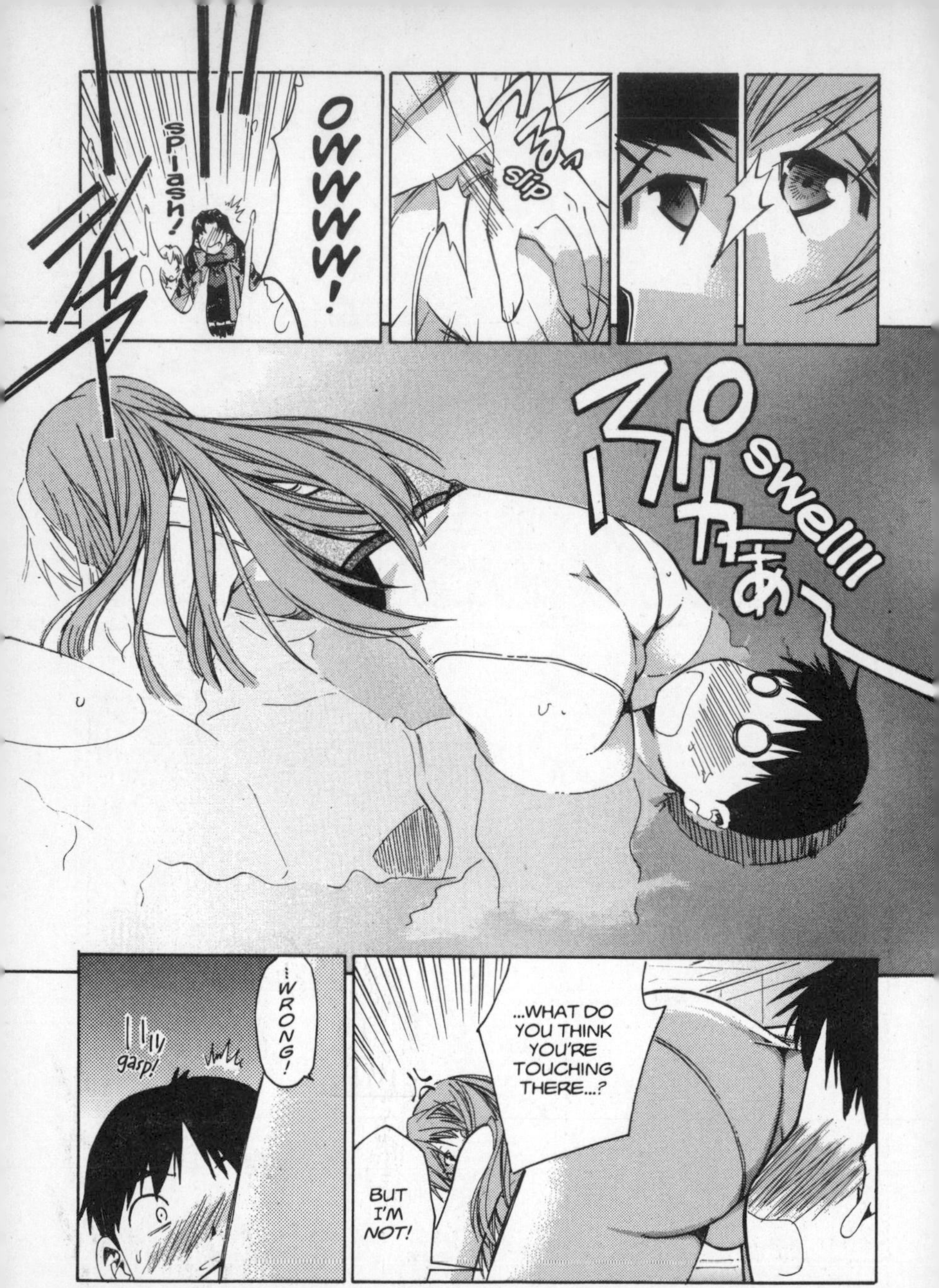
slip
OWWWWW!
splash!
swellll
...WHAT DO YOU THINK YOU'RE TOUCHING THERE...?
BUT I'M NOT!
...WRONG!
gasp!

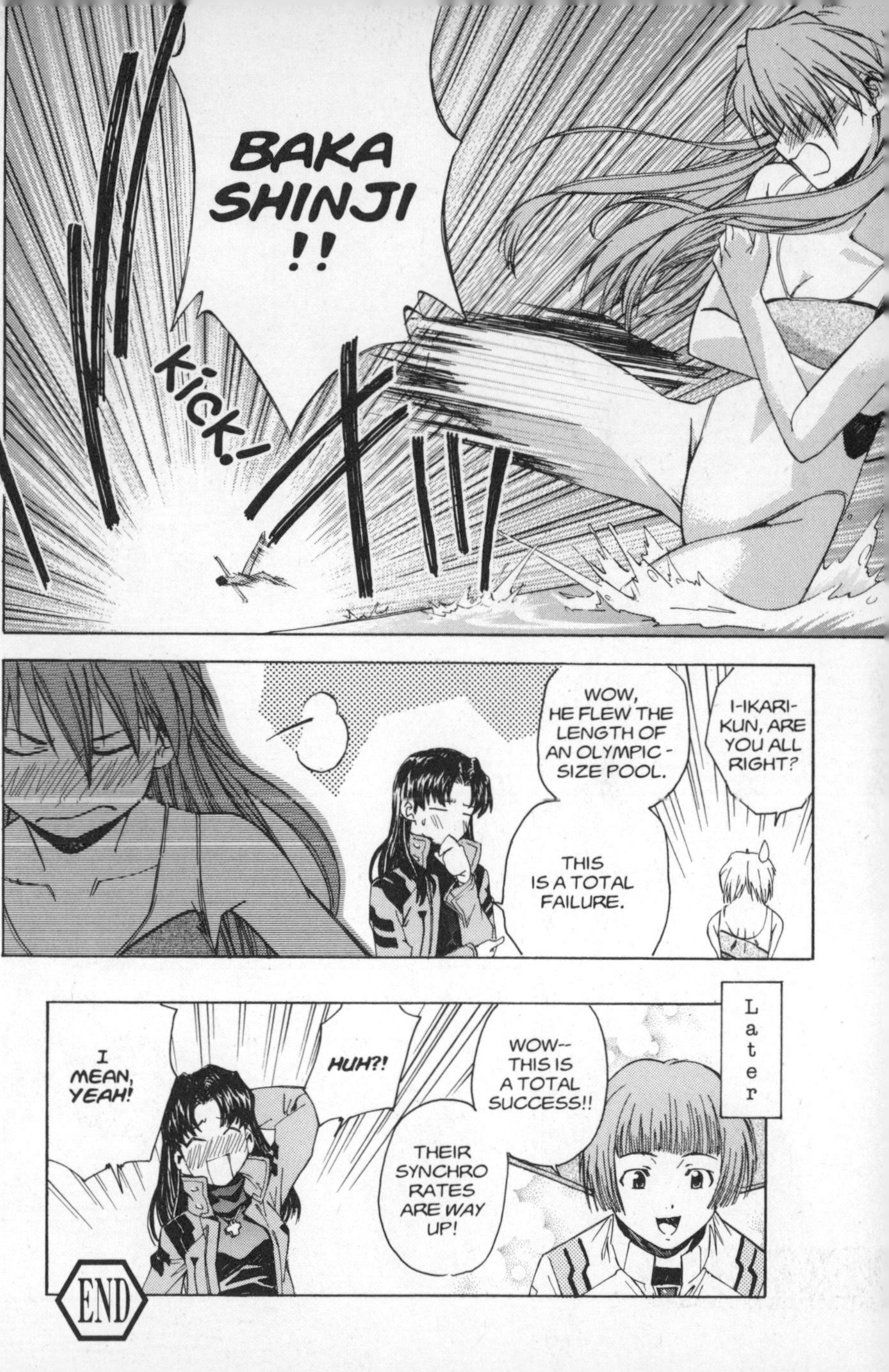
BAKA SHINJI !!
KICK!
I-IKARI-KUN, ARE YOU ALL RIGHT?
WOW, HE FLEW THE LENGTH OF AN OLYMPIC-SIZE POOL.
THIS IS A TOTAL FAILURE.
Later
WOW-- THIS IS A TOTAL SUCCESS!!
THEIR SYNCHRO RATES ARE WAY UP!
HUH?!
I MEAN, YEAH!
END

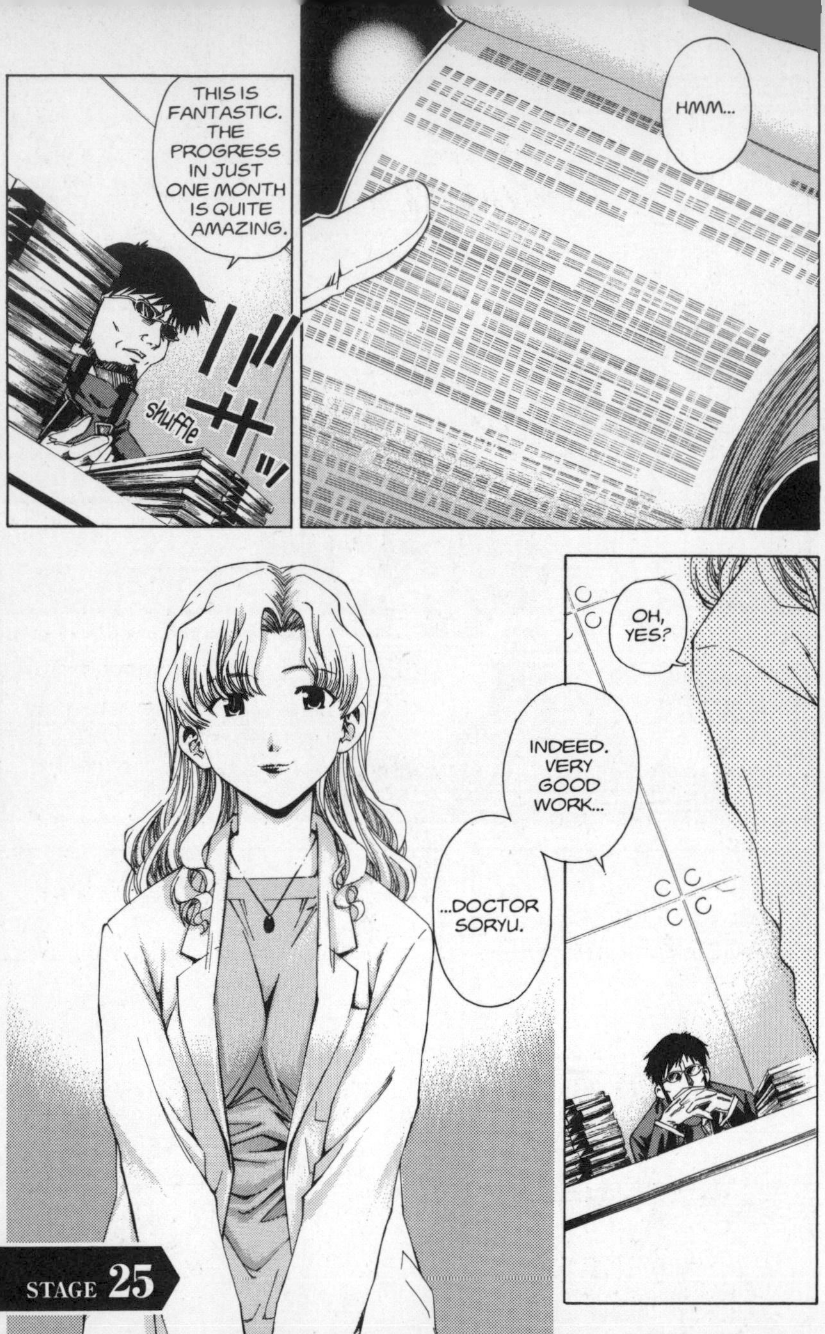
HMM...
THIS IS FANTASTIC. THE PROGRESS IN JUST ONE MONTH IS QUITE AMAZING.
shuffle
OH, YES?
INDEED. VERY GOOD WORK...
...DOCTOR SORYU.

STAGE 25

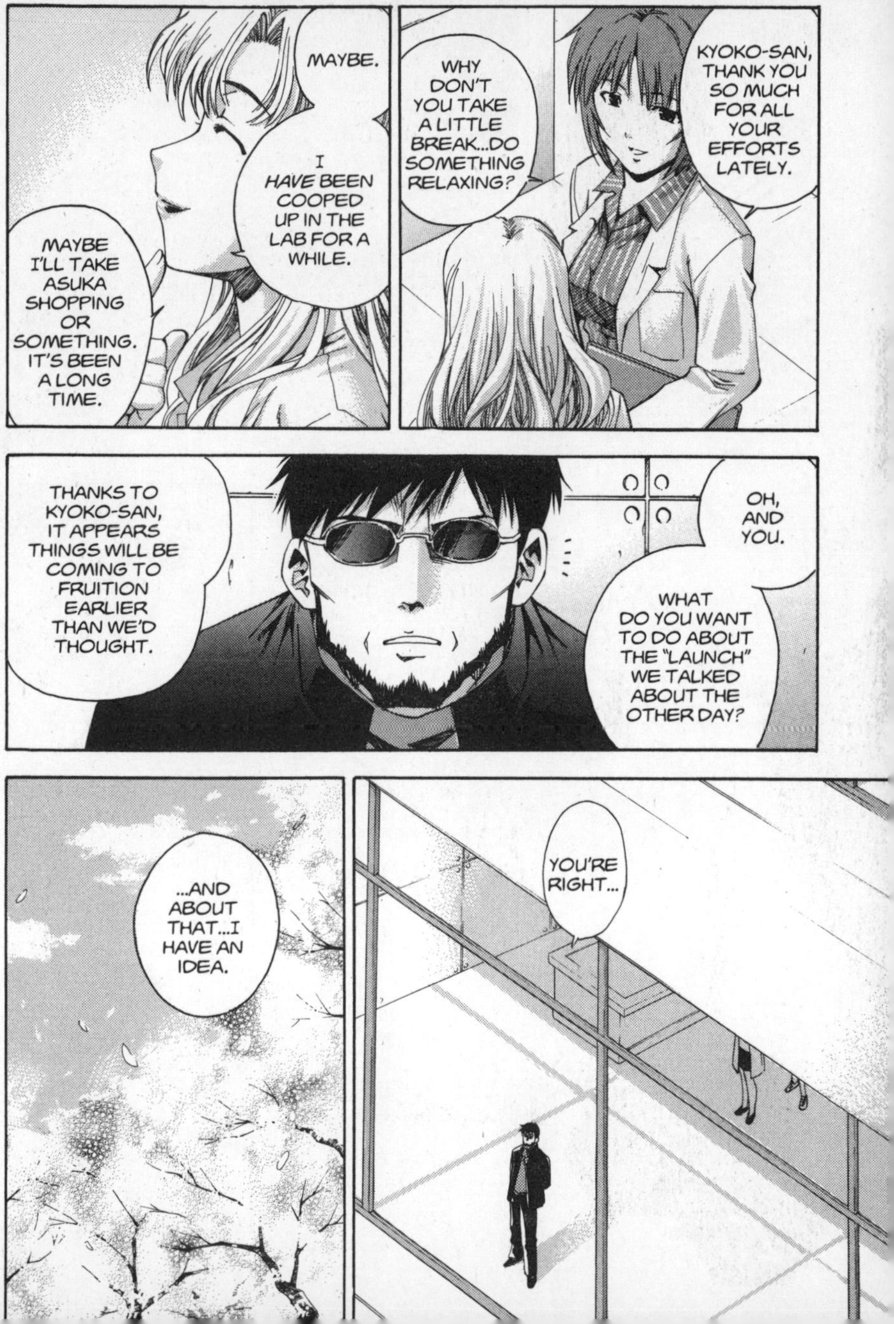
KYOKO-SAN, THANK YOU SO MUCH FOR ALL YOUR EFFORTS LATELY.
WHY DON'T YOU TAKE A LITTLE BREAK...DO SOMETHING RELAXING?
MAYBE.
I *HAVE* BEEN COOPED UP IN THE LAB FOR A WHILE.
MAYBE I'LL TAKE ASUKA SHOPPING OR SOMETHING. IT'S BEEN A LONG TIME.
OH, AND YOU.
WHAT DO YOU WANT TO DO ABOUT THE "LAUNCH" WE TALKED ABOUT THE OTHER DAY?
THANKS TO KYOKO-SAN, IT APPEARS THINGS WILL BE COMING TO FRUITION EARLIER THAN WE'D THOUGHT.
YOU'RE RIGHT...
...AND ABOUT THAT...I HAVE AN IDEA.

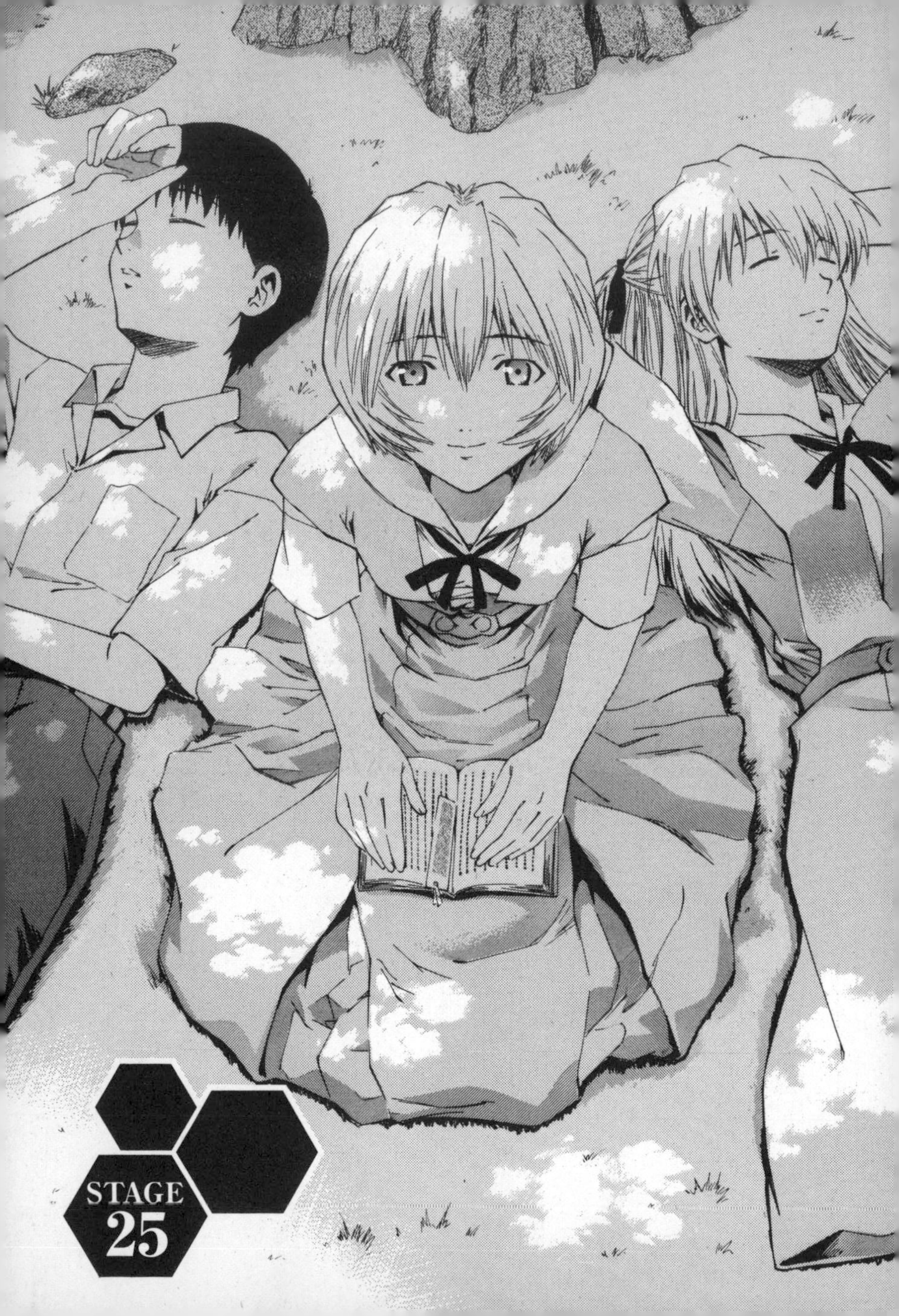
STAGE
25

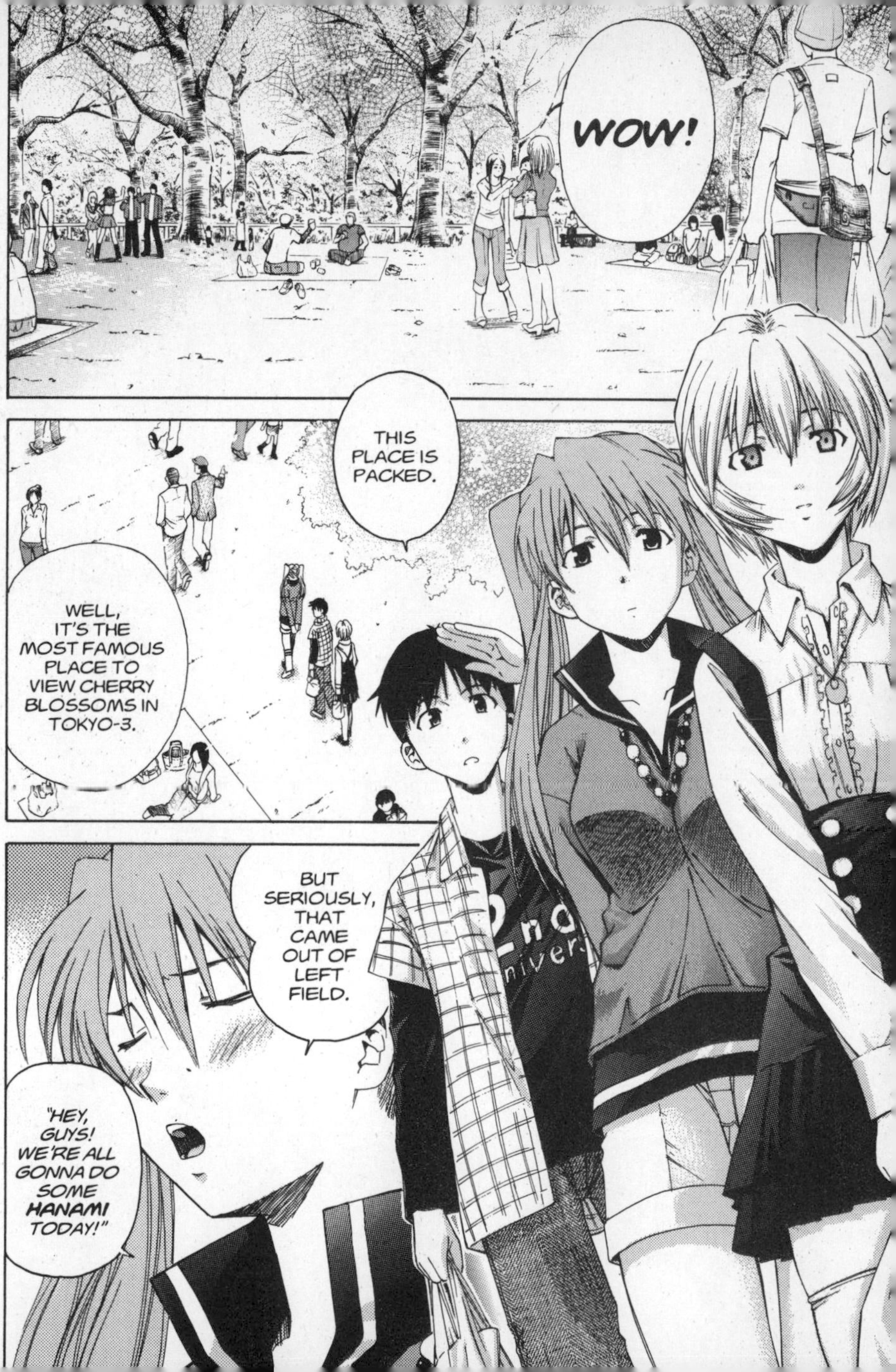
WOW!
THIS PLACE IS PACKED.
WELL, IT'S THE MOST FAMOUS PLACE TO VIEW CHERRY BLOSSOMS IN TOKYO-3.
BUT SERIOUSLY, THAT CAME OUT OF LEFT FIELD.
"HEY, GUYS! WE'RE ALL GONNA DO SOME **HANAMI** TODAY!"

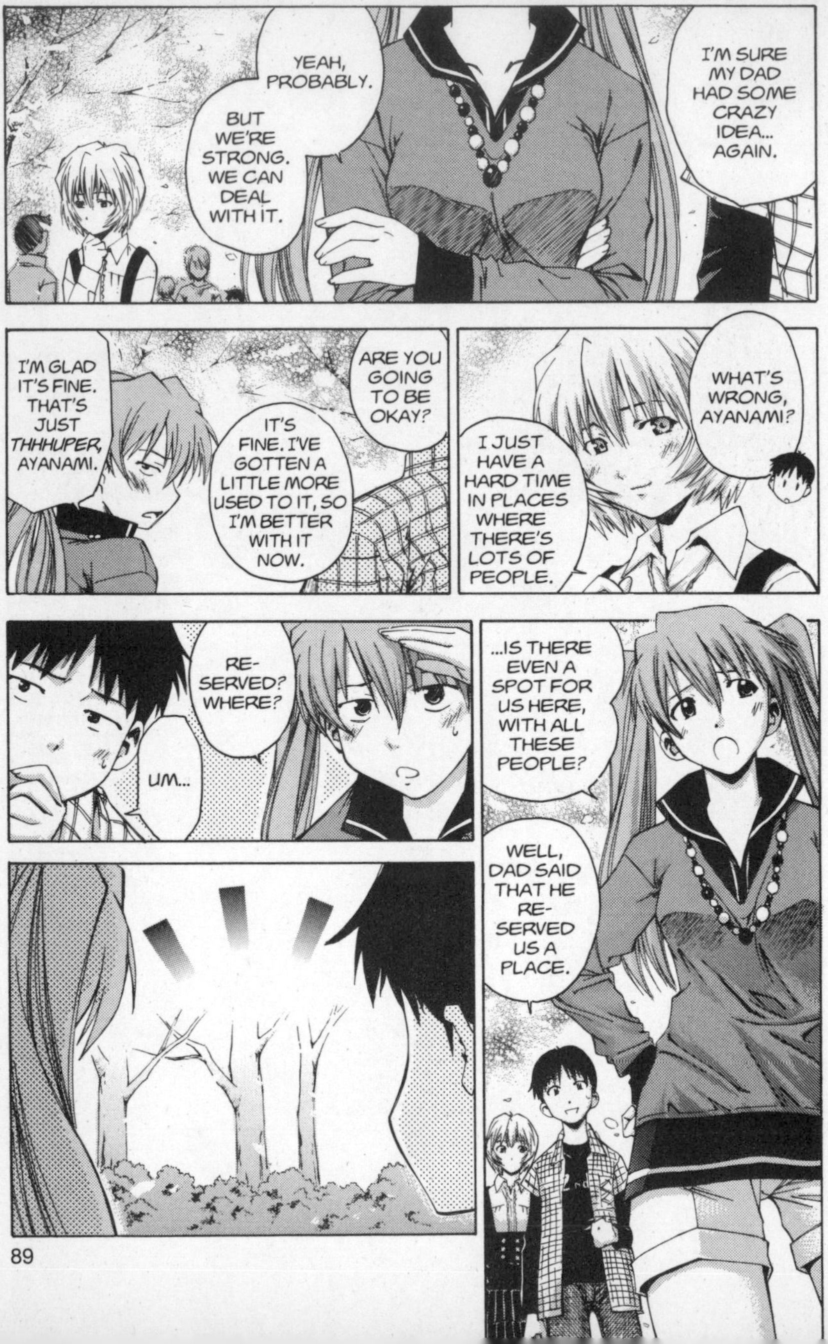
I'M SURE MY DAD HAD SOME CRAZY IDEA... AGAIN.
YEAH, PROBABLY.
BUT WE'RE STRONG. WE CAN DEAL WITH IT.
WHAT'S WRONG, AYANAMI?
I JUST HAVE A HARD TIME IN PLACES WHERE THERE'S LOTS OF PEOPLE.
ARE YOU GOING TO BE OKAY?
IT'S FINE. I'VE GOTTEN A LITTLE MORE USED TO IT, SO I'M BETTER WITH IT NOW.
I'M GLAD IT'S FINE. THAT'S JUST THHHUPER, AYANAMI.
...IS THERE EVEN A SPOT FOR US HERE, WITH ALL THESE PEOPLE?
WELL, DAD SAID THAT HE RE-SERVED US A PLACE.
RE-SERVED? WHERE?
UM...

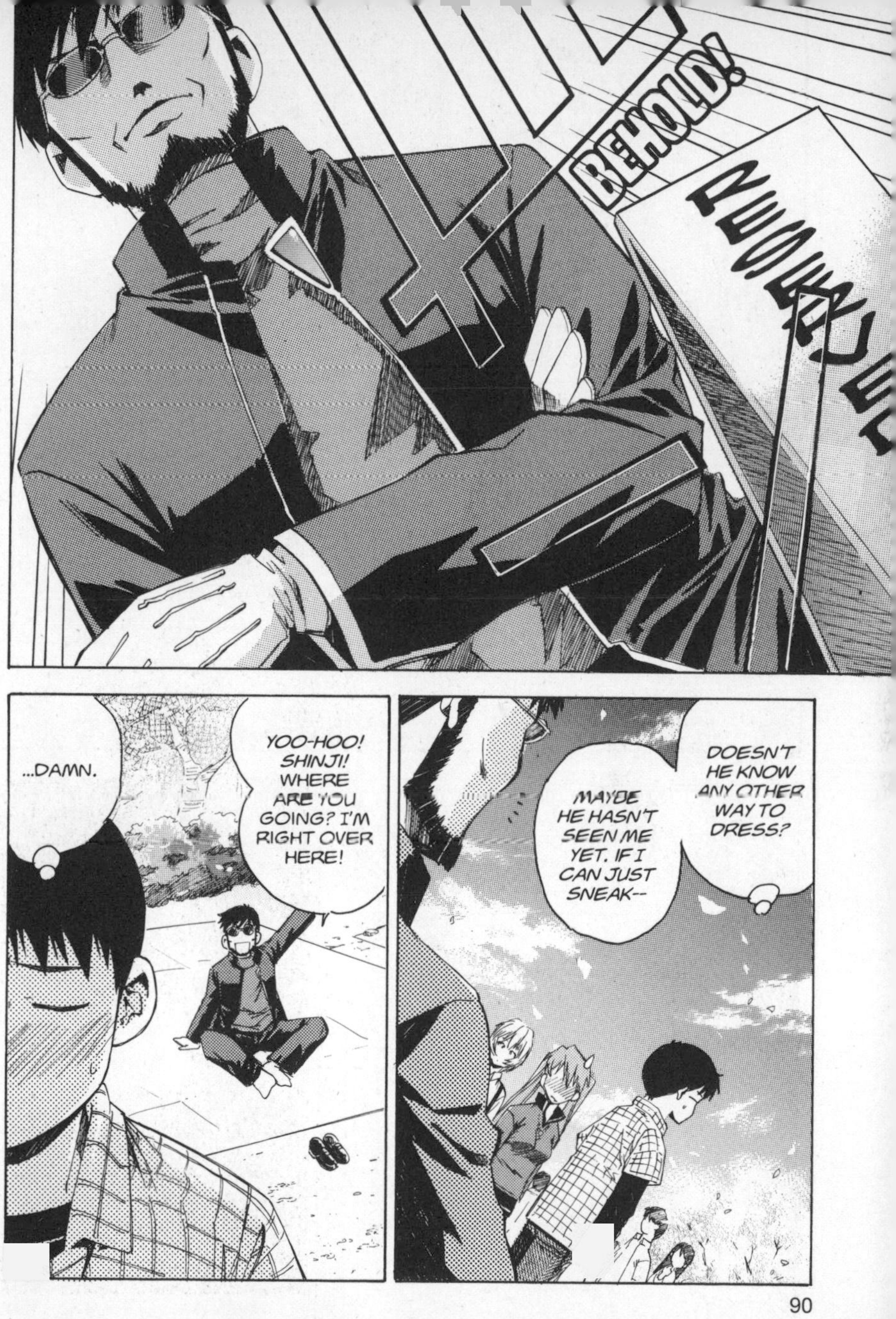
BEHOLD!
DOESN'T HE KNOW ANY OTHER WAY TO DRESS?
MAYBE HE HASN'T SEEN ME YET. IF I CAN JUST SNEAK--
YOO-HOO! SHINJI! WHERE ARE YOU GOING? I'M RIGHT OVER HERE!
...DAMN.

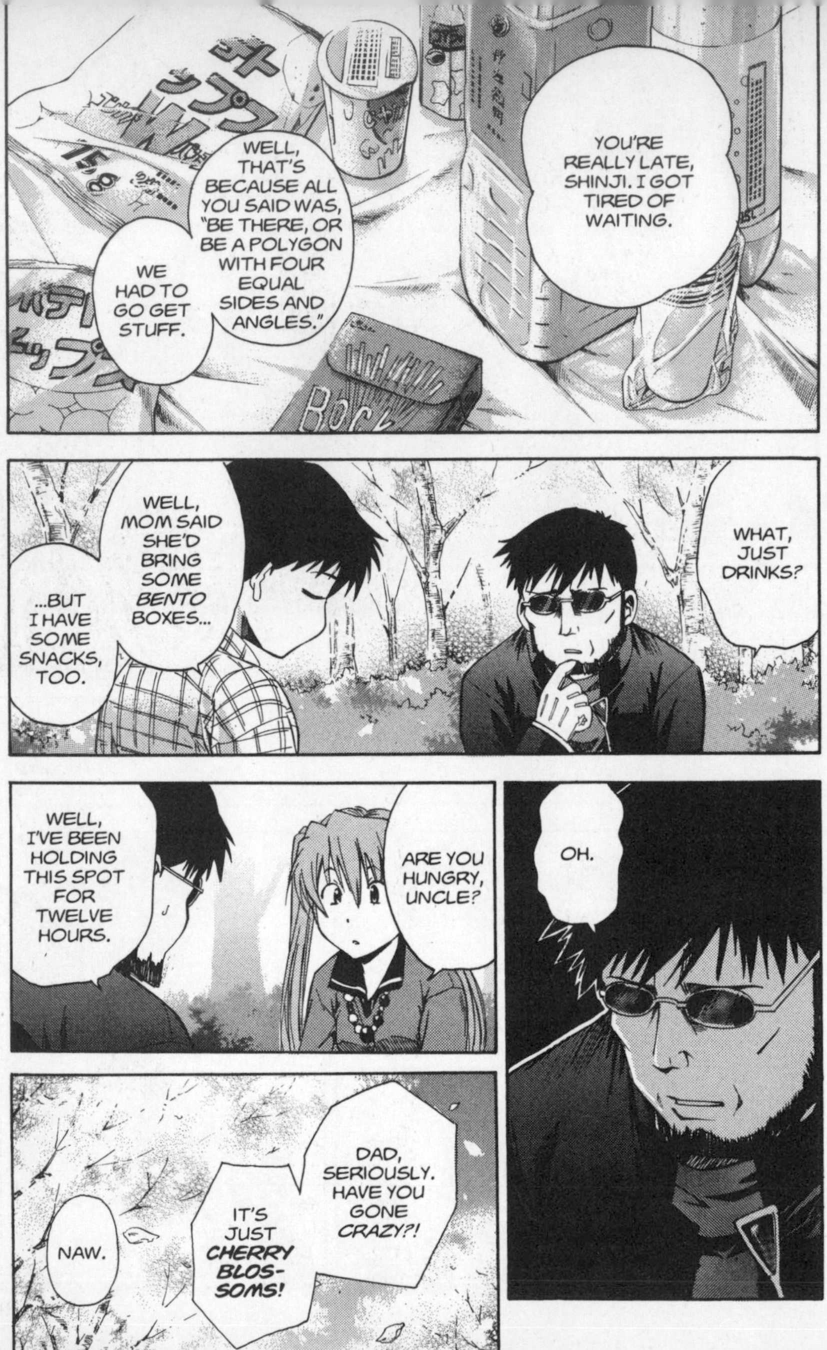
YOU'RE REALLY LATE, SHINJI. I GOT TIRED OF WAITING.
WELL, THAT'S BECAUSE ALL YOU SAID WAS, "BE THERE, OR BE A POLYGON WITH FOUR EQUAL SIDES AND ANGLES."
WE HAD TO GO GET STUFF.
WHAT, JUST DRINKS?
WELL, MOM SAID SHE'D BRING SOME BENTO BOXES...
...BUT I HAVE SOME SNACKS, TOO.
OH.
ARE YOU HUNGRY, UNCLE?
WELL, I'VE BEEN HOLDING THIS SPOT FOR TWELVE HOURS.
DAD, SERIOUSLY. HAVE YOU GONE CRAZY?!
IT'S JUST CHERRY BLOSSOMS!
NAW.

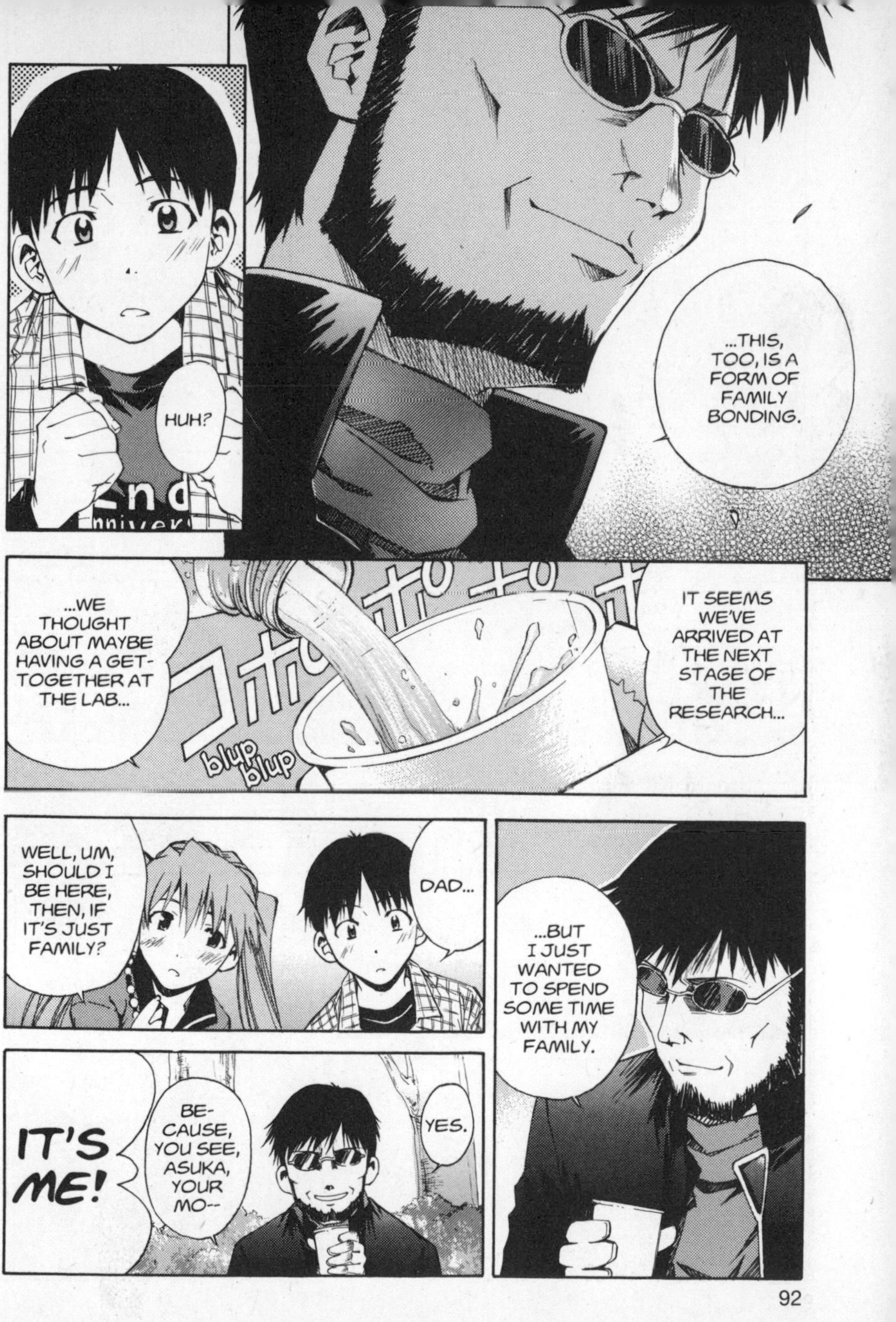
...THIS, TOO, IS A FORM OF FAMILY BONDING.
HUH?
IT SEEMS WE'VE ARRIVED AT THE NEXT STAGE OF THE RESEARCH...
...WE THOUGHT ABOUT MAYBE HAVING A GET-TOGETHER AT THE LAB...
blup blup
...BUT I JUST WANTED TO SPEND SOME TIME WITH MY FAMILY.
DAD...
WELL, UM, SHOULD I BE HERE, THEN, IF IT'S JUST FAMILY?
YES.
BE-CAUSE, YOU SEE, ASUKA, YOUR MO--
IT'S ME!

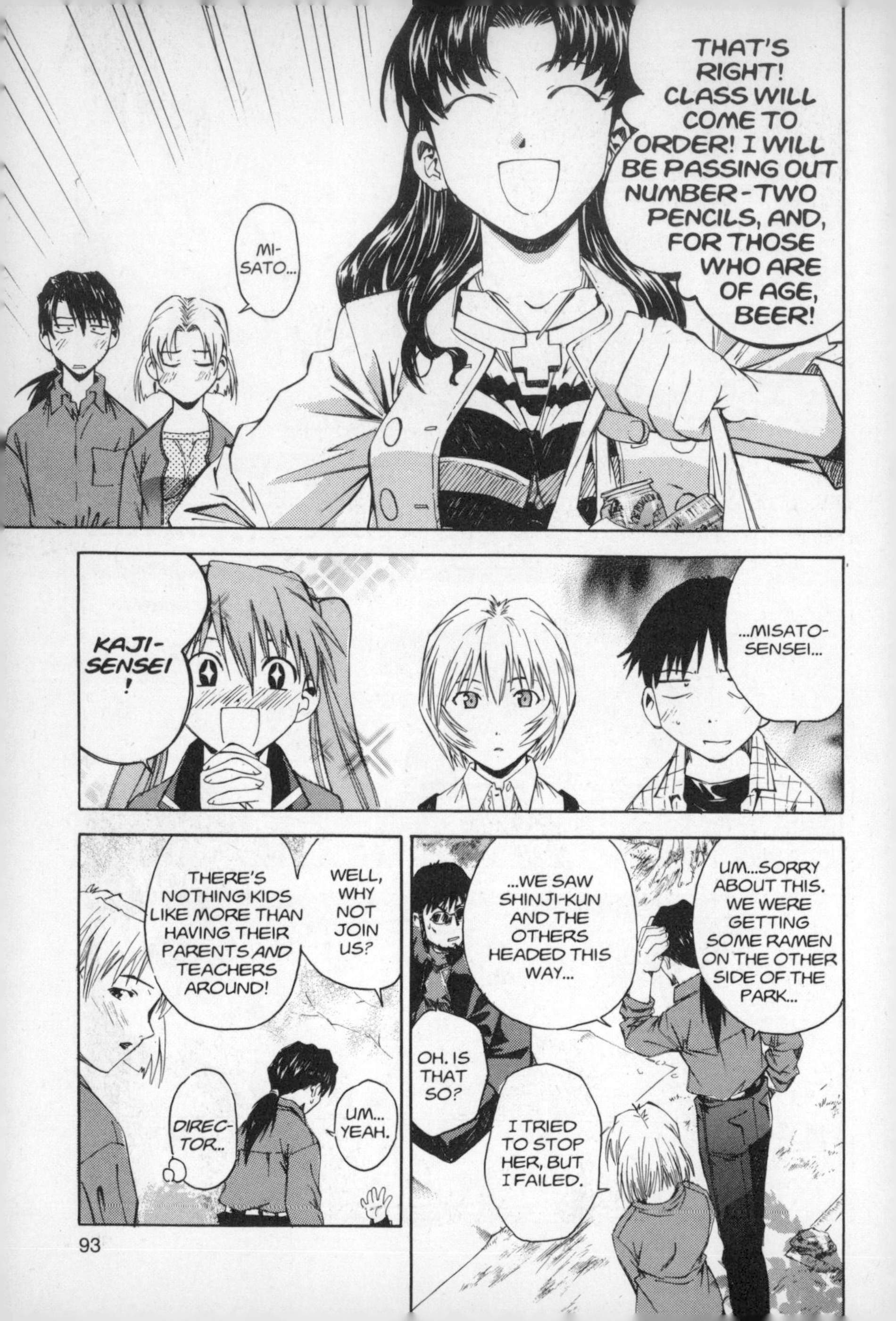
THAT'S RIGHT! CLASS WILL COME TO ORDER! I WILL BE PASSING OUT NUMBER-TWO PENCILS, AND, FOR THOSE WHO ARE OF AGE, BEER!
MI-SATO...
...MISATO-SENSEI...
KAJI-SENSEI!
UM...SORRY ABOUT THIS. WE WERE GETTING SOME RAMEN ON THE OTHER SIDE OF THE PARK...
...WE SAW SHINJI-KUN AND THE OTHERS HEADED THIS WAY...
OH. IS THAT SO?
I TRIED TO STOP HER, BUT I FAILED.
WELL, WHY NOT JOIN US?
THERE'S NOTHING KIDS LIKE MORE THAN HAVING THEIR PARENTS AND TEACHERS AROUND!
UM... YEAH.
DIRECTOR...

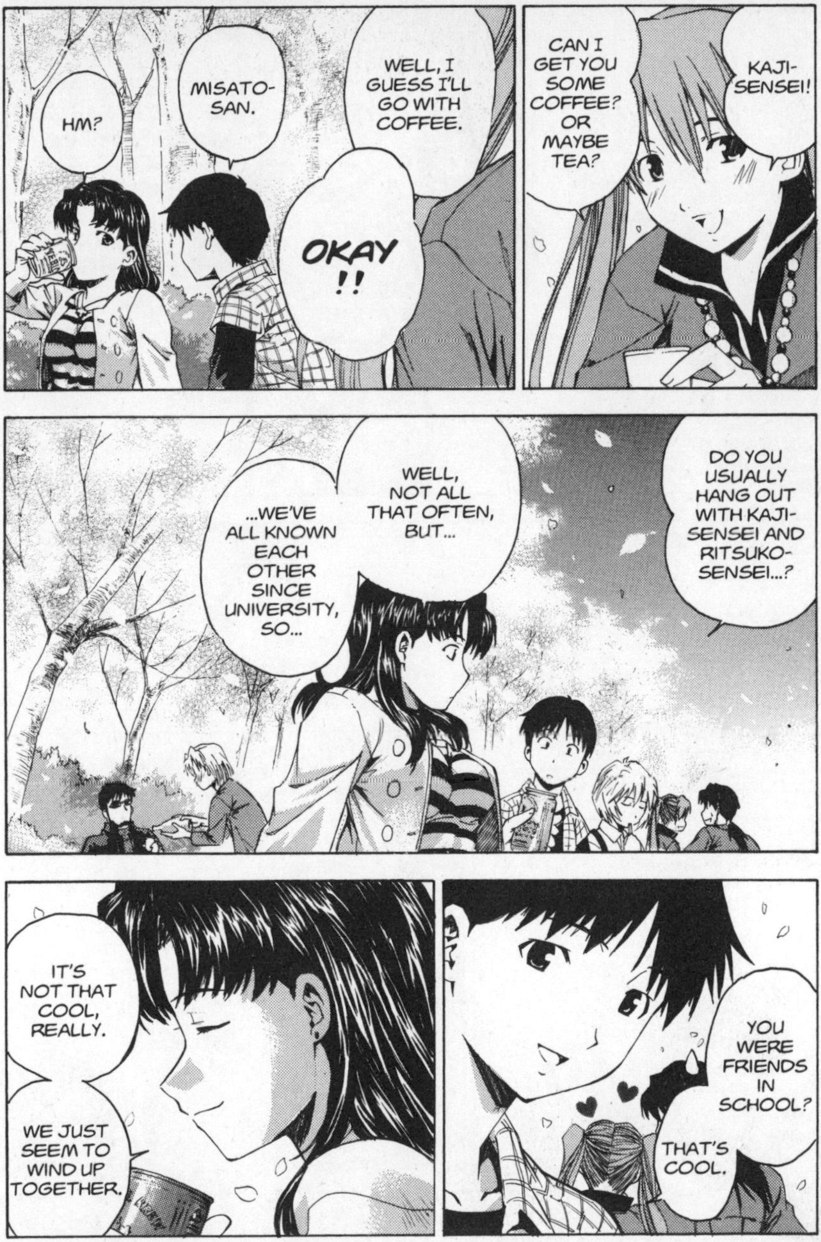
KAJI-SENSEI!
CAN I GET YOU SOME COFFEE? OR MAYBE TEA?
WELL, I GUESS I'LL GO WITH COFFEE.
OKAY !!
MISATO-SAN.
HM?
DO YOU USUALLY HANG OUT WITH KAJI-SENSEI AND RITSUKO-SENSEI...?
WELL, NOT ALL THAT OFTEN, BUT...
...WE'VE ALL KNOWN EACH OTHER SINCE UNIVERSITY, SO...
YOU WERE FRIENDS IN SCHOOL?
THAT'S COOL.
IT'S NOT THAT COOL, REALLY.
WE JUST SEEM TO WIND UP TOGETHER.

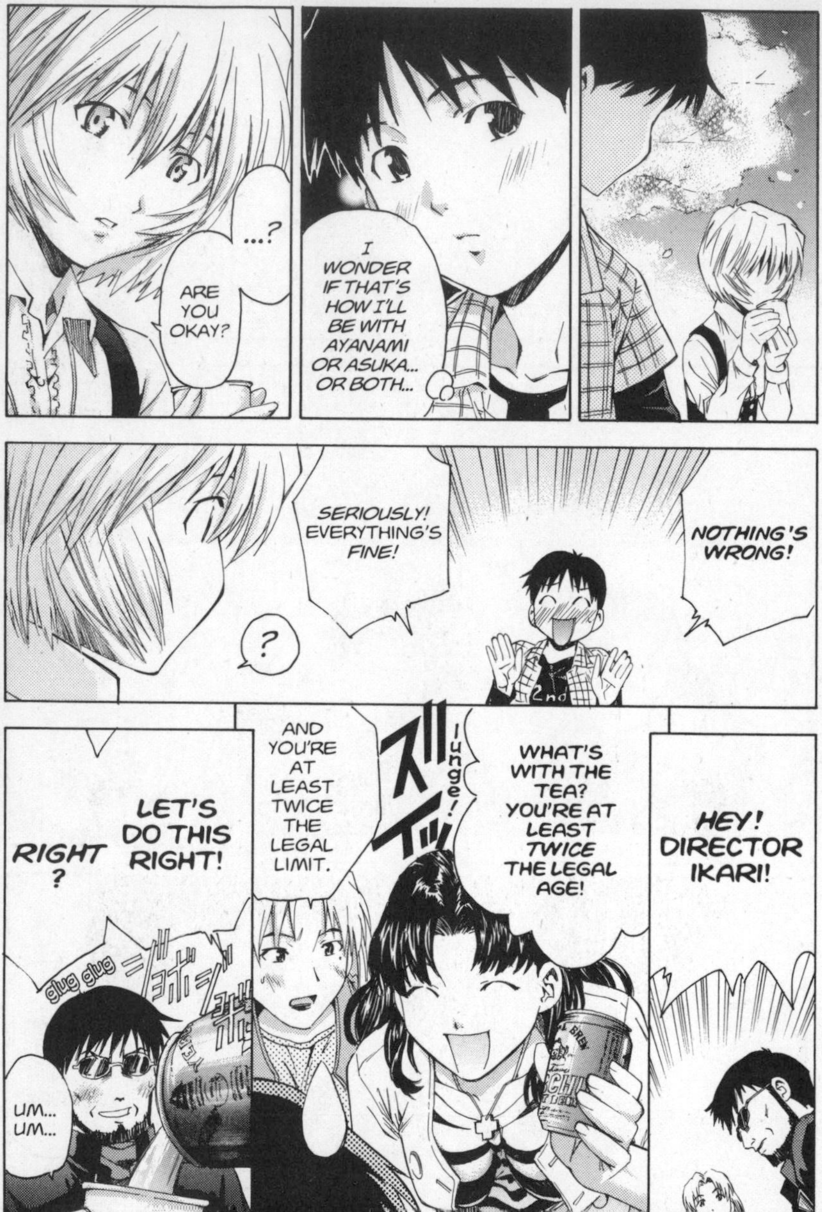
I WONDER IF THAT'S HOW I'LL BE WITH AYANAMI OR ASUKA... OR BOTH...
...?
ARE YOU OKAY?
NOTHING'S WRONG!
SERIOUSLY! EVERYTHING'S FINE!
?
HEY! DIRECTOR IKARI!
WHAT'S WITH THE TEA? YOU'RE AT LEAST TWICE THE LEGAL AGE!
lunge!
AND YOU'RE AT LEAST TWICE THE LEGAL LIMIT.
LET'S DO THIS RIGHT!
RIGHT?
glug glug
UM... UM...

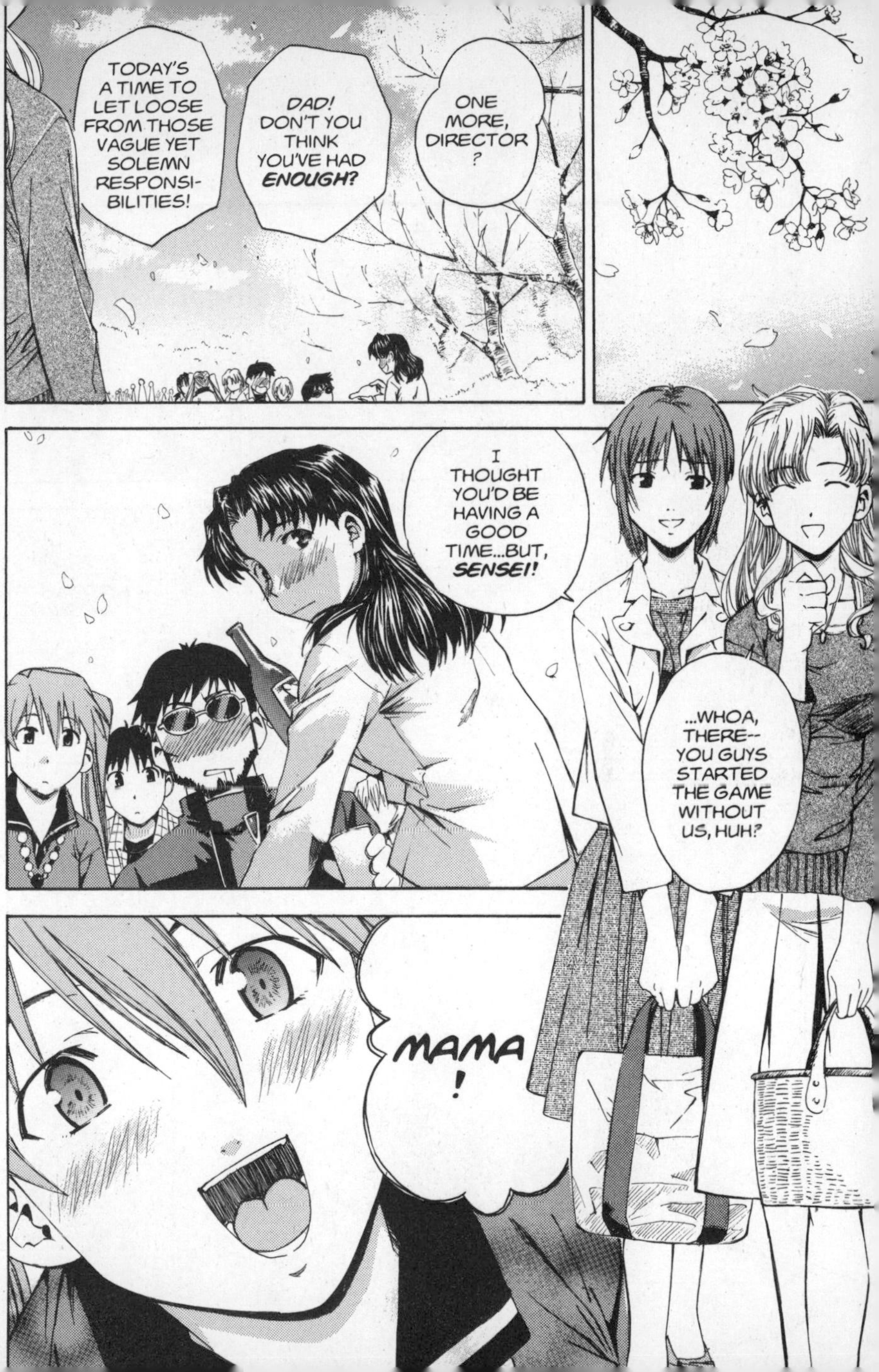
ONE MORE, DIRECTOR?
DAD! DON'T YOU THINK YOU'VE HAD ENOUGH?
TODAY'S A TIME TO LET LOOSE FROM THOSE VAGUE YET SOLEMN RESPONSIBILITIES!
I THOUGHT YOU'D BE HAVING A GOOD TIME...BUT, SENSEI!
...WHOA, THERE-- YOU GUYS STARTED THE GAME WITHOUT US, HUH?
MAMA!

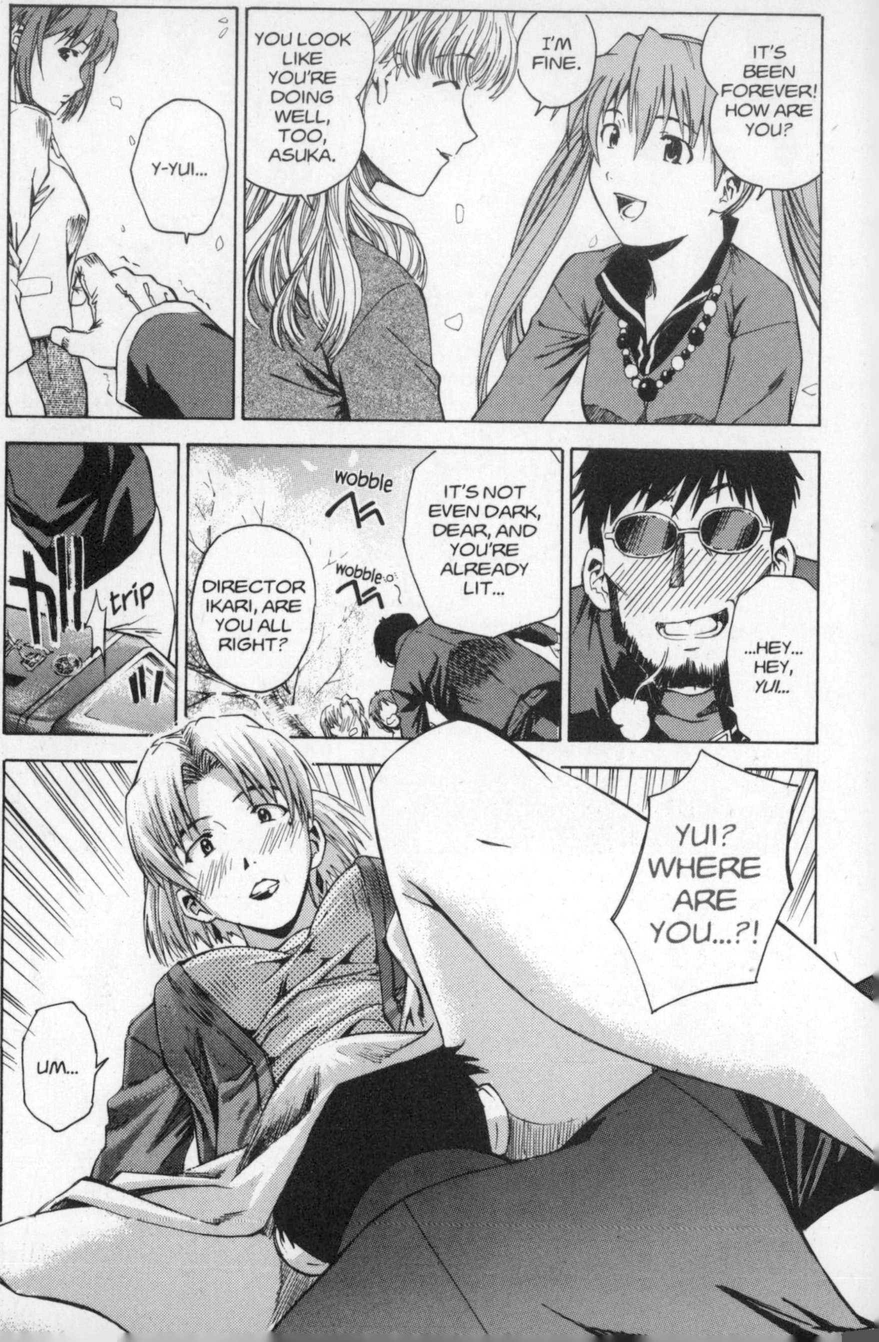
IT'S BEEN FOREVER! HOW ARE YOU?
I'M FINE.
YOU LOOK LIKE YOU'RE DOING WELL, TOO, ASUKA.
Y-YUI...
...HEY... HEY, YUI...
IT'S NOT EVEN DARK, DEAR, AND YOU'RE ALREADY LIT...
wobble
wobble
DIRECTOR IKARI, ARE YOU ALL RIGHT?
trip
YUI? WHERE ARE YOU...?!
UM...

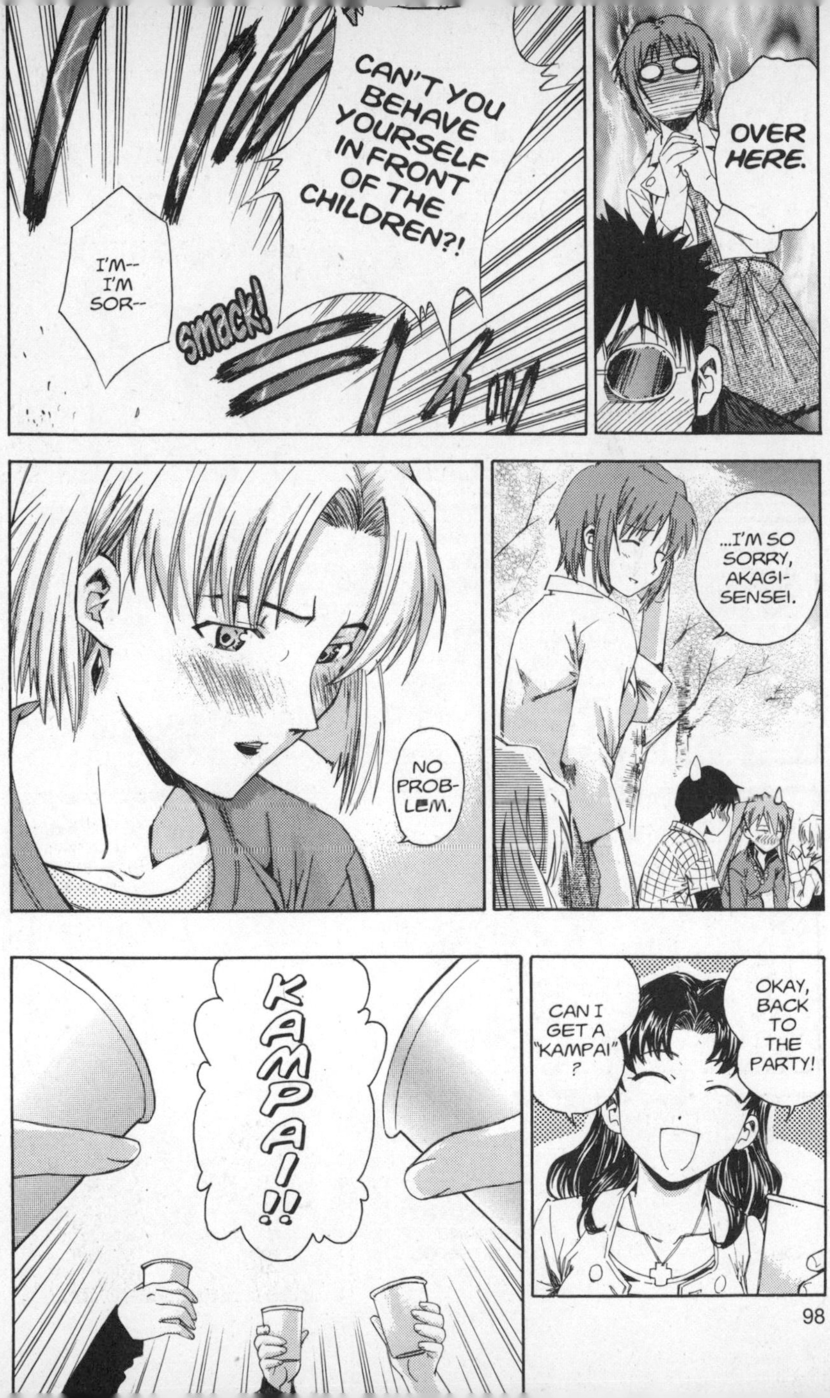
OVER HERE.
CAN'T YOU BEHAVE YOURSELF IN FRONT OF THE CHILDREN?!
I'M-- I'M SOR--
smack!
...I'M SO SORRY, AKAGI-SENSEI.
NO PROB-LEM.
OKAY, BACK TO THE PARTY!
CAN I GET A "KAMPAI"?
KAMPAI!!

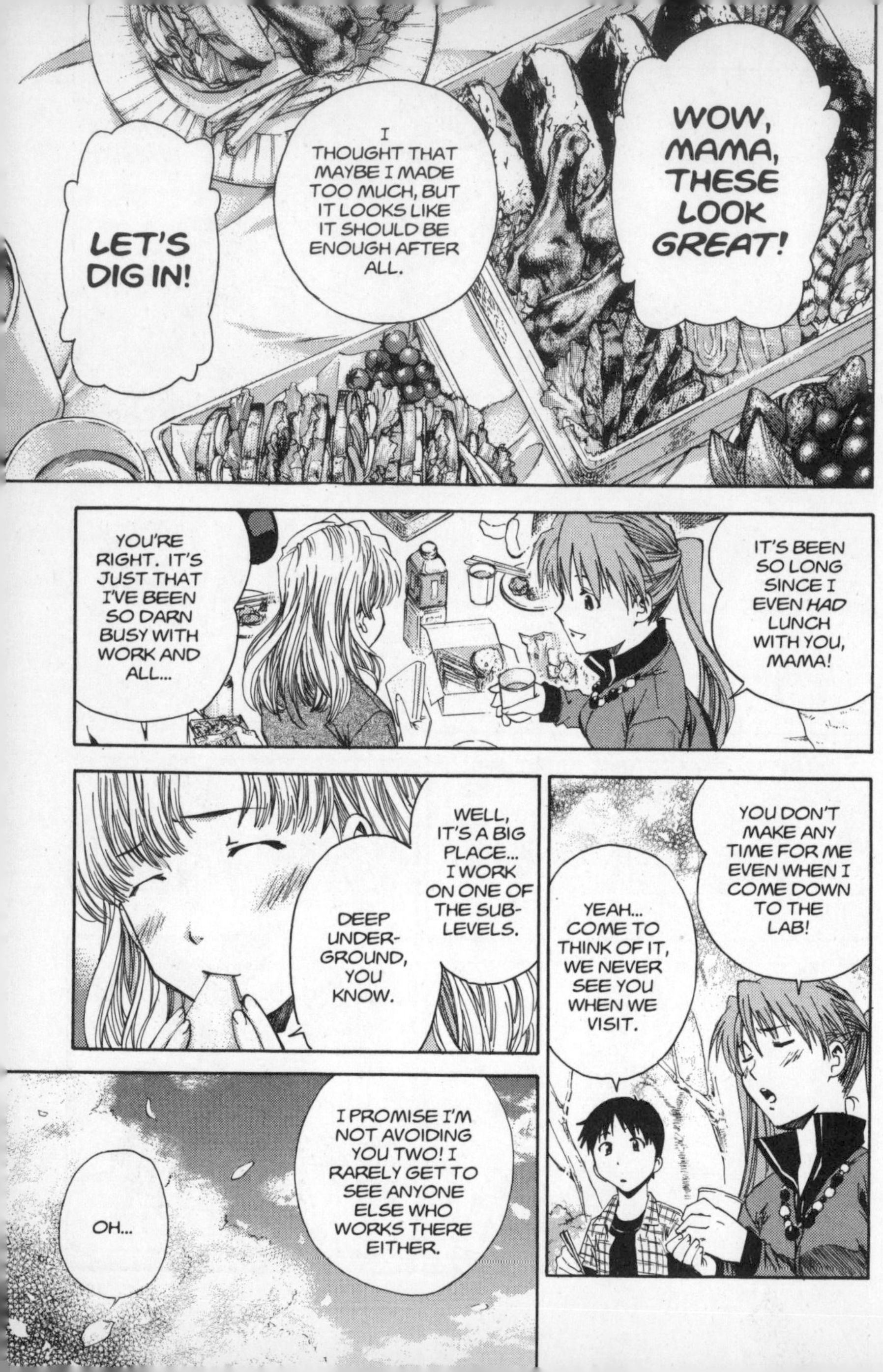
WOW, MAMA, THESE LOOK GREAT!
I THOUGHT THAT MAYBE I MADE TOO MUCH, BUT IT LOOKS LIKE IT SHOULD BE ENOUGH AFTER ALL.
LET'S DIG IN!
IT'S BEEN SO LONG SINCE I EVEN *HAD* LUNCH WITH YOU, MAMA!
YOU'RE RIGHT. IT'S JUST THAT I'VE BEEN SO DARN BUSY WITH WORK AND ALL...
YOU DON'T MAKE ANY TIME FOR ME EVEN WHEN I COME DOWN TO THE LAB!
YEAH... COME TO THINK OF IT, WE NEVER SEE YOU WHEN WE VISIT.
WELL, IT'S A BIG PLACE... I WORK ON ONE OF THE SUB-LEVELS.
DEEP UNDER-GROUND, YOU KNOW.
I PROMISE I'M NOT AVOIDING YOU TWO! I RARELY GET TO SEE ANYONE ELSE WHO WORKS THERE EITHER.
OH...

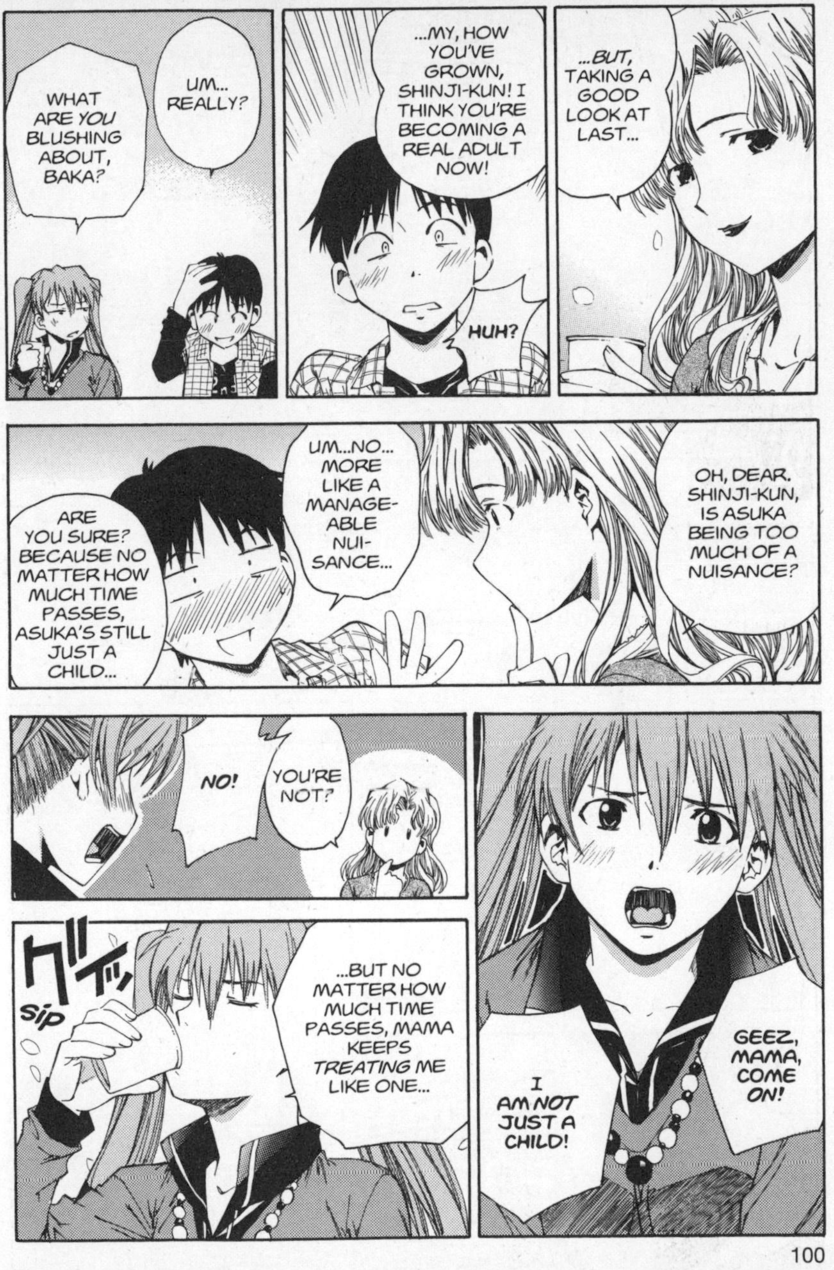
...BUT, TAKING A GOOD LOOK AT LAST...
...MY, HOW YOU'VE GROWN, SHINJI-KUN! I THINK YOU'RE BECOMING A REAL ADULT NOW!
HUH?
UM... REALLY?
WHAT ARE YOU BLUSHING ABOUT, BAKA?
OH, DEAR. SHINJI-KUN, IS ASUKA BEING TOO MUCH OF A NUISANCE?
UM...NO... MORE LIKE A MANAGE-ABLE NUI-SANCE...
ARE YOU SURE? BECAUSE NO MATTER HOW MUCH TIME PASSES, ASUKA'S STILL JUST A CHILD...
GEEZ, MAMA, COME ON!
I AM NOT JUST A CHILD!
YOU'RE NOT?
NO!
グビッ
sip
...BUT NO MATTER HOW MUCH TIME PASSES, MAMA KEEPS TREATING ME LIKE ONE...

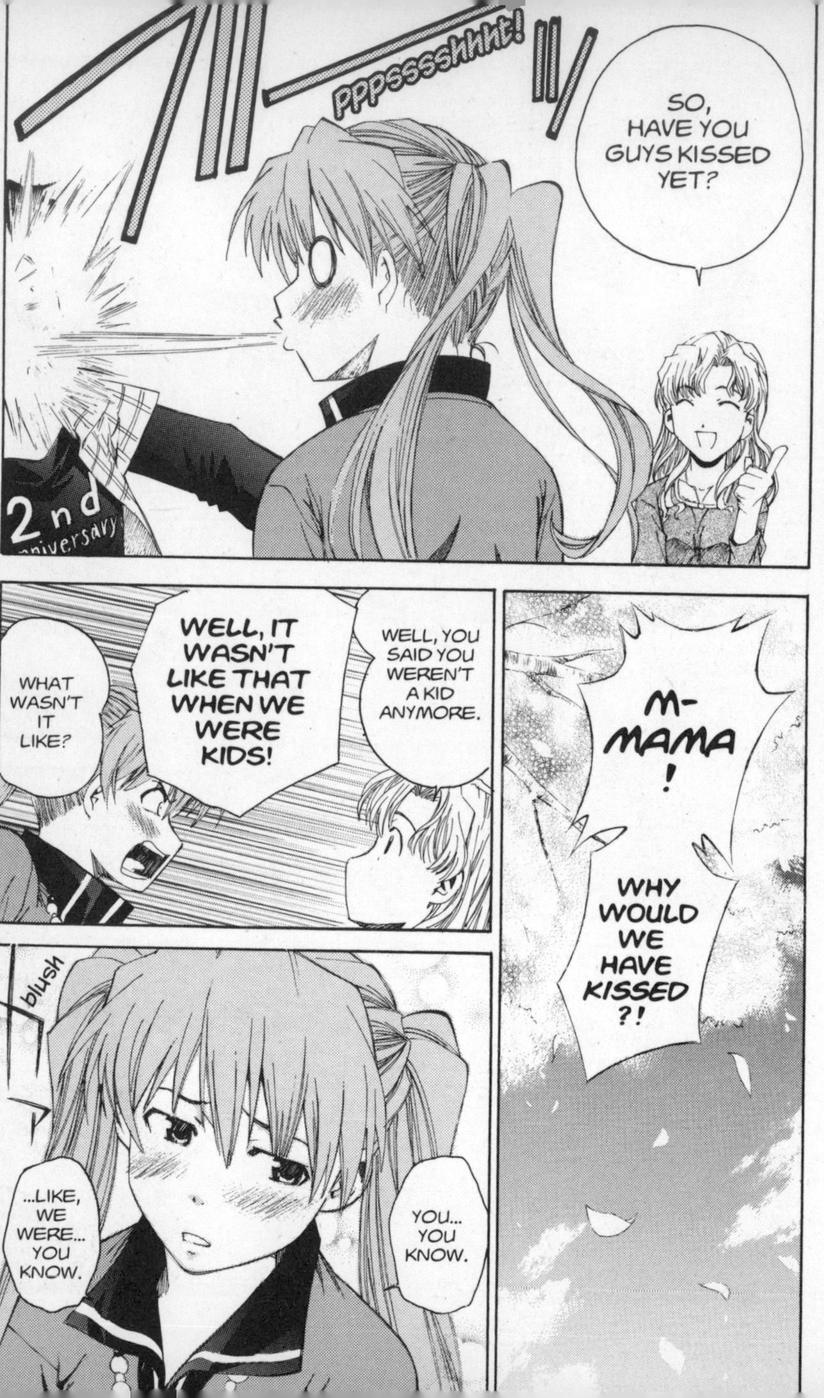
SO, HAVE YOU GUYS KISSED YET?
PPPSSSSHHHT!
M-MAMA!
WHY WOULD WE HAVE KISSED?!
WELL, YOU SAID YOU WEREN'T A KID ANYMORE.
WELL, IT WASN'T LIKE THAT WHEN WE WERE KIDS!
WHAT WASN'T IT LIKE?
blush
YOU... YOU KNOW.
...LIKE, WE WERE... YOU KNOW.

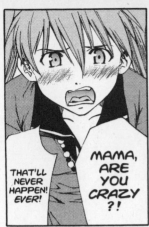

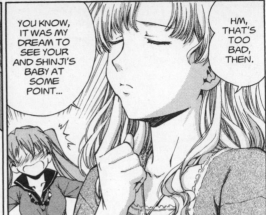

HM, THAT'S TOO BAD, THEN.
YOU KNOW, IT WAS MY DREAM TO SEE YOUR AND SHINJI'S BABY AT SOME POINT...
MAMA, ARE YOU CRAZY?!
THAT'LL NEVER HAPPEN! EVER!
YOU SURE?
REMEMBER HOW MANY TIMES YOU SAID YOU WANTED TO MARRY SHINJI-KUN WHEN YOU WERE LITTLE?
I NEVER SAID THAT!
WHAT I MEANT WAS SHINJI'S SO GODDAMN HOPELESS THAT I WANTED TO ALWAYS BE AROUND SO HE DOESN'T DO SOMETHING TOO BAKA FOR HUMANITY TO WITHSTAND!
THERE, THERE, KYOKO-SAN.
YOU KNOW, ASUKA-CHAN HAS GROWN UP QUITE A BIT. I'VE BEEN WATCHING HER.
...YOU'RE RIGHT.
sigh

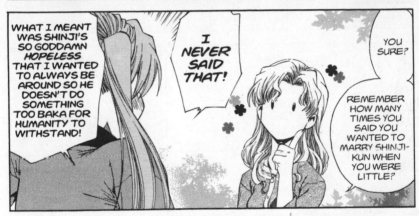

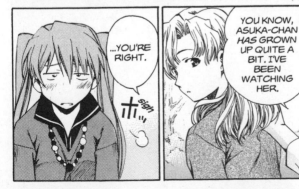

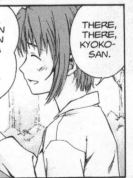

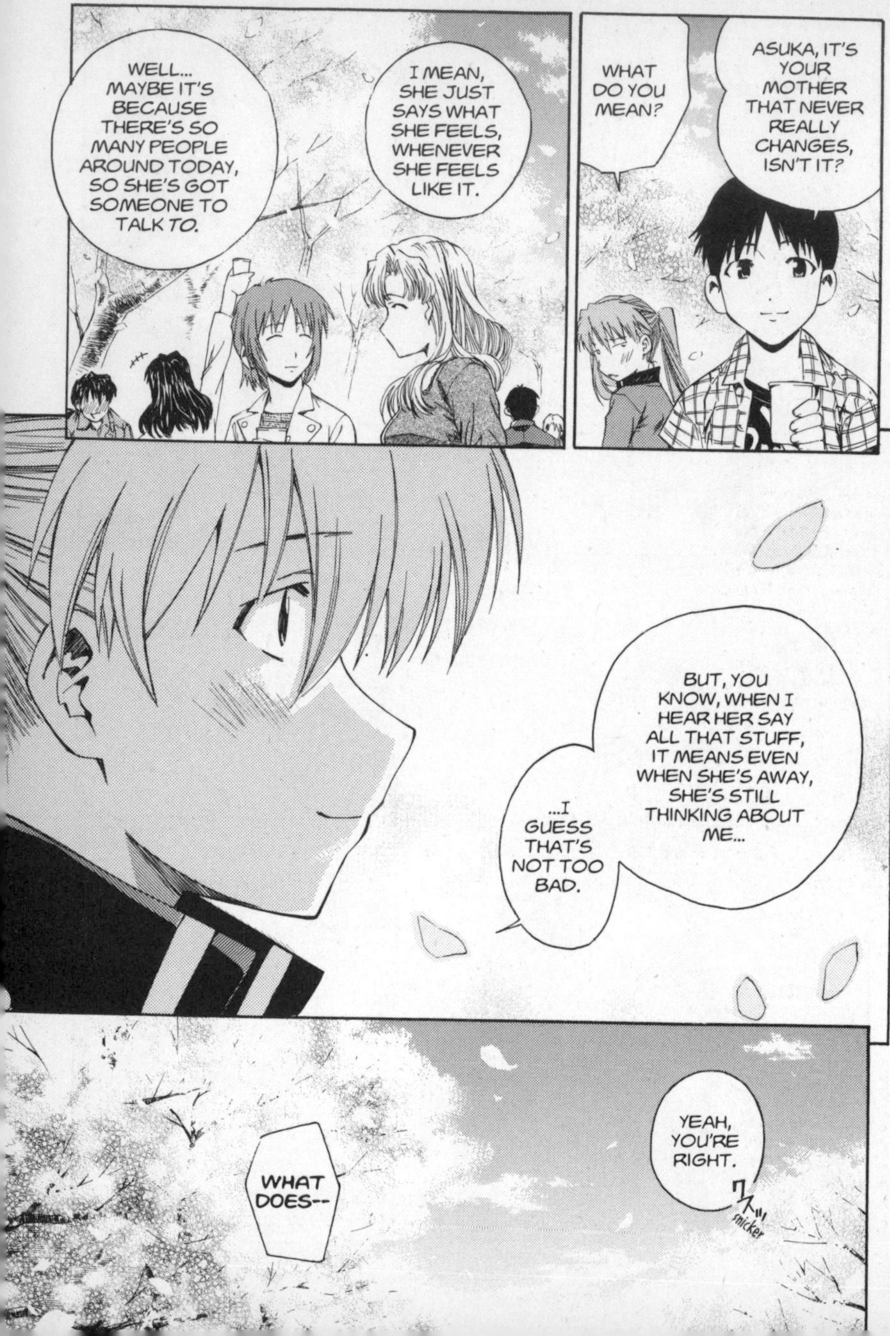
ASUKA, IT'S YOUR MOTHER THAT NEVER REALLY CHANGES, ISN'T IT?
WHAT DO YOU MEAN?
I MEAN, SHE JUST SAYS WHAT SHE FEELS, WHENEVER SHE FEELS LIKE IT.
WELL... MAYBE IT'S BECAUSE THERE'S SO MANY PEOPLE AROUND TODAY, SO SHE'S GOT SOMEONE TO TALK TO.
BUT, YOU KNOW, WHEN I HEAR HER SAY ALL THAT STUFF, IT MEANS EVEN WHEN SHE'S AWAY, SHE'S STILL THINKING ABOUT ME...
...I GUESS THAT'S NOT TOO BAD.
YEAH, YOU'RE RIGHT.
snicker
WHAT DOES--

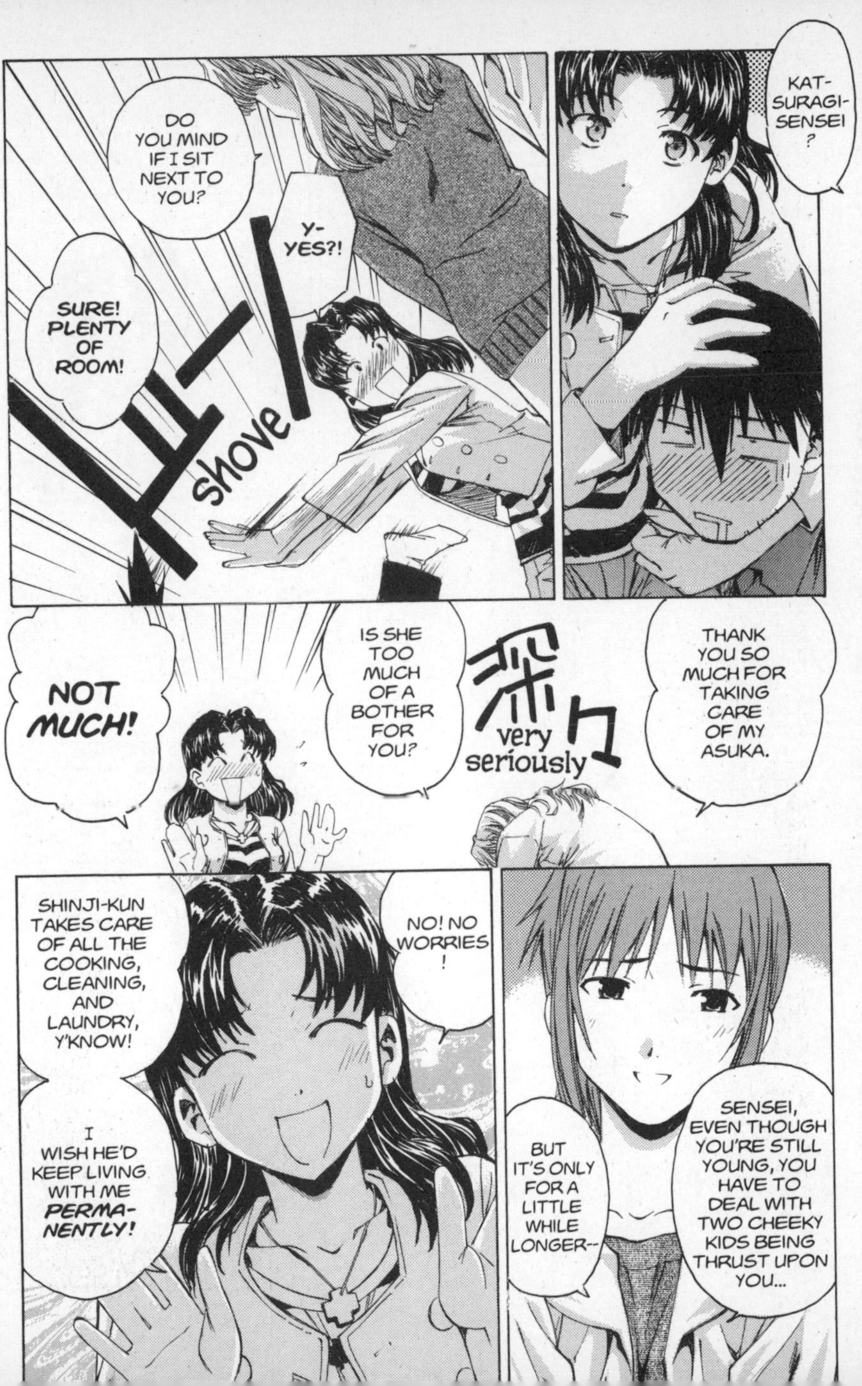
KAT-SURAGI-SENSEI?
DO YOU MIND IF I SIT NEXT TO YOU?
Y-YES?!
SURE! PLENTY OF ROOM!
shove
THANK YOU SO MUCH FOR TAKING CARE OF MY ASUKA.
very seriously
IS SHE TOO MUCH OF A BOTHER FOR YOU?
NOT MUCH!
SENSEI, EVEN THOUGH YOU'RE STILL YOUNG, YOU HAVE TO DEAL WITH TWO CHEEKY KIDS BEING THRUST UPON YOU...
BUT IT'S ONLY FOR A LITTLE WHILE LONGER--
NO! NO WORRIES!
SHINJI-KUN TAKES CARE OF ALL THE COOKING, CLEANING, AND LAUNDRY, Y'KNOW!
I WISH HE'D KEEP LIVING WITH ME PERMANENTLY!

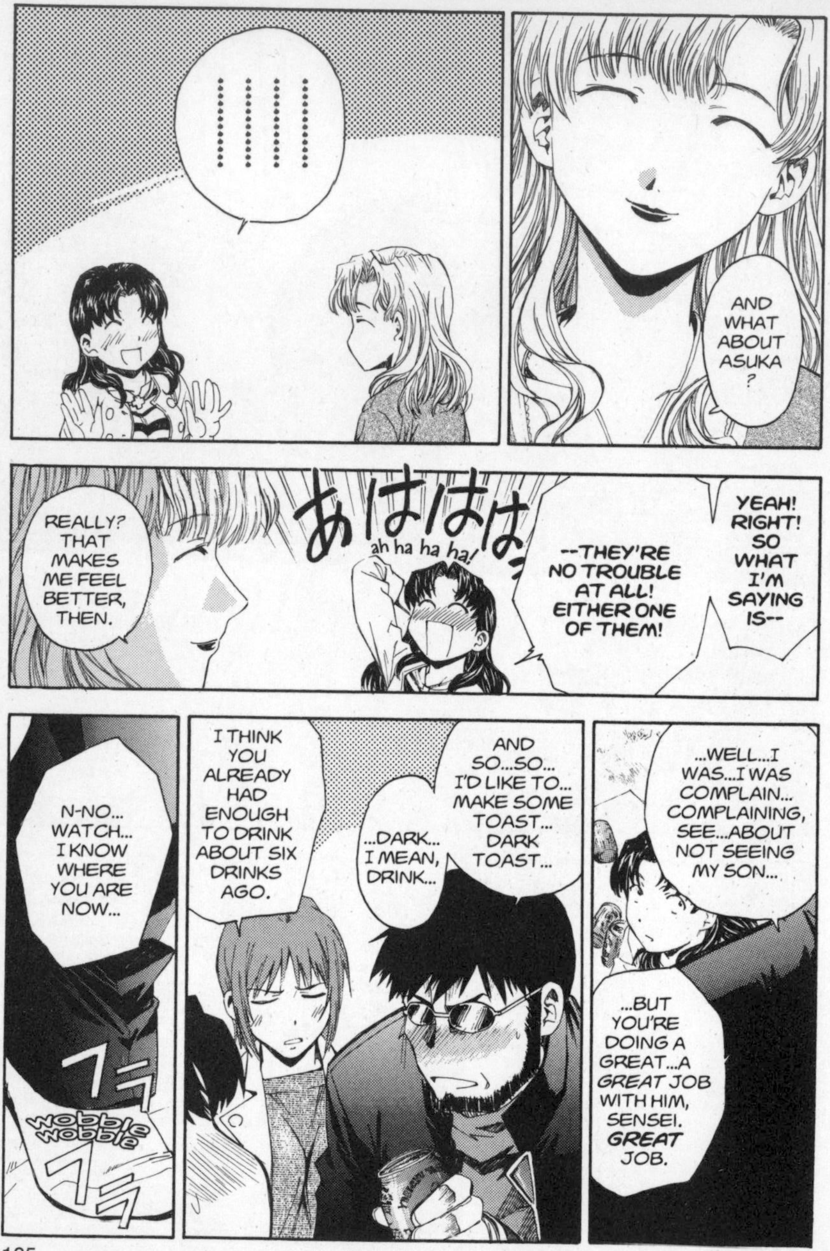
AND WHAT ABOUT ASUKA ?
YEAH! RIGHT! SO WHAT I'M SAYING IS--
--THEY'RE NO TROUBLE AT ALL! EITHER ONE OF THEM!
あははは
ah ha ha ha!
REALLY? THAT MAKES ME FEEL BETTER, THEN.
...WELL...I WAS...I WAS COMPLAIN... COMPLAINING, SEE...ABOUT NOT SEEING MY SON...
...BUT YOU'RE DOING A GREAT...A *GREAT* JOB WITH HIM, SENSEI. **GREAT** JOB.
AND SO...SO... I'D LIKE TO... MAKE SOME TOAST... DARK TOAST...
...DARK... I MEAN, DRINK...
I THINK YOU ALREADY HAD ENOUGH TO DRINK ABOUT SIX DRINKS AGO.
N-NO... WATCH... I KNOW WHERE YOU ARE NOW...
フラ
wobble wobble
フラ

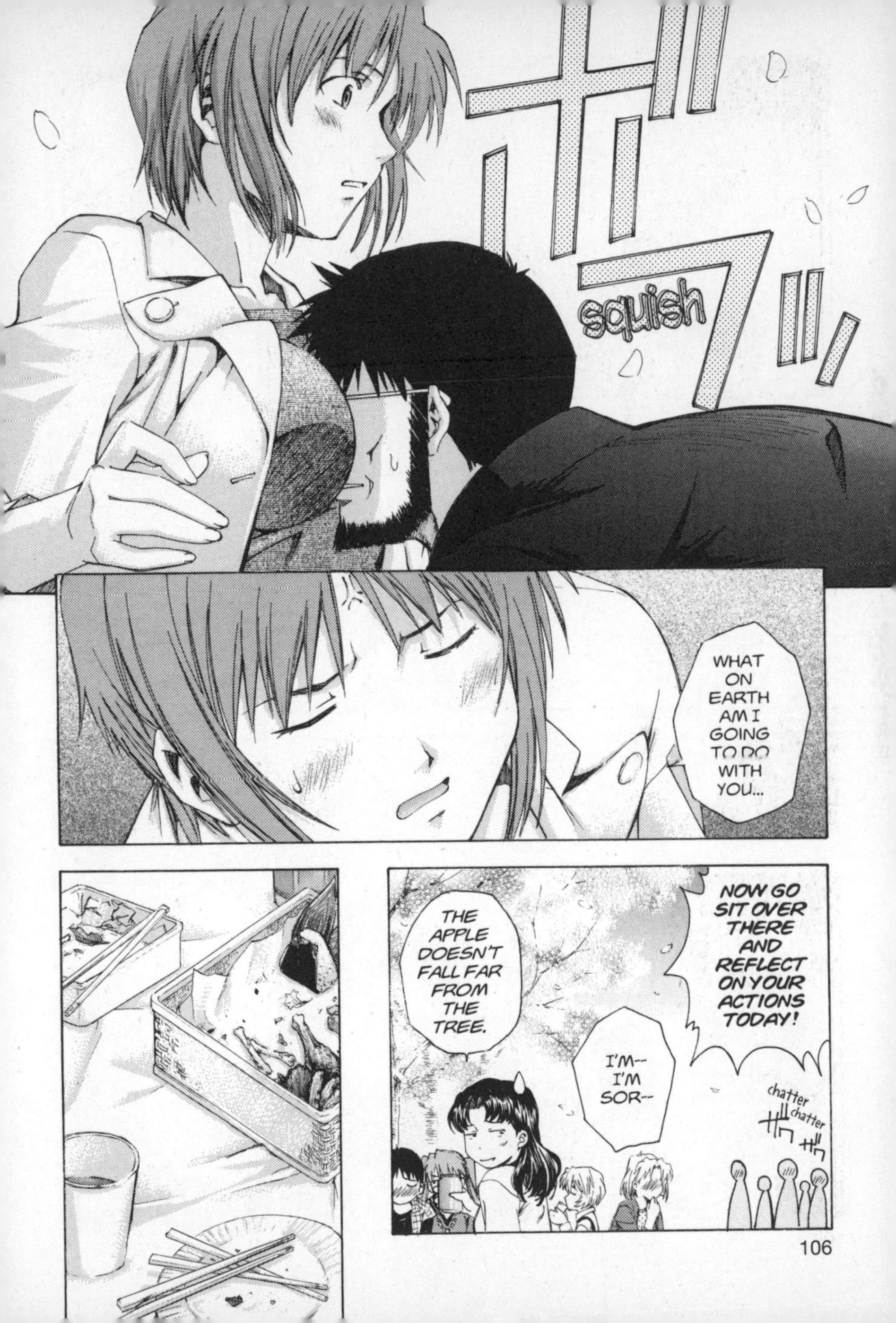
squish
WHAT ON EARTH AM I GOING TO DO WITH YOU...
NOW GO SIT OVER THERE AND REFLECT ON YOUR ACTIONS TODAY!
THE APPLE DOESN'T FALL FAR FROM THE TREE.
I'M-- I'M SOR--
chatter chatter

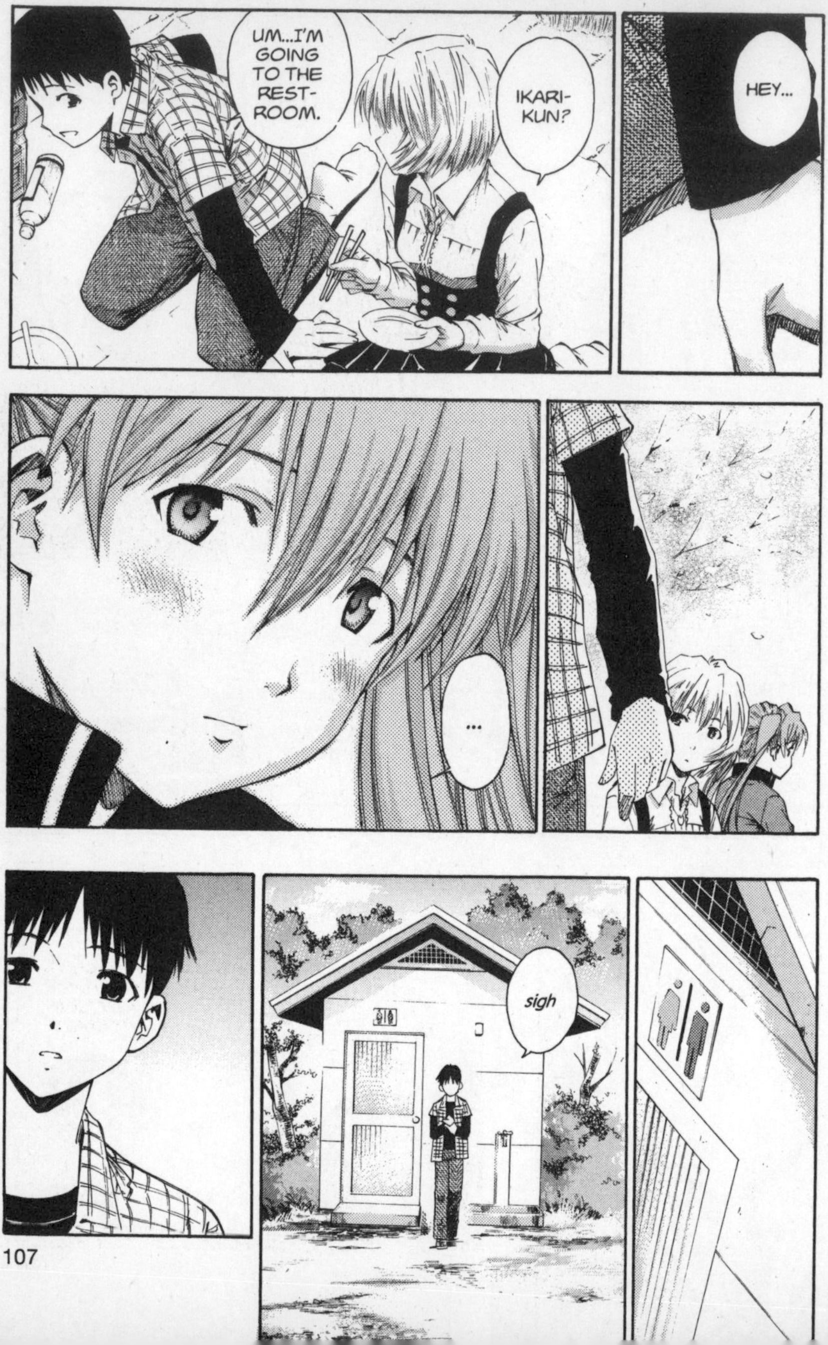
HEY...
IKARI-KUN?
UM...I'M GOING TO THE REST-ROOM.
...
sigh

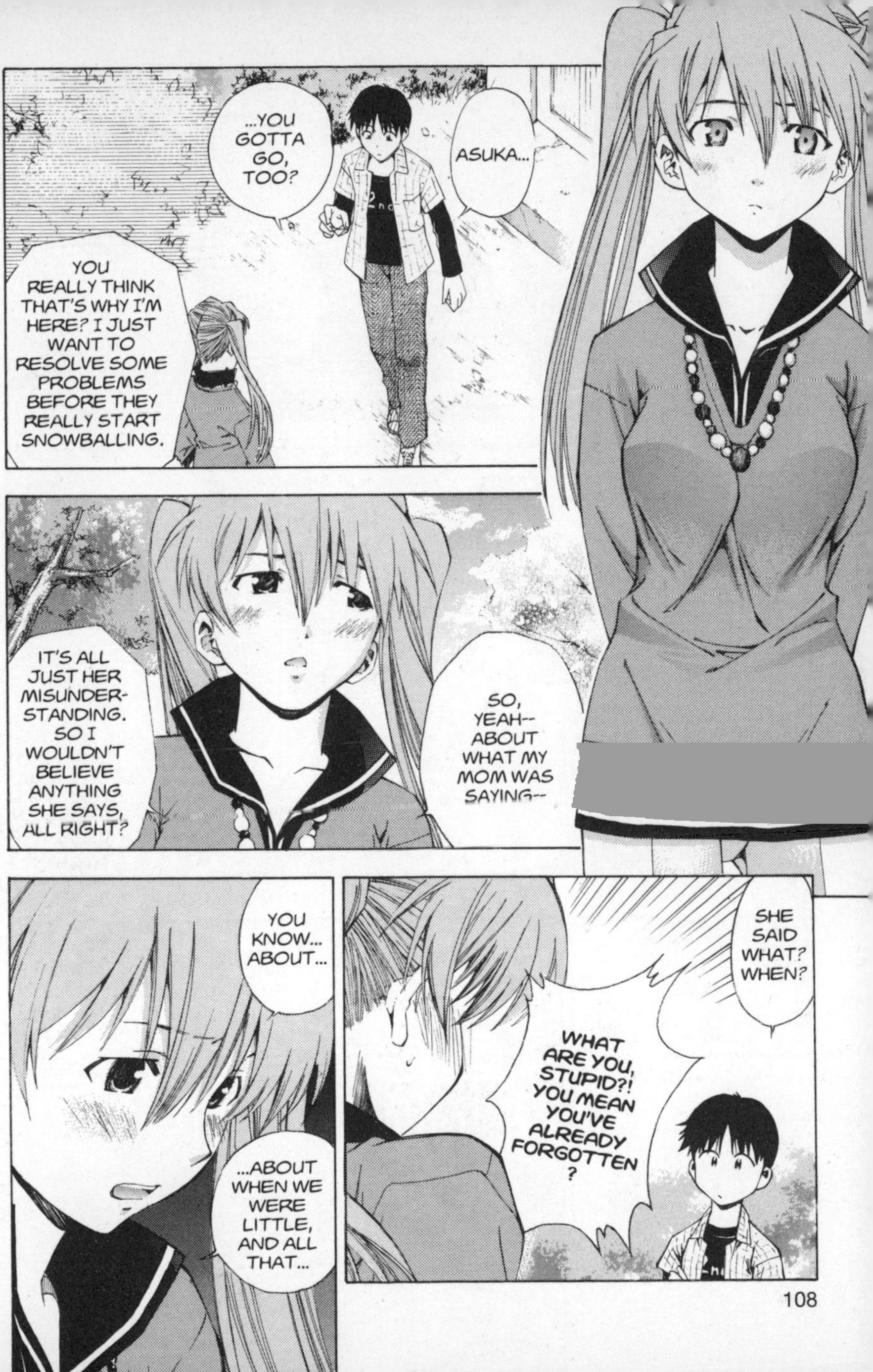
ASUKA...
...YOU GOTTA GO, TOO?
YOU REALLY THINK THAT'S WHY I'M HERE? I JUST WANT TO RESOLVE SOME PROBLEMS BEFORE THEY REALLY START SNOWBALLING.
SO, YEAH-- ABOUT WHAT MY MOM WAS SAYING--
IT'S ALL JUST HER MISUNDER-STANDING. SO I WOULDN'T BELIEVE ANYTHING SHE SAYS, ALL RIGHT?
SHE SAID WHAT? WHEN?
WHAT ARE YOU, STUPID?! YOU MEAN YOU'VE ALREADY FORGOTTEN?
YOU KNOW... ABOUT...
...ABOUT WHEN WE WERE LITTLE, AND ALL THAT...

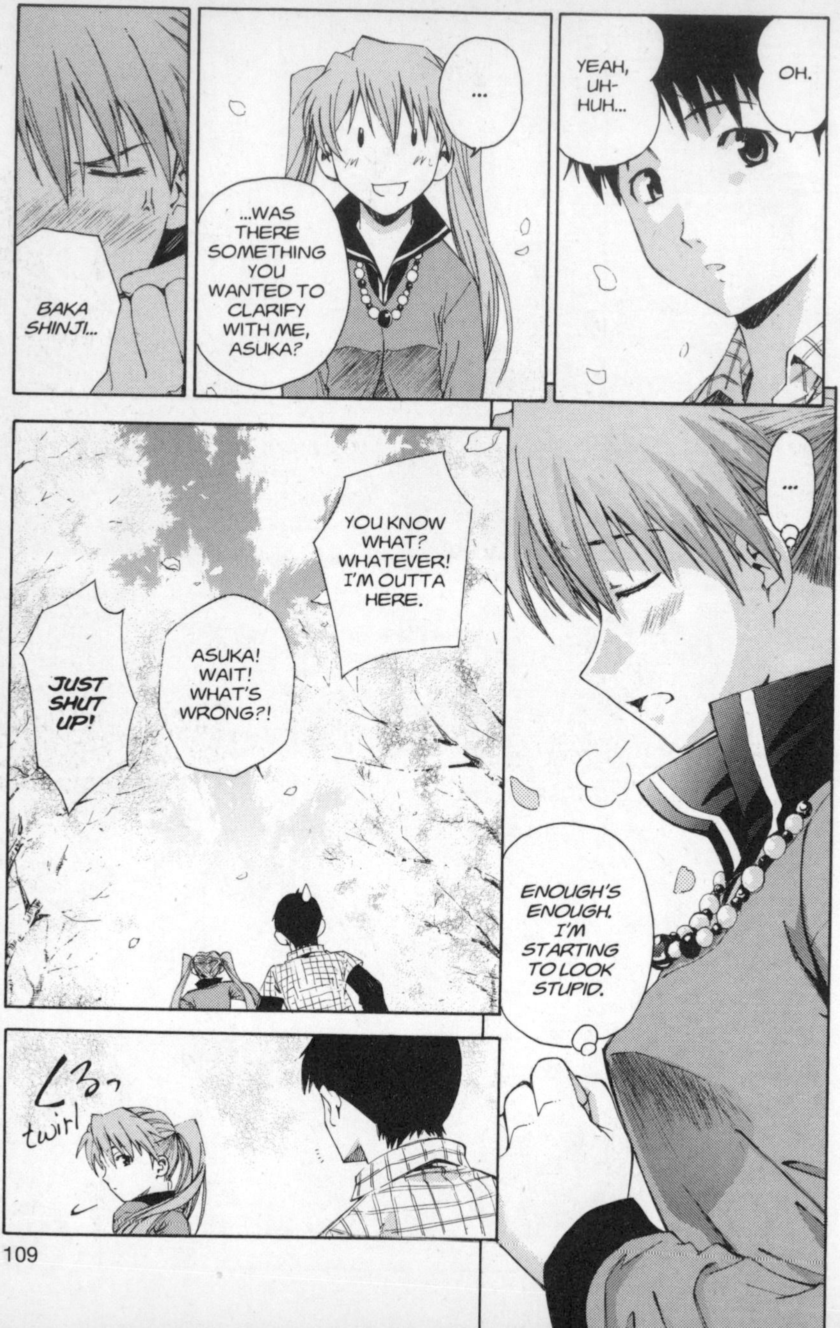
OH.
YEAH, UH-HUH...
...
...WAS THERE SOMETHING YOU WANTED TO CLARIFY WITH ME, ASUKA?
BAKA SHINJI...
...
ENOUGH'S ENOUGH. I'M STARTING TO LOOK STUPID.
YOU KNOW WHAT? WHATEVER! I'M OUTTA HERE.
ASUKA! WAIT! WHAT'S WRONG?!
JUST SHUT UP!
くるっ
twirl

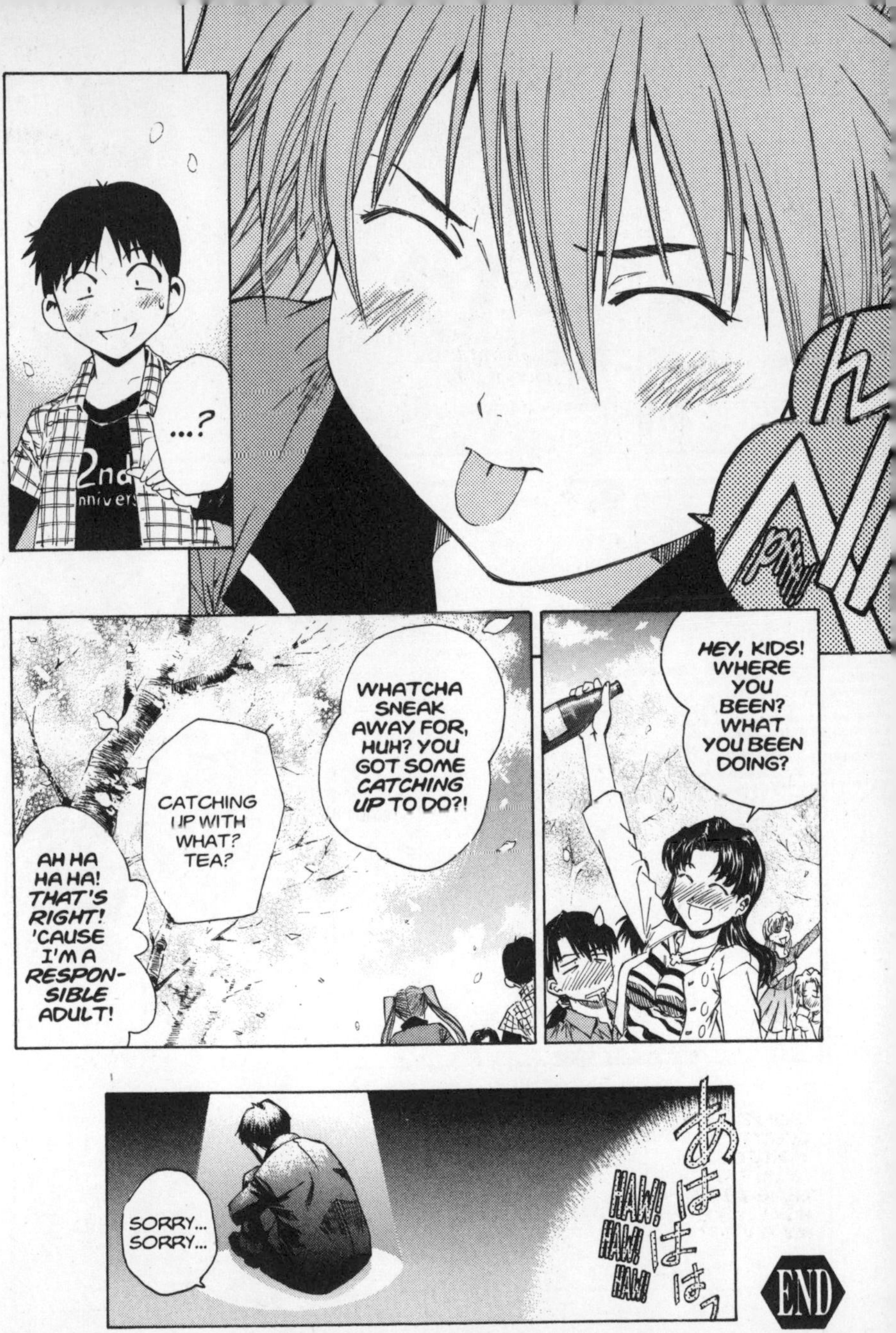
...?
HEY, KIDS! WHERE YOU BEEN? WHAT YOU BEEN DOING?
WHATCHA SNEAK AWAY FOR, HUH? YOU GOT SOME CATCHING UP TO DO?!
CATCHING UP WITH WHAT? TEA?
AH HA HA HA! THAT'S RIGHT! 'CAUSE I'M A RESPONSIBLE ADULT!
あははっ
HAW! HAW! HAW!
SORRY... SORRY...
END

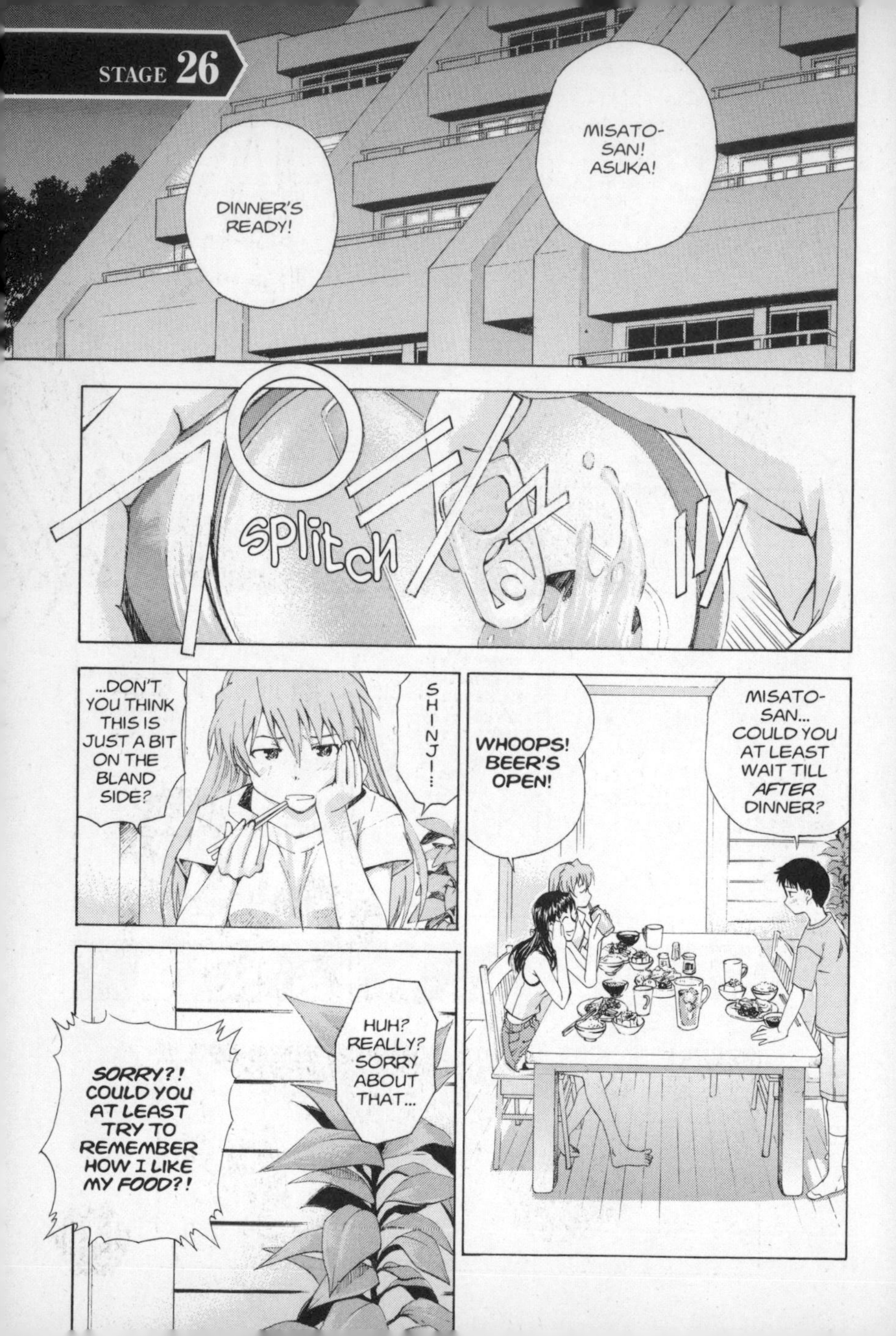
STAGE 26
MISATO-SAN! ASUKA!
DINNER'S READY!
splitch
MISATO-SAN... COULD YOU AT LEAST WAIT TILL *AFTER* DINNER?
WHOOPS! BEER'S OPEN!
SHINJI!...
...DON'T YOU THINK THIS IS JUST A BIT ON THE BLAND SIDE?
HUH? REALLY? SORRY ABOUT THAT...
SORRY?! COULD YOU AT LEAST TRY TO REMEMBER HOW I LIKE *MY FOOD*?!

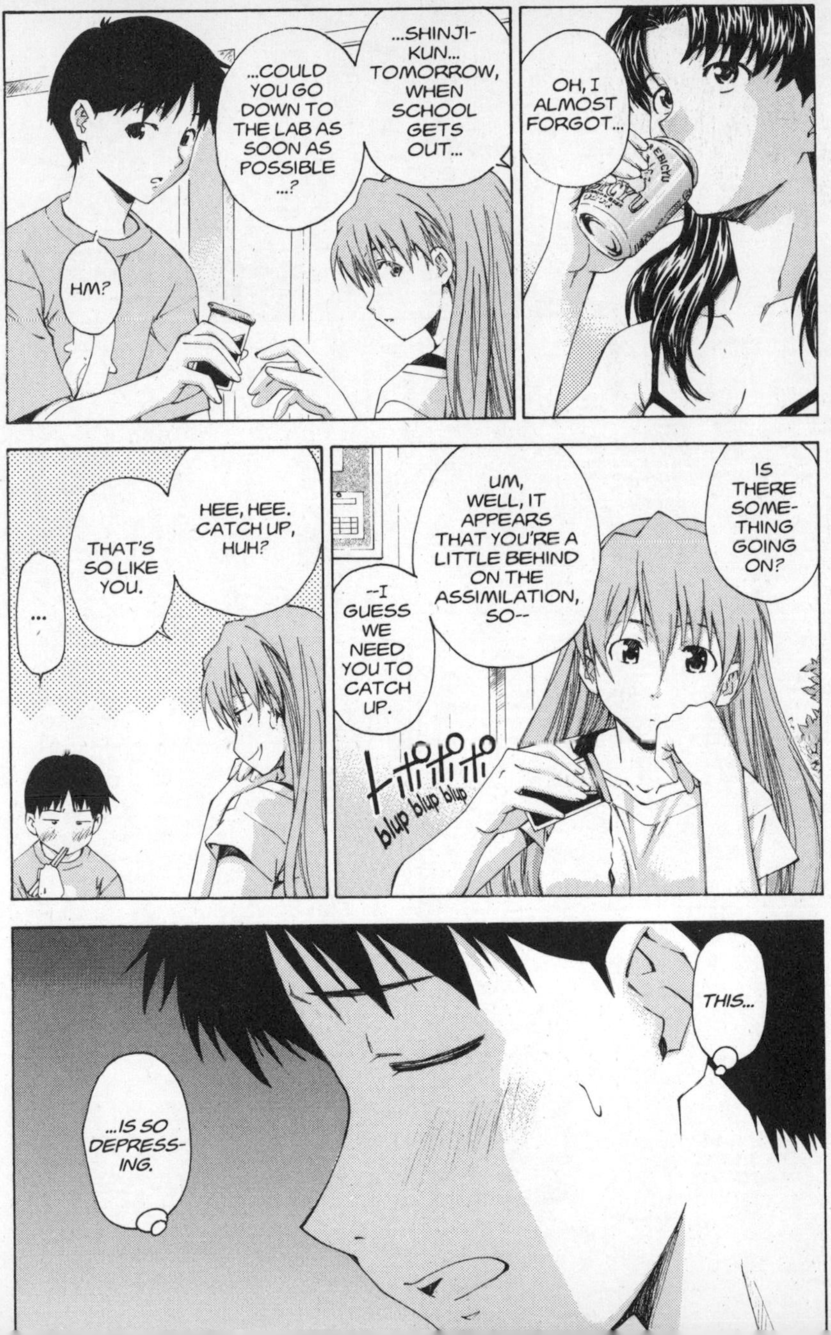
OH, I ALMOST FORGOT...
...SHINJI-KUN... TOMORROW, WHEN SCHOOL GETS OUT...
...COULD YOU GO DOWN TO THE LAB AS SOON AS POSSIBLE ...?
HM?
IS THERE SOMETHING GOING ON?
UM, WELL, IT APPEARS THAT YOU'RE A LITTLE BEHIND ON THE ASSIMILATION, SO--
--I GUESS WE NEED YOU TO CATCH UP.
blup blup blup
HEE, HEE. CATCH UP, HUH?
THAT'S SO LIKE YOU.
...
THIS...
...IS SO DEPRESSING.

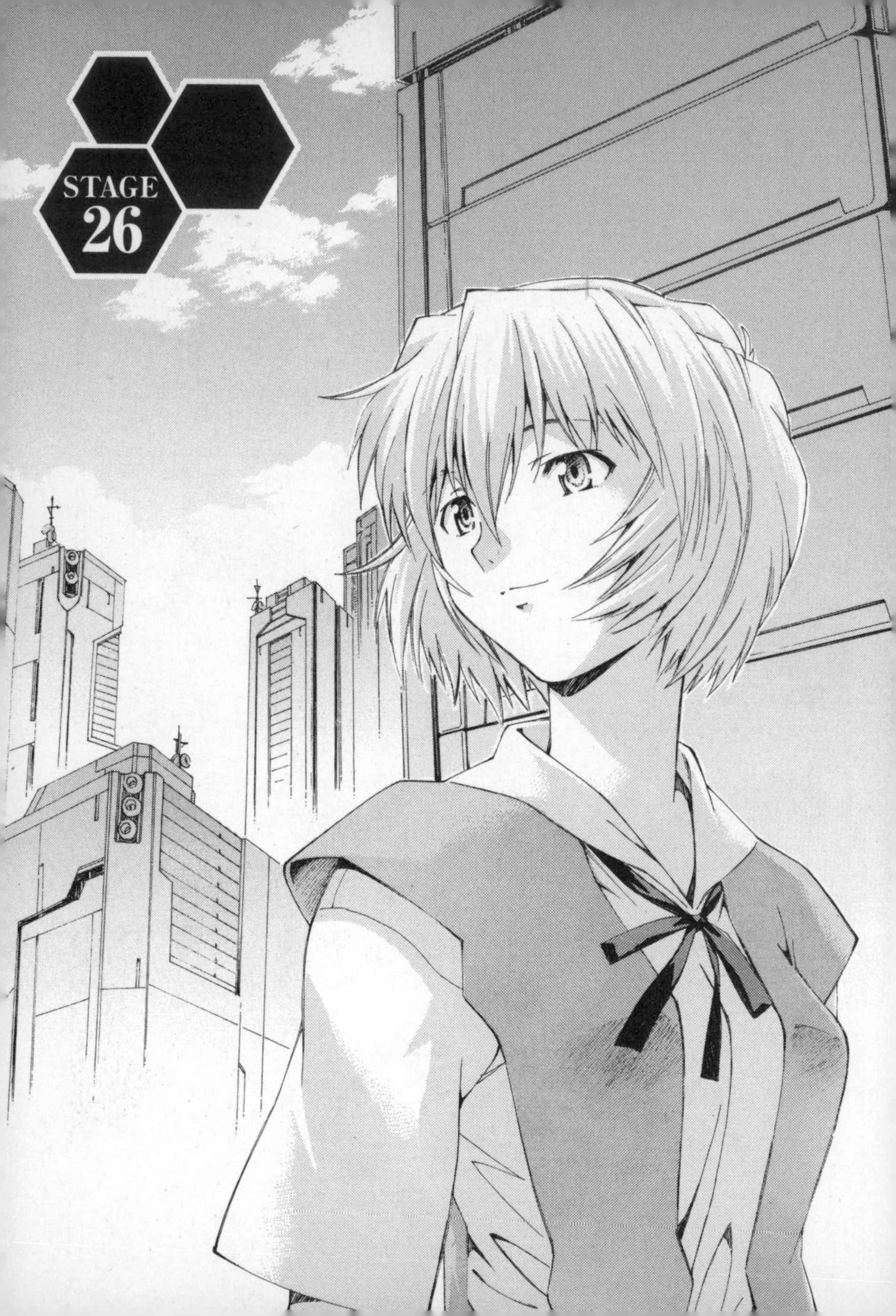
STAGE
26

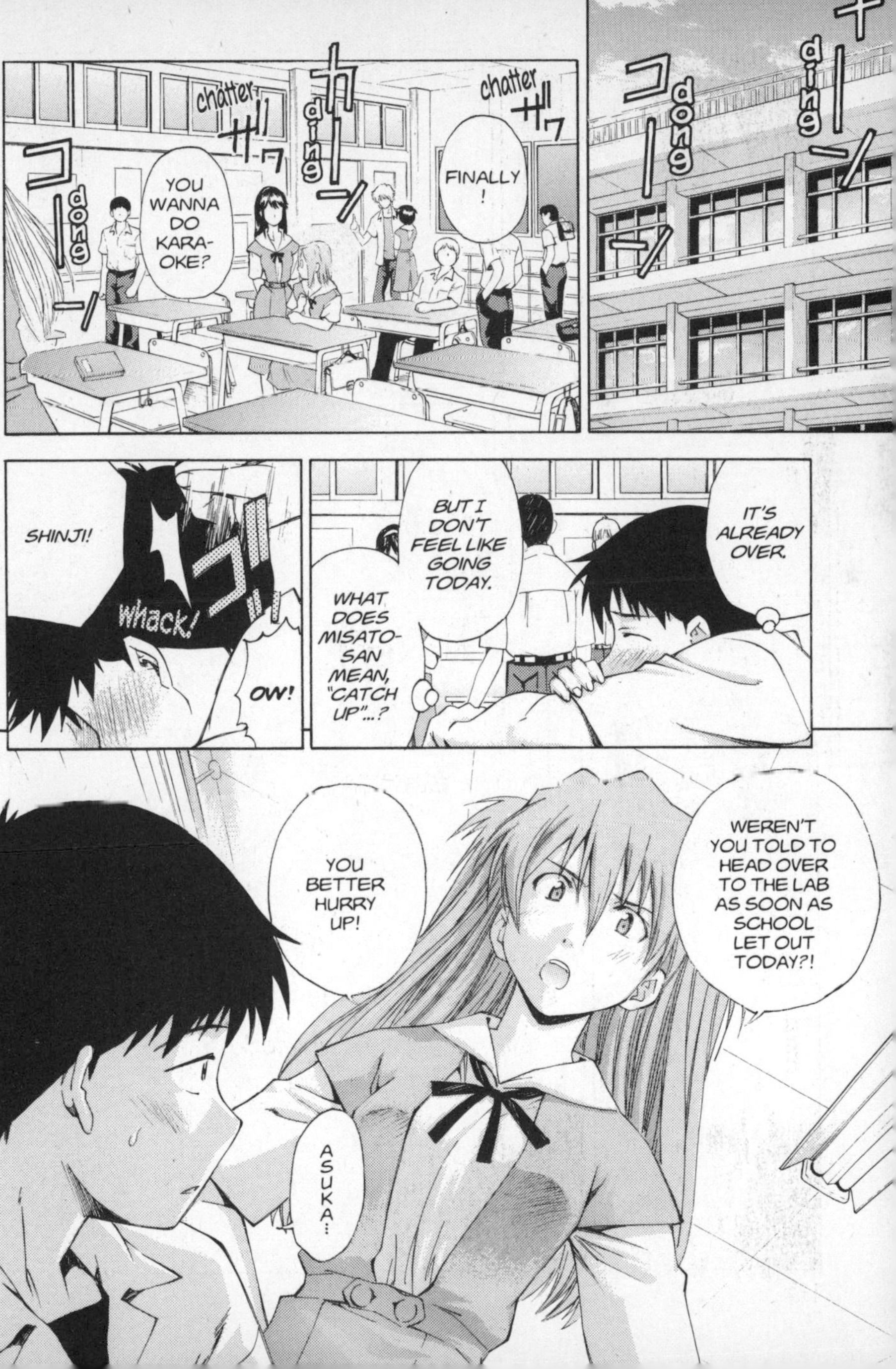
ding dong
chatter
FINALLY!
ding
YOU WANNA DO KARA-OKE?
chatter
dong
IT'S ALREADY OVER.
BUT I DON'T FEEL LIKE GOING TODAY.
WHAT DOES MISATO-SAN MEAN, "CATCH UP"...?
SHINJI!
whack!
OW!
WEREN'T YOU TOLD TO HEAD OVER TO THE LAB AS SOON AS SCHOOL LET OUT TODAY?!
YOU BETTER HURRY UP!
ASUKA...

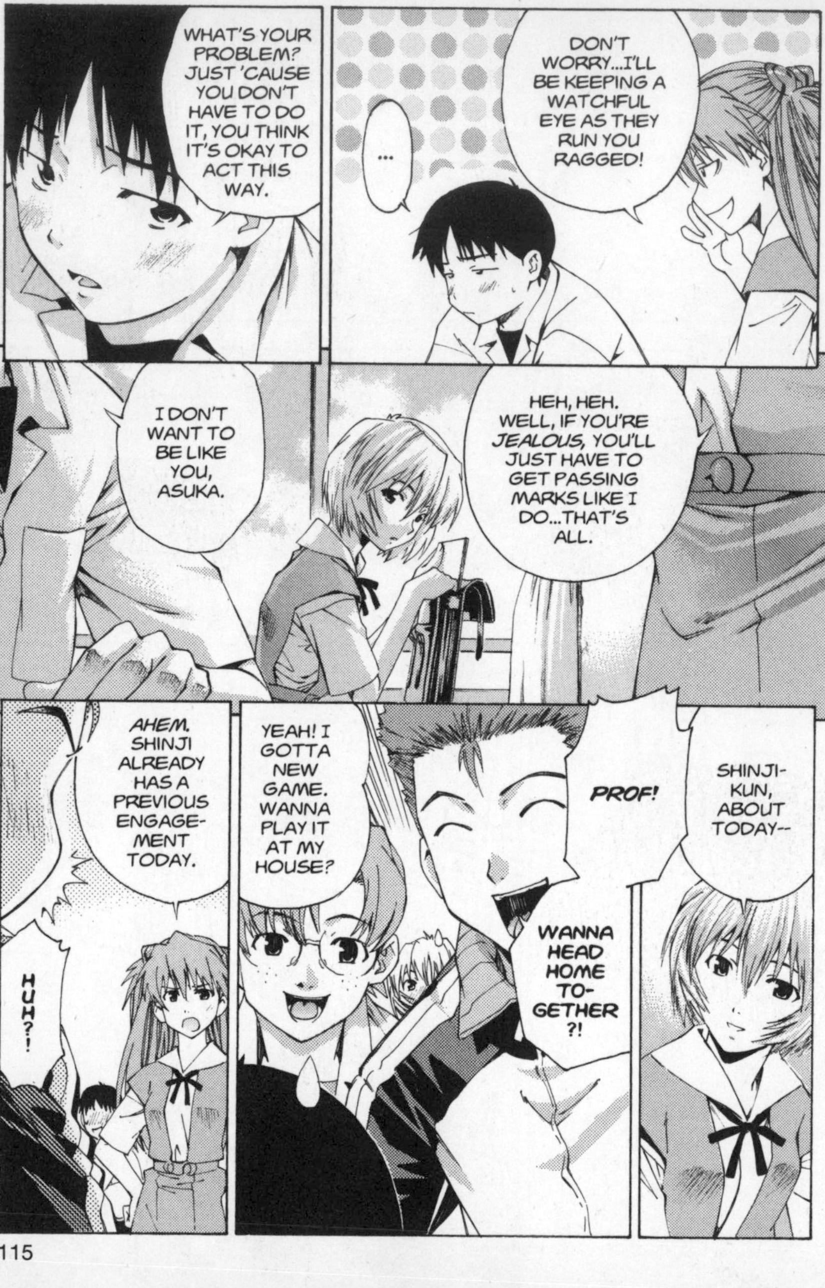
DON'T WORRY...I'LL BE KEEPING A WATCHFUL EYE AS THEY RUN YOU RAGGED!
...
WHAT'S YOUR PROBLEM? JUST 'CAUSE YOU DON'T HAVE TO DO IT, YOU THINK IT'S OKAY TO ACT THIS WAY.
HEH, HEH. WELL, IF YOU'RE *JEALOUS,* YOU'LL JUST HAVE TO GET PASSING MARKS LIKE I DO...THAT'S ALL.
I DON'T WANT TO BE LIKE YOU, ASUKA.
SHINJI-KUN, ABOUT TODAY--
PROF!
WANNA HEAD HOME TO-GETHER ?!
YEAH! I GOTTA NEW GAME. WANNA PLAY IT AT MY HOUSE?
AHEM. SHINJI ALREADY HAS A PREVIOUS ENGAGE-MENT TODAY.
HUH?!

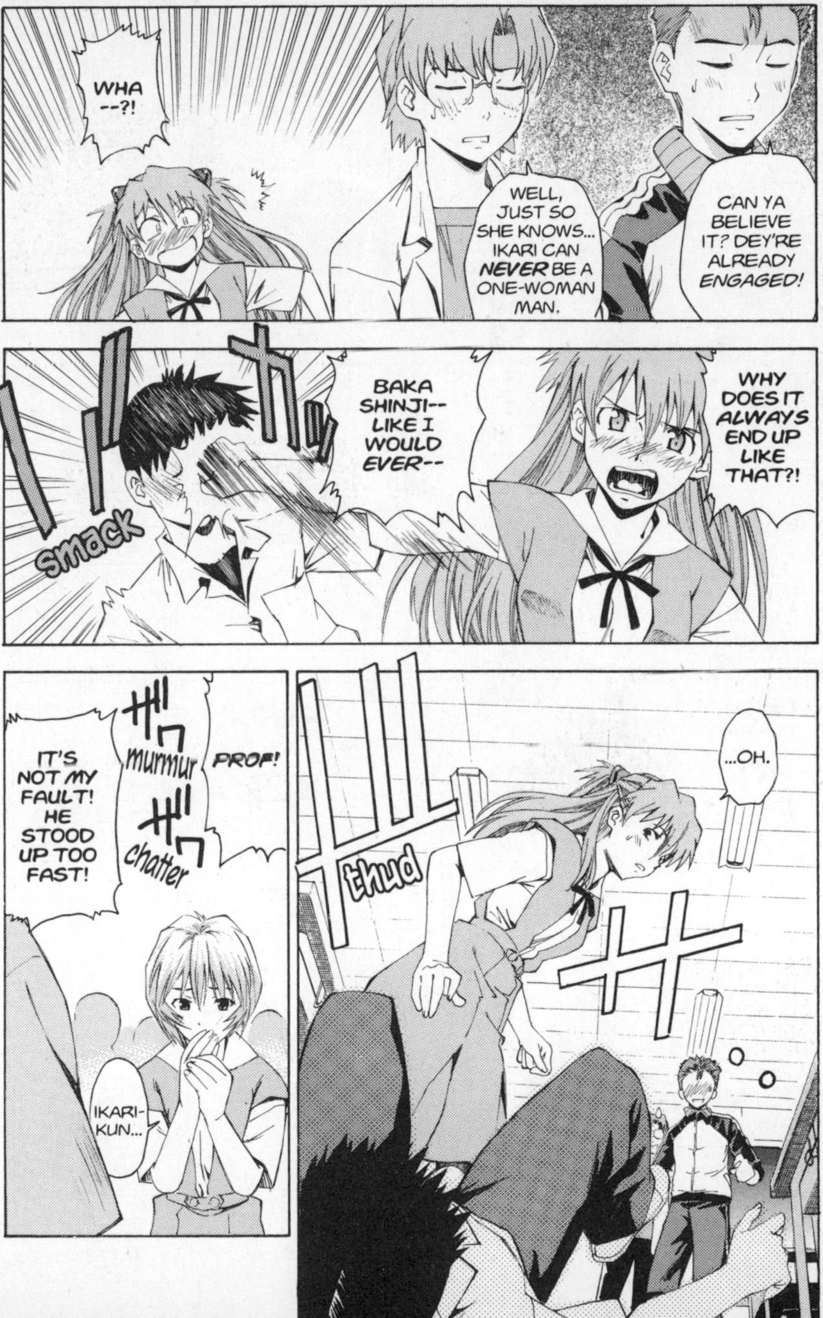
CAN YA BELIEVE IT? DEY'RE ALREADY ENGAGED!
WELL, JUST SO SHE KNOWS... IKARI CAN NEVER BE A ONE-WOMAN MAN.
WHA --?!
WHY DOES IT ALWAYS END UP LIKE THAT?!
BAKA SHINJI-- LIKE I WOULD EVER--
smack
...OH.
thud
PROF!
murmur
chatter
IT'S NOT MY FAULT! HE STOOD UP TOO FAST!
IKARI-KUN...

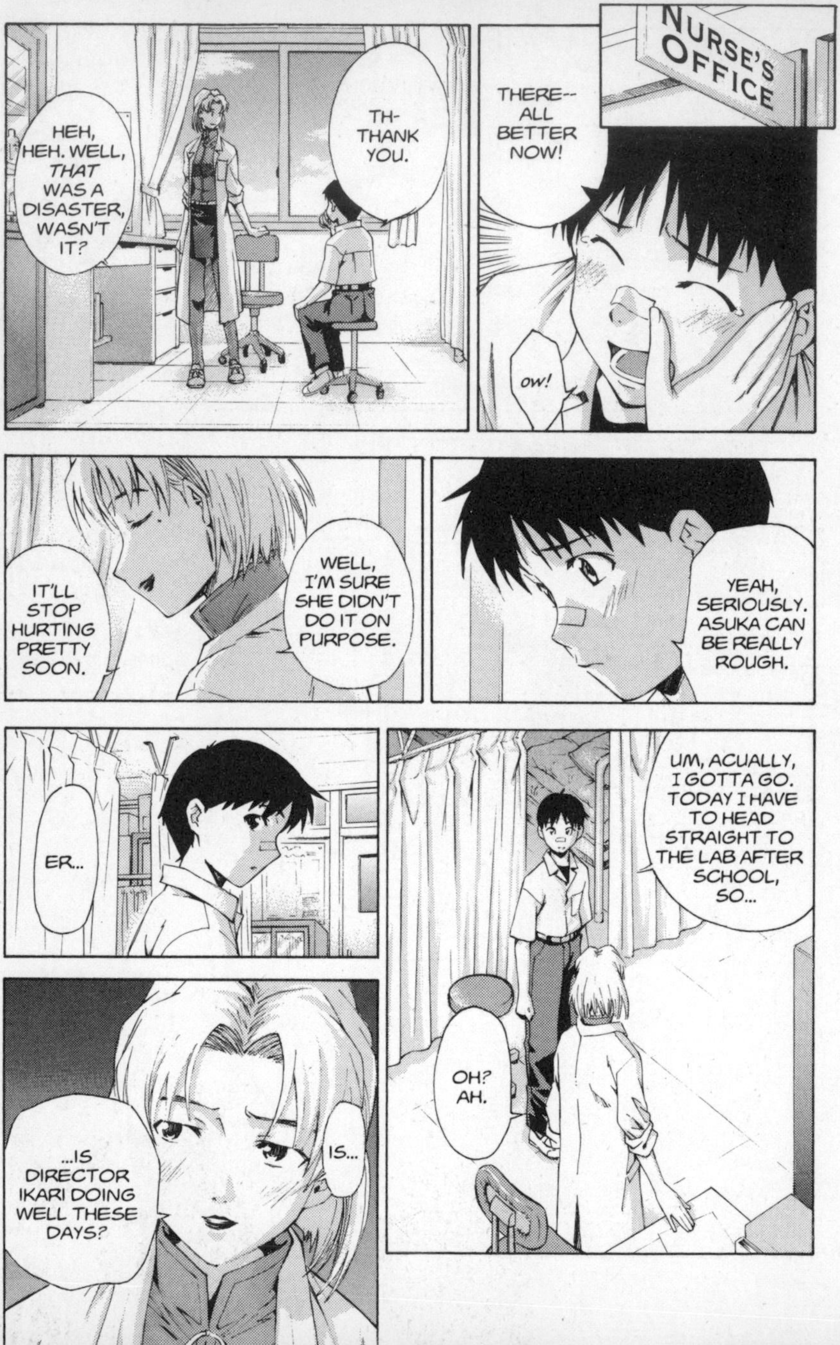
NURSE'S OFFICE
THERE-- ALL BETTER NOW!
OW!
TH- THANK YOU.
HEH, HEH. WELL, *THAT* WAS A DISASTER, WASN'T IT?
YEAH, SERIOUSLY. ASUKA CAN BE REALLY ROUGH.
WELL, I'M SURE SHE DIDN'T DO IT ON PURPOSE.
IT'LL STOP HURTING PRETTY SOON.
UM, ACUALLY, I GOTTA GO. TODAY I HAVE TO HEAD STRAIGHT TO THE LAB AFTER SCHOOL, SO...
OH? AH.
ER...
IS...
...IS DIRECTOR IKARI DOING WELL THESE DAYS?

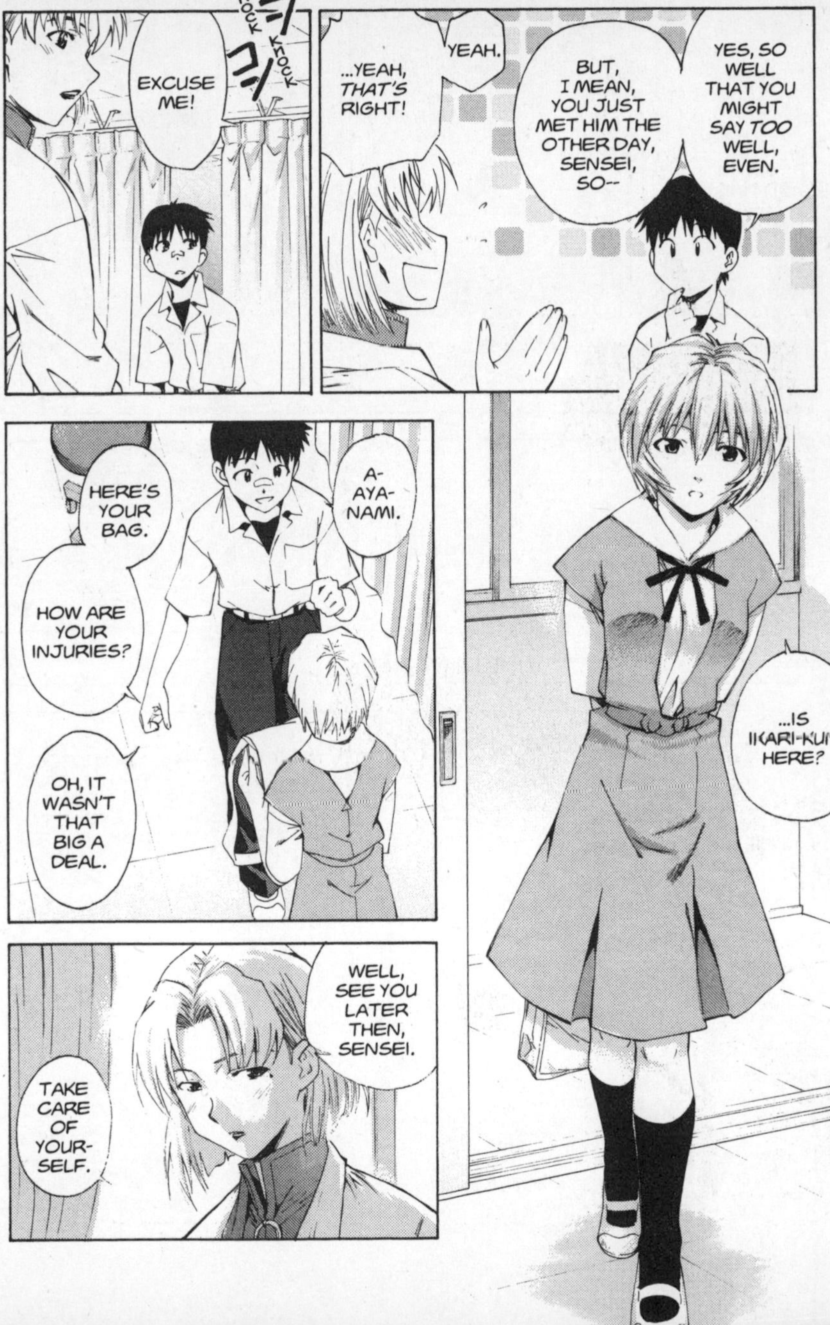
YES, SO WELL THAT YOU MIGHT SAY *TOO* WELL, EVEN.
BUT, I MEAN, YOU JUST MET HIM THE OTHER DAY, SENSEI, SO--
YEAH.
...YEAH, *THAT'S* RIGHT!
KNOCK KNOCK
EXCUSE ME!
...IS IKARI-KUN HERE?
A- AYA- NAMI.
HERE'S YOUR BAG.
HOW ARE YOUR INJURIES?
OH, IT WASN'T THAT BIG A DEAL.
WELL, SEE YOU LATER THEN, SENSEI.
TAKE CARE OF YOUR- SELF.

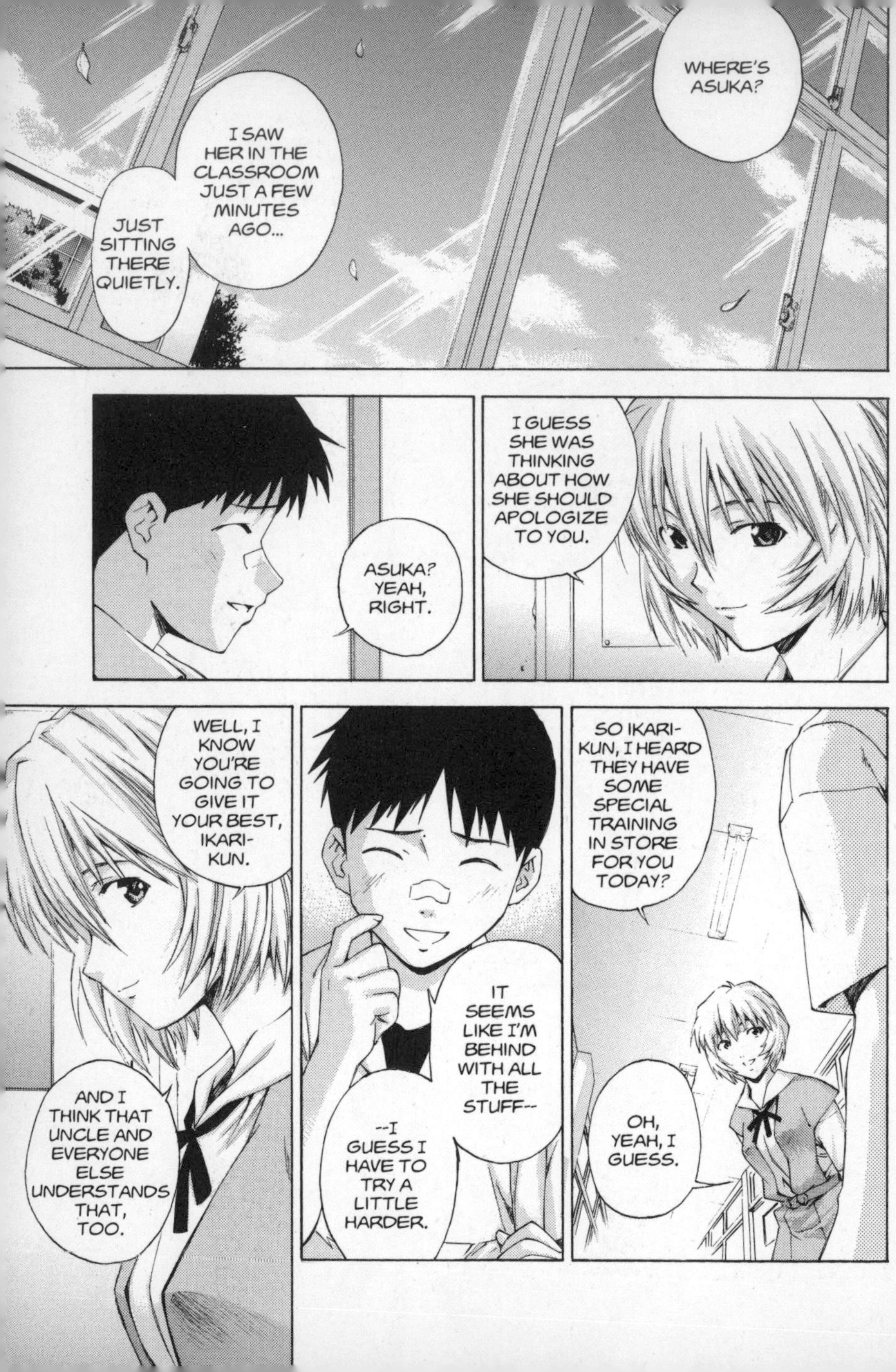
WHERE'S ASUKA?
I SAW HER IN THE CLASSROOM JUST A FEW MINUTES AGO...
JUST SITTING THERE QUIETLY.
I GUESS SHE WAS THINKING ABOUT HOW SHE SHOULD APOLOGIZE TO YOU.
ASUKA? YEAH, RIGHT.
SO IKARI-KUN, I HEARD THEY HAVE SOME SPECIAL TRAINING IN STORE FOR YOU TODAY?
OH, YEAH, I GUESS.
IT SEEMS LIKE I'M BEHIND WITH ALL THE STUFF--
--I GUESS I HAVE TO TRY A LITTLE HARDER.
WELL, I KNOW YOU'RE GOING TO GIVE IT YOUR BEST, IKARI-KUN.
AND I THINK THAT UNCLE AND EVERYONE ELSE UNDERSTANDS THAT, TOO.

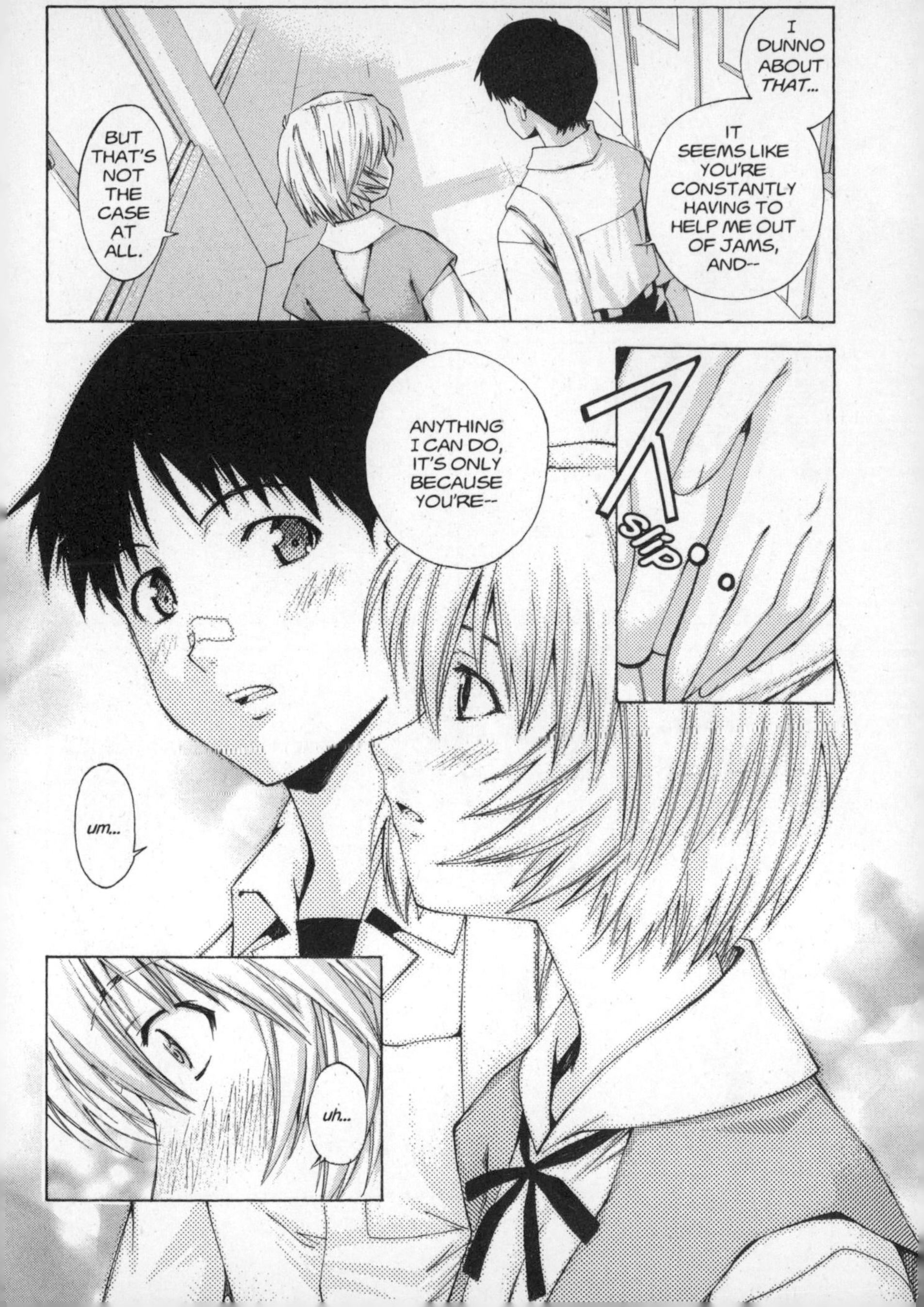
I DUNNO ABOUT THAT...
IT SEEMS LIKE YOU'RE CONSTANTLY HAVING TO HELP ME OUT OF JAMS, AND--
BUT THAT'S NOT THE CASE AT ALL.
slip
ANYTHING I CAN DO, IT'S ONLY BECAUSE YOU'RE--
um...
uh...

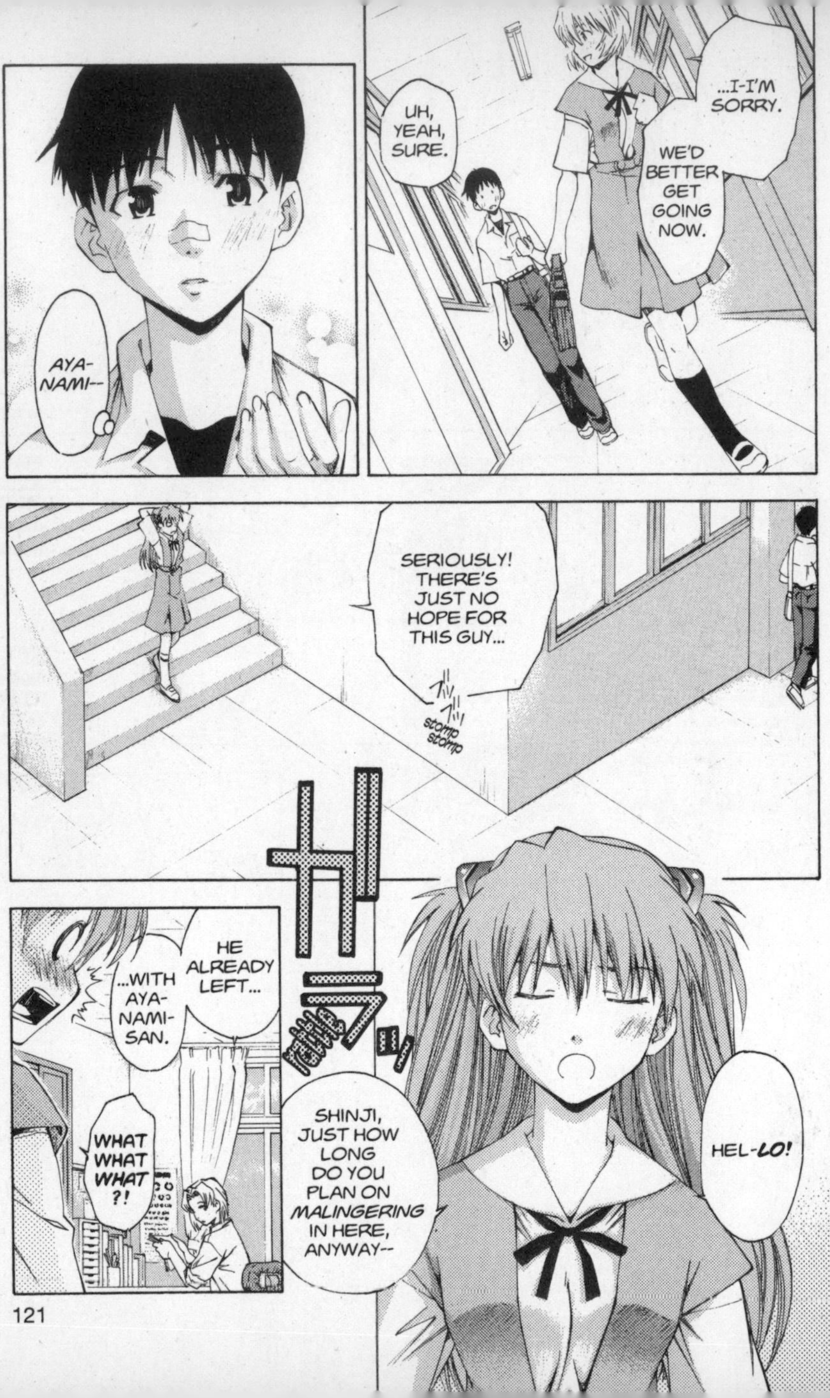

...I-I'M SORRY.
WE'D BETTER GET GOING NOW.
UH, YEAH, SURE.
AYA-NAMI--
SERIOUSLY! THERE'S JUST NO HOPE FOR THIS GUY...
stomp stomp
rattle
HEL-*LO*!
SHINJI, JUST HOW LONG DO YOU PLAN ON *MALINGERING* IN HERE, ANYWAY--
HE ALREADY LEFT...
...WITH AYA-NAMI-SAN.
WHAT WHAT *WHAT* ?!

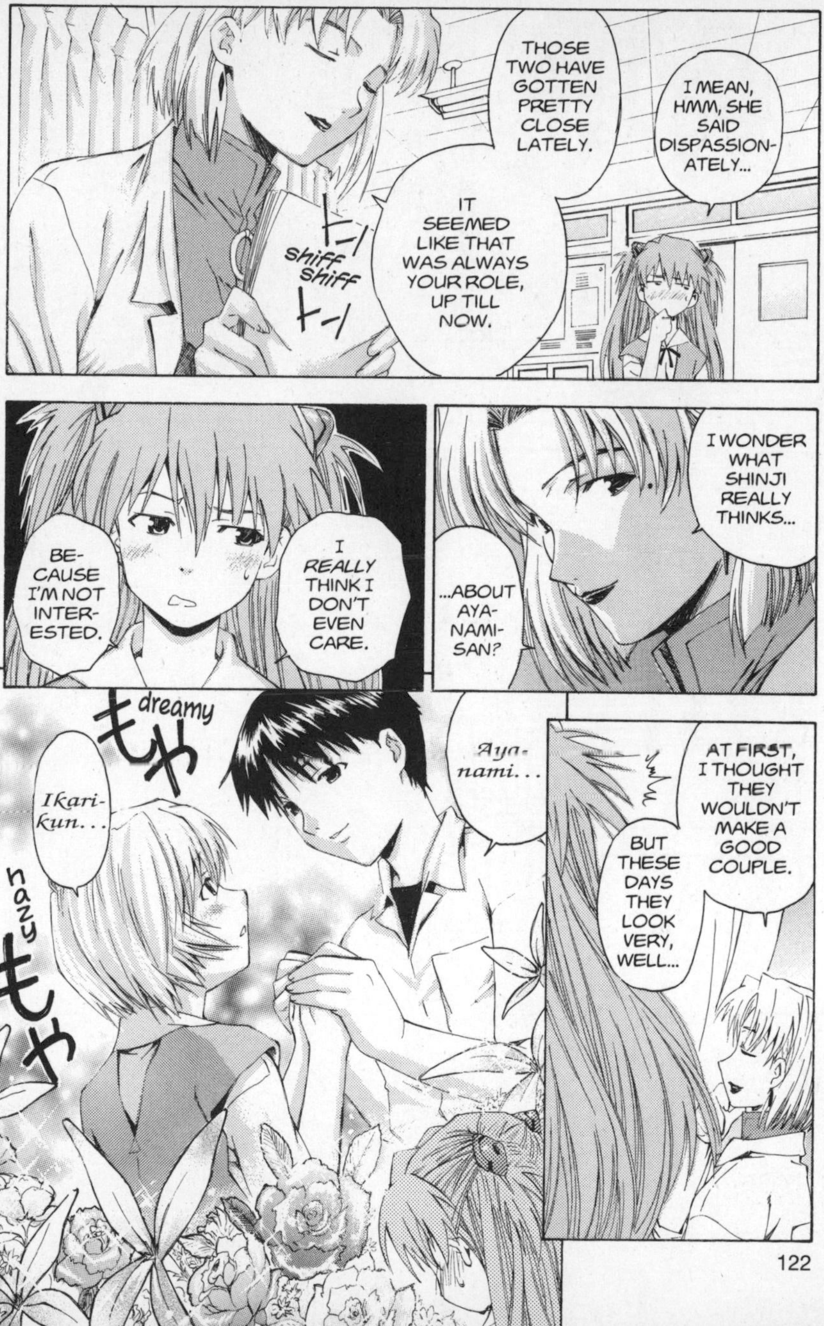
THOSE TWO HAVE GOTTEN PRETTY CLOSE LATELY.
I MEAN, HMM, SHE SAID DISPASSION-ATELY...
IT SEEMED LIKE THAT WAS ALWAYS YOUR ROLE, UP TILL NOW.
shiff shiff
I WONDER WHAT SHINJI REALLY THINKS...
...ABOUT AYA-NAMI-SAN?
I REALLY THINK I DON'T EVEN CARE.
BE-CAUSE I'M NOT INTER-ESTED.
AT FIRST, I THOUGHT THEY WOULDN'T MAKE A GOOD COUPLE.
BUT THESE DAYS THEY LOOK VERY, WELL...
Aya-nami...
dreamy
Ikari-kun...
hazy

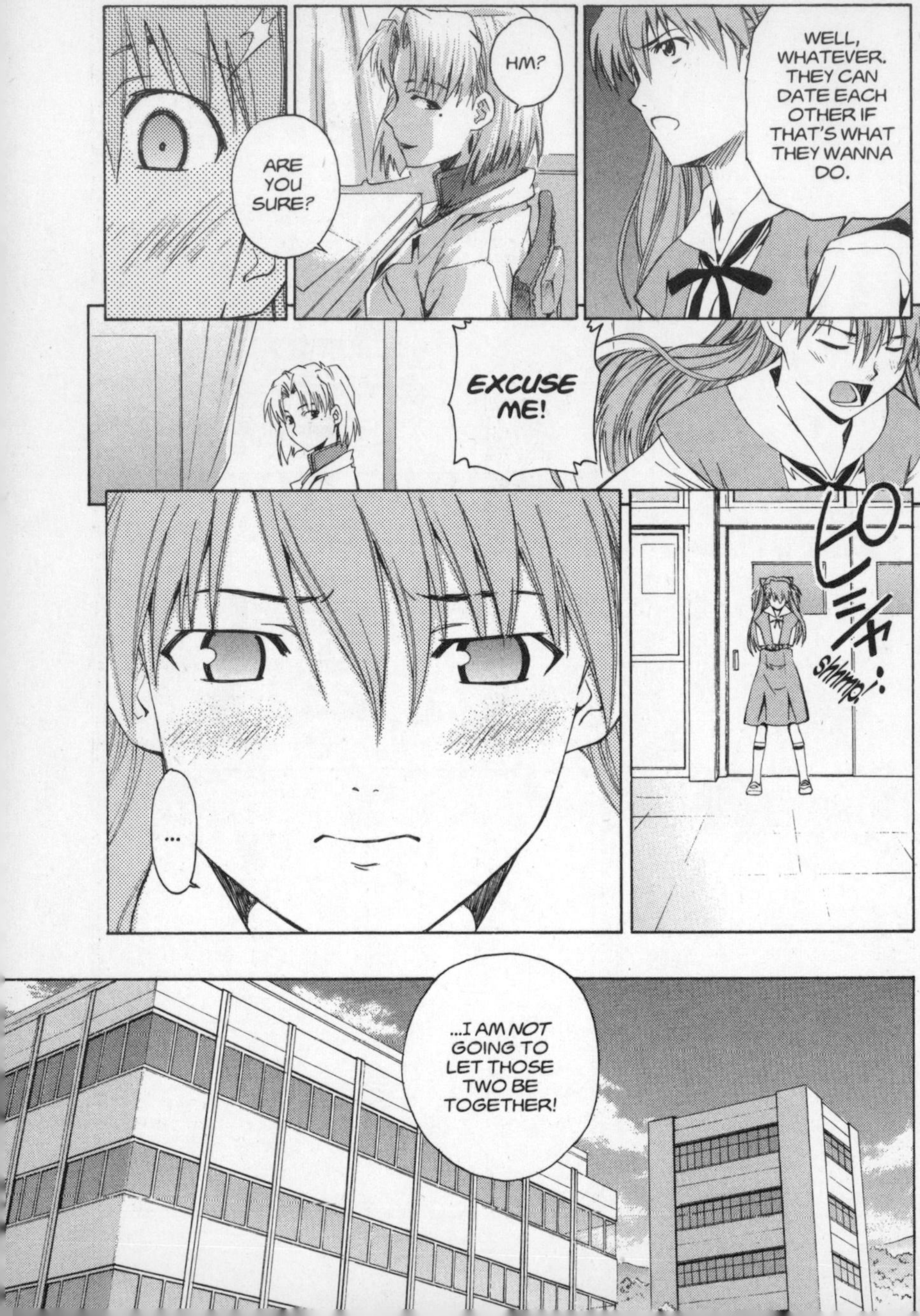
WELL, WHATEVER. THEY CAN DATE EACH OTHER IF THAT'S WHAT THEY WANNA DO.
HM?
ARE YOU SURE?
EXCUSE ME!
shhmp!
...
...I AM NOT GOING TO LET THOSE TWO BE TOGETHER!

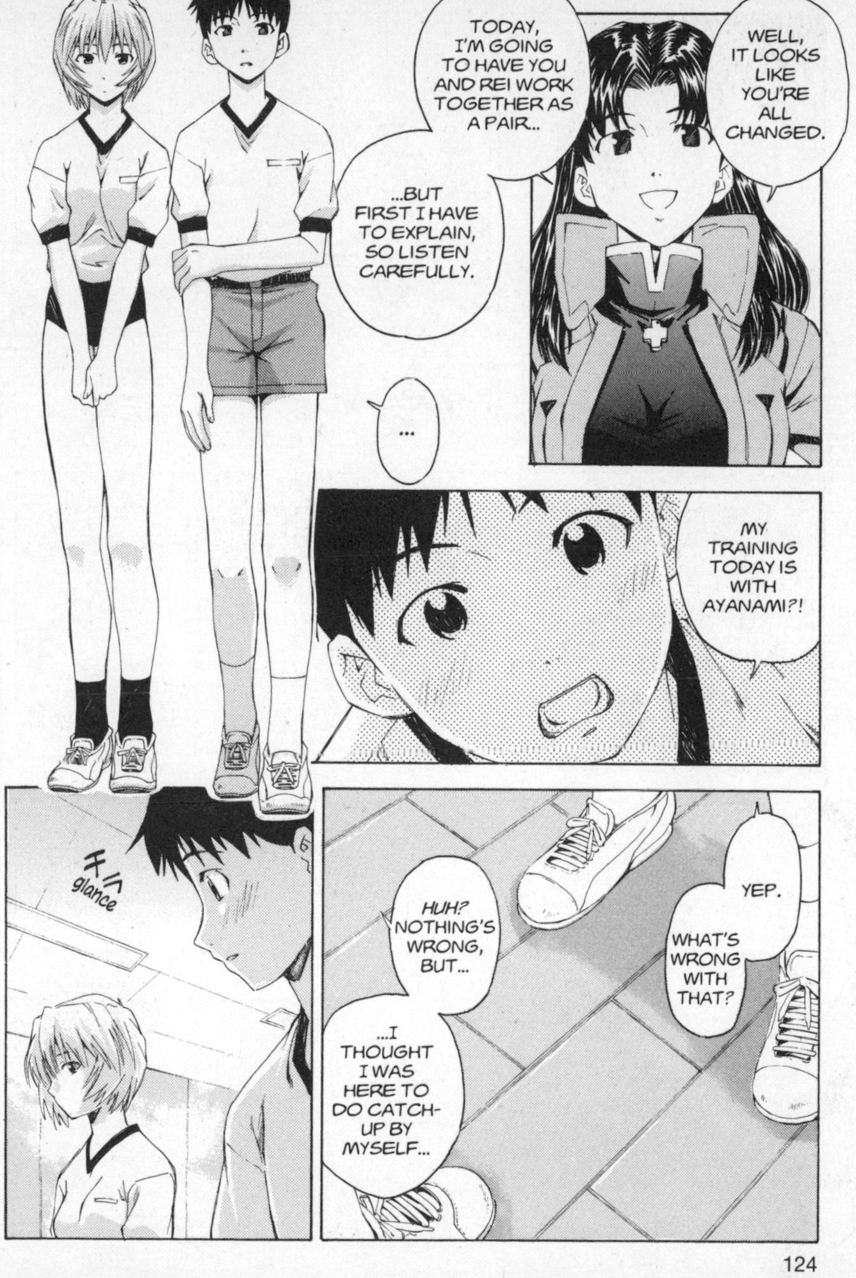
WELL, IT LOOKS LIKE YOU'RE ALL CHANGED.
TODAY, I'M GOING TO HAVE YOU AND REI WORK TOGETHER AS A PAIR...
...BUT FIRST I HAVE TO EXPLAIN, SO LISTEN CAREFULLY.
...
MY TRAINING TODAY IS WITH AYANAMI?!
YEP.
WHAT'S WRONG WITH THAT?
HUH? NOTHING'S WRONG, BUT...
...I THOUGHT I WAS HERE TO DO CATCH-UP BY MYSELF...
チラ
glance

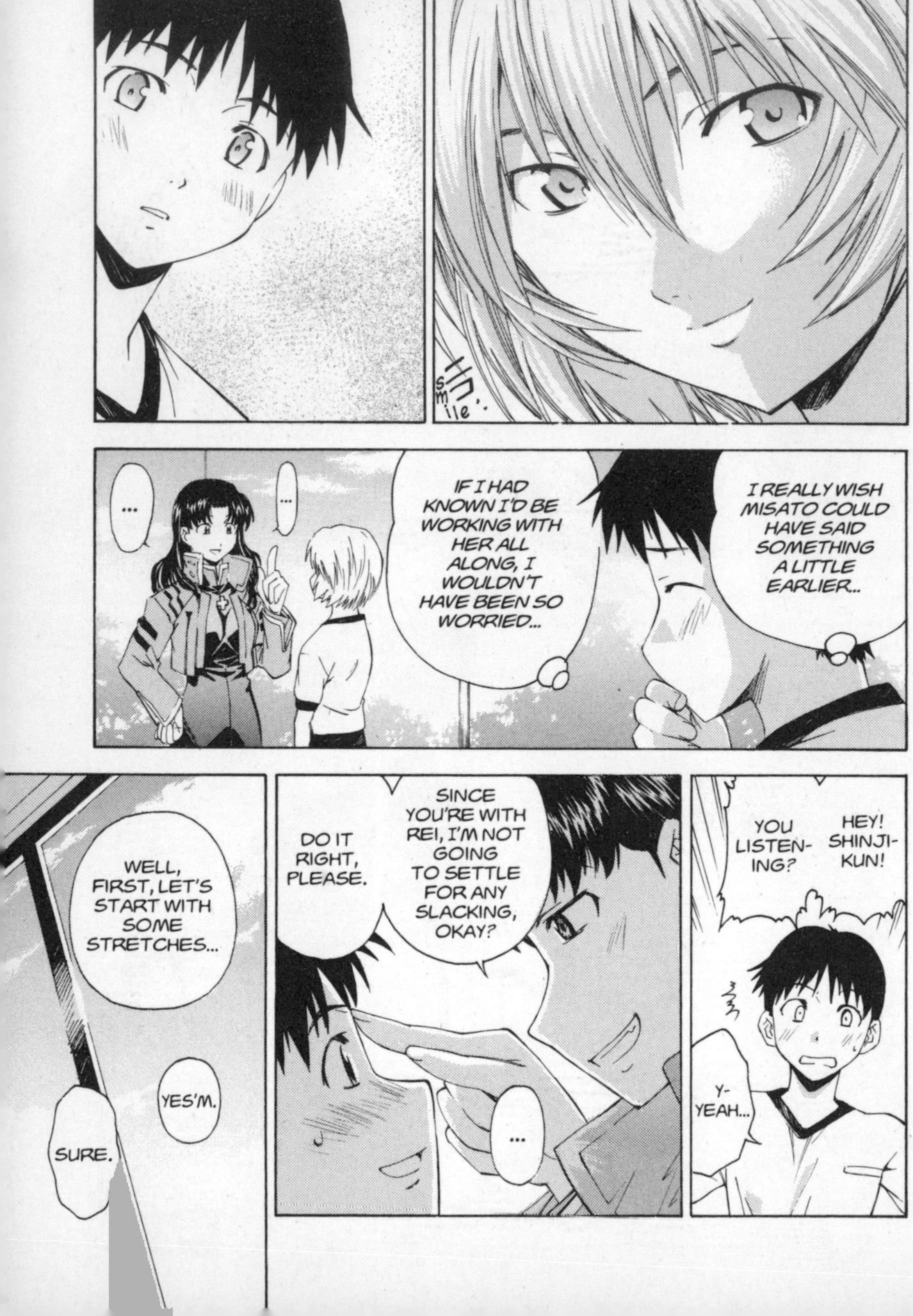
smile
I REALLY WISH MISATO COULD HAVE SAID SOMETHING A LITTLE EARLIER...
IF I HAD KNOWN I'D BE WORKING WITH HER ALL ALONG, I WOULDN'T HAVE BEEN SO WORRIED...
...
...
HEY! SHINJI-KUN!
YOU LISTENING?
Y-YEAH...
SINCE YOU'RE WITH REI, I'M NOT GOING TO SETTLE FOR ANY SLACKING, OKAY?
DO IT RIGHT, PLEASE.
...
WELL, FIRST, LET'S START WITH SOME STRETCHES...
YES'M.
SURE.

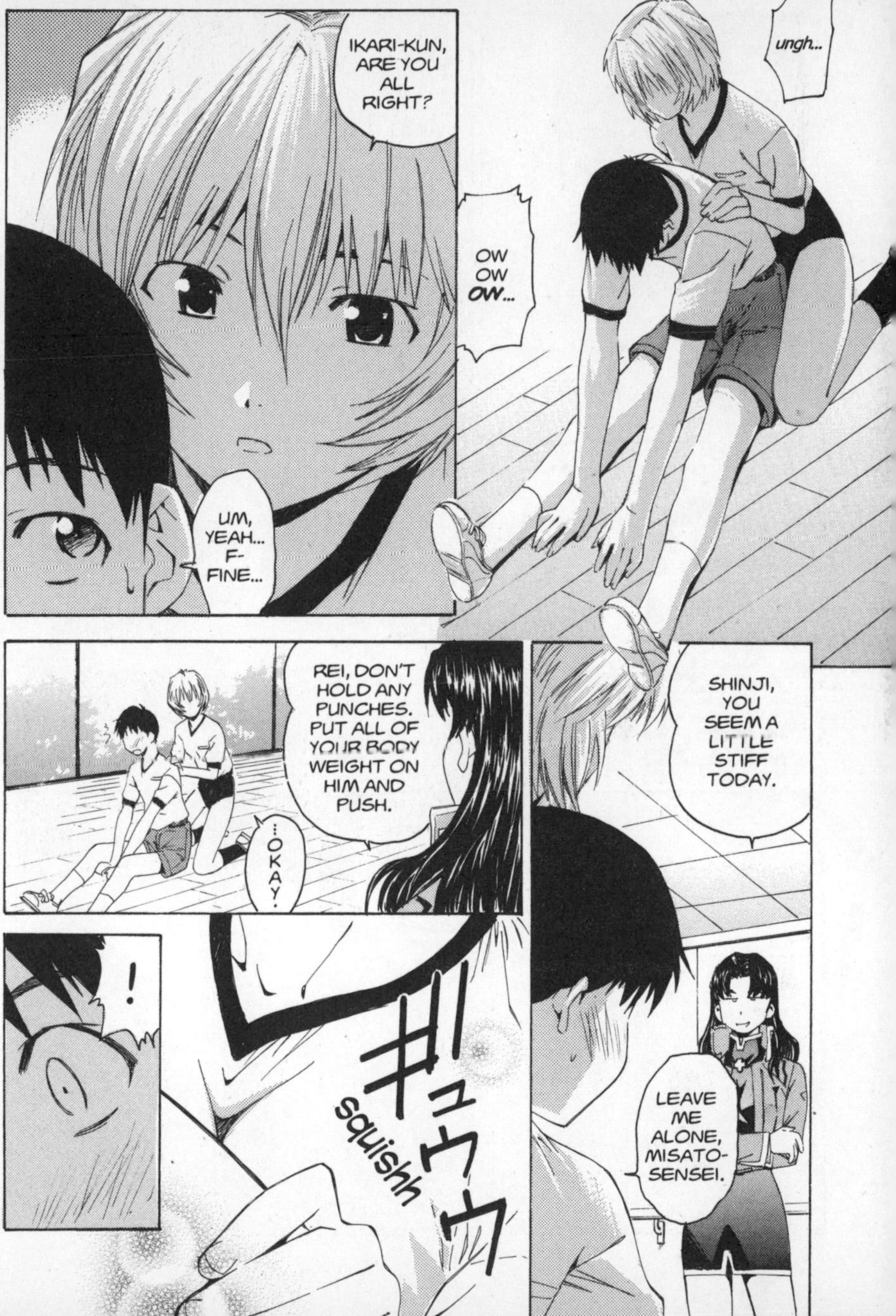
ungh...
OW OW OW...
IKARI-KUN, ARE YOU ALL RIGHT?
UM, YEAH... F-FINE...
SHINJI, YOU SEEM A LITTLE STIFF TODAY.
LEAVE ME ALONE, MISATO-SENSEI.
REI, DON'T HOLD ANY PUNCHES. PUT ALL OF YOUR BODY WEIGHT ON HIM AND PUSH.
...OKAY.
!
ギュウウ
squishh

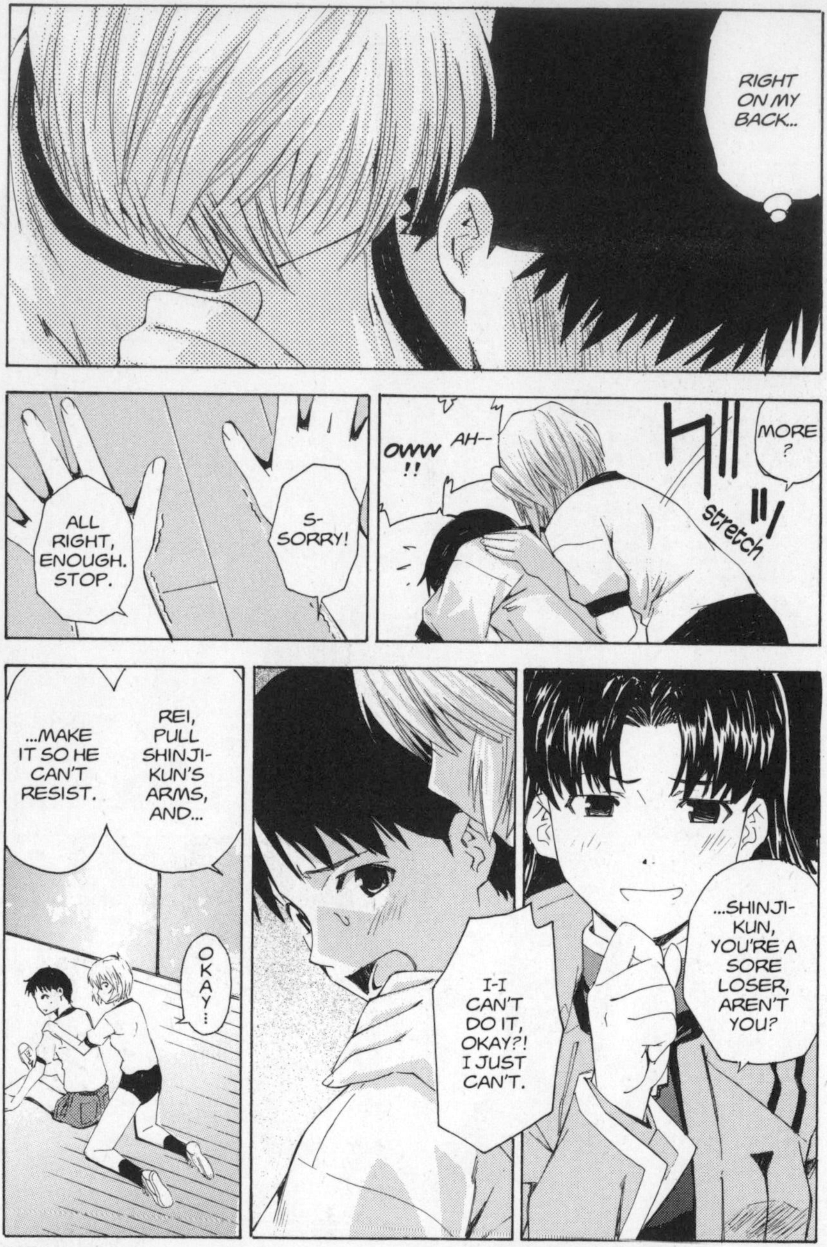
RIGHT ON MY BACK...
MORE?
stretch
AH--
OWW!!
S-SORRY!
ALL RIGHT, ENOUGH. STOP.
...SHINJI-KUN, YOU'RE A SORE LOSER, AREN'T YOU?
I-I CAN'T DO IT, OKAY?! I JUST CAN'T.
REI, PULL SHINJI-KUN'S ARMS, AND...
...MAKE IT SO HE CAN'T RESIST.
OKAY...

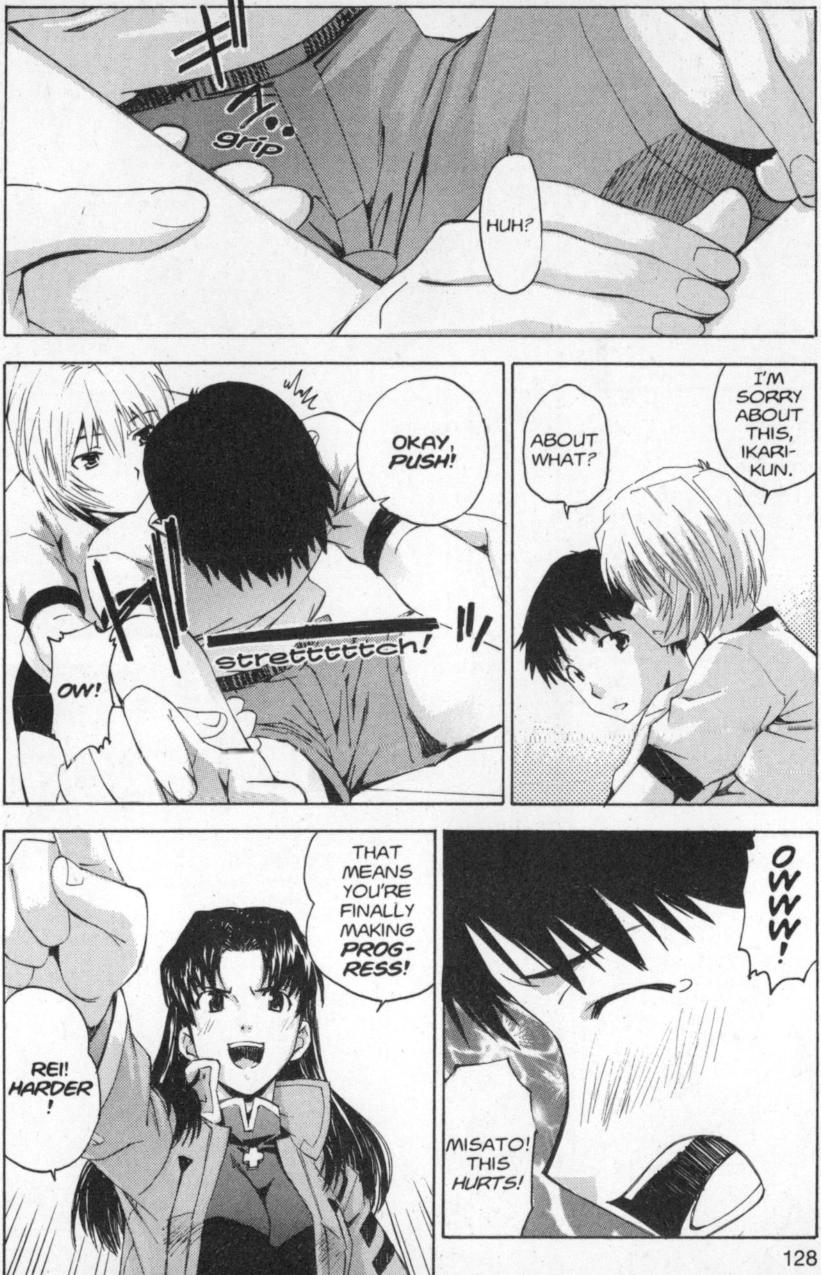
grip
HUH?
I'M SORRY ABOUT THIS, IKARI-KUN.
ABOUT WHAT?
OKAY, PUSH!
stretttttch!
OW!
OWWW!
MISATO! THIS HURTS!
THAT MEANS YOU'RE FINALLY MAKING PROG-RESS!
REI! HARDER!

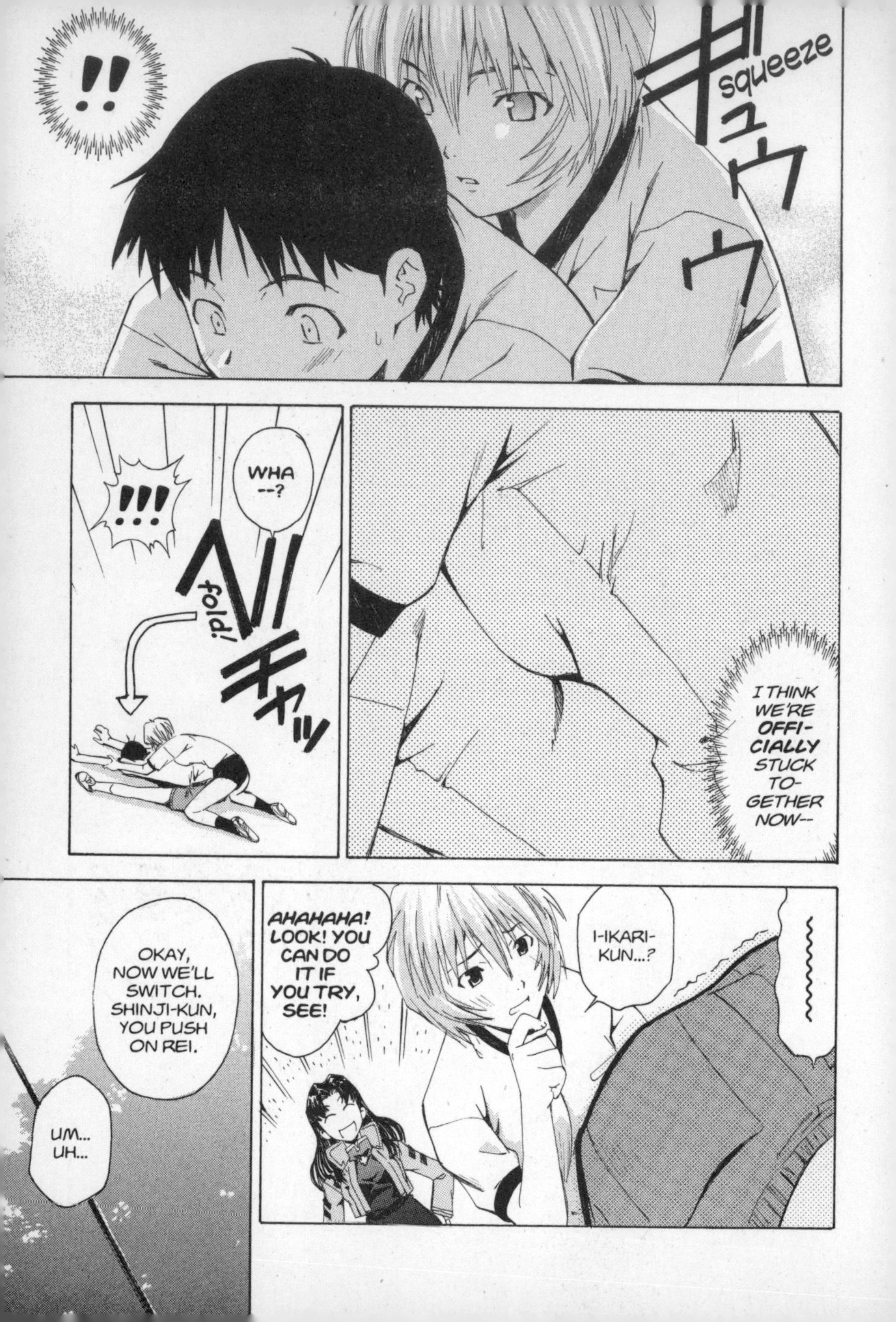
!!
squeeze
I THINK WE'RE OFFICIALLY STUCK TOGETHER NOW--
WHA--?
!!!
fold!
I-IKARI-KUN...?
AHAHAHA! LOOK! YOU CAN DO IT IF YOU TRY, SEE!
OKAY, NOW WE'LL SWITCH. SHINJI-KUN, YOU PUSH ON REI.
UM... UH...

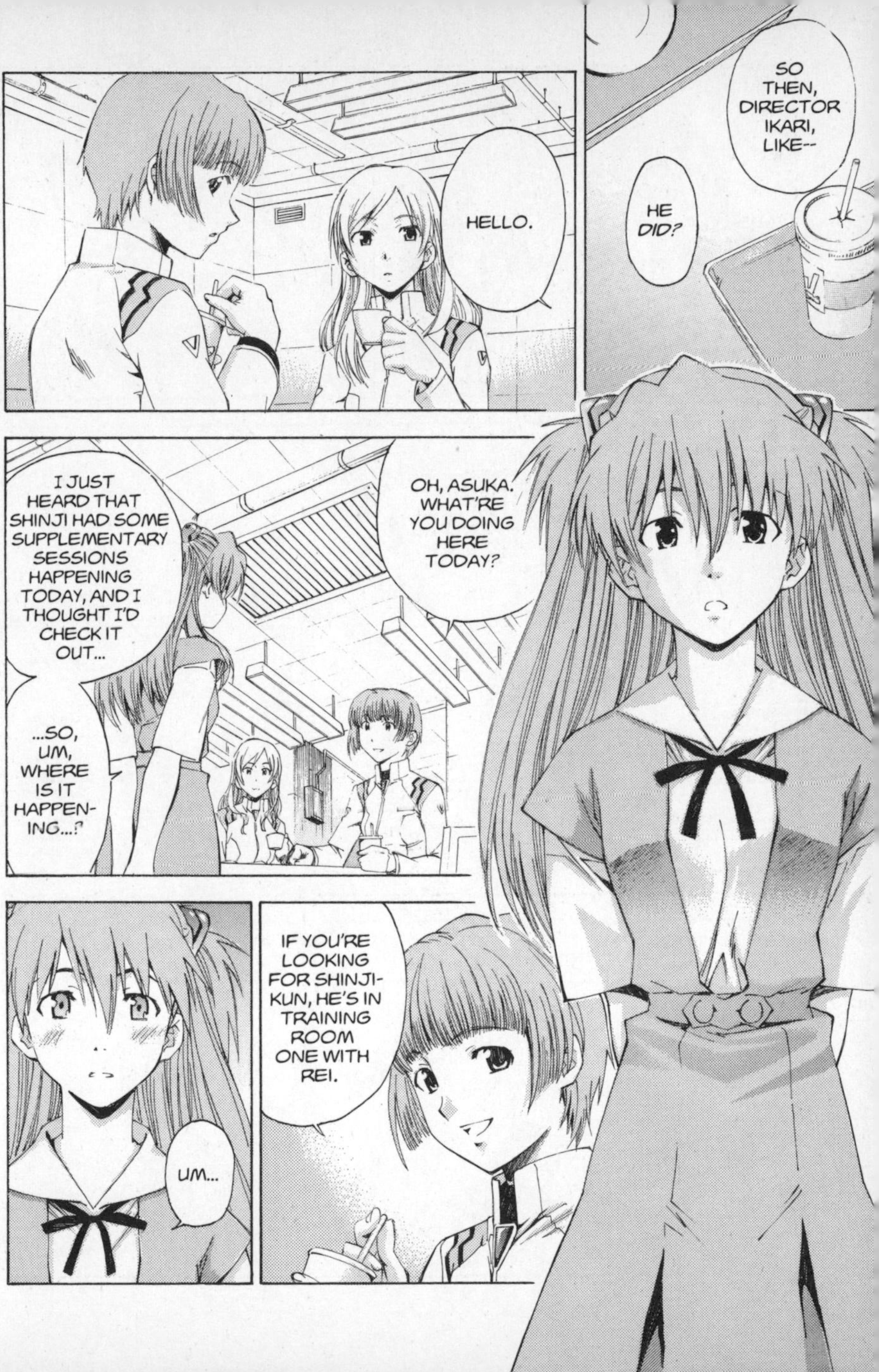
SO THEN, DIRECTOR IKARI, LIKE--
HE DID?
HELLO.
OH, ASUKA. WHAT'RE YOU DOING HERE TODAY?
I JUST HEARD THAT SHINJI HAD SOME SUPPLEMENTARY SESSIONS HAPPENING TODAY, AND I THOUGHT I'D CHECK IT OUT...
...SO, UM, WHERE IS IT HAPPEN-ING...?
IF YOU'RE LOOKING FOR SHINJI-KUN, HE'S IN TRAINING ROOM ONE WITH REI.
UM...

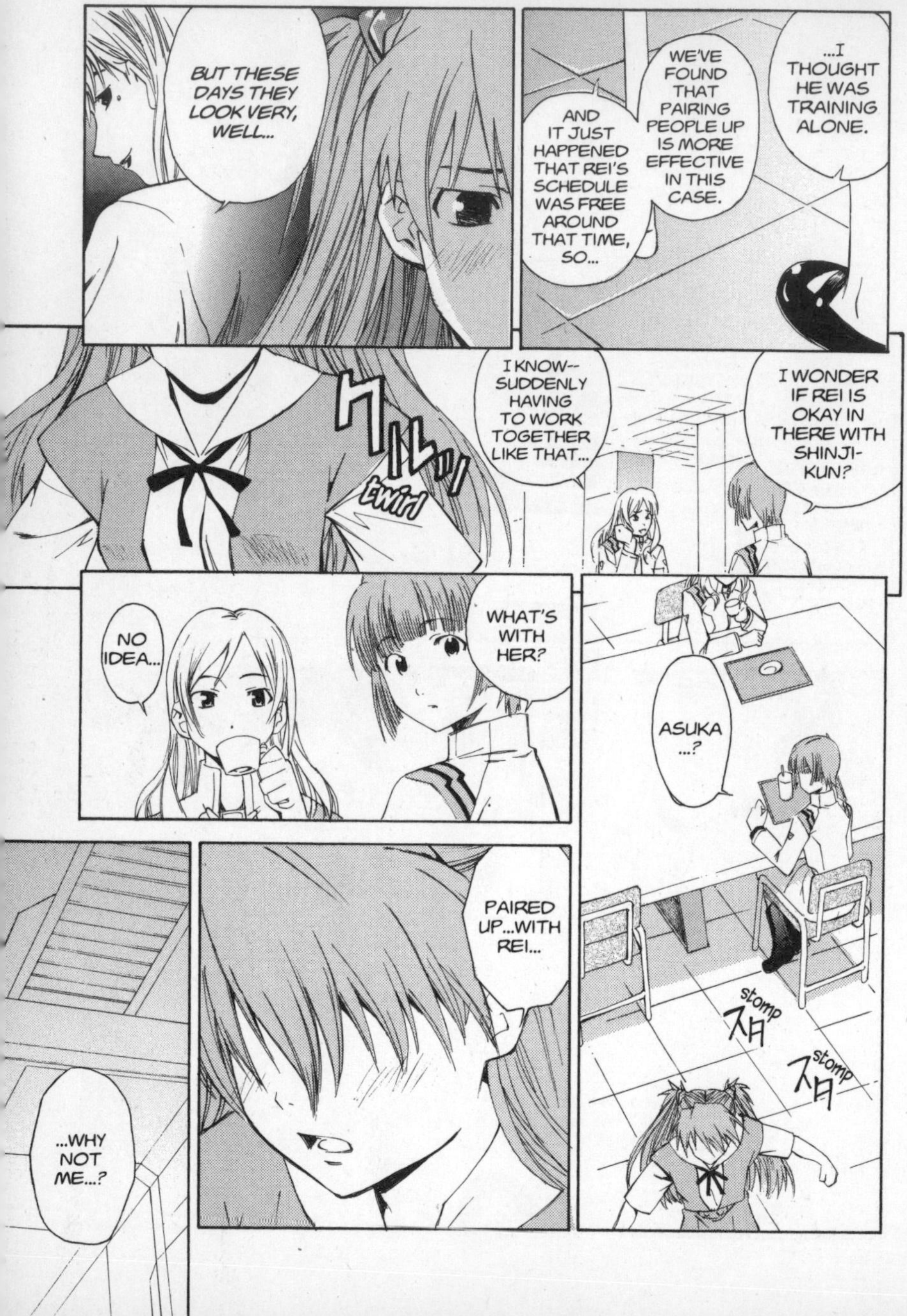
...I THOUGHT HE WAS TRAINING ALONE.
WE'VE FOUND THAT PAIRING PEOPLE UP IS MORE EFFECTIVE IN THIS CASE.
AND IT JUST HAPPENED THAT REI'S SCHEDULE WAS FREE AROUND THAT TIME, SO...
BUT THESE DAYS THEY LOOK VERY, WELL...
I WONDER IF REI IS OKAY IN THERE WITH SHINJI-KUN?
I KNOW-- SUDDENLY HAVING TO WORK TOGETHER LIKE THAT...
twirl
ASUKA ...?
stomp
stomp
WHAT'S WITH HER?
NO IDEA...
PAIRED UP...WITH REI...
...WHY NOT ME...?

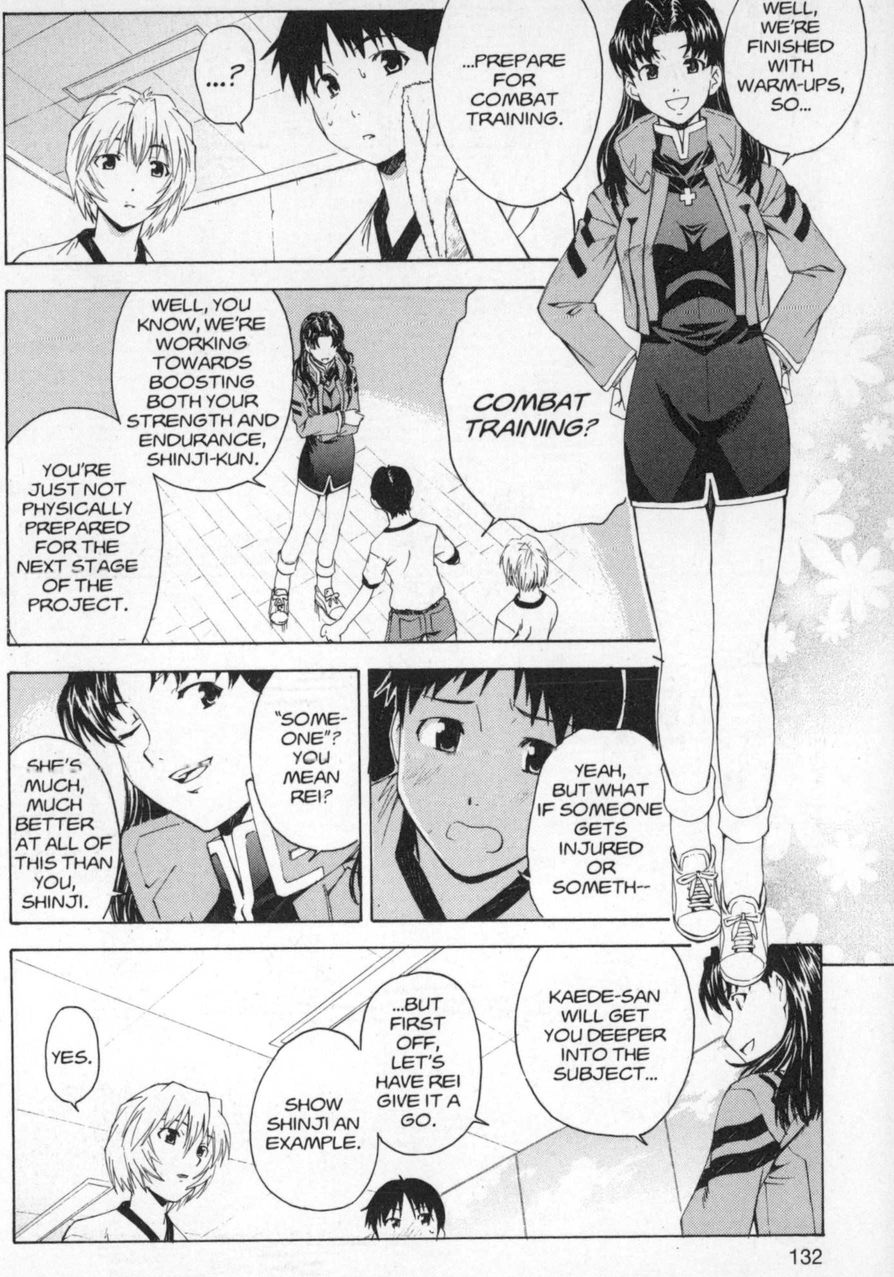
WELL, WE'RE FINISHED WITH WARM-UPS, SO...
...PREPARE FOR COMBAT TRAINING.
...?
COMBAT TRAINING?
WELL, YOU KNOW, WE'RE WORKING TOWARDS BOOSTING BOTH YOUR STRENGTH AND ENDURANCE, SHINJI-KUN.
YOU'RE JUST NOT PHYSICALLY PREPARED FOR THE NEXT STAGE OF THE PROJECT.
YEAH, BUT WHAT IF SOMEONE GETS INJURED OR SOMETH--
"SOME-ONE"? YOU MEAN REI?
SHE'S MUCH, MUCH BETTER AT ALL OF THIS THAN YOU, SHINJI.
KAEDE-SAN WILL GET YOU DEEPER INTO THE SUBJECT...
...BUT FIRST OFF, LET'S HAVE REI GIVE IT A GO.
SHOW SHINJI AN EXAMPLE.
YES.

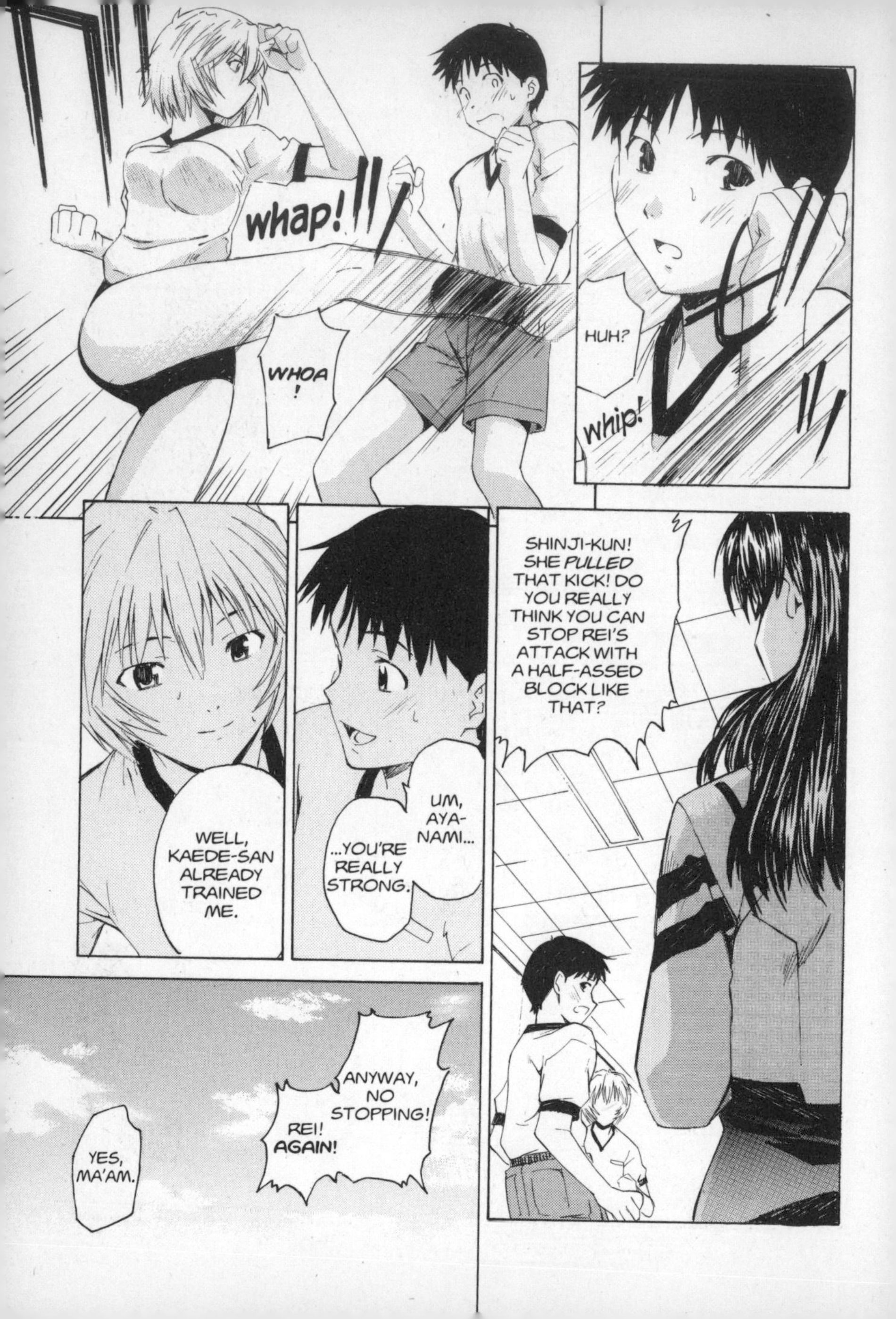
HUH?
whip!
whap!
WHOA!
SHINJI-KUN! SHE *PULLED* THAT KICK! DO YOU REALLY THINK YOU CAN STOP REI'S ATTACK WITH A HALF-ASSED BLOCK LIKE THAT?
UM, AYA-NAMI...
...YOU'RE REALLY STRONG.
WELL, KAEDE-SAN ALREADY TRAINED ME.
ANYWAY, NO STOPPING!
REI! **AGAIN!**
YES, MA'AM.

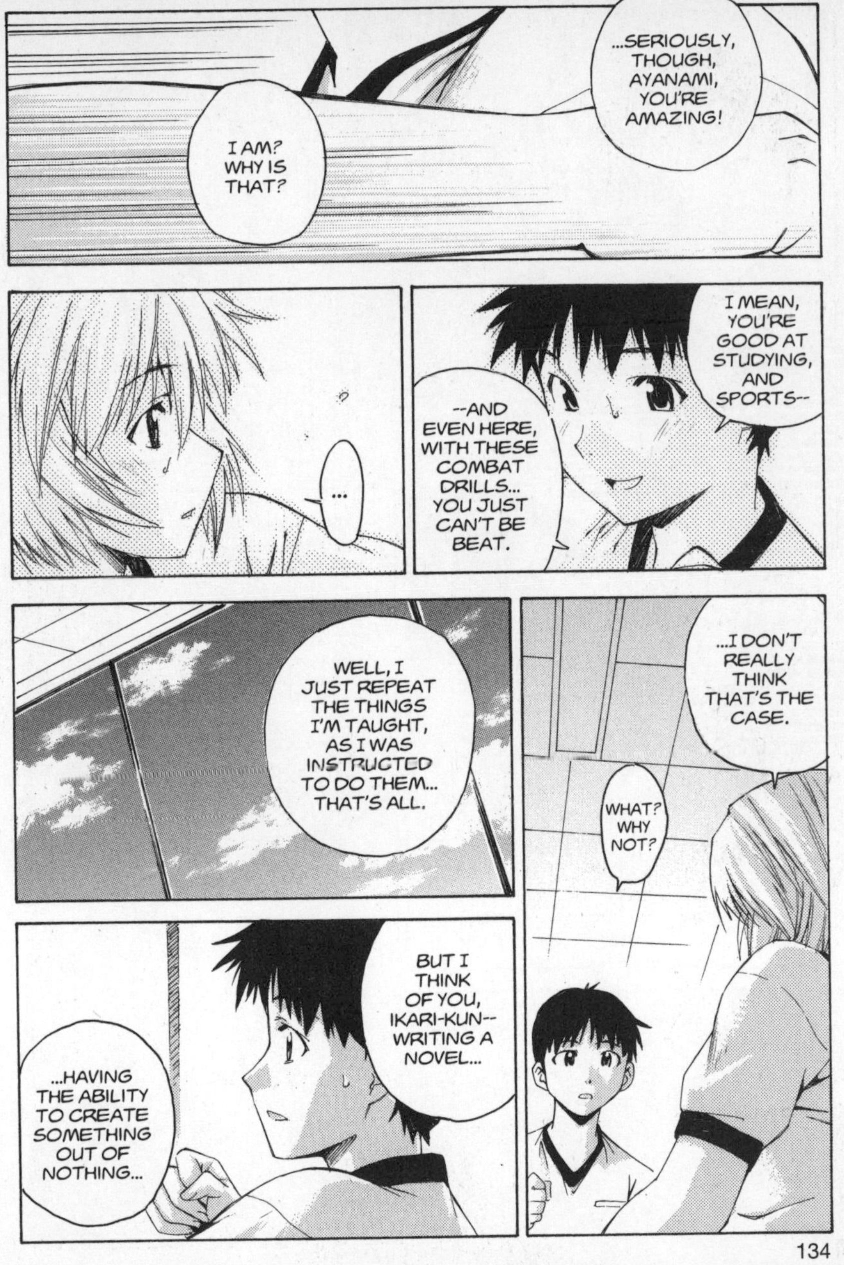
...SERIOUSLY, THOUGH, AYANAMI, YOU'RE AMAZING!
I AM? WHY IS THAT?
I MEAN, YOU'RE GOOD AT STUDYING, AND SPORTS--
--AND EVEN HERE, WITH THESE COMBAT DRILLS... YOU JUST CAN'T BE BEAT.
...
...I DON'T REALLY THINK THAT'S THE CASE.
WHAT? WHY NOT?
WELL, I JUST REPEAT THE THINGS I'M TAUGHT, AS I WAS INSTRUCTED TO DO THEM... THAT'S ALL.
BUT I THINK OF YOU, IKARI-KUN-- WRITING A NOVEL...
...HAVING THE ABILITY TO CREATE SOMETHING OUT OF NOTHING...

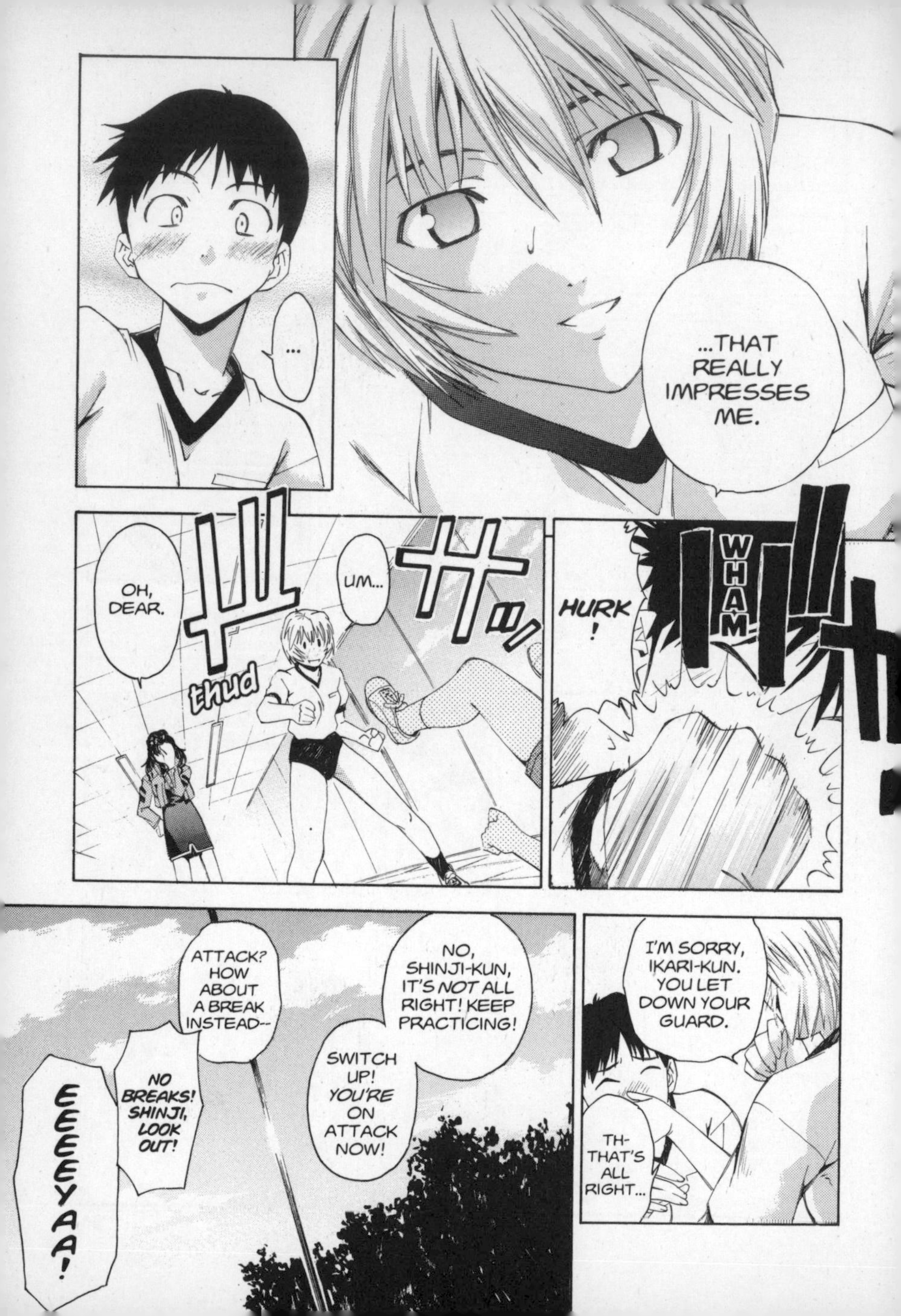
...THAT REALLY IMPRESSES ME.
...
WHAM
HURK!
UM...
OH, DEAR.
thud
I'M SORRY, IKARI-KUN. YOU LET DOWN YOUR GUARD.
TH-THAT'S ALL RIGHT...
NO, SHINJI-KUN, IT'S *NOT* ALL RIGHT! KEEP PRACTICING!
SWITCH UP! *YOU'RE* ON ATTACK NOW!
ATTACK? HOW ABOUT A BREAK INSTEAD--
NO BREAKS! SHINJI, LOOK OUT!
EEEEYAA!

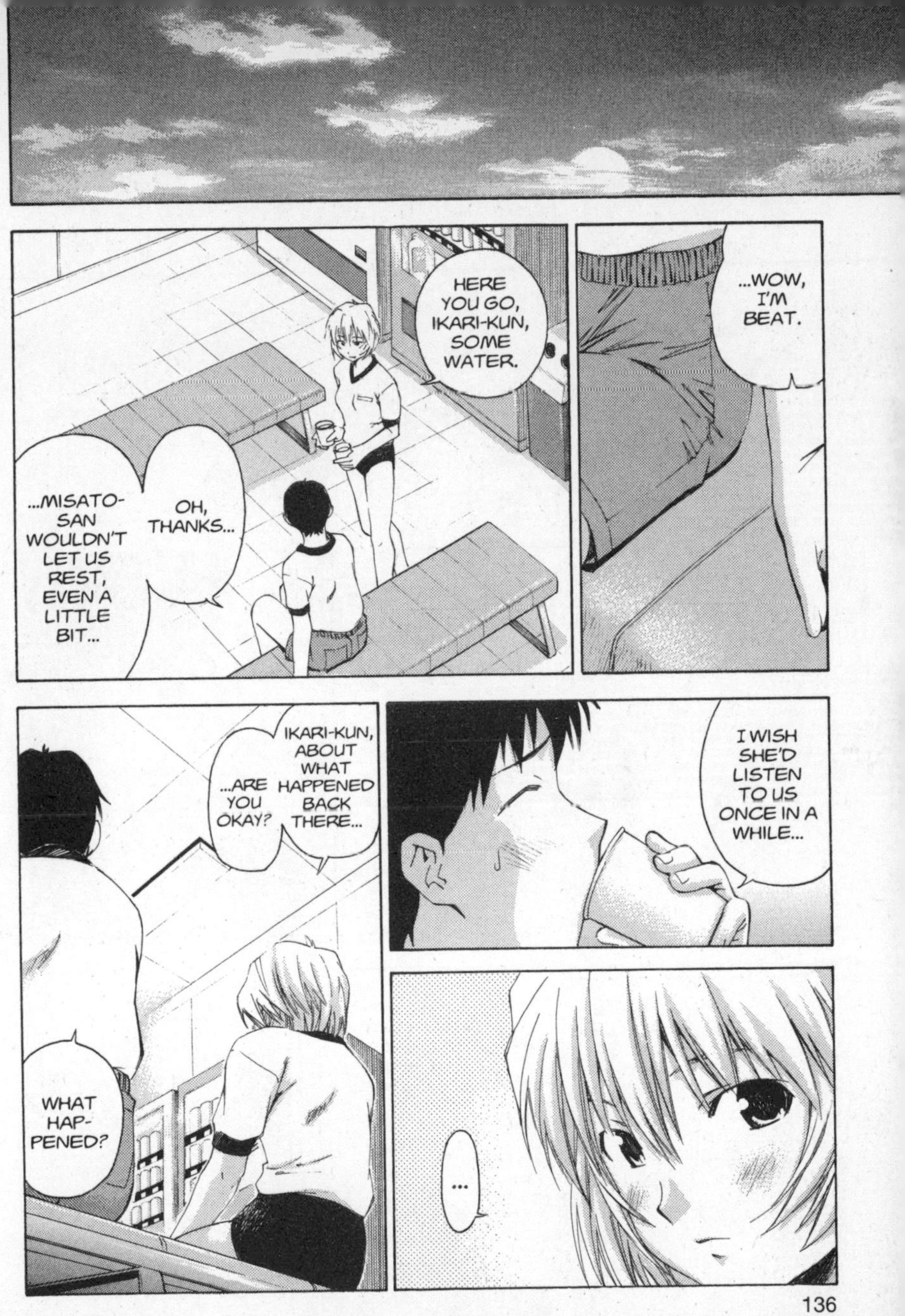
...WOW, I'M BEAT.
HERE YOU GO, IKARI-KUN, SOME WATER.
OH, THANKS...
...MISATO-SAN WOULDN'T LET US REST, EVEN A LITTLE BIT...
I WISH SHE'D LISTEN TO US ONCE IN A WHILE...
...
IKARI-KUN, ABOUT WHAT HAPPENED BACK THERE...
...ARE YOU OKAY?
WHAT HAP-PENED?

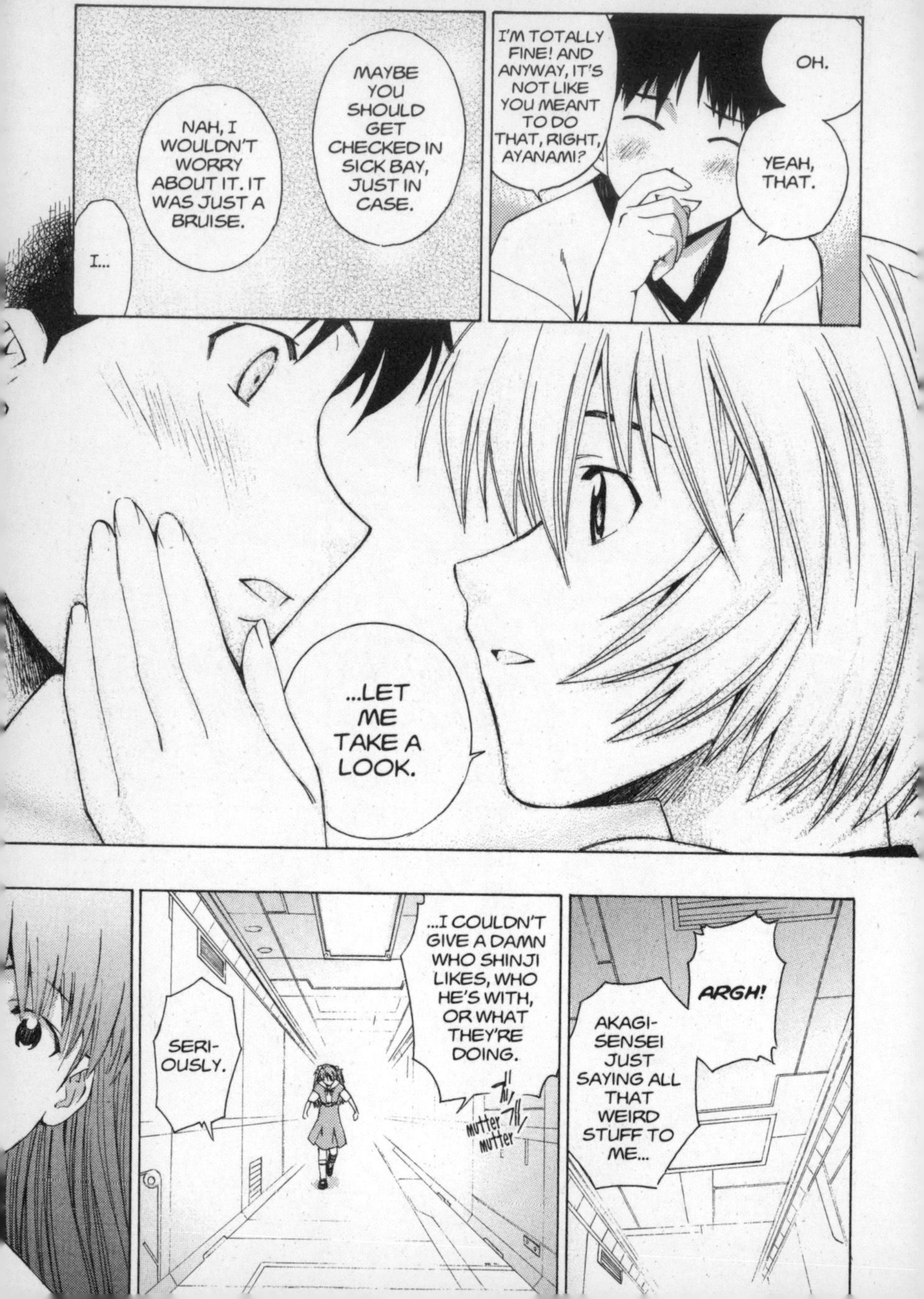
OH.
YEAH, THAT.
I'M TOTALLY FINE! AND ANYWAY, IT'S NOT LIKE YOU MEANT TO DO THAT, RIGHT, AYANAMI?
MAYBE YOU SHOULD GET CHECKED IN SICK BAY, JUST IN CASE.
NAH, I WOULDN'T WORRY ABOUT IT. IT WAS JUST A BRUISE.
I...
...LET ME TAKE A LOOK.
ARGH!
AKAGI-SENSEI JUST SAYING ALL THAT WEIRD STUFF TO ME...
...I COULDN'T GIVE A DAMN WHO SHINJI LIKES, WHO HE'S WITH, OR WHAT THEY'RE DOING.
SERI-OUSLY.
mutter mutter

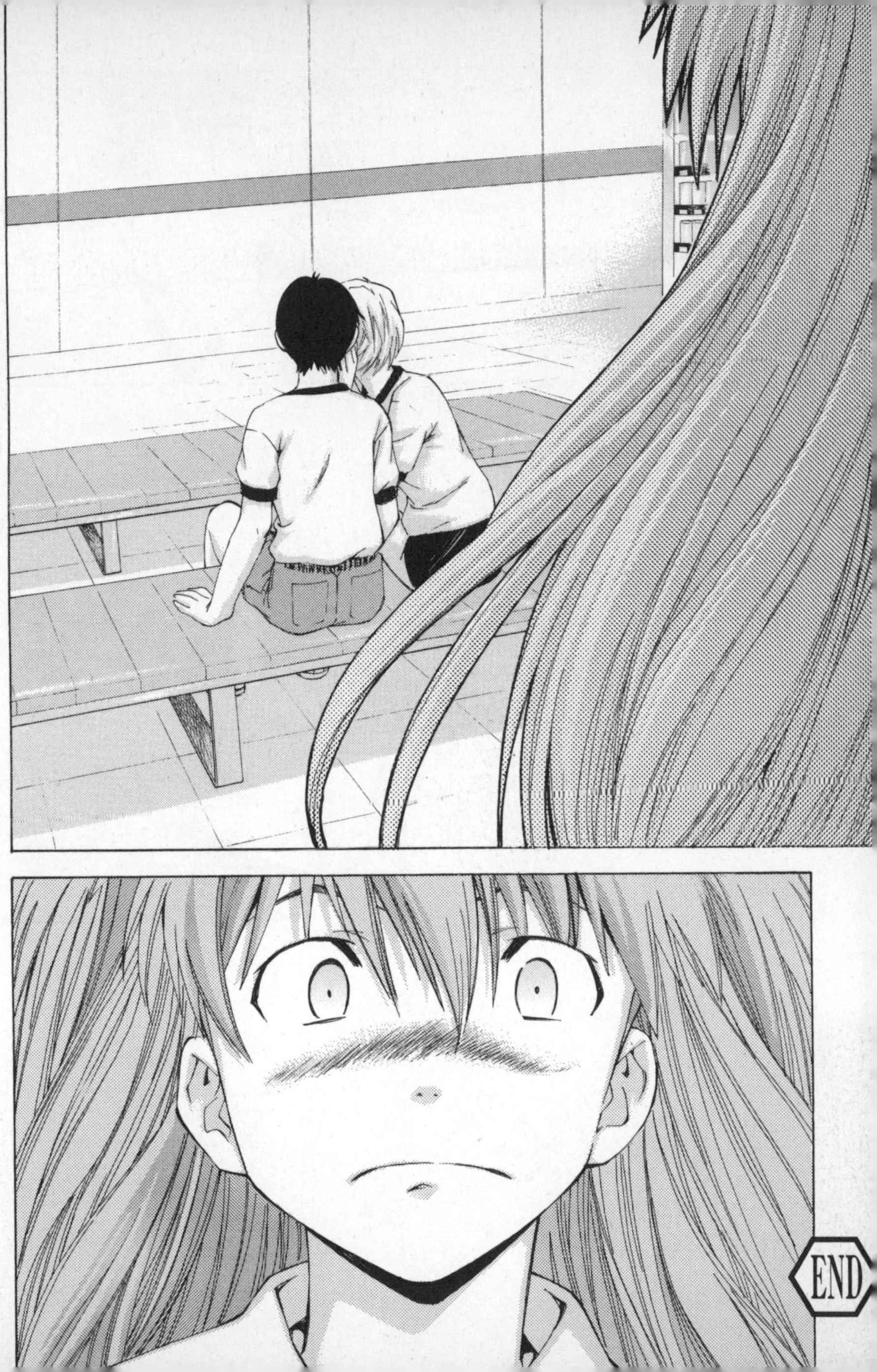
END

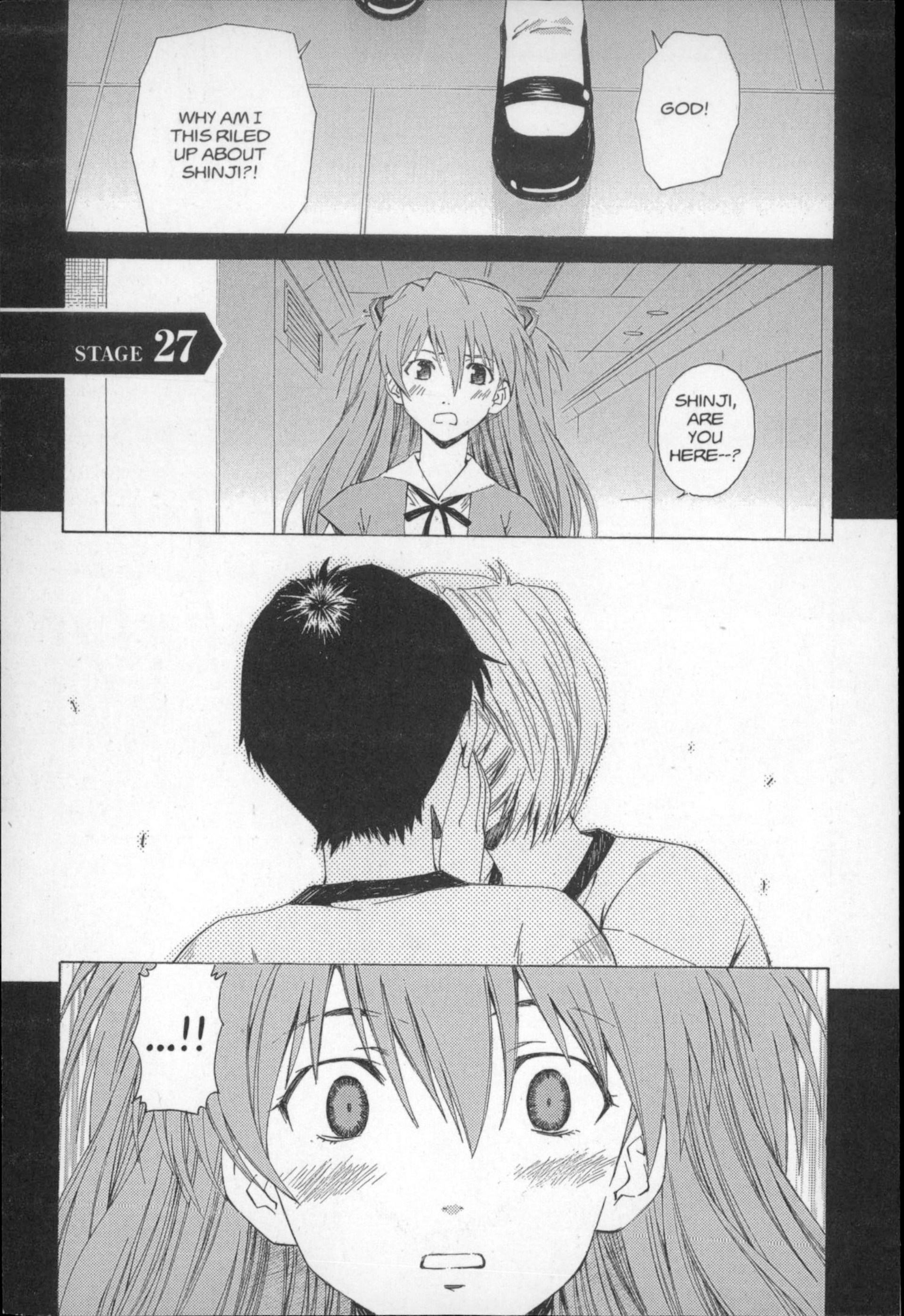
GOD!
WHY AM I THIS RILED UP ABOUT SHINJI?!
STAGE 27
SHINJI, ARE YOU HERE--?
...!!

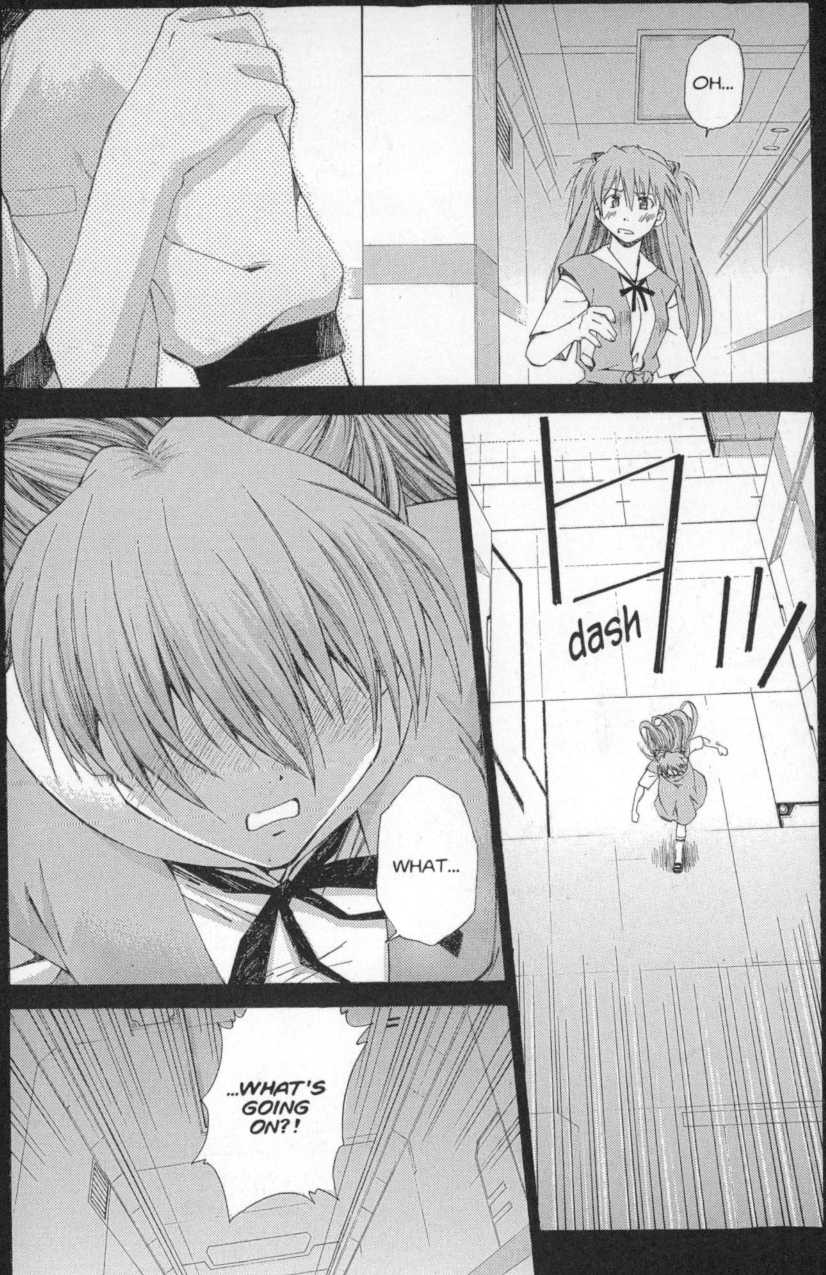
OH...
dash
WHAT...
...WHAT'S GOING ON?!

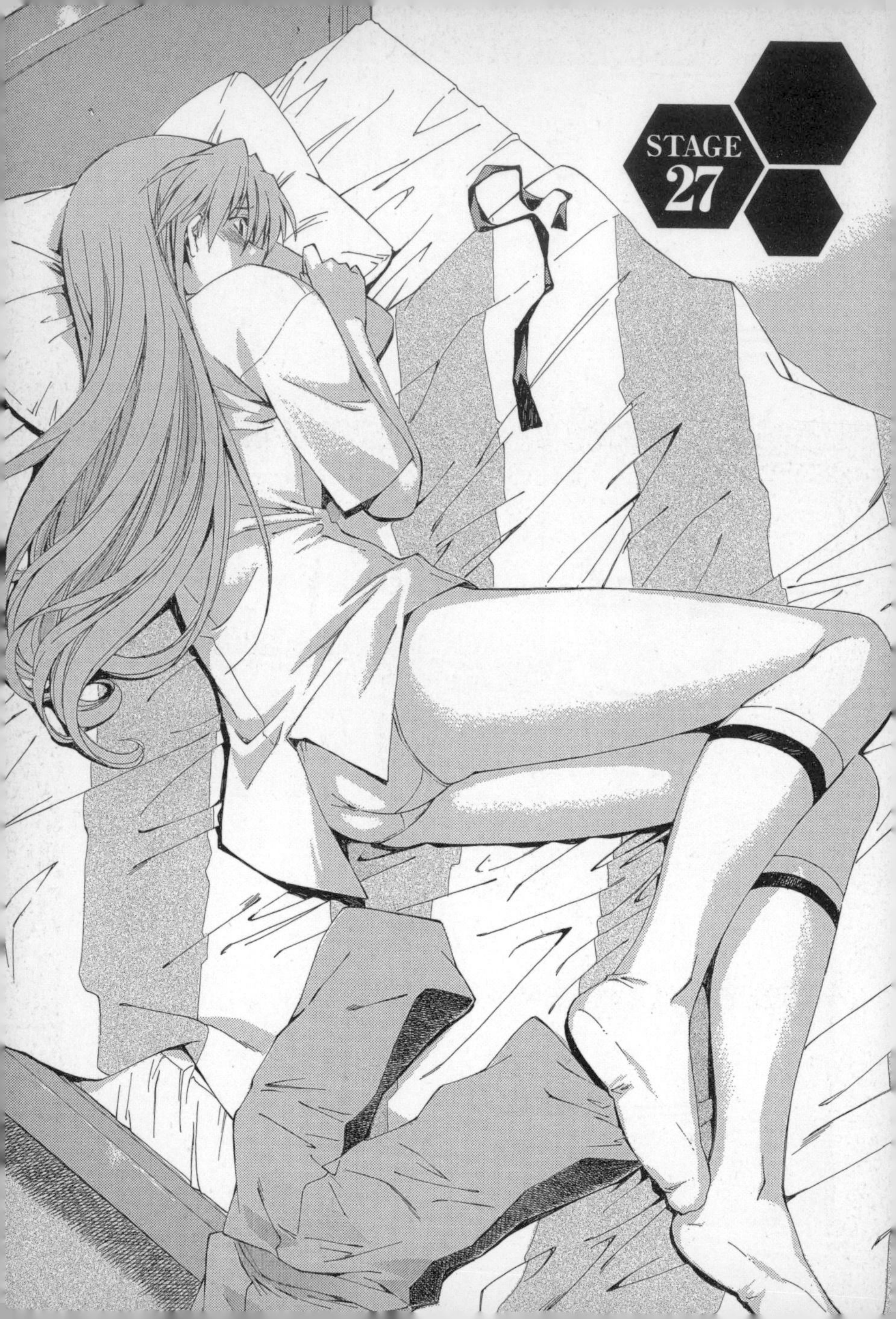
STAGE
27

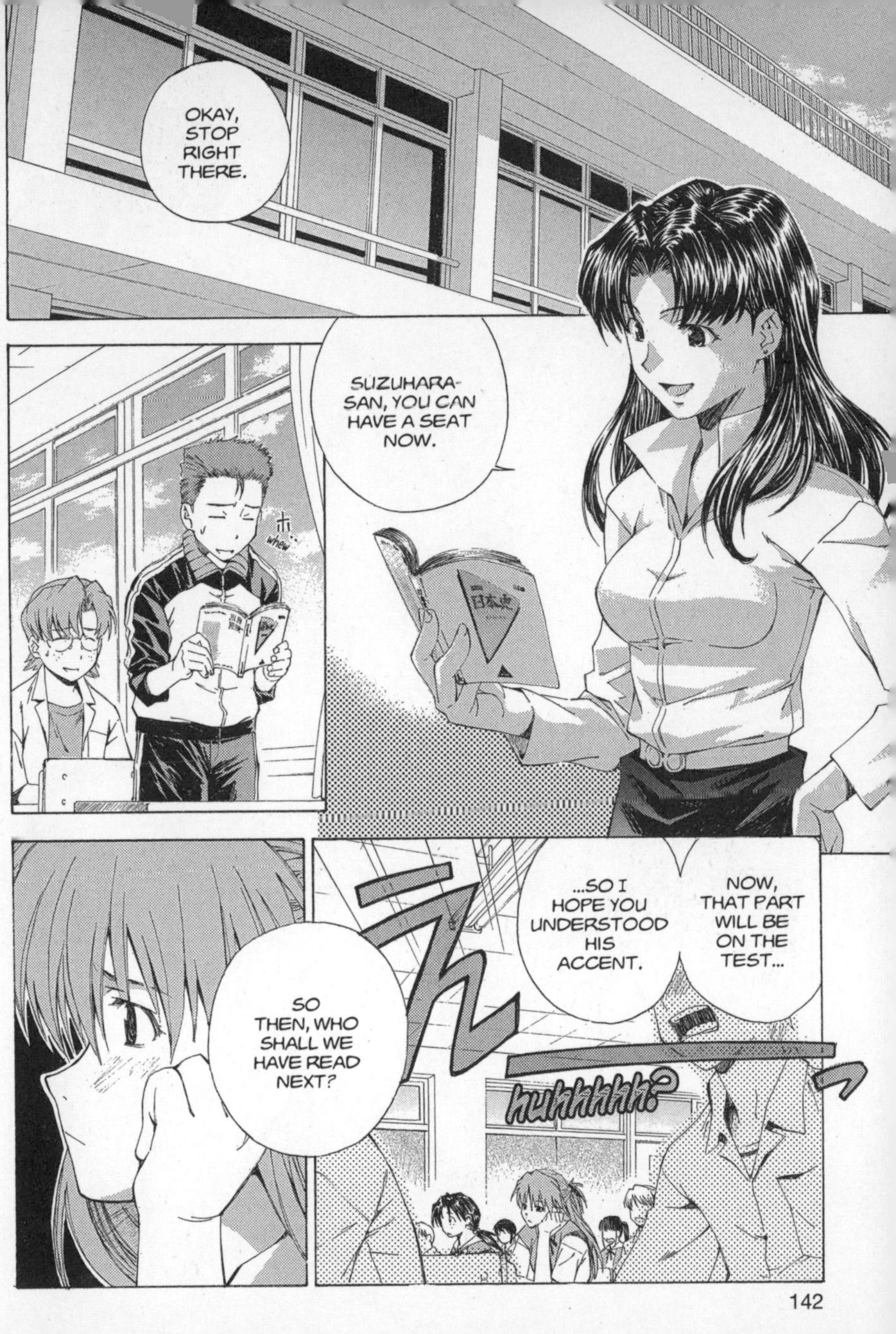
OKAY, STOP RIGHT THERE.
SUZUHARA-SAN, YOU CAN HAVE A SEAT NOW.
ホ.. whew
NOW, THAT PART WILL BE ON THE TEST...
...SO I HOPE YOU UNDERSTOOD HIS ACCENT.
SO THEN, WHO SHALL WE HAVE READ NEXT?
huhhhhhh?

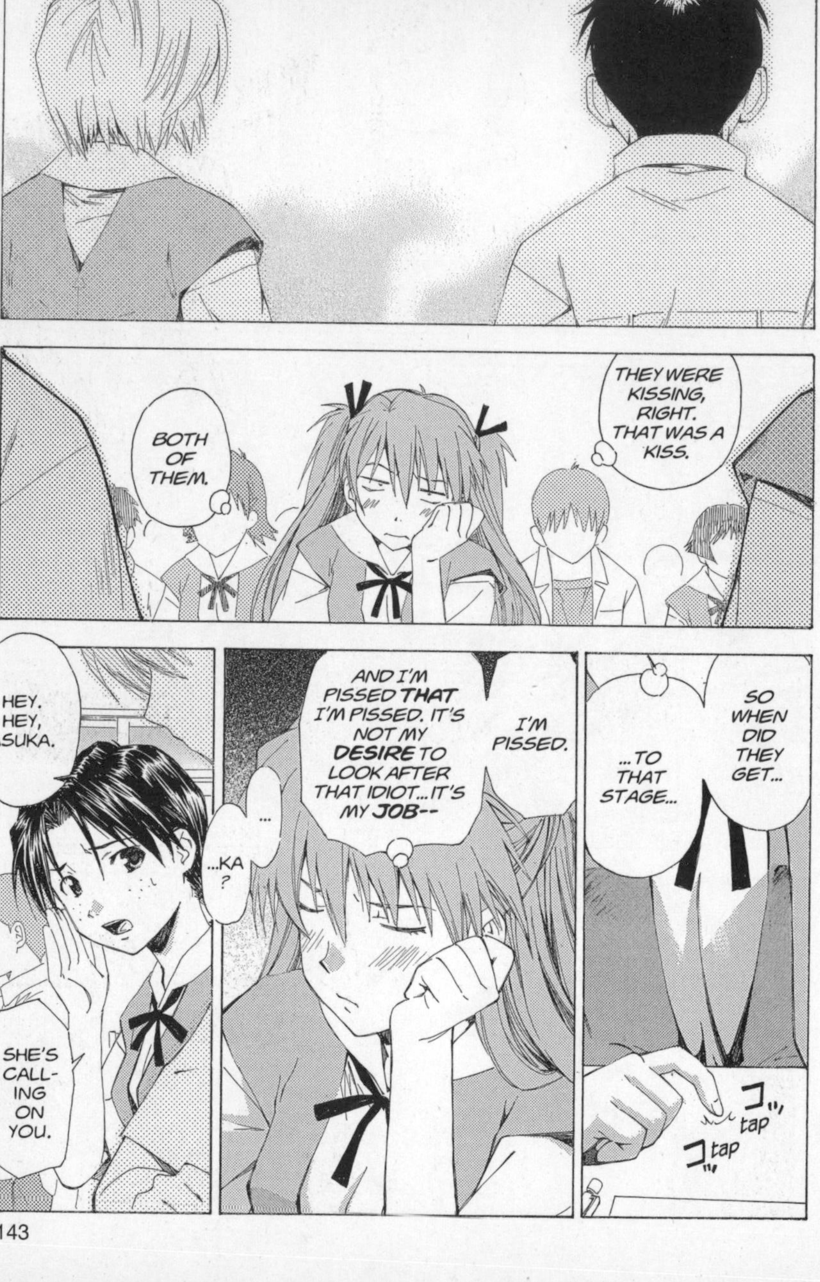

THEY WERE KISSING, RIGHT. THAT WAS A KISS.
BOTH OF THEM.
SO WHEN DID THEY GET...
...TO THAT STAGE...
tap
tap
I'M PISSED.
AND I'M PISSED **THAT** I'M PISSED. IT'S NOT MY **DESIRE** TO LOOK AFTER THAT IDIOT...IT'S MY **JOB**--
...
...KA?
HEY. HEY, ASUKA.
SHE'S CALLING ON YOU.

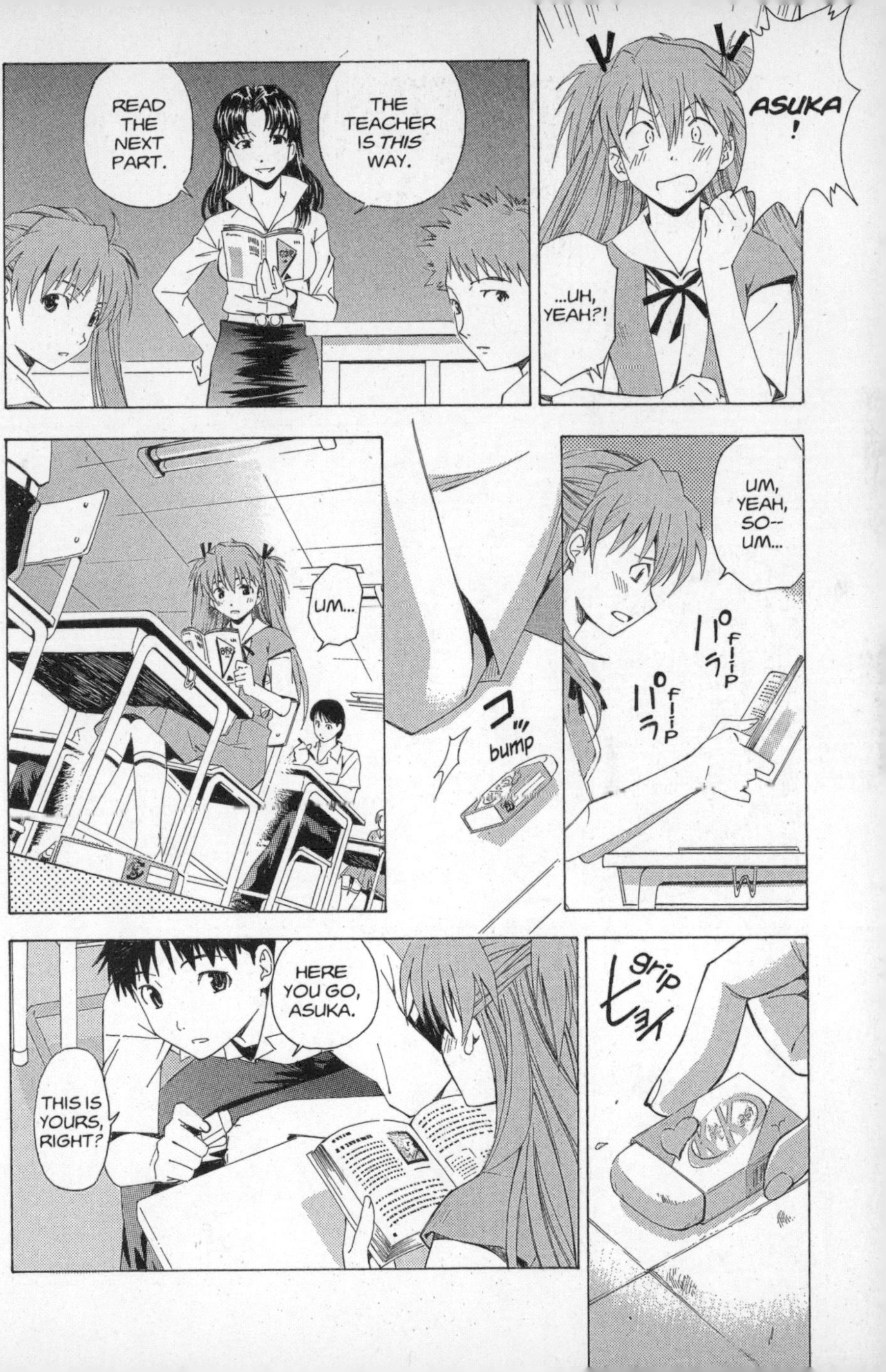
ASUKA!
...UH, YEAH?!
THE TEACHER IS *THIS* WAY.
READ THE NEXT PART.
UM, YEAH, SO-- UM...
パラ flip
パラ flip
コッ bump
UM...
ヒョイ grip
HERE YOU GO, ASUKA.
THIS IS YOURS, RIGHT?

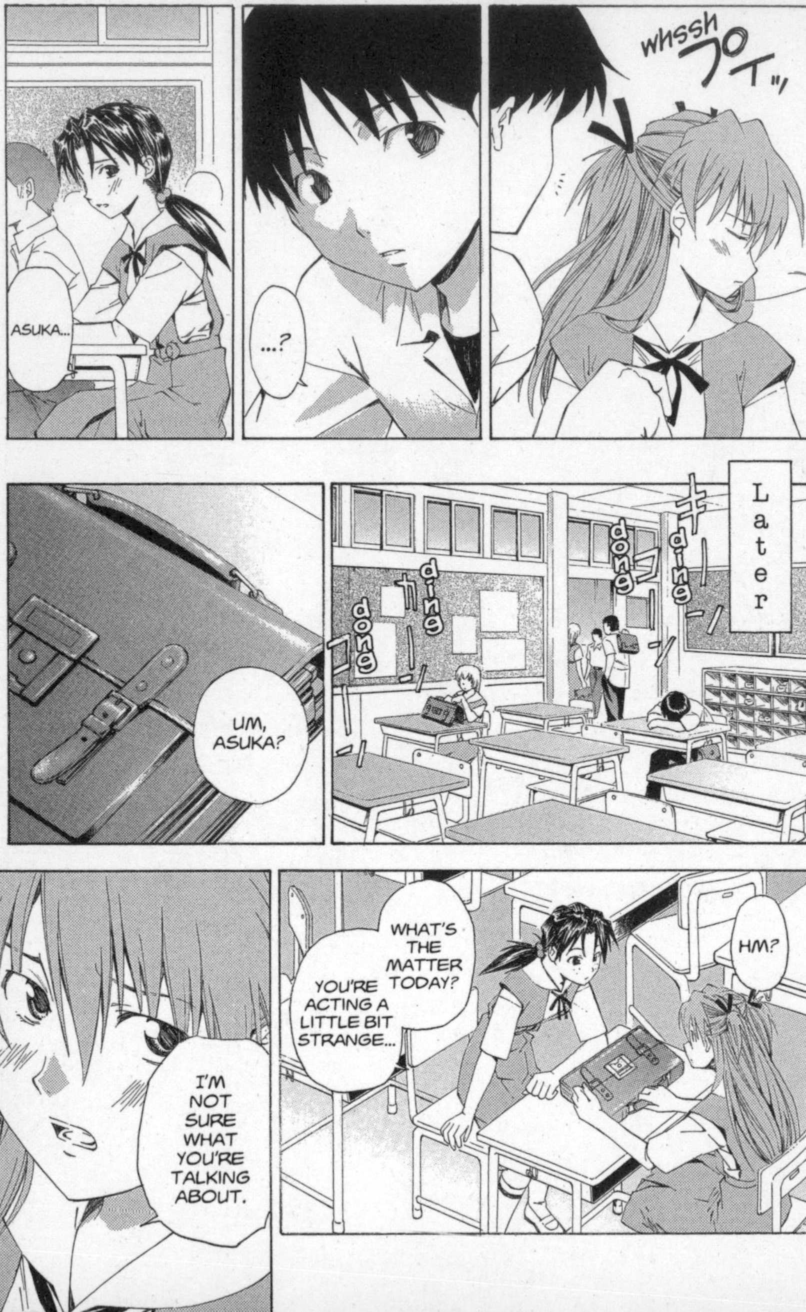
whssh
プイッ
...?
ASUKA...
Later
ding
dong
ding
dong
UM, ASUKA?
HM?
WHAT'S THE MATTER TODAY?
YOU'RE ACTING A LITTLE BIT STRANGE...
I'M NOT SURE WHAT YOU'RE TALKING ABOUT.

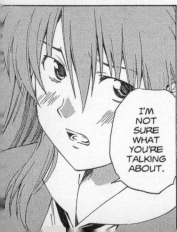

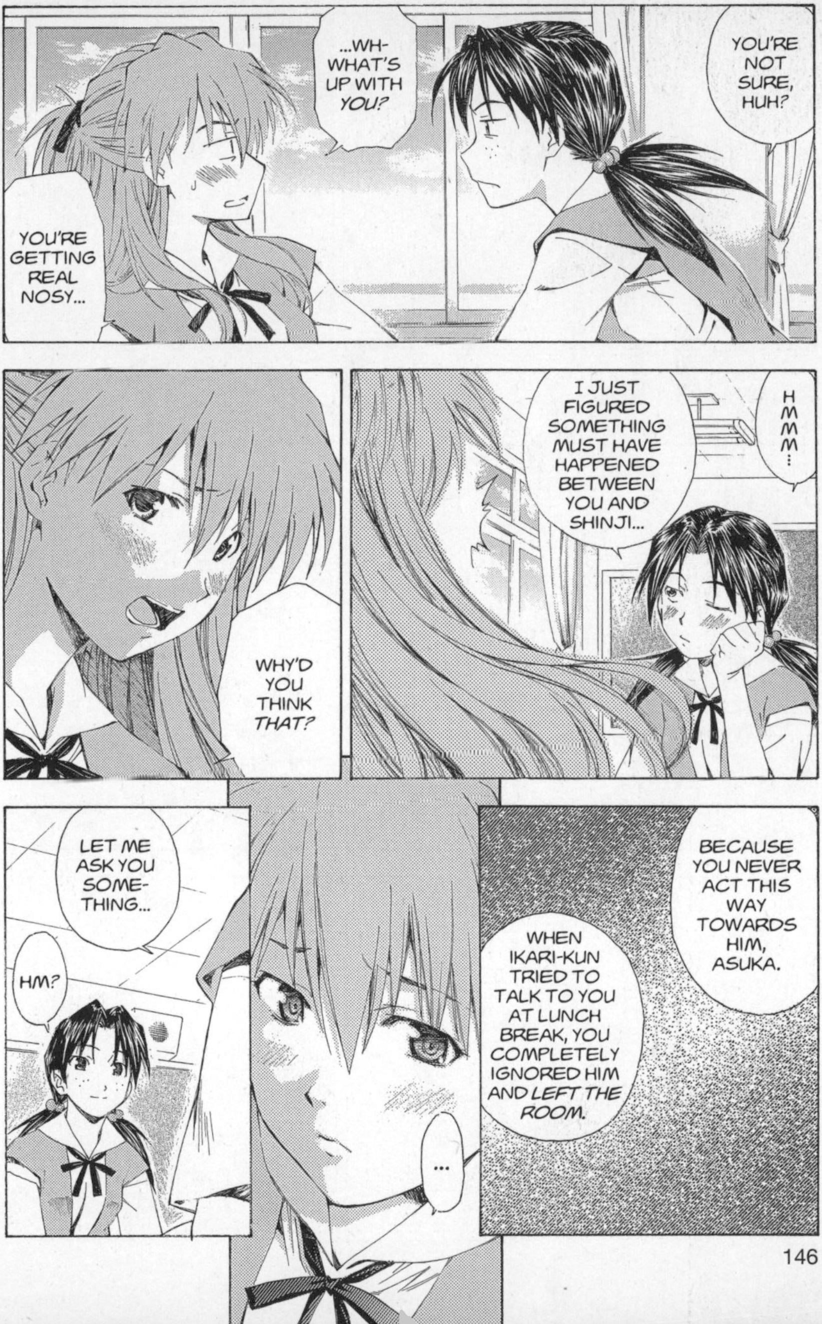
YOU'RE NOT SURE, HUH?
...WH-WHAT'S UP WITH *YOU?*
YOU'RE GETTING REAL NOSY...
HMMM...
I JUST FIGURED SOMETHING MUST HAVE HAPPENED BETWEEN YOU AND SHINJI...
WHY'D YOU THINK *THAT?*
BECAUSE YOU NEVER ACT THIS WAY TOWARDS HIM, ASUKA.
WHEN IKARI-KUN TRIED TO TALK TO YOU AT LUNCH BREAK, YOU COMPLETELY IGNORED HIM AND *LEFT THE ROOM.*
...
LET ME ASK YOU SOME-THING...
HM?

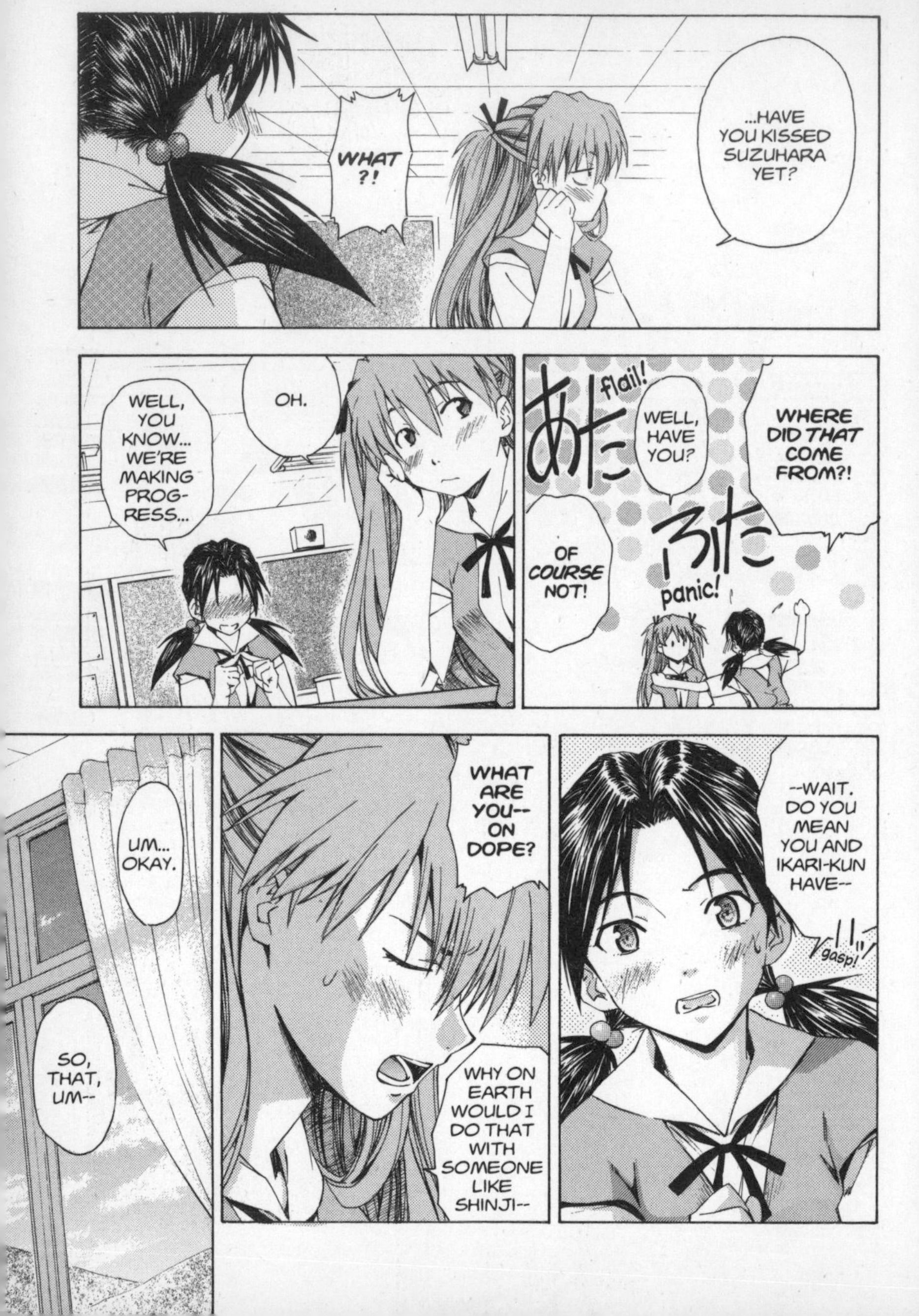
...HAVE YOU KISSED SUZUHARA YET?
WHAT ?!
WHERE DID *THAT* COME FROM?!
WELL, HAVE YOU?
OF COURSE NOT!
flail!
panic!
OH.
WELL, YOU KNOW... WE'RE MAKING PROG-RESS...
--WAIT. DO YOU MEAN YOU AND IKARI-KUN HAVE--
gasp!
WHAT ARE YOU-- ON DOPE?
WHY ON EARTH WOULD I DO THAT WITH SOMEONE LIKE SHINJI--
UM... OKAY.
SO, THAT, UM--

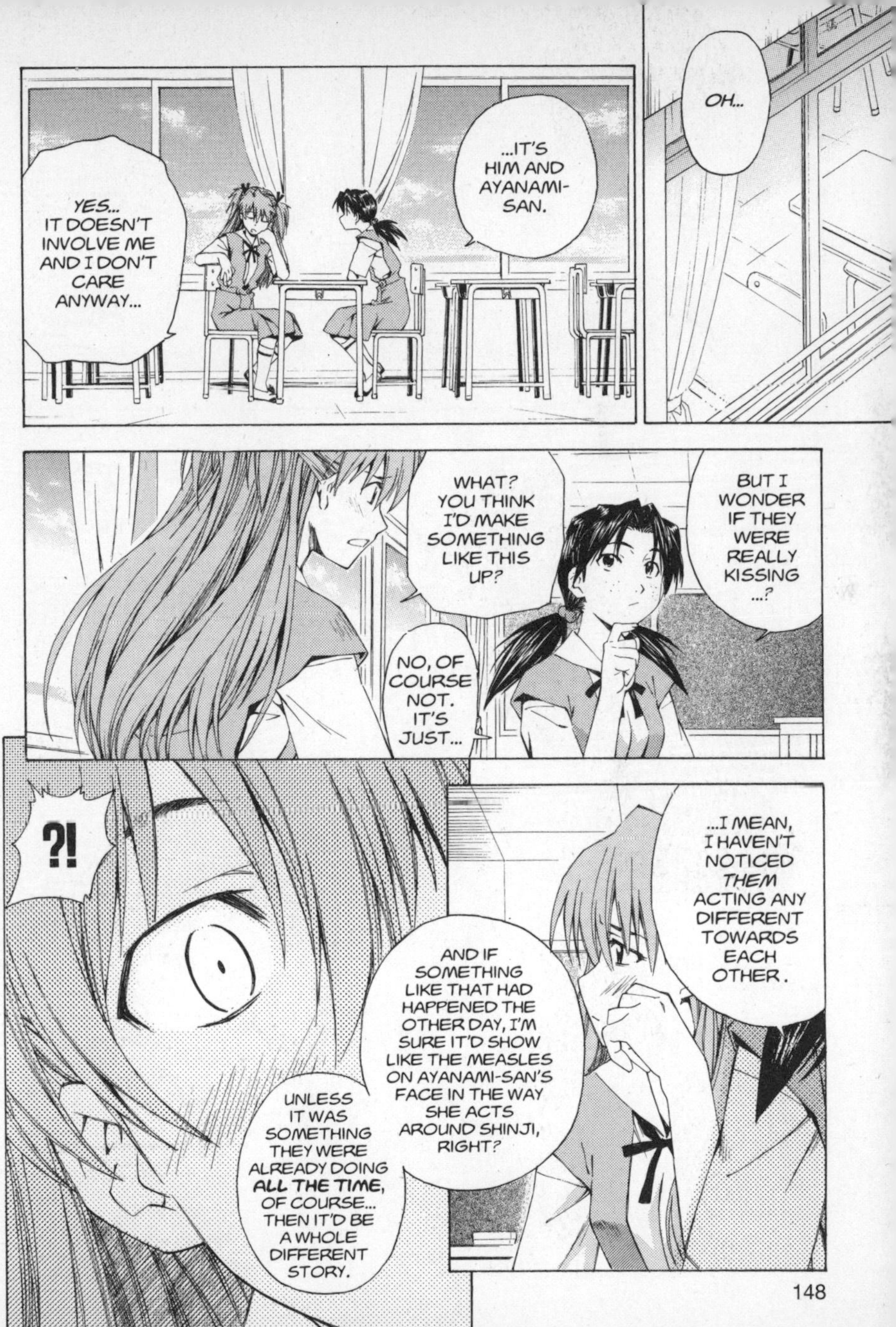
OH...
...IT'S HIM AND AYANAMI-SAN.
YES... IT DOESN'T INVOLVE ME AND I DON'T CARE ANYWAY...
BUT I WONDER IF THEY WERE REALLY KISSING ...?
WHAT? YOU THINK I'D MAKE SOMETHING LIKE THIS UP?
NO, OF COURSE NOT. IT'S JUST...
...I MEAN, I HAVEN'T NOTICED *THEM* ACTING ANY DIFFERENT TOWARDS EACH OTHER.
AND IF SOMETHING LIKE THAT HAD HAPPENED THE OTHER DAY, I'M SURE IT'D SHOW LIKE THE MEASLES ON AYANAMI-SAN'S FACE IN THE WAY SHE ACTS AROUND SHINJI, RIGHT?
?!
UNLESS IT WAS SOMETHING THEY WERE ALREADY DOING **ALL THE TIME**, OF COURSE... THEN IT'D BE A WHOLE DIFFERENT STORY.

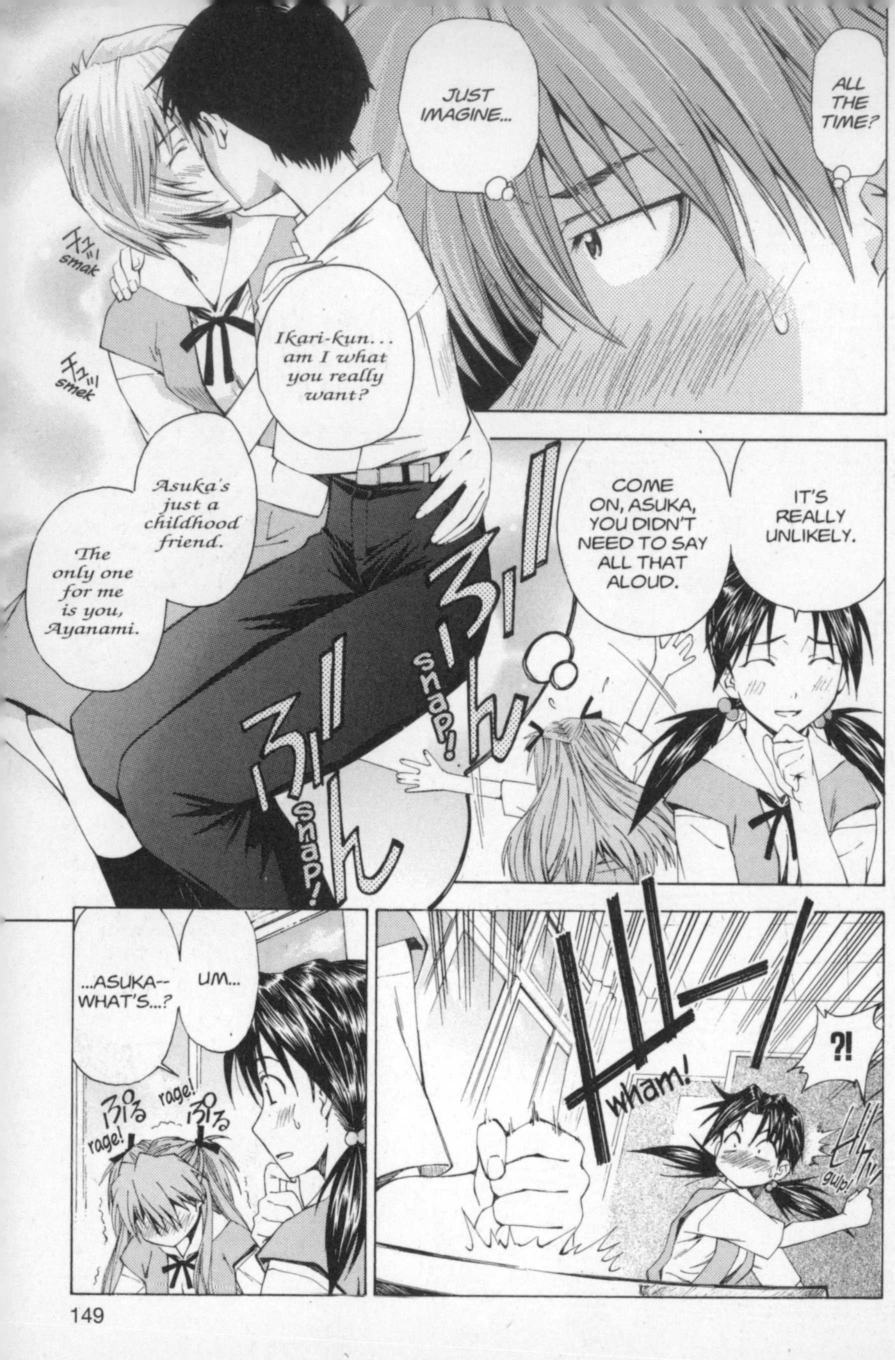
ALL THE TIME?
JUST IMAGINE...
IT'S REALLY UNLIKELY.
COME ON, ASUKA, YOU DIDN'T NEED TO SAY ALL THAT ALOUD.
smak
smek
Ikari-kun... am I what you really want?
Asuka's just a childhood friend.
The only one for me is you, Ayanami.
snap!
snap!
?!
wham!
gulp!
UM...
...ASUKA-- WHAT'S...?
rage!
rage!

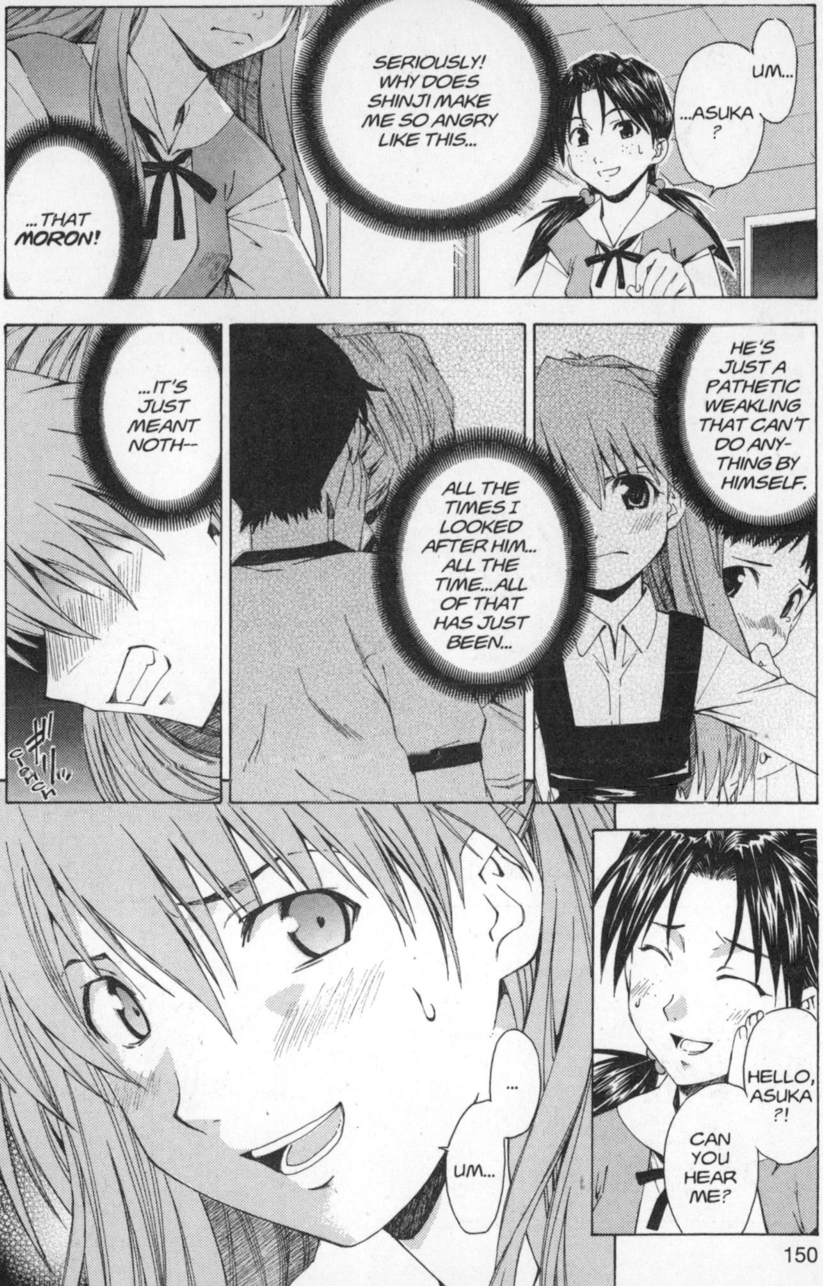
UM...
...ASUKA?
SERIOUSLY! WHY DOES SHINJI MAKE ME SO ANGRY LIKE THIS...
...THAT MORON!
HE'S JUST A PATHETIC WEAKLING THAT CAN'T DO ANYTHING BY HIMSELF.
ALL THE TIMES I LOOKED AFTER HIM... ALL THE TIME...ALL OF THAT HAS JUST BEEN...
...IT'S JUST MEANT NOTH--
HELLO, ASUKA?!
CAN YOU HEAR ME?
...
UM...

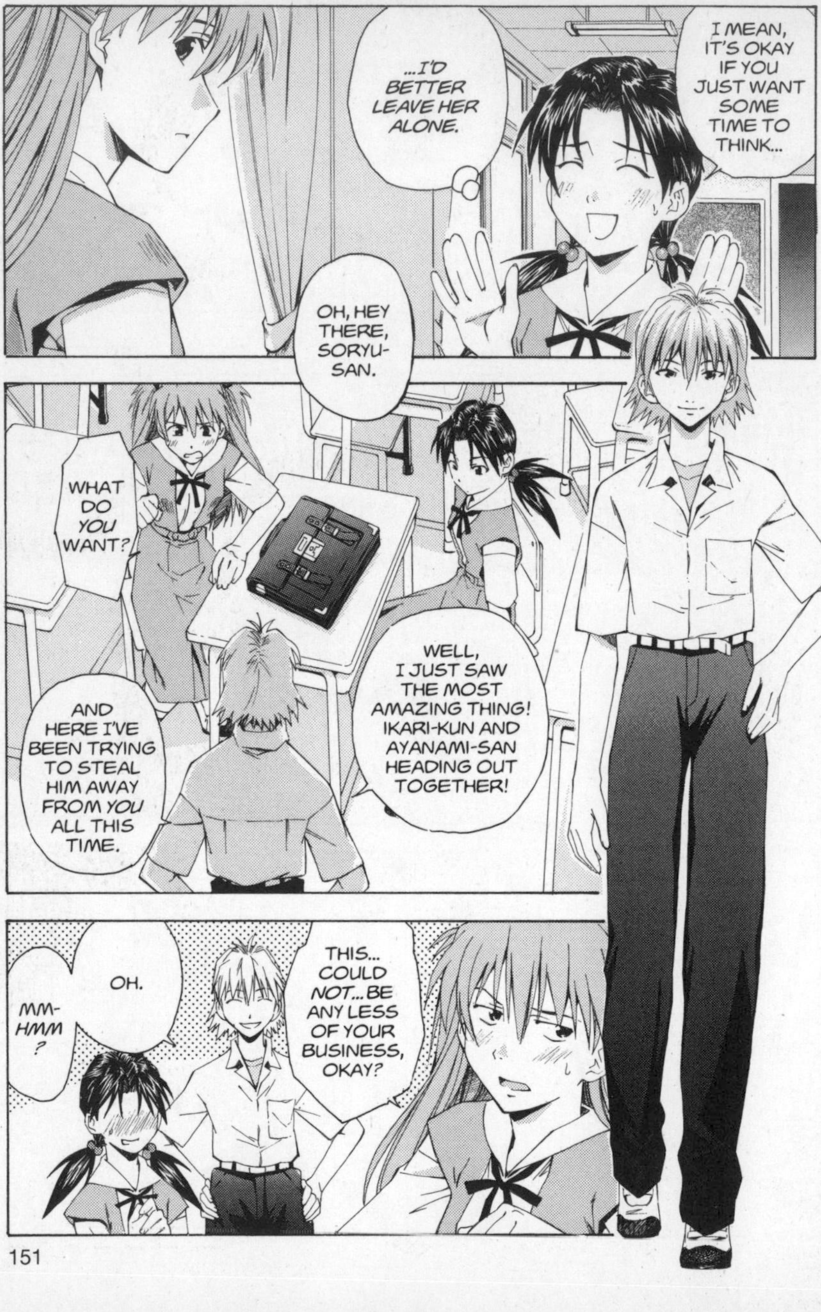
I MEAN, IT'S OKAY IF YOU JUST WANT SOME TIME TO THINK...
...I'D BETTER LEAVE HER ALONE.
OH, HEY THERE, SORYU-SAN.
WHAT DO YOU WANT?
WELL, I JUST SAW THE MOST AMAZING THING! IKARI-KUN AND AYANAMI-SAN HEADING OUT TOGETHER!
AND HERE I'VE BEEN TRYING TO STEAL HIM AWAY FROM YOU ALL THIS TIME.
THIS... COULD NOT...BE ANY LESS OF YOUR BUSINESS, OKAY?
OH.
MM-HMM?

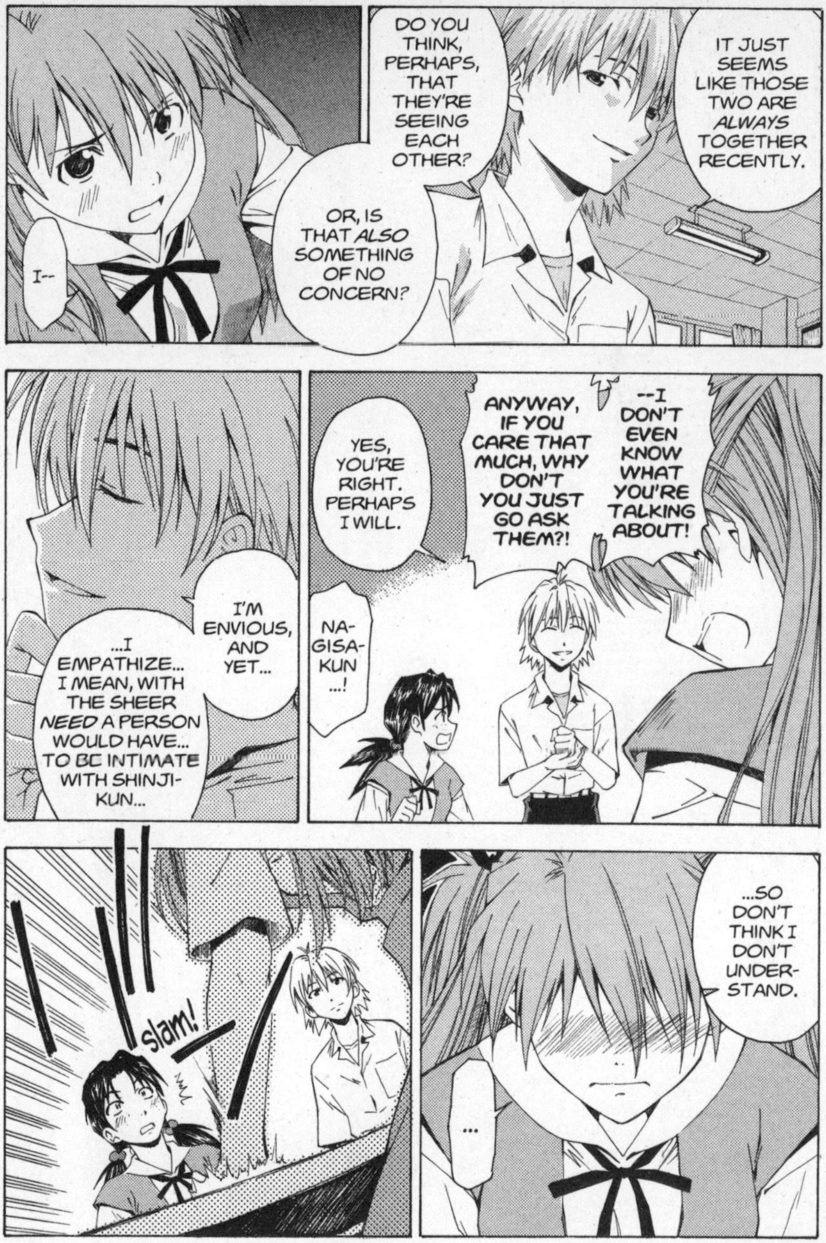
IT JUST SEEMS LIKE THOSE TWO ARE *ALWAYS* TOGETHER RECENTLY.
DO YOU THINK, PERHAPS, THAT THEY'RE SEEING EACH OTHER?
OR, IS THAT *ALSO* SOMETHING OF NO CONCERN?
I--
--I DON'T EVEN KNOW WHAT YOU'RE TALKING ABOUT!
ANYWAY, IF YOU CARE THAT MUCH, WHY DON'T YOU JUST GO ASK THEM?!
YES, YOU'RE RIGHT. PERHAPS I WILL.
NA-GISA-KUN ...!
I'M ENVIOUS, AND YET...
...I EMPATHIZE... I MEAN, WITH THE SHEER *NEED* A PERSON WOULD HAVE... TO BE INTIMATE WITH SHINJI-KUN...
...SO DON'T THINK I DON'T UNDER-STAND.
...
slam!

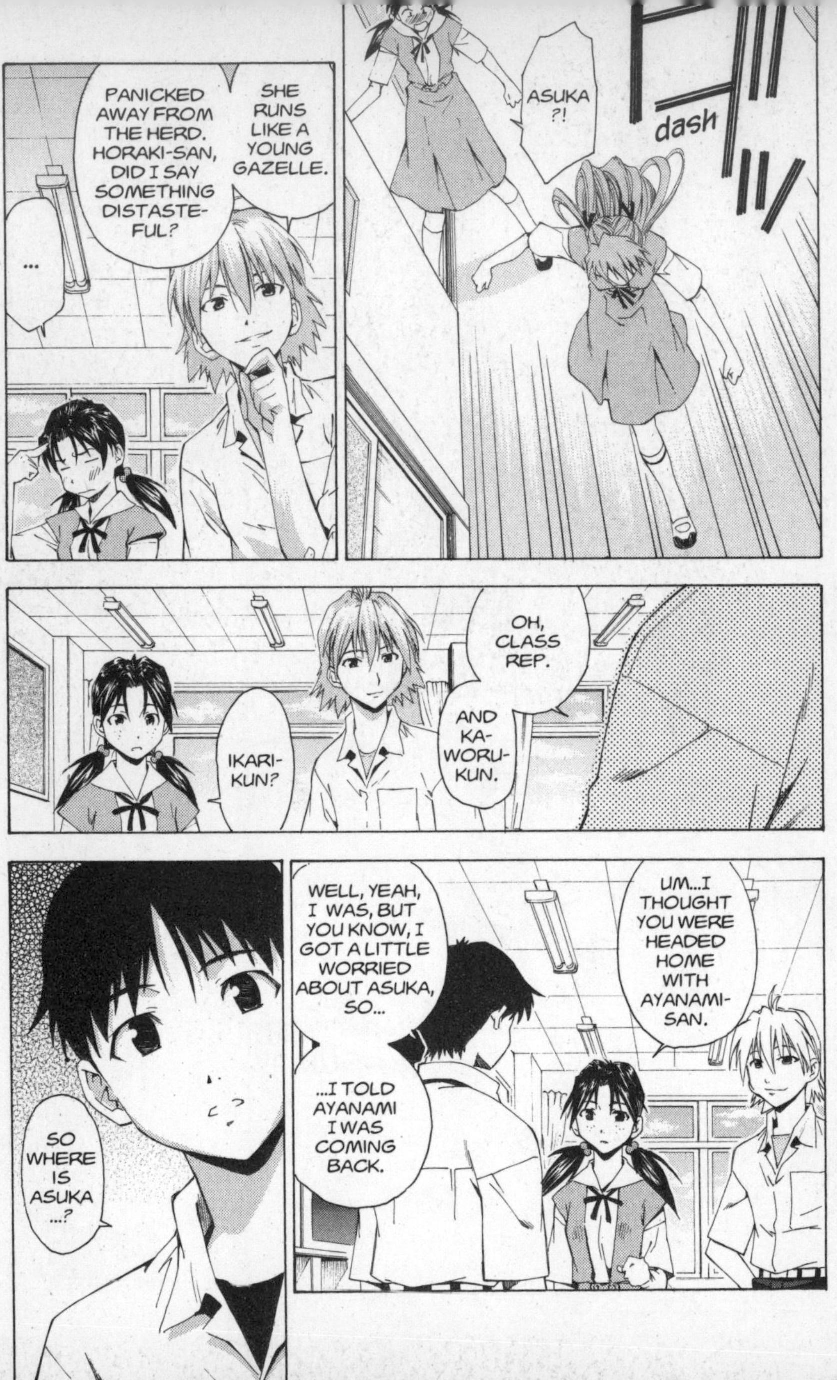
dash
ASUKA?!
SHE RUNS LIKE A YOUNG GAZELLE.
PANICKED AWAY FROM THE HERD. HORAKI-SAN, DID I SAY SOMETHING DISTASTE-FUL?
...
OH, CLASS REP.
AND KA-WORU-KUN.
IKARI-KUN?
UM...I THOUGHT YOU WERE HEADED HOME WITH AYANAMI-SAN.
WELL, YEAH, I WAS, BUT YOU KNOW, I GOT A LITTLE WORRIED ABOUT ASUKA, SO...
...I TOLD AYANAMI I WAS COMING BACK.
SO WHERE IS ASUKA ...?

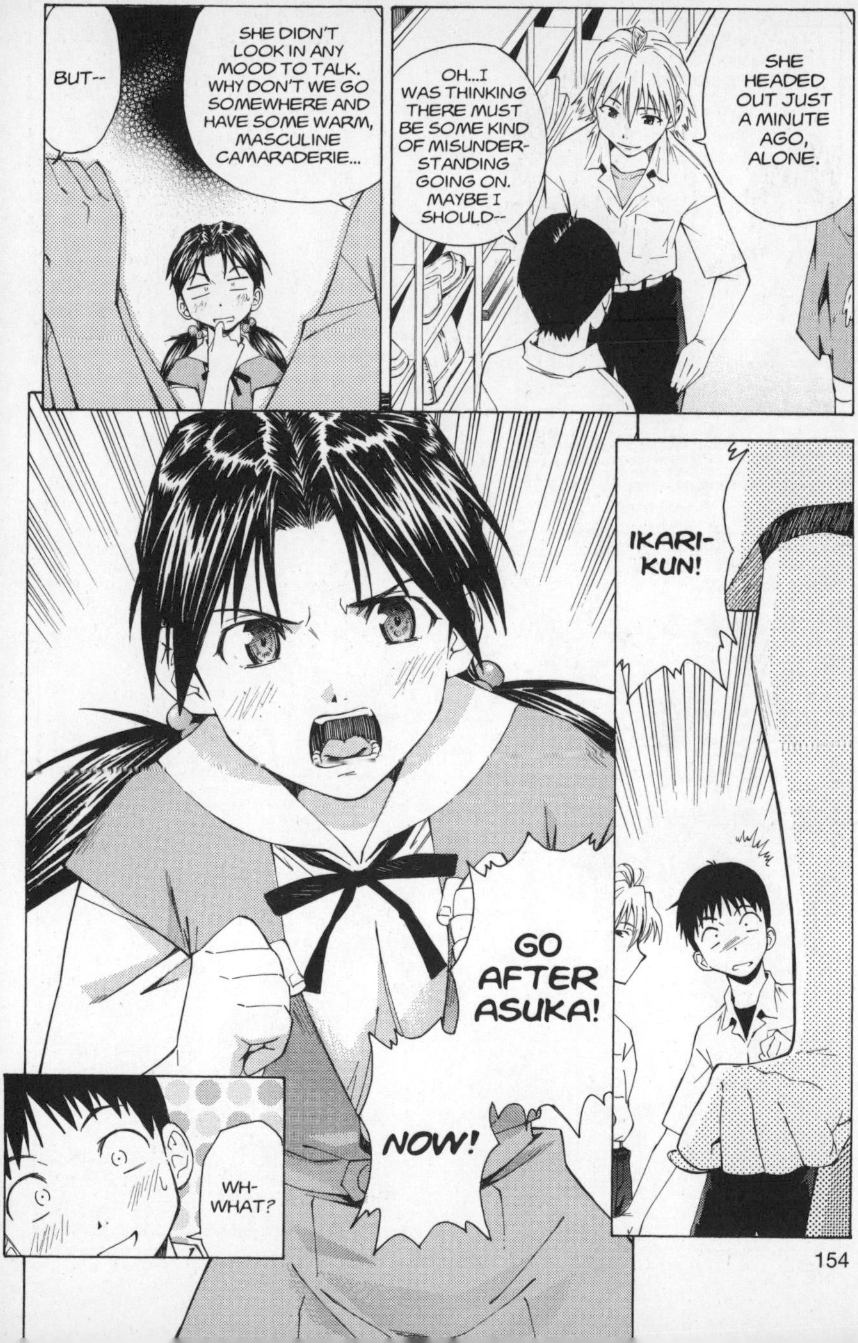
SHE HEADED OUT JUST A MINUTE AGO, ALONE.
OH...I WAS THINKING THERE MUST BE SOME KIND OF MISUNDER-STANDING GOING ON. MAYBE I SHOULD--
SHE DIDN'T LOOK IN ANY MOOD TO TALK. WHY DON'T WE GO SOMEWHERE AND HAVE SOME WARM, MASCULINE CAMARADERIE...
BUT--
IKARI-KUN!
GO AFTER ASUKA!
NOW!
WH-WHAT?

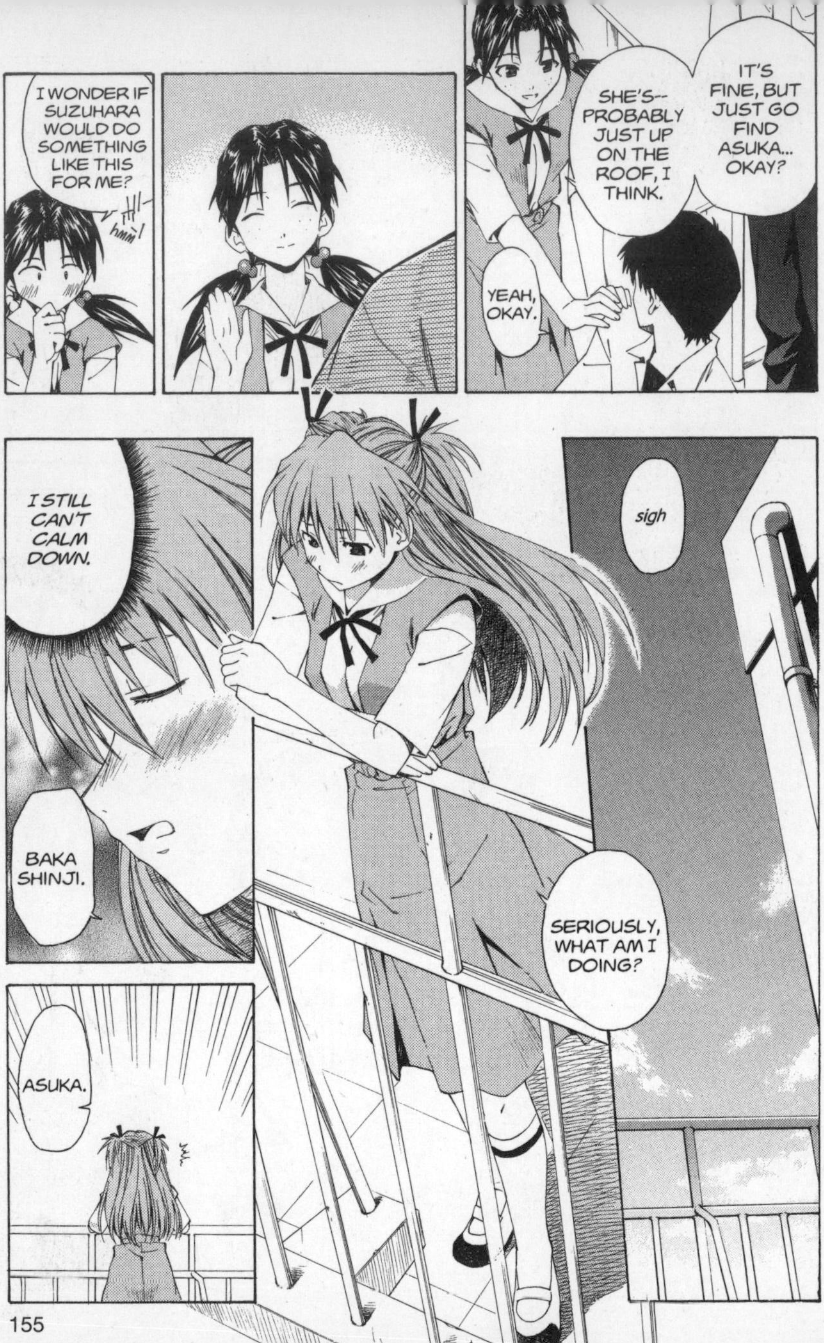

IT'S FINE, BUT JUST GO FIND ASUKA... OKAY?
SHE'S-- PROBABLY JUST UP ON THE ROOF, I THINK.
YEAH, OKAY.
I WONDER IF SUZUHARA WOULD DO SOMETHING LIKE THIS FOR ME?
sigh
SERIOUSLY, WHAT AM I DOING?
I STILL CAN'T CALM DOWN.
BAKA SHINJI.
ASUKA.

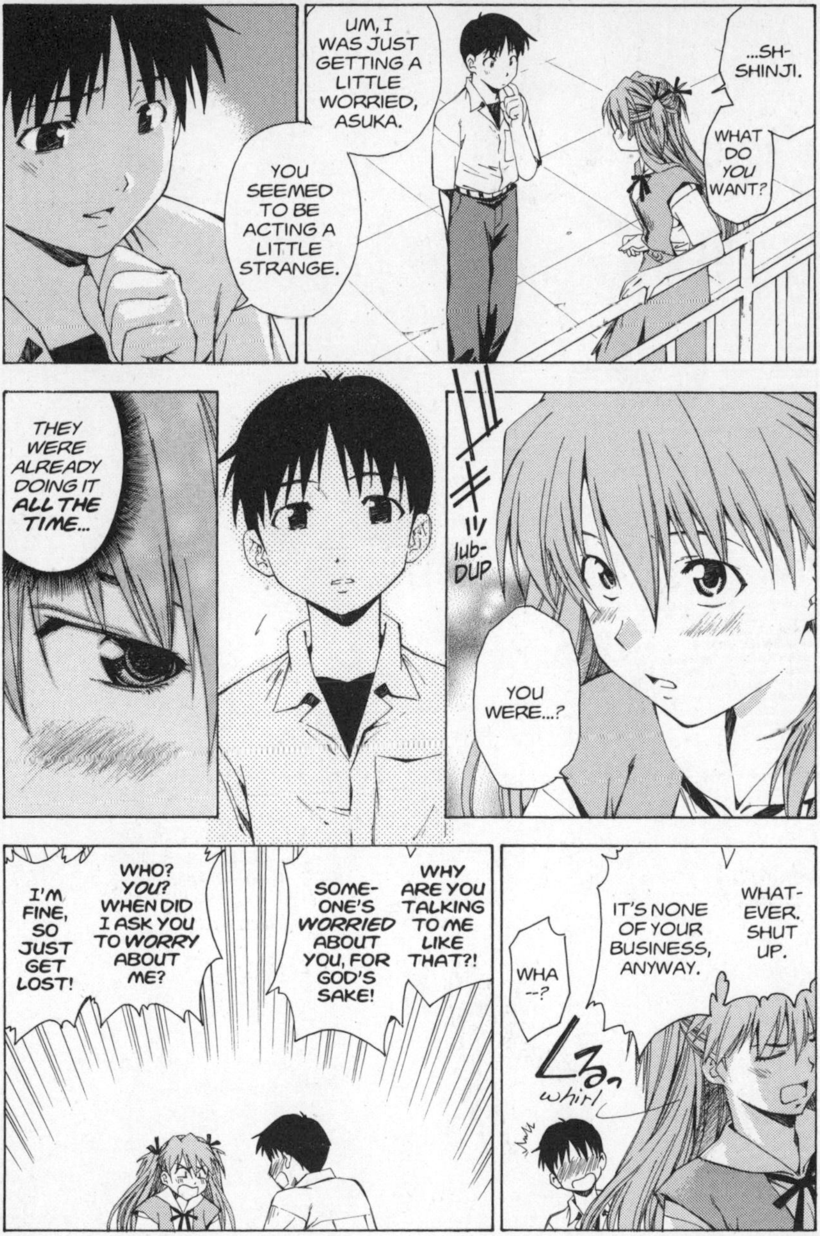
...SH-SHINJI.
WHAT DO YOU WANT?
UM, I WAS JUST GETTING A LITTLE WORRIED, ASUKA.
YOU SEEMED TO BE ACTING A LITTLE STRANGE.
lub-DUP
YOU WERE...?
THEY WERE ALREADY DOING IT ALL THE TIME...
WHAT-EVER. SHUT UP.
IT'S NONE OF YOUR BUSINESS, ANYWAY.
WHA--?
whirl
WHY ARE YOU TALKING TO ME LIKE THAT?!
SOME-ONE'S WORRIED ABOUT YOU, FOR GOD'S SAKE!
WHO? YOU? WHEN DID I ASK YOU TO WORRY ABOUT ME?
I'M FINE, SO JUST GET LOST!

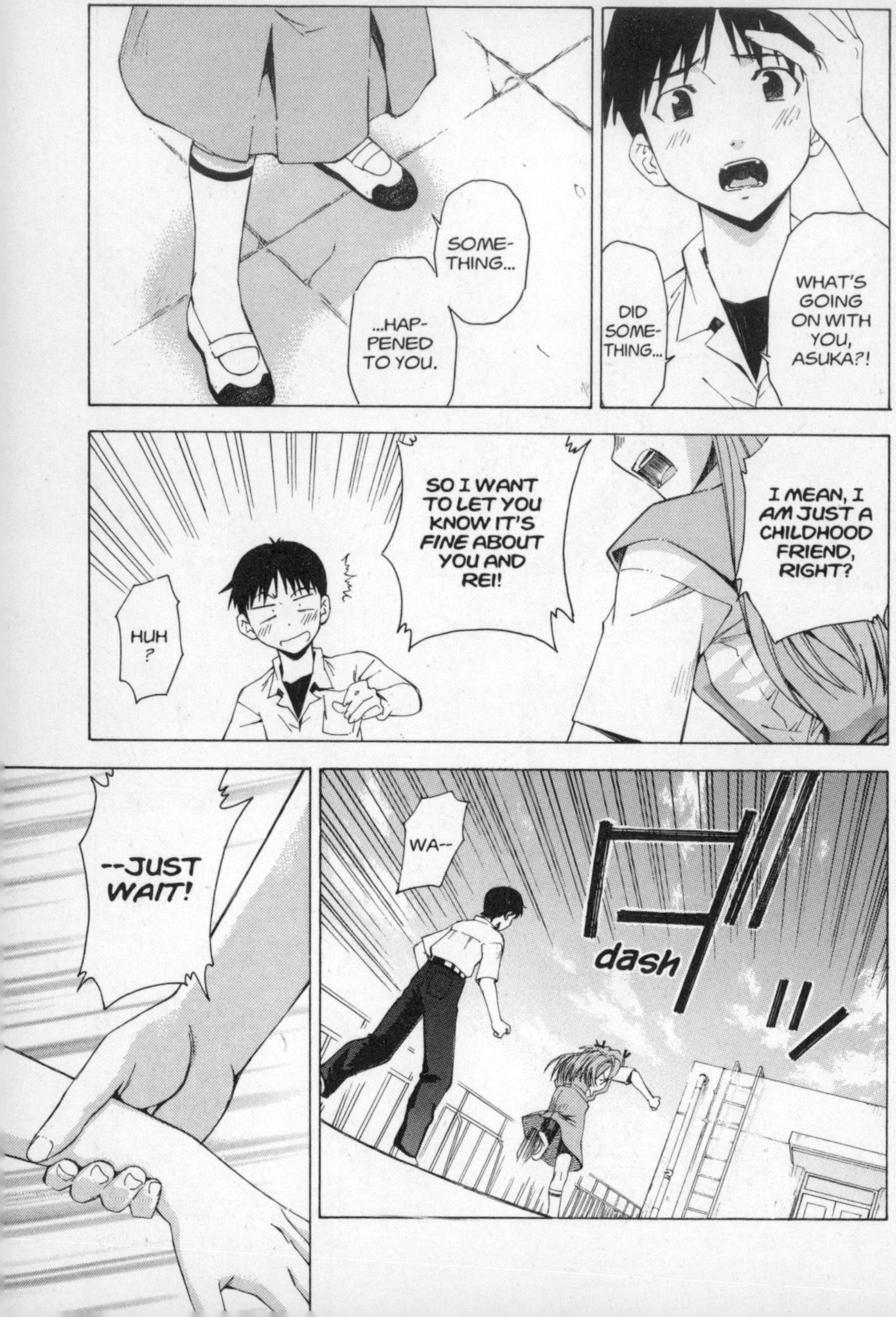
WHAT'S GOING ON WITH YOU, ASUKA?!
DID SOMETHING...
SOME-THING...
...HAP-PENED TO YOU.
I MEAN, I AM JUST A CHILDHOOD FRIEND, RIGHT?
SO I WANT TO LET YOU KNOW IT'S *FINE* ABOUT YOU AND REI!
HUH ?
WA--
dash
--JUST WAIT!

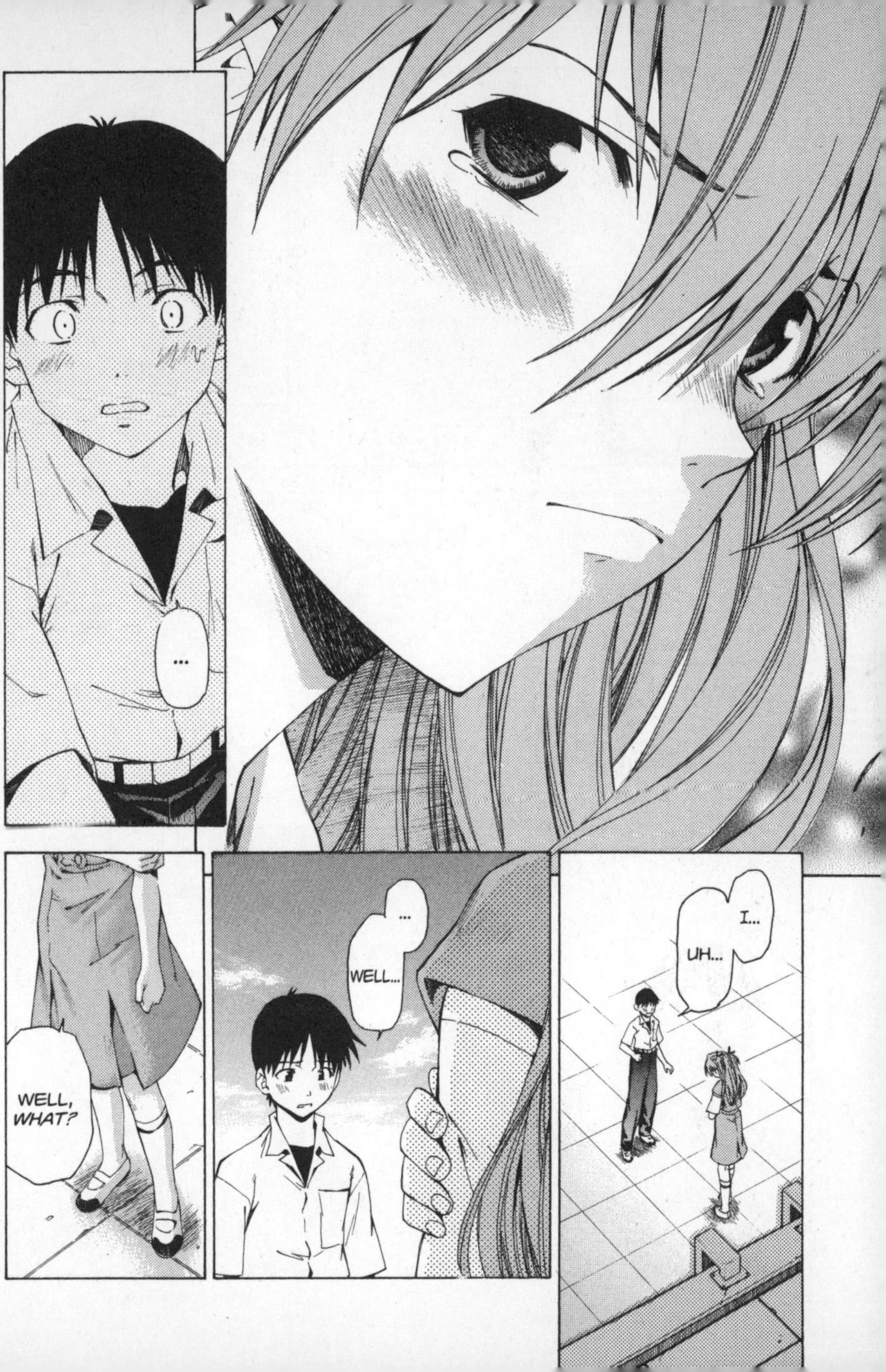
...
I...
UH...
...
WELL...
WELL, WHAT?

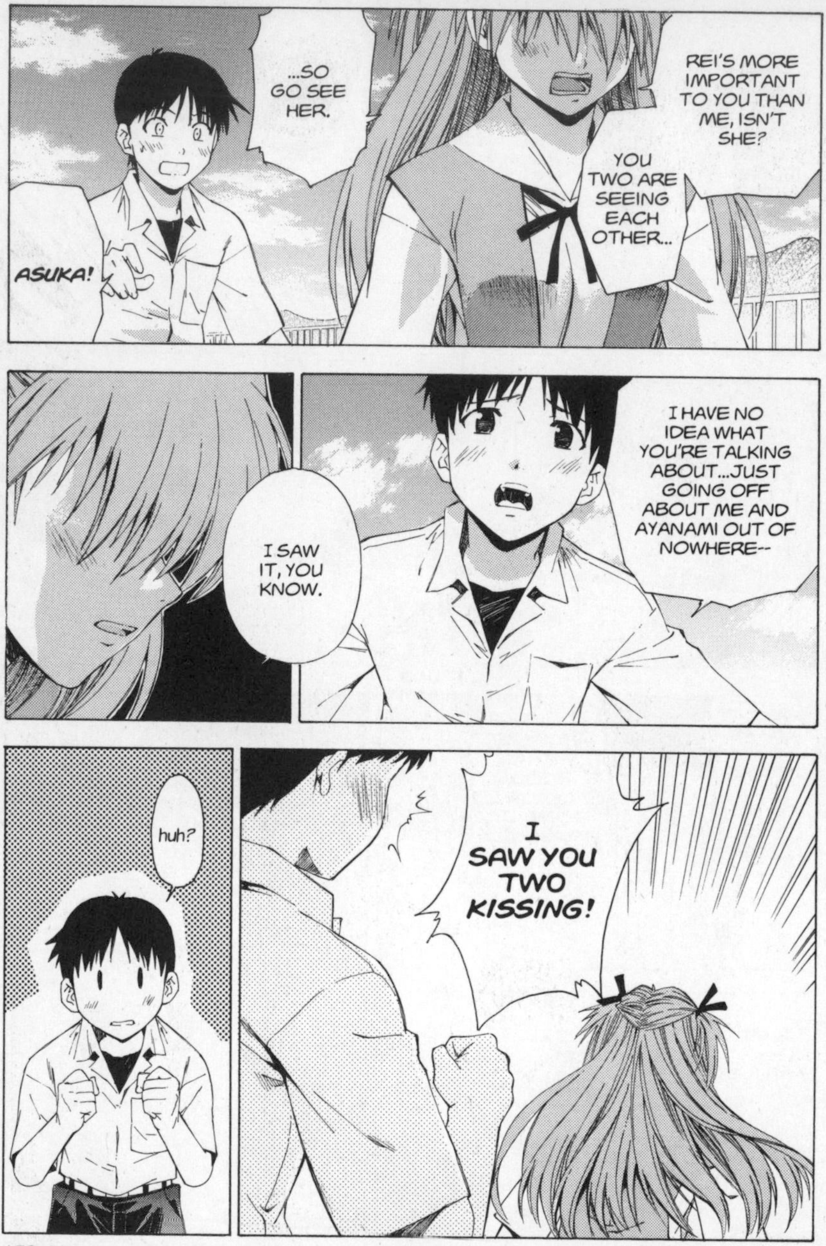
REI'S MORE IMPORTANT TO YOU THAN ME, ISN'T SHE?
YOU TWO ARE SEEING EACH OTHER...
...SO GO SEE HER.
ASUKA!
I HAVE NO IDEA WHAT YOU'RE TALKING ABOUT...JUST GOING OFF ABOUT ME AND AYANAMI OUT OF NOWHERE--
I SAW IT, YOU KNOW.
I SAW YOU TWO KISSING!
huh?

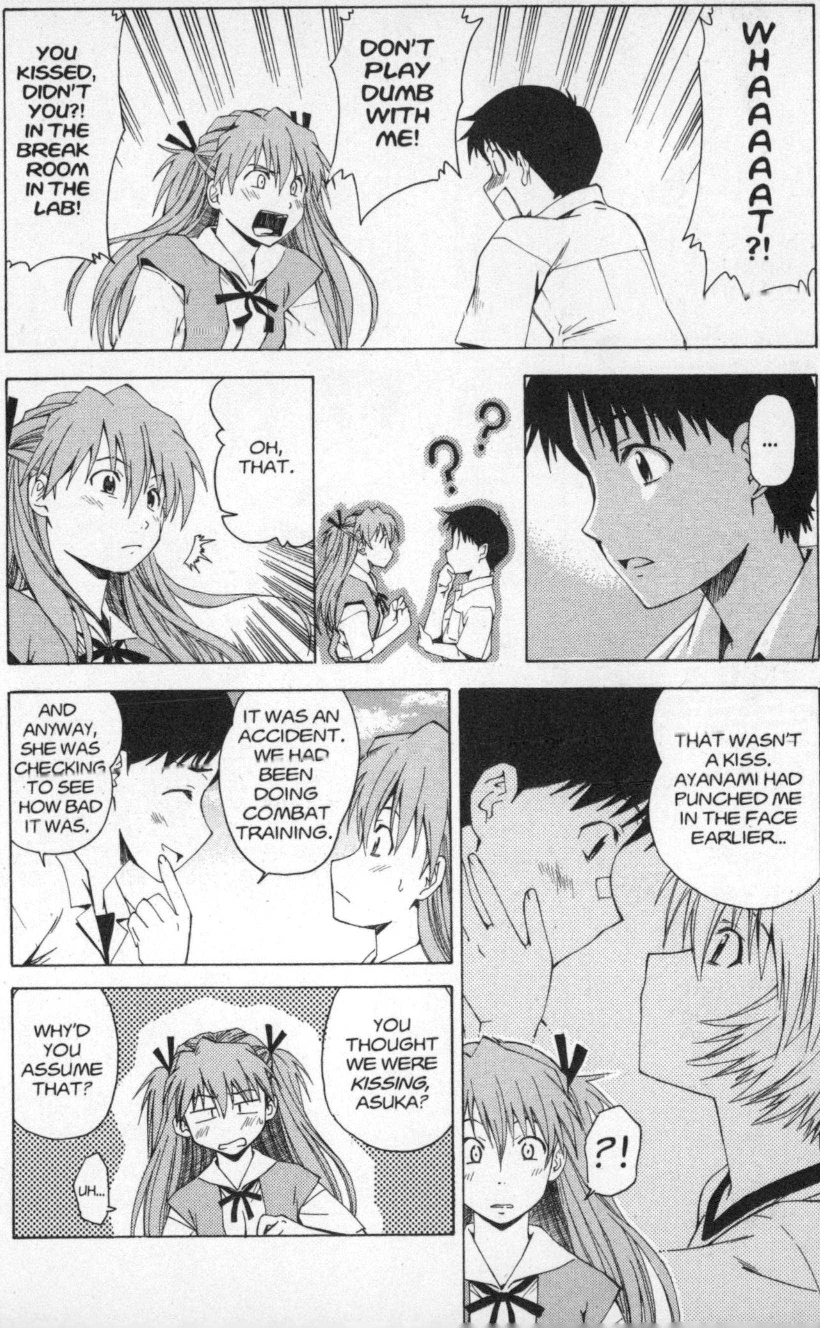
WHAAAAAAT?!
DON'T PLAY DUMB WITH ME!
YOU KISSED, DIDN'T YOU?! IN THE BREAK ROOM IN THE LAB!
...
OH, THAT.
THAT WASN'T A KISS. AYANAMI HAD PUNCHED ME IN THE FACE EARLIER...
?!
IT WAS AN ACCIDENT. WE HAD BEEN DOING COMBAT TRAINING.
AND ANYWAY, SHE WAS CHECKING TO SEE HOW BAD IT WAS.
YOU THOUGHT WE WERE *KISSING*, ASUKA?
WHY'D YOU ASSUME THAT?
UH...

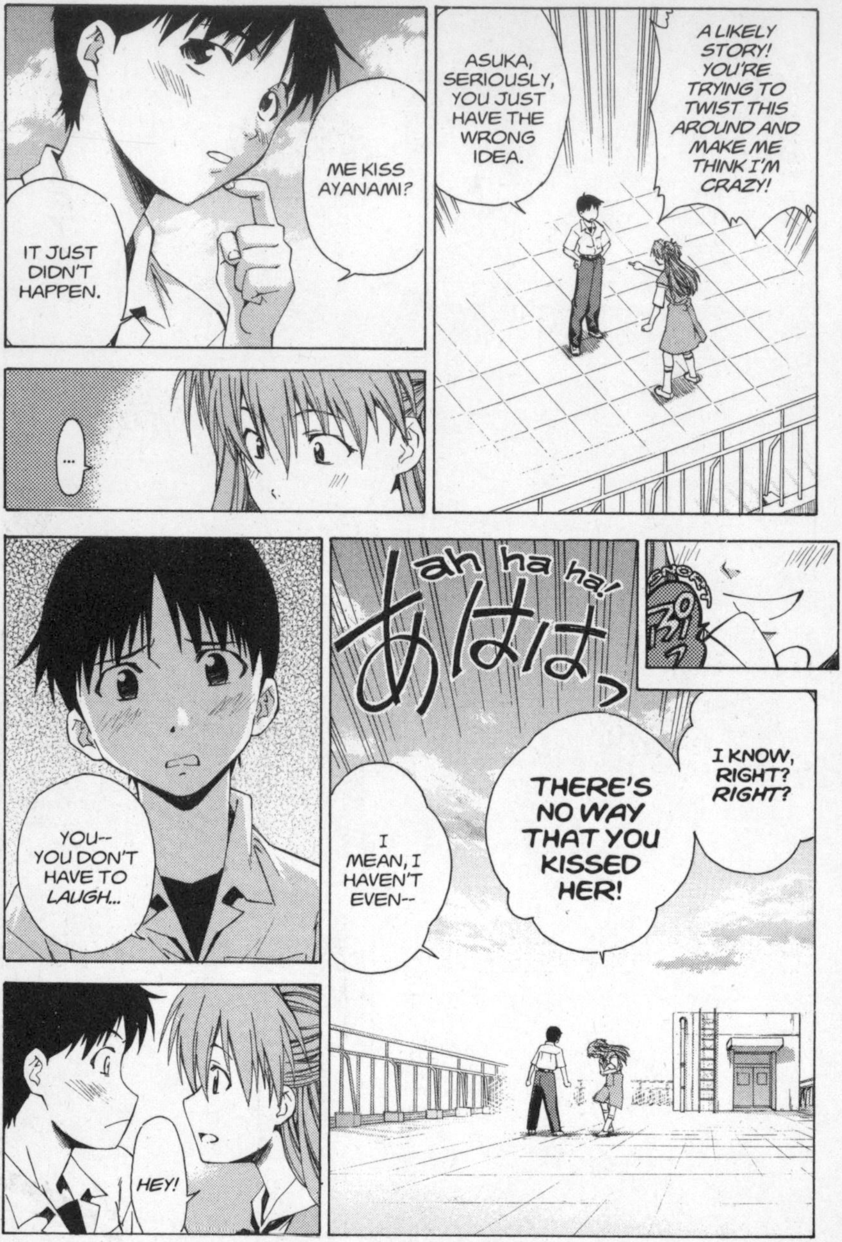
A LIKELY STORY! YOU'RE TRYING TO TWIST THIS AROUND AND MAKE ME THINK I'M CRAZY!
ASUKA, SERIOUSLY, YOU JUST HAVE THE WRONG IDEA.
ME KISS AYANAMI?
IT JUST DIDN'T HAPPEN.
...
SNORT
ぷっ
ah ha ha!
あはは
I KNOW, RIGHT? RIGHT?
THERE'S NO WAY THAT YOU KISSED HER!
I MEAN, I HAVEN'T EVEN--
YOU-- YOU DON'T HAVE TO LAUGH...
HEY!

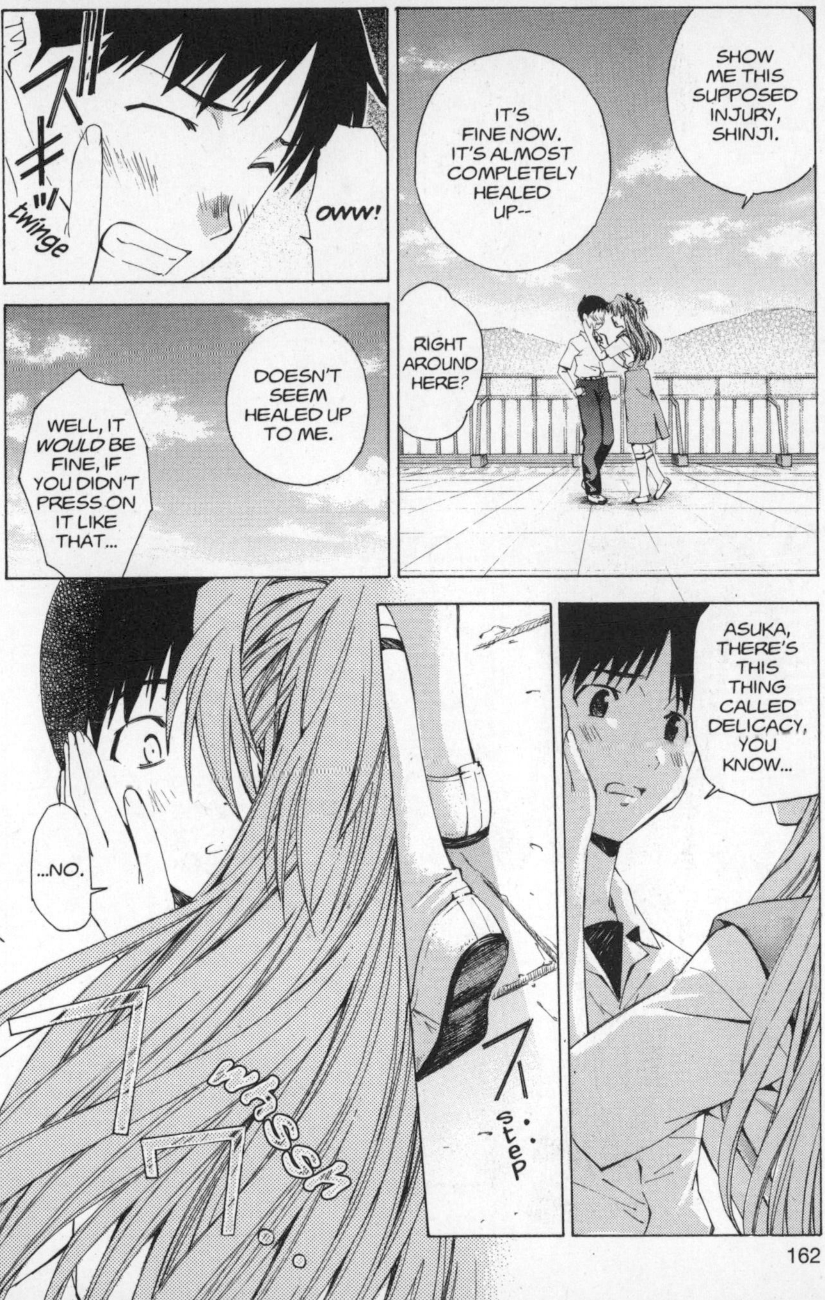
SHOW ME THIS SUPPOSED INJURY, SHINJI.
IT'S FINE NOW. IT'S ALMOST COMPLETELY HEALED UP--
RIGHT AROUND HERE?
twinge
OWW!
DOESN'T SEEM HEALED UP TO ME.
WELL, IT *WOULD* BE FINE, IF YOU DIDN'T PRESS ON IT LIKE THAT...
ASUKA, THERE'S THIS THING CALLED DELICACY, YOU KNOW...
step
whssh
...NO.

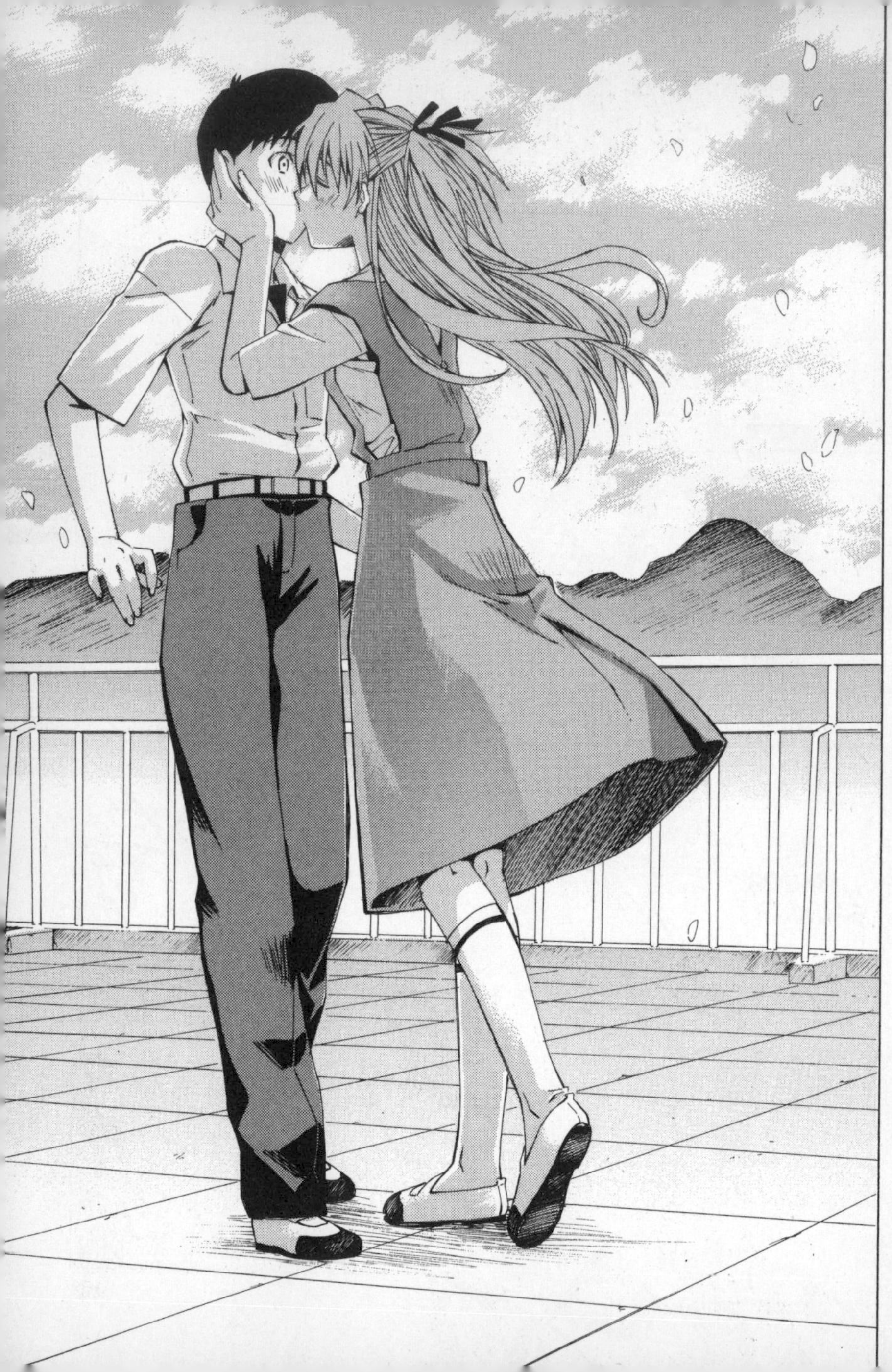

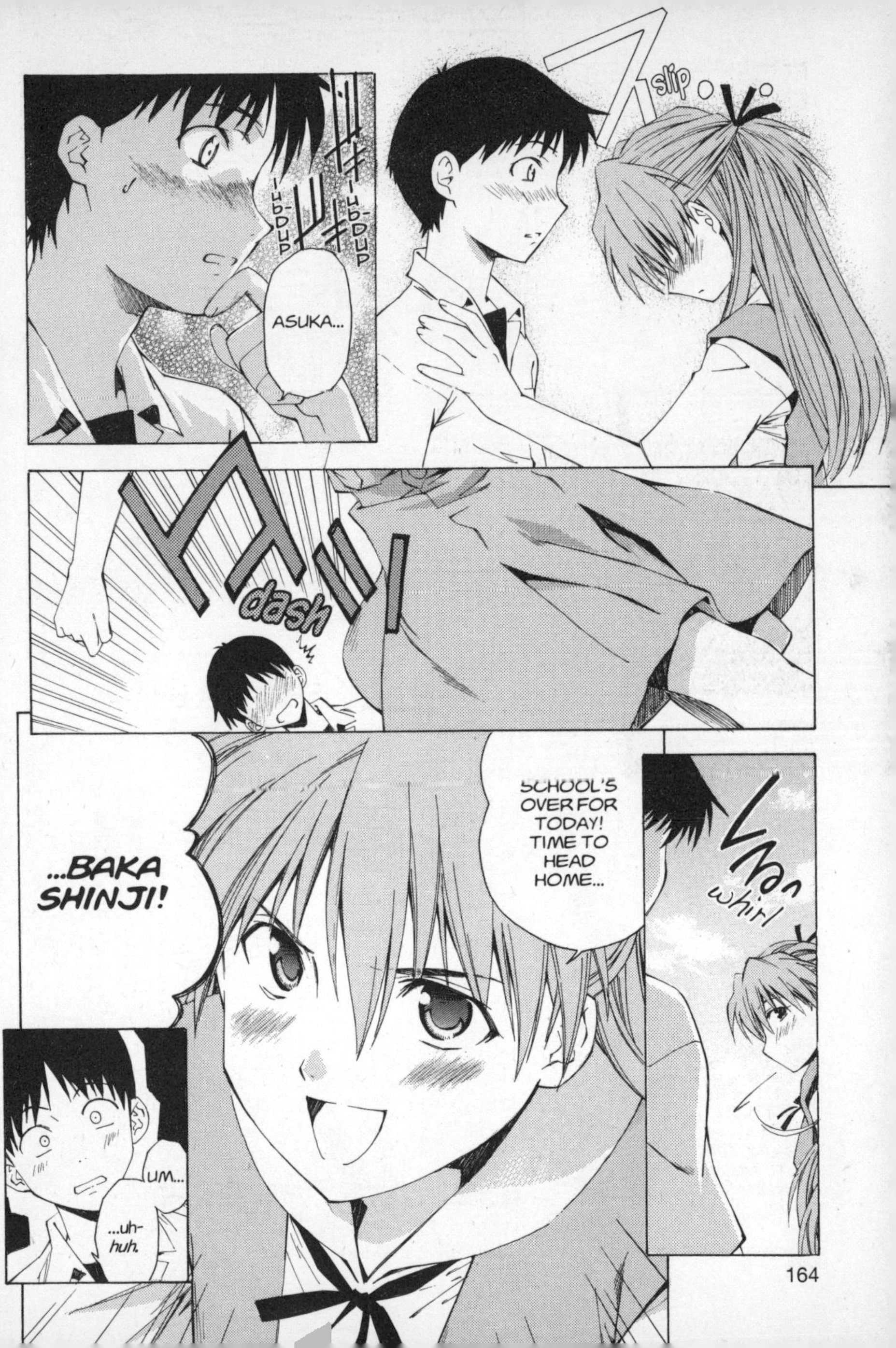

slip
dub-DUP
dub-DUP
ASUKA...
dash
whirl
SCHOOL'S OVER FOR TODAY! TIME TO HEAD HOME...
...BAKA SHINJI!
um...
...uh-huh.

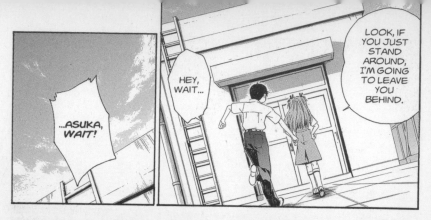

...ASUKA, WAIT!

HEY, WAIT...

LOOK, IF YOU JUST STAND AROUND, I'M GOING TO LEAVE YOU BEHIND.

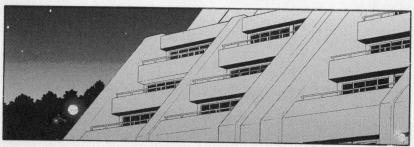

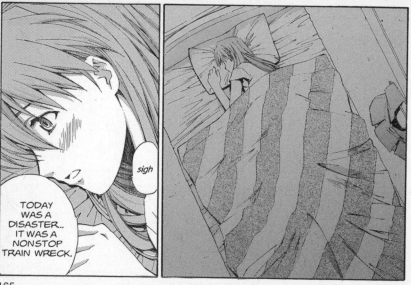

sigh

TODAY WAS A DISASTER... IT WAS A NONSTOP TRAIN WRECK.

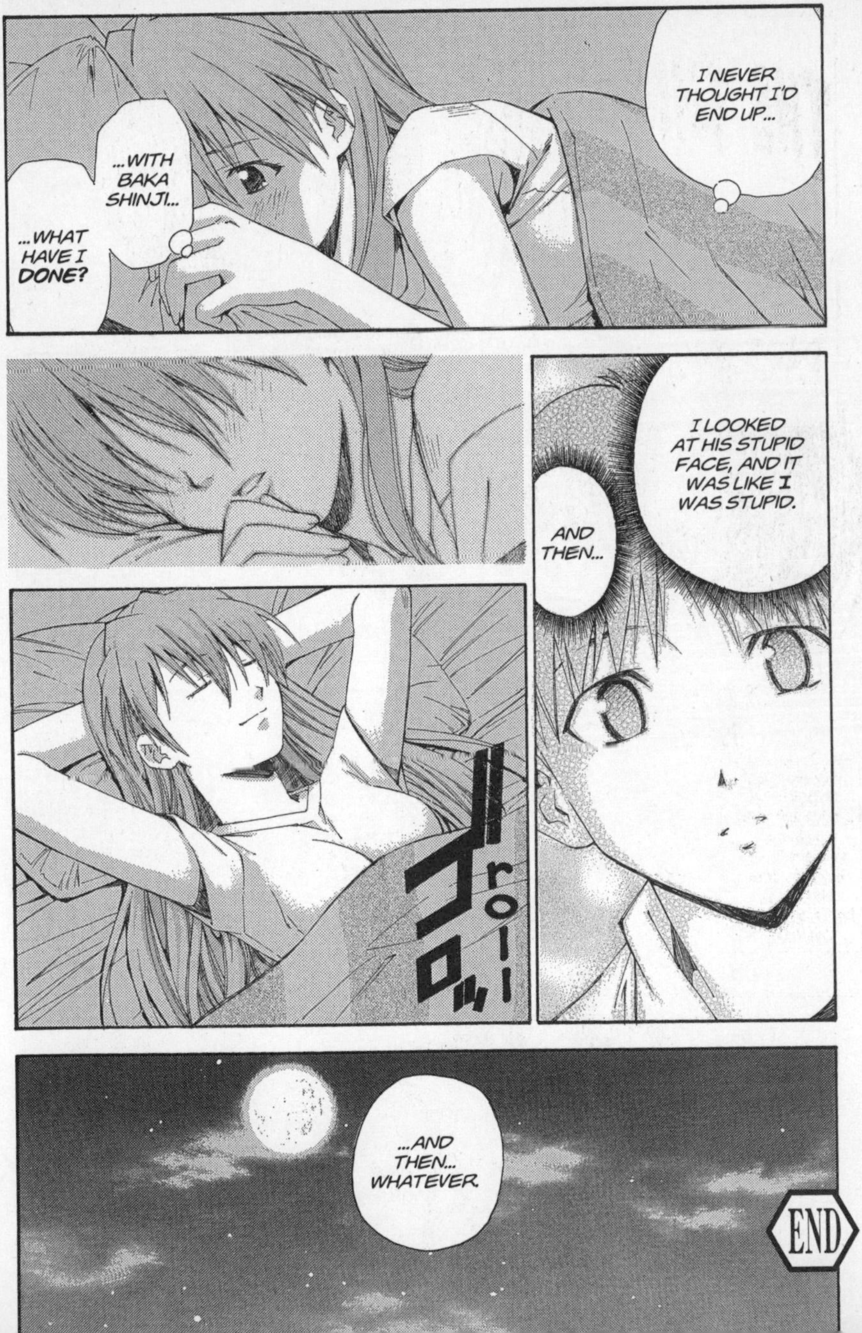
I NEVER THOUGHT I'D END UP...
...WITH BAKA SHINJI...
...WHAT HAVE I DONE?
I LOOKED AT HIS STUPID FACE, AND IT WAS LIKE I WAS STUPID.
AND THEN...
roll
...AND THEN... WHATEVER.
END

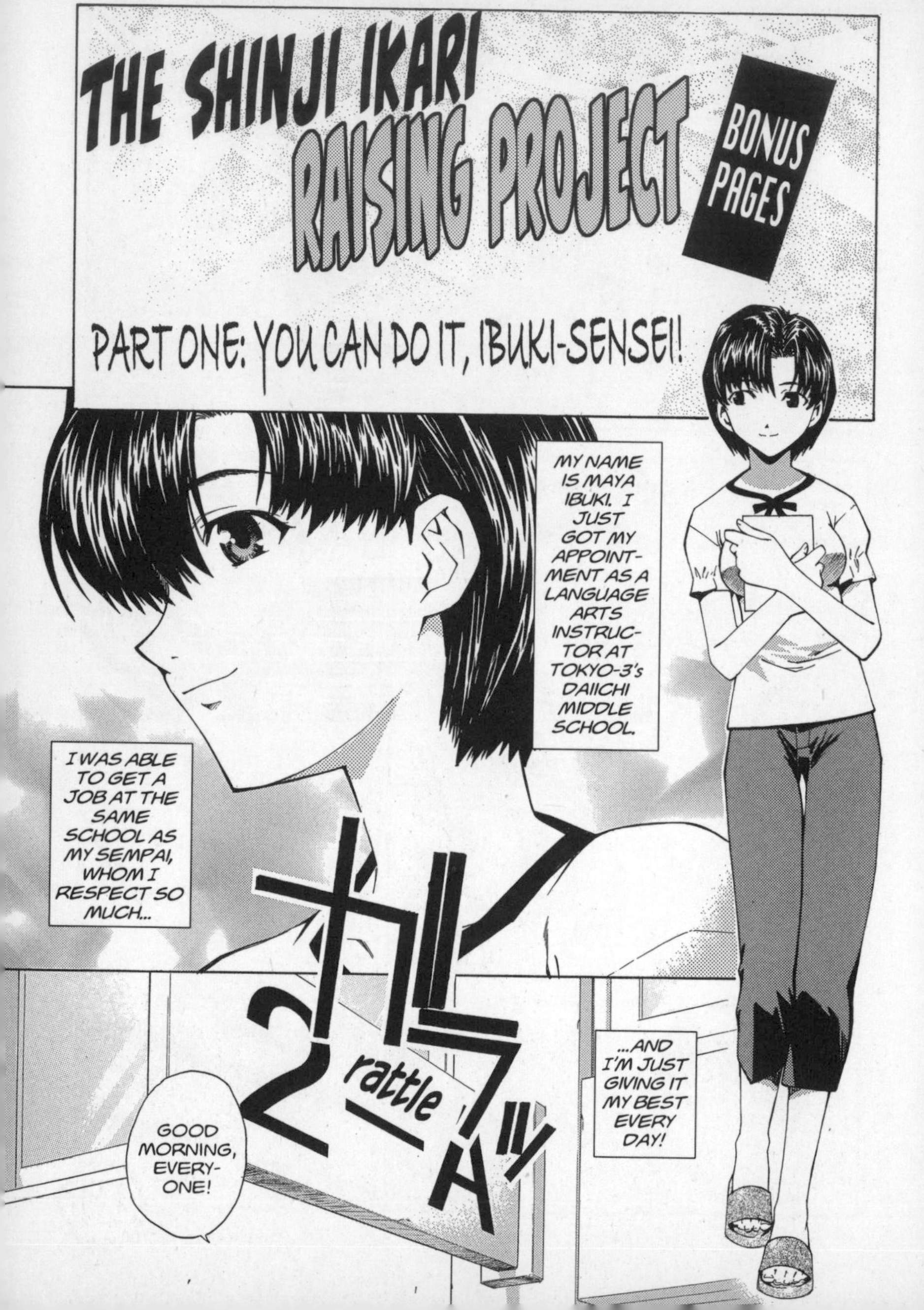
THE SHINJI IKARI RAISING PROJECT
BONUS PAGES
PART ONE: YOU CAN DO IT, IBUKI-SENSEI!
MY NAME IS MAYA IBUKI. I JUST GOT MY APPOINTMENT AS A LANGUAGE ARTS INSTRUCTOR AT TOKYO-3's DAIICHI MIDDLE SCHOOL.
I WAS ABLE TO GET A JOB AT THE SAME SCHOOL AS MY SEMPAI, WHOM I RESPECT SO MUCH...
...AND I'M JUST GIVING IT MY BEST EVERY DAY!
rattle
GOOD MORNING, EVERY-ONE!

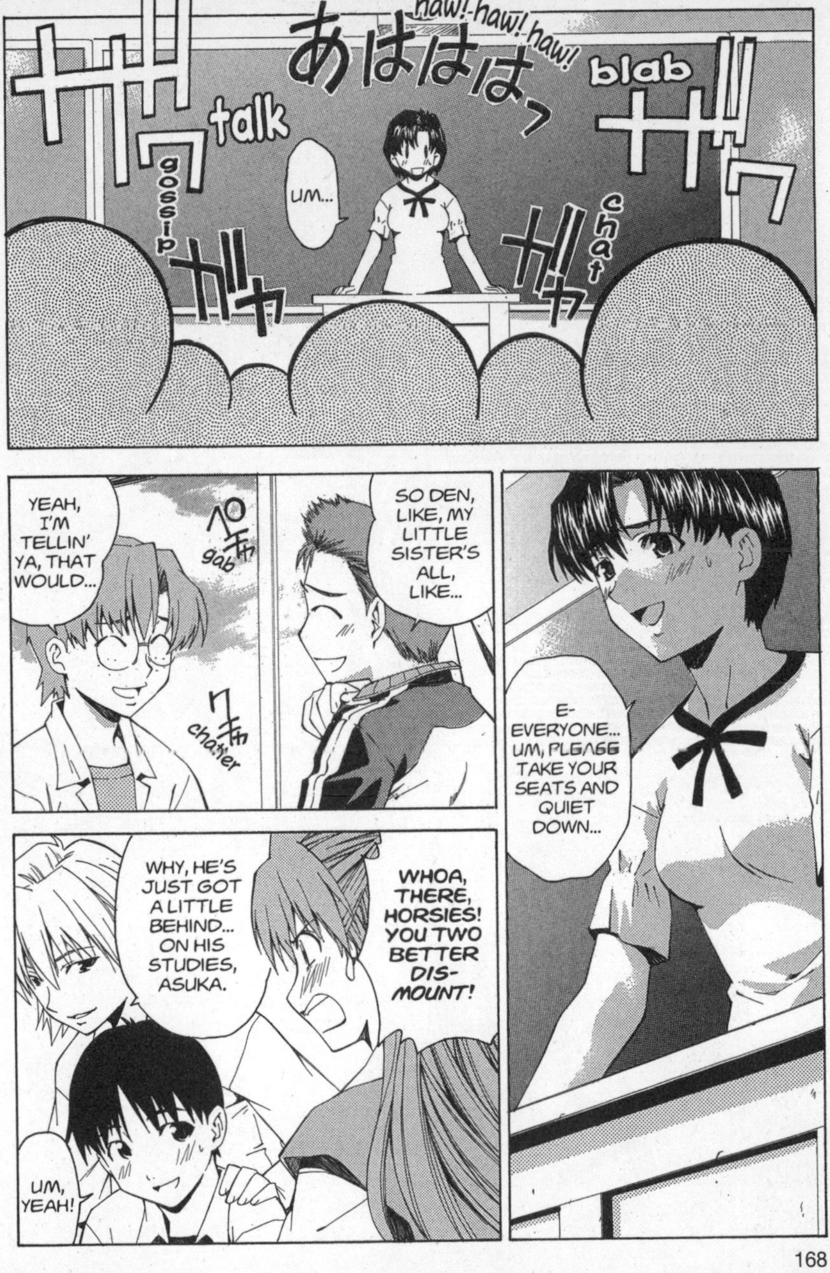
blab
ザワ
haw!-haw! haw!
あははっ
chat
ガヤ
UM...
talk
ザワ
gossip
ガヤ
E-EVERYONE... UM, PLEASE TAKE YOUR SEATS AND QUIET DOWN...
SO DEN, LIKE, MY LITTLE SISTER'S ALL, LIKE...
ワキャ chatter
YEAH, I'M TELLIN' YA, THAT WOULD...
ヘキャ gab
WHOA, THERE, HORSIES! YOU TWO BETTER DIS-MOUNT!
WHY, HE'S JUST GOT A LITTLE BEHIND... ON HIS STUDIES, ASUKA.
UM, YEAH!

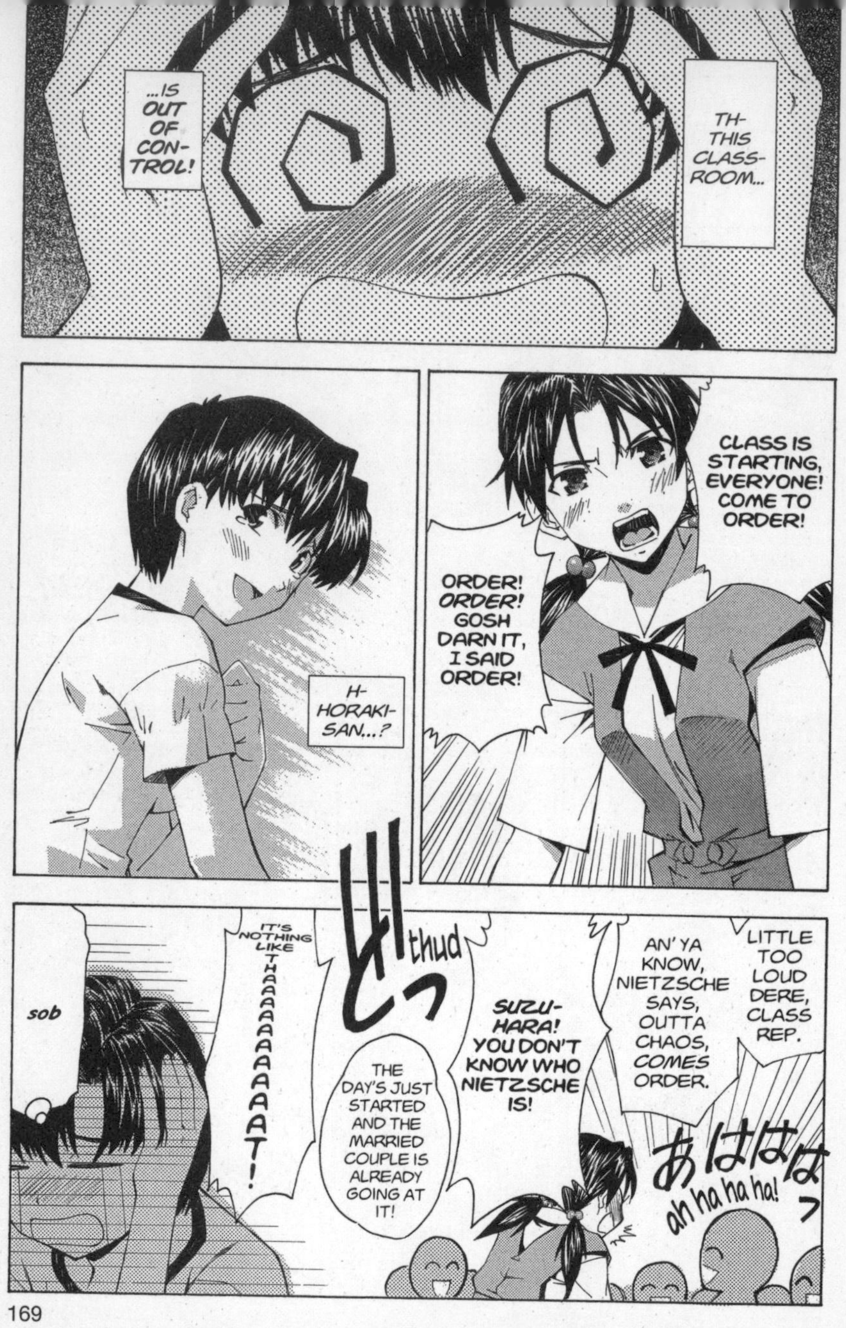
TH-THIS CLASSROOM...
...IS OUT OF CONTROL!
CLASS IS STARTING, EVERYONE! COME TO ORDER!
ORDER! ORDER! GOSH DARN IT, I SAID ORDER!
H-HORAKI-SAN...?
LITTLE TOO LOUD DERE, CLASS REP.
AN' YA KNOW, NIETZSCHE SAYS, OUTTA CHAOS, COMES ORDER.
SUZUHARA! YOU DON'T KNOW WHO NIETZSCHE IS!
どっ
thud
IT'S NOTHING LIKE THAAAAAAAAAAAAT!
あははは
ah ha ha ha!
THE DAY'S JUST STARTED AND THE MARRIED COUPLE IS ALREADY GOING AT IT!
sob

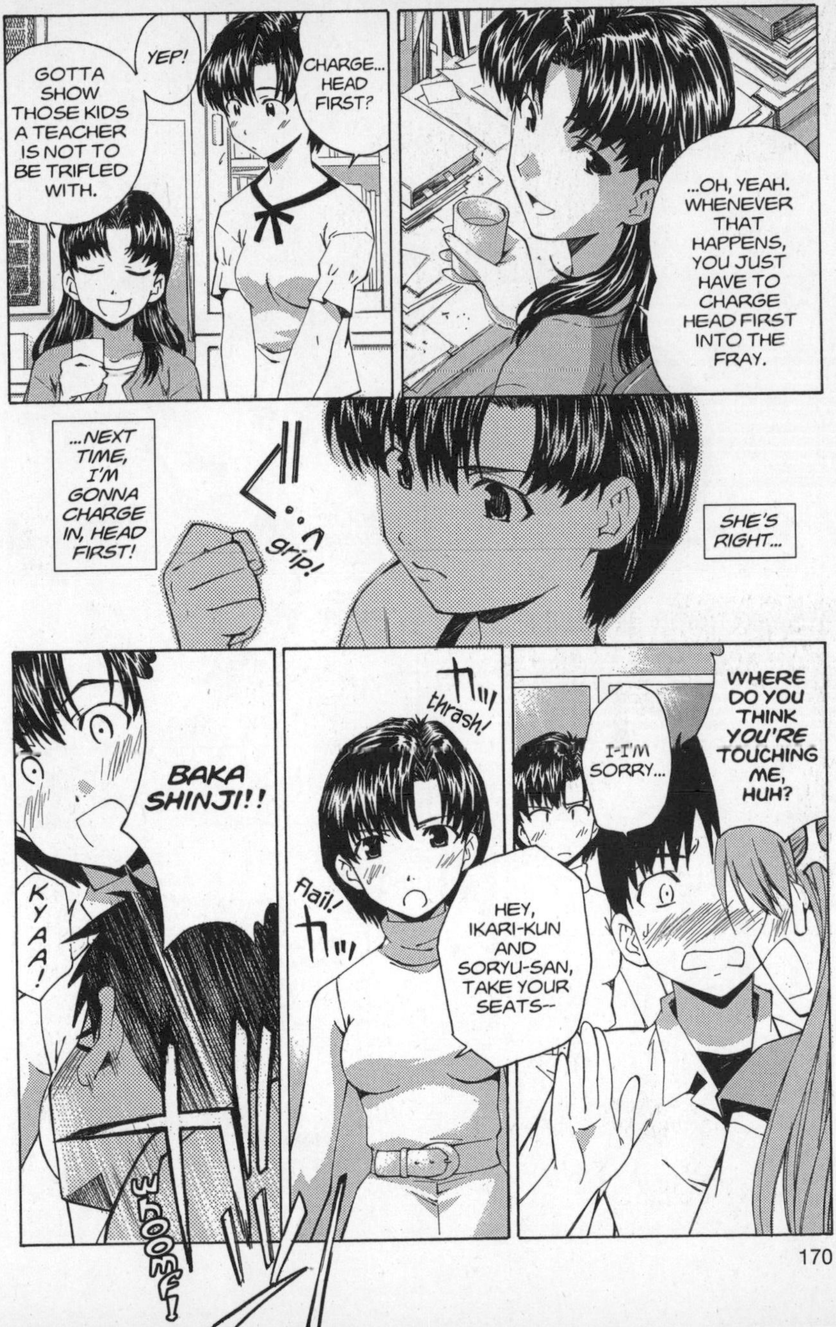
...OH, YEAH. WHENEVER THAT HAPPENS, YOU JUST HAVE TO CHARGE HEAD FIRST INTO THE FRAY.
CHARGE... HEAD FIRST?
YEP!
GOTTA SHOW THOSE KIDS A TEACHER IS NOT TO BE TRIFLED WITH.
SHE'S RIGHT...
grip!
...NEXT TIME, I'M GONNA CHARGE IN, HEAD FIRST!
WHERE DO YOU THINK YOU'RE TOUCHING ME, HUH?
I-I'M SORRY...
thrash!
flail!
HEY, IKARI-KUN AND SORYU-SAN, TAKE YOUR SEATS--
BAKA SHINJI!!
KYAA!
whoomf!

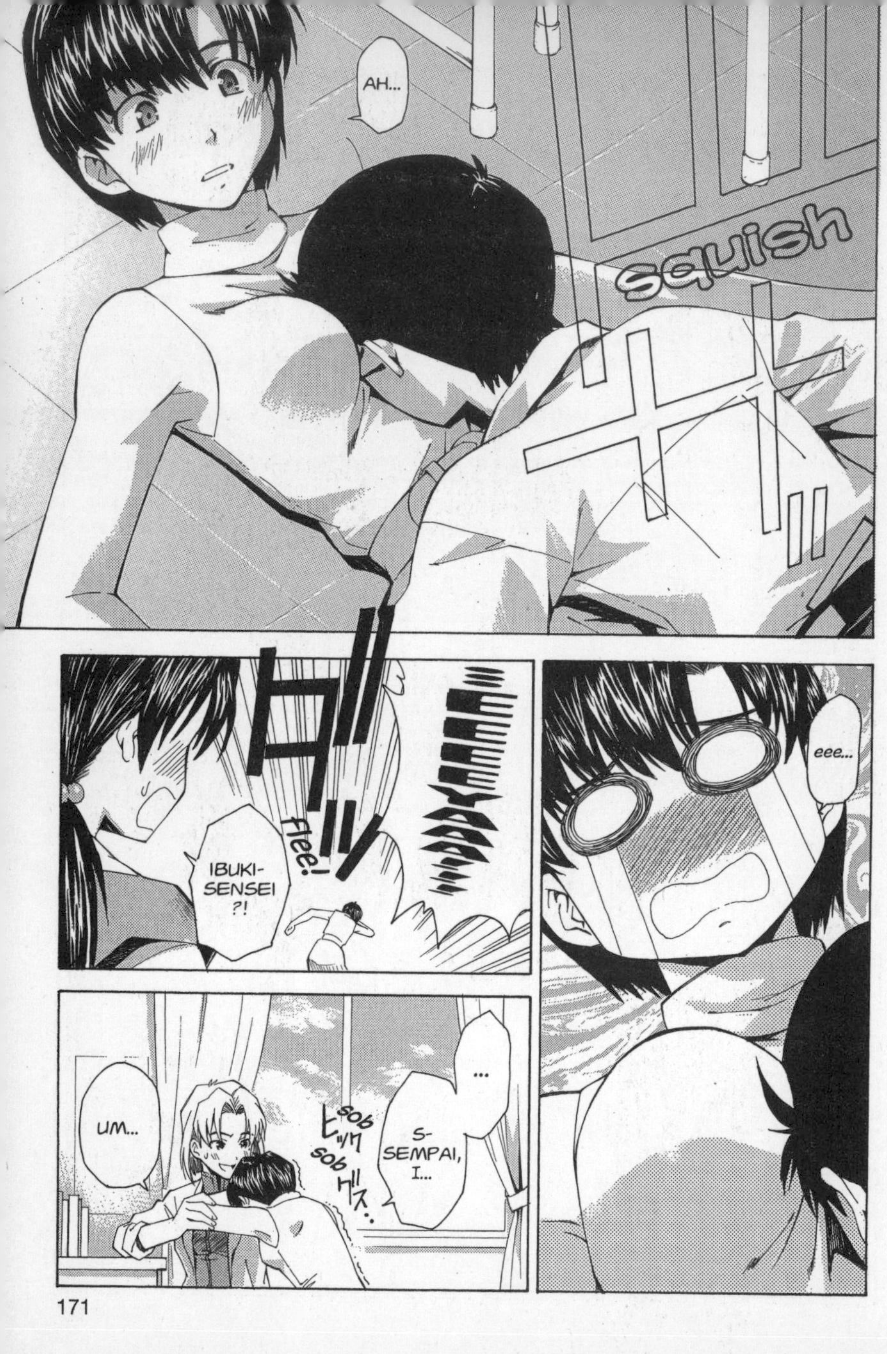
AH...
squish
eee...
IBUKI-SENSEI ?!
flee!
S-SEMPAI, I...
...
sob
sob
UM...

PART TWO: THE MELANCHOLY OF VICE DIRECTOR FUYUTSUKI

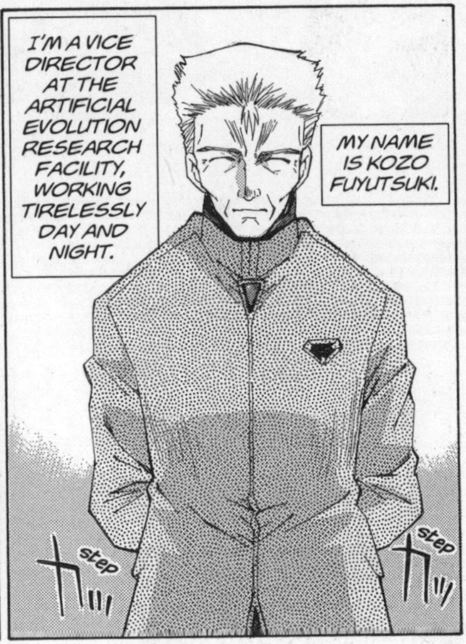
MY NAME IS KOZO FUYUTSUKI.
I'M A VICE DIRECTOR AT THE ARTIFICIAL EVOLUTION RESEARCH FACILITY, WORKING TIRELESSLY DAY AND NIGHT.
step
step

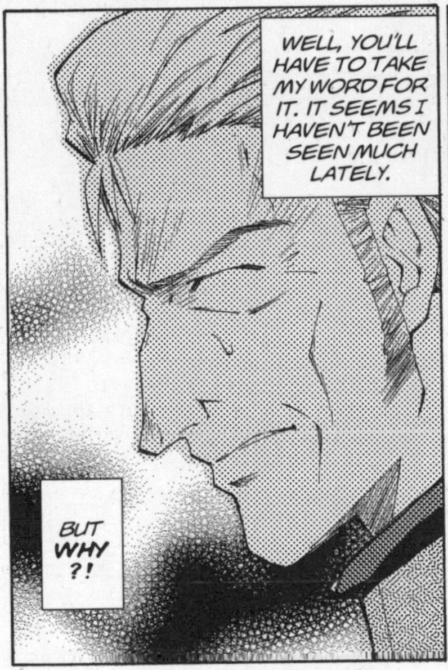
WELL, YOU'LL HAVE TO TAKE MY WORD FOR IT. IT SEEMS I HAVEN'T BEEN SEEN MUCH LATELY.
BUT WHY?!

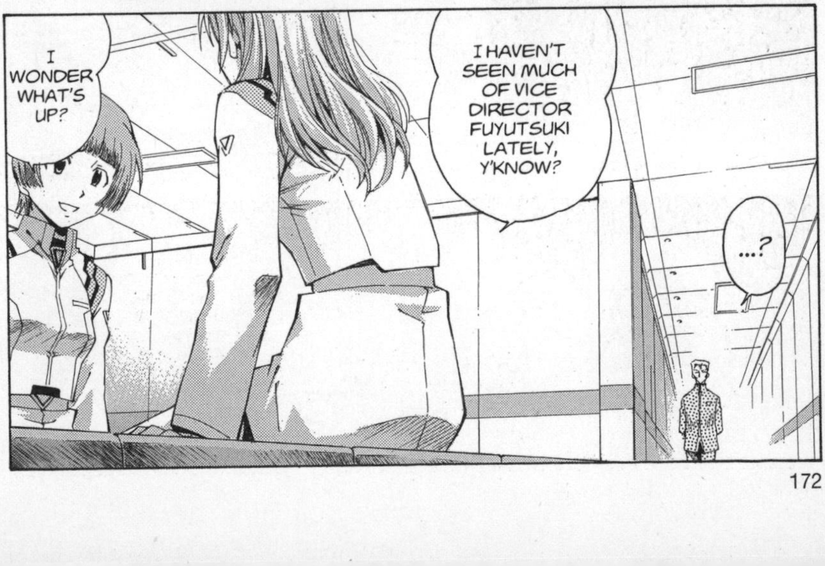
I HAVEN'T SEEN MUCH OF VICE DIRECTOR FUYUTSUKI LATELY, Y'KNOW?
I WONDER WHAT'S UP?
...?

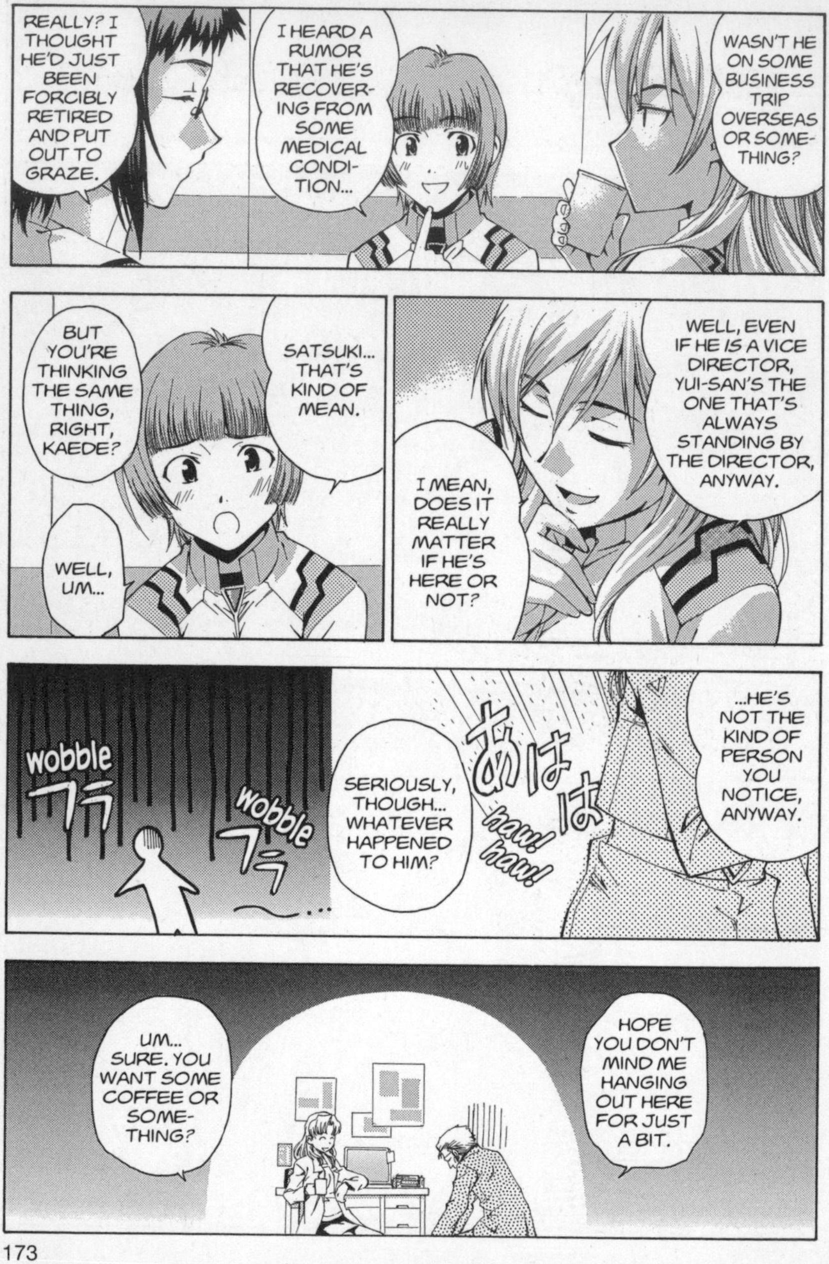
WASN'T HE ON SOME BUSINESS TRIP OVERSEAS OR SOMETHING?
I HEARD A RUMOR THAT HE'S RECOVERING FROM SOME MEDICAL CONDITION...
REALLY? I THOUGHT HE'D JUST BEEN FORCIBLY RETIRED AND PUT OUT TO GRAZE.
WELL, EVEN IF HE *IS* A VICE DIRECTOR, YUI-SAN'S THE ONE THAT'S ALWAYS STANDING BY THE DIRECTOR, ANYWAY.
I MEAN, DOES IT REALLY MATTER IF HE'S HERE OR NOT?
SATSUKI... THAT'S KIND OF MEAN.
BUT YOU'RE THINKING THE SAME THING, RIGHT, KAEDE?
WELL, UM...
...HE'S NOT THE KIND OF PERSON YOU NOTICE, ANYWAY.
あはは
haw! haw!
SERIOUSLY, THOUGH... WHATEVER HAPPENED TO HIM?
wobble
フラ
wobble
フラ
HOPE YOU DON'T MIND ME HANGING OUT HERE FOR JUST A BIT.
UM... SURE. YOU WANT SOME COFFEE OR SOMETHING?

PART THREE: WAIT! WE HAVE ANOTHER APPEARANCE!

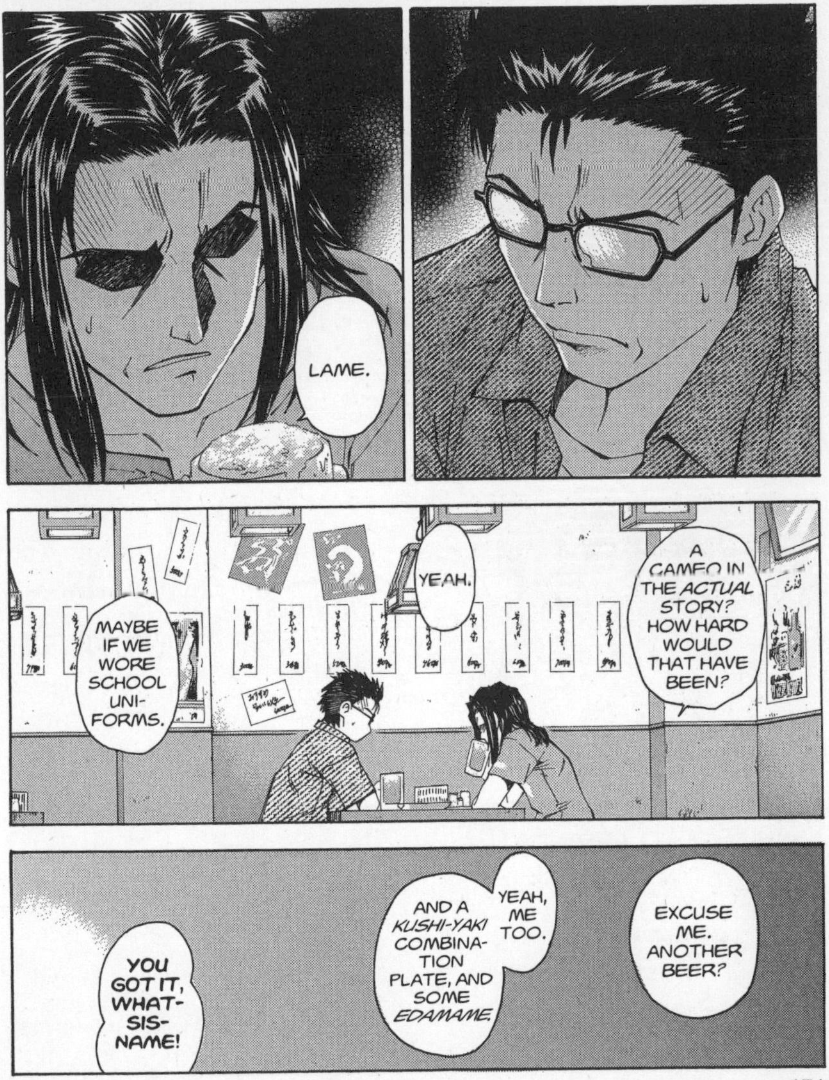
LAME.
A CAMEO IN THE ACTUAL STORY? HOW HARD WOULD THAT HAVE BEEN?
YEAH.
MAYBE IF WE WORE SCHOOL UNIFORMS.
EXCUSE ME. ANOTHER BEER?
YEAH, ME TOO.
AND A KUSHI-YAKI COMBINATION PLATE, AND SOME EDAMAME.
YOU GOT IT, WHATSISNAME!

AFTERWORD

Since this manga began, I've often been asked, either by my assistants or the people I meet, "So...who is your favorite Eva character?"

What a question like this typically means is, "Who's your favorite Eva character—Asuka or Rei?" The truth is, though, when I watched the anime, I liked a character best who doesn't show up much in this manga at all.

That's why I came up with those "special stages" as a bonus at the end of vol. 4, in honor of that particular person. I'm really hoping I can find a way to drum up a proper role for them in the actual story itself . . .

-Osamu Takahashi

~STAFF~
Kasumiryo
Miki
Kanna
Takuji
Yukiko Sasahara

COVER DESIGN
Seki Shindo

See you in vol. 5 . . .

EDITOR
CARL GUSTAV HORN

EDITORIAL ASSISTANT
ANNIE GULLION

DESIGNER
STEPHEN REICHERT

PUBLISHER
MIKE RICHARDSON

English-language version produced by Dark Horse Comics

Neon Genesis Evangelion: The Shinji Ikari Raising Project Vol. 4

Published by
Dark Horse Manga
A division of Dark Horse Comics, Inc.
10956 SE Main Street
Milwaukie, OR 97222

darkhorse.com

To find a comics shop in your area, call the Comic Shop Locator Service toll-free at 1-888-266-4226

First edition: April 2010
ISBN: 978-1-59582-454-7

1 3 5 7 9 10 8 6 4 2
Printed at Worldcolor Press, Inc., Leominster, MA, USA

publisher Mike Richardson • **executive vice president** Neil Hankerson • **chief financial officer** Tom Weddle • **vice
president of publishing** Randy Stradley • **vice president of business development** Michael Martens • **vice president of
marketing, sales, and licensing** Anita Nelson • **vice president of product development** David Scroggy • **vice president
of information technology** Dale LaFountain • **director of purchasing** Darlene Vogel • **general counsel** Ken Lizzi • **editorial
director** Davey Estrada • **senior managing editor** Scott Allie • **senior books editor** Chris Warner • **executive editor** Diana
Schutz • **director of design and production** Cary Grazzini • **art director** Lia Ribacchi • **director of scheduling** Cara Niece

MISATO'S FAN SERVICE CENTER

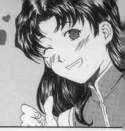

c/o Dark Horse Comics • 10956 SE Main Street • Milwaukie, OR 97222 • evangelion@darkhorse.com

Welcome to the incredible future year 2010! By the way, I see that at 96,000 copies sold, the #1 Blu-ray release of 2009 in Japan was *Evangelion 1.11,* the remix of the previous *Eva 1.0* DVD—which was itself Amazon Japan's top-selling DVD of 2008. Which is great, except that the Blu-ray edition of *Lupin III: The Castle of Cagliostro* only came in at #5 with 11,000. That is, in the words of *Loveline,* "unacceptable."

(I just had to instantly stop at this point and imagine an all-*Evangelion* episode of *Loveline,* where every caller of the evening is a different character seeking help with their particular problems. Adam Corolla must make a return appearance for this occasion. "Uh, yeah . . . first, turn down that SDAT player. Now, uh, 'Shinji.' Here's the deal—" Good times.)

Back on topic—don't those *Eva* fans in Japan know that *Lupin III* is one of Yoshiyuki Sadamoto's favorite anime, and that Fujiko was one of the inspirations for Misato? (Fortunately, only one of them. If Fujiko had been the *only* inspiration for Misato, she would have sold the positron cannon to the highest foreign bidder). And *Lupin III: The Castle of Cagliostro* is anime's greatest pure adventure film—it's really anime's *Raiders of the Lost Ark,* and it's a movie every fan should see. Oh yeah, it was also the first movie ever made by some guy named Hayao Miyazaki.

I know there are some *Eva* fans out there who don't need to be told, because I ran into two at a party this last Anime Weekend Atlanta, one cosplaying as Fujiko, and one crossplaying as Lupin. It turned out Sarah and Zelda were both students from the Savannah College of Art and Design, SCAD, a school that's got a good reputation at Dark Horse; Chris Warner, one of the founding figures of the

company and editor of *Berserk* and *Oldboy* (as well as *Lone Wolf and Cub, Ghost in the Shell,* and many comics that aren't Japanese ^_^), has lectured there.

Well, after I got over tripping about discussing episode 99 of the second *Lupin III* TV series with someone who wasn't even born when it came out (when *Lupin* finally showed on Adult Swim back in 2003, I thought the world had ended. Back in the '80s, I used to dream it would be on TV here. I mean I would *literally* have dreams where I'd wake up in the middle of the night, go downstairs, and it'd be on some late-night TV channel. What an otaku.), the conversation turned, as all conversations with me must, to *Evangelion.* Before long, I was saying, "You've got to write all this up for me as an essay and send this in to Misato's Fan Service Center. Please?" And so—

What *Neon Genesis Evangelion* Means to Me
The Nerdiest Essay You Will Ever Read
By Sarah "Shinji" Myer

I first discovered *Neon Genesis Evangelion* during a trip to Hollywood Video in the decidedly non-anime-friendly town of Shrewsbury, Pennsylvania. Intrigued by the cover art, I rented VHS volumes 1 and 2. I was not expecting to experience the level of drama and tension, the moments of silent introspection, and the intense, psychologically driven violence found within those two hours of the anime that would change my life forever.

At the time, I was a twelve-year-old entering the seventh grade at Hereford Middle School. Not only was I literally the only person in my entire grade who openly liked anime, I was also one of very few nonwhite students in the school and

school district. Having been adopted from South Korea as a very young infant and raised by white American parents, I had always been different in my hometown. For me, being an artist and anime fan was hardly anything unusual when I took into account just how *different* I was to begin with. When I discovered *Evangelion*, I'd been adjusting to the influx of new experiences and social changes which came with middle-school life.

The first night after watching *Eva*, I had a nightmare in which I had to evacuate whilst Sachiel, the third Angel, was invading and destroying my town. I remember feeling terrified but ultimately frustrated because I couldn't get to my Eva unit to counter the attack. Prior to this experience, I'd never seen an anime powerful enough to fuel such a vivid nightmare. Little did I know that my *Eva*-fueled nightmare was a figurative prognosis of that which was to come, a connection made within my mind that my heart had yet to truly understand.

I identified with the character Shinji on many levels. For one, Shinji himself didn't feel he was anything special, though he was forced to live his life within the confines of some very special circumstances. I'd been known as "the artist" amongst my classmates and my family for nearly all my life at that point, and I could identify with the pressures associated with being able to do something that was exclusively associated with one's self. Though this sounds terribly narcissistic, I assure you that it was merely due to the external circumstance of having few other artists in my school. I took great pride in my art (one could say, at times as passionately as Asuka prized her status as Unit 02's pilot) but found it difficult to find value in myself as a person beyond my identity as an artist.

As I met new people and made new friends in school, it became apparent that some of them only associated with me because they wanted me to draw things for them. Others, as I painfully discovered, befriended me so that I could be their "unusual" or "rare" novelty due to my unusual physical appearance (many of the people in my hometown had never actually encountered an Asian person before meeting me). They used my talents for their own means, expected me to drop whatever I was doing at any moment during the school day to draw "something cool" for them, and viewed me only as a tool.

Initially, I turned to *Evangelion* for a dose of escapism as with any entertaining anime or TV show, but when it became excruciatingly clear that Shinji's hard-won and unstable identity as the pilot of Evangelion Unit 01 would not last . . . I knew something had to give, and after episode 16, it did. Maybe it was just good luck that I went through some of the roughest years of my life when my progress in watching the *Evangelion* series took a turn for the more intense.

Shinji's frustration and outbursts (a rather tame way of putting it) regarding his hatred for his identity being purely wrapped up in his pilot status were something I could relate to; thus, I'd begun to feel that I no longer wanted to put up with people treating me unfairly and using me for art, for not valuing me for who I was. I cut ties with those who I believed were not my true friends, and vowed to live a life only for what made me happy. I hurt a few people who didn't deserve it along the way, but I also freed myself from those who would bring me down. At times I was overly selfish with my newfound "code," but I don't regret it one bit in the end. It helped me understand the fine balance between protecting oneself from hurt and pain and harming others inadvertently in exchange.

The last two episodes of *Evangelion* are something that I always believed were clear as day to anyone who would watch them. Imagine my surprise when, while cosplaying Shinji at numerous conventions between 2001 and 2004, I was approached by many other fans who would ask me, "What the hell was up with that weird ending to the *Eva* TV series?"

I'd always felt that Shinji's realization that he could be whatever he wanted to, and did not have to live only by his identity as a pilot, was a message that one can make their life whatever they choose as long as they have the will to work for it and to live by their own values. Whether it be avoidance of pain (a common theme with Misato, who embodied "The Pleasure Principle"), emotional distance (Rei to a degree), or outright rejection of anyone who is not "good enough" to mask deep emotional hurt

(Asuka and Gendo), everyone has a stigma—a challenge—to deal with in life.

On a personal level, the struggles of those characters were so real to me that I began to pity myself a little less and think more about how I could share those amazing anime experiences with others. It sounds nerdy as hell, but it was all out of a pure, unbridled enthusiasm for storytelling drawn by one's own hand! And I realized, upon watching the marker-colored and pencil-drawn animated scenes in the last two *Eva* episodes, that I could not have been more fortunate. I *was* an artist. It was what I loved to do, and had done since I was only four years old. It was this level of awareness that *Eva* brought to me that spurred me to finally and confidently embrace my identity as myself, the artist.

Sure, I'd aspired to be an animator or cartoonist since I was very young, but it was the sheer level of sincerity in *Evangelion* as a story about the human condition that made me *proud* to be an artist. I think that *Evangelion* is what ultimately drove me to take those true steps into my career. Thinking of *Eva* and the message that Anno tried to express to the world through it was what drove me to fill out my application to the Savannah College of Art and Design in early 2004. Shinji's acceptance of emotional pain in order to experience the love of important people in his life one more time during Third Impact strengthened my resolve when I found that quite a few professors and students in the sequential art (comics) department of SCAD hated and misunderstood all anime and manga. There is no sweet without bitter, no light without shadow. If everyone loved what I loved, I wouldn't have much to fight for and my life and passion for drawing would have very little conviction. Devoid of that passion, I would not be me. My identity and self-worth stand side by side with my art and my capacity to welcome others into my heart, and I fully accept that to the core.

I'm a fan of a wide variety of anime, both old and new, but none have remained such a driving force in my life as *Evangelion*. I can wholeheartedly say that *Evangelion* instantly puts my problems into perspective as soon as I'm feeling sorry for myself. I look at what Shinji, Asuka, and Misato have had

to overcome and realize that my problems are easily solvable by doing what I feel is right. When I'm asked by fellow fans, "What was up with *The End of Evangelion*?" I tell them that I think Misato's last words to Shinji in the elevator scene sum it up best. Her admission that she's regretted too much in her life and her subsequent insistence that Shinji make his own decisions and live or die by them without looking back was akin to religion to me. The lyrics to the theme song, "Cruel Angel's Thesis," mention a bible of sorts as an allusion to one's purpose in life.

Regardless of actual religious beliefs, I think that anyone can relate to the idea of living by a set of values only understandable to oneself. No one else can dictate what is best for you, because you are the only person who can truly understand where you've come from and where you need to be. When I was a young teenager and felt down about something, my dad would affectionately call me Shinji and would tell me that I could do it. My nickname amongst my closest friends in high school and college was Shinji. When I graduated from SCAD in 2008 and walked across the stage to accept my diploma in sequential art, I heard a group of voices shout, "*Go Shinji!*" from both my parents' location in the audience and from the sequential art professors' section. That identity will always be within me as a reminder to give everything my best even when things look bleak.

As I go forward into my career as a comic artist (and hopefully as an artist in animation someday), I always try to remember that *Evangelion* essentially saved me from a potentially life-crippling depression. In effect, the sincerity and emotional conviction of *Evangelion* may very well have saved my life. I am now happily working towards my artistic goals, working towards going back to school for my master's degree in Japan. I find myself surrounded by wonderful and supportive friends and parents who understand my passion for creating comics, and I see the positive things in my life more so than the negative.

Because of this, I feel I owe it to myself and to the ones I love to step forward, pilot the Eva because I must, and live my life with sincerity without ever betraying my dreams. I strive to

create something just as sincere through my art, so that I may one day inspire others the way that Anno's *Evangelion* has inspired me. For deep down inside, I will always be the pilot of Evangelion Unit 01, Shinji Ikari.

—Sarah "Shinji" Myer

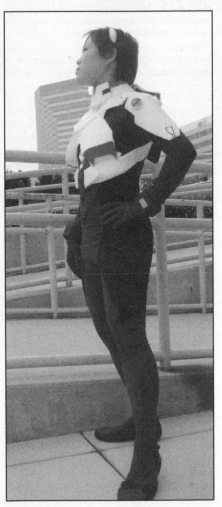

Well, I think this is the best letter we've received so far. There are many ways to look at *Evangelion*, but for me, the simplest and strongest one is what Sarah talks about—the fact of its sincerity, the rare sense that the artists who made it, and particularly Hideaki Anno, were trying to express something personal and real, instead of just making an anime show for the sake of making one, because they've got a season to fill. Warren Ellis recently talked about an interview *Vice* magazine conducted with David Simon, the guy who cowrote HBO's *The Wire* and *Generation Kill*, where Simon said that before they started to write . . .

" . . . we'd discuss what we were trying to say . . . We weren't cynical about having been given ten, twelve, thirteen hours—whatever we had for any season from HBO. All of that was an incredible gift. So godammit, you better have something to say. That sounds really simple, but it's actually a conversation that I don't think happens on a lot of serialized drama. Certainly not on American television. I think that a lot of people believe that our job as TV writers is to get the show up as a franchise, and get as many viewers, as many eyeballs, as we can, and keep them. What we were asking was, 'What should we spend twelve hours of television saying?'"

And I thought, of course, of Hideaki Anno's famous essay, "What Were We Trying to Make Here?" written and published several months before the premiere of *Evangelion* (you can find it in the back of vol. 1 of the original manga by Yoshiyuki Sadamoto, if for some strange reason you don't already have it ^_^). Too many people tried to imitate *Eva* by saying, "Hey, let's make a cryptic and angsty series, too."

But I think what really made *Eva* appeal to so many people (including many people who didn't usually watch anime) was its *sincerity*—it showed how insincere most anime really is, how most of it is just going through the motions, when what anime needs most—what any medium of art needs above all—is a sense of life, of human communication, a sense there was an actual person behind it trying to say something that was important to them. It doesn't have to be something dark—just something real. Why use anime, or any art form, to escape, when you could use it to see and to speak?

A person who speaks just with art alone (because he

sent no letter ^_^) is Isaac LaRussa (cool name—it sounds like someone from *Baccano!*), who sent this drawing of *Evangelion*'s classic pilot trio from Oceanside, California. Thank you very much!

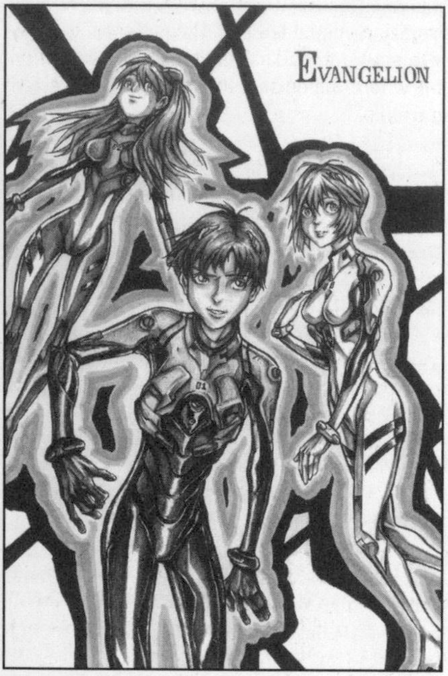
EVANGELION

And once again, Canada comes through for MFSC, with this next letter from Ben Kellett:

I just want to say "thank you" for bringing Neon Genesis Evangelion: The Shinji Ikari Raising Project *to North America. I love the original* Eva *series (and have been inspired to rewatch it after reading volume 1 of this latest manga). It is so different from any other series, mecha or otherwise, anime or not. It has its . . . I like to call them WTF moments (something Gainax is famous for), but it's a good kind of WTF. The psychological drama and tragedy are what make it so special, easily one of the greatest anime of all time (and I know that a lot of people agree).*

However, it's great to be able to read about these characters in a less tragic, more normal circumstance. The last two episodes of Eva *. . . I won't lie; they weren't, for me, as great as the rest of the series. Fortunately,* The End of Evangelion *makes up for it, and serves as a great transition between Shinji's whining and the Human Instrumentality Project, which was lacking in the original series. However, one thing I did enjoy about the final two episodes was the segment where they explored a possible alternate reality, the reality that this manga is based on.*

So once again, thank you for bringing us this manga series to enjoy in English. I eagerly await all future volumes.

On another note, in addition to inspiring me to rewatch the original series, reading this manga also inspired me to do my first piece of Eva *fan art, something that I inexplicably never got around to doing before. I hope you enjoy it as much as I enjoyed creating it. It is a depiction of my favorite character from the series: Rei.*

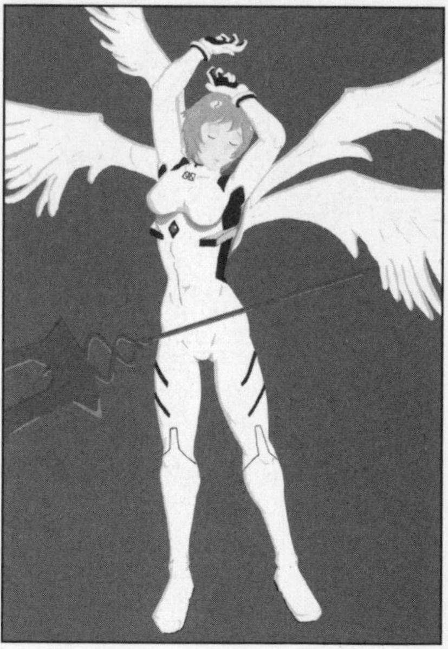

Rei is a popular character, to be sure. ^_^ I personally (as noted below) find the last two episodes of the TV series very interesting, and

think that particular ending is the more important one if you look at *Evangelion* from a psychological perspective—since it's very human in scale, concentrating purely on what the characters think about their experiences and what they've gone through, without the distracting elements of apocalypse seen in the film. ^_^

Sarah, Isaac, and Ben are our winners for this volume, and will each receive the Mari Makinami figurines featured in vol. 3's MFSC. Yes, yes, you're saying—but what's in it for *me* if I send something in for the *next* volume? We draw back our curtain to present—

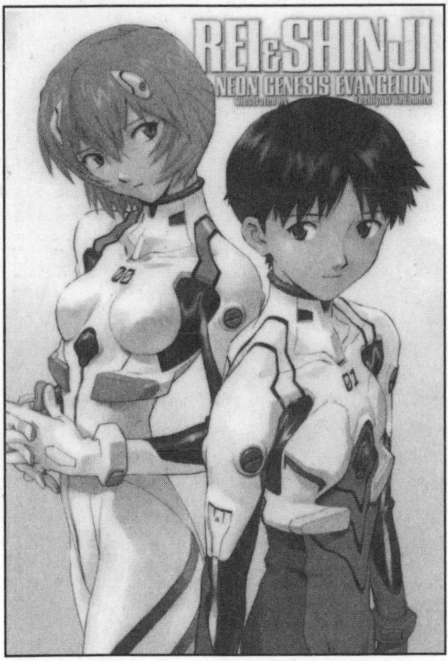
REI & SHINJI
NEON GENESIS EVANGELION

Why, it's Asuka's favorite couple, Rei and Shinji! This *shitajiki* (pencil board, designed so you can lay a sheet of paper over it as you write—does anyone ever actually do that, though?) was done by Yoshiyuki Sadamoto as an exclusive for *Shonen Ace* magazine, the original home of *Evangelion*. But we got three extra, to be given to three people in vol. 5 . . . and if you're reading this, you may get to be that person!

Some comments from the translator, talked over by the editor: on page 1, panel 1, Yui refers to Gendo, as she typically does, as "*anta*," one of the many forms in Japanese of the word "you," and one typically used by someone's spouse or partner. Come to think of it, isn't that the same *anta* as in *anta baka?* I think there's hope for Asuka yet.

Speaking of which, on page 7, panel 4, the term Asuka uses to describe her role in Shinji's life is *kantoku*, which is the same word used to describe a film or TV director. It's used as an honorific the way *sensei* is, so that Hideaki Anno is often described in print or addressed in interviews as "Anno-*kantoku*." Of course, it's also used for such supervisory roles as the coach of a sports team, but it's very meta, and thus, very *Eva*, for Asuka to use such a word here. I'm half expecting her to stand over Shinji as he sits in a folding chair on stage and declare, "But it's a false happiness!"

(Since the last two episodes of *Evangelion* are basically in the form of a stage play, don't you think it'd be an interesting fan project to actually *perform* 25 and 26 together as a stage play? Has anyone done that? I can't have been the only anime fan who was in the drama club in high school. I would have tried to put on some sort of anime play back then, but back then it was all transforming mecha, and as you know, you need a big budget for those.)

On page 9, panel 2, the idea that the staff of NERV—I mean, the Artificial Evolution Laboratory—could just suddenly gallivant off to an island retreat is not *quite* as contrived as it may sound; there's a whole chain of small islands that people take day trips to on ferries, stretching for hundreds of kilometers due south of Sagami Bay, which is near to both Tokyo-3 (on its northwest side) and Tokyo (Tokyo Bay branches off of northeastern Sagami Bay). In real life these islands are under the administration of Tokyo, so it's not illogical that after the regrettable incidents of 2000 (was there a Second Impact in *The Shinji Ikari Raising Project*?) they might have passed to the administration of Tokyo-3. See? Contrived, but not quite as contrived as it may sound.

Page 10, panel 1—that was really more of a "*bam!*" sound, but, you know.

On page 25, panel 4, Asuka said in the original that she had the better *sutairu,* which is the Japanese way of pronouncing "style," and has been adopted into Japanese to mean a person's figure or the build of their body.

On page 33, panel 5, we can see this is a correct calendar for Valentine's Day, 2015, which will be on a Saturday (actually, it will be the same calendar as 2009); note the last day of the week on this particular wall calendar is a Sunday. The fact they're going to school on a Saturday isn't so much the mystery here (this is Japan, where a half day in school on Saturdays is common), as the coy appearance of Unit 02 on the calendar. Yeah, I get that it's the second month of the year . . .

This chapter, of course, deals with Valentine's Day, and the particular way it's observed in Japan. The "obligatory" Meiji chocolate bar (kind of like buying a Hershey's bar for someone in the U.S.) Asuka gets Shinji is what they call *giri-choco* in Japan, "*giri*" meaning something you do out of obligation, not necessarily personal sentiment. But then, as Asuka complains on page 39, in Japan, Valentine's Day is *specifically* for girls giving boys candy (ideally, homemade chocolate). Boys are supposed to reciprocate exactly one month later on March fourteenth, the so-called "White Day," first popularized by Japanese candy companies in the 1970s; this is what Asuka alludes to on page 51. It's supposedly named for the white chocolate they suggest you buy, although, frankly, these days many girls would prefer to receive Abercrombie and Fitch. Their first store in Japan opened just this last December. On page 42, Asuka said in the original Japanese that she'd never have to experience the feelings of *motenai* boys, meaning "not *moteru*"—to be attractive or hot.

Regarding page 91, panel 4, it's always good to mention again that, although in this manga Rei and Shinji are supposed to be distant cousins, Gendo is *not* Rei and Asuka's uncle, nor Yui their auntie— they just call them that sometimes. The translator notes that while he was living in Japan, he did in fact pull two separate twelve-hour shifts out of

the seventy-two total needed for his group to hold down a prime spot for a *hanami,* a cherry blossom viewing party, in Shinjuku-Gyoen park in Tokyo. Such *hanami* are sometimes (especially in comedy manga) seen as a suitable occasion for *bureikou,* meaning that you temporarily drop formal speech and regard for whether someone is considered socially above or below you, and just converse as equals. On page 94, panel 2, the editor thought it was interesting that Shinji addressed Misato as "Misato-san" rather than "Misato-sensei." Perhaps it's because they live together, or the fact he's asking her a semipersonal question? In panel 5, by the way, Misato describes her relationship with Kaji and Ritsuko as *kusare-en,* meaning an undesirable but inseparable relationship.

On page 169, panel 1, Maya (I'm being familiar, here, aren't I? I mean, Ibuki-sensei) calls this situation a *gakkyu houkai,* which the translator calls "another one of those social phenomena that is better left in Japanese. It's a complete breakdown of cohesion in the classroom, when chaos erupts and, aside from disbanding the class, cannot be reversed until the group disperses." The editor points out that this phenomenon is called in America a *normal classroom.*

One last thing! Remember how we mentioned last volume that in August we're going to be starting a new *shojo* Eva manga series, *Evangelion: Campus Apocalypse*? On the next page, you'll see a preview image from *Campus Apocalypse* vol. 1 by the artist, MingMing! "The name's Ikari . . . Shinji Ikari." *Anta baka!* Who said you were allowed to look so cool, Shinji?! See you in vol. 5 . . .

—CGH

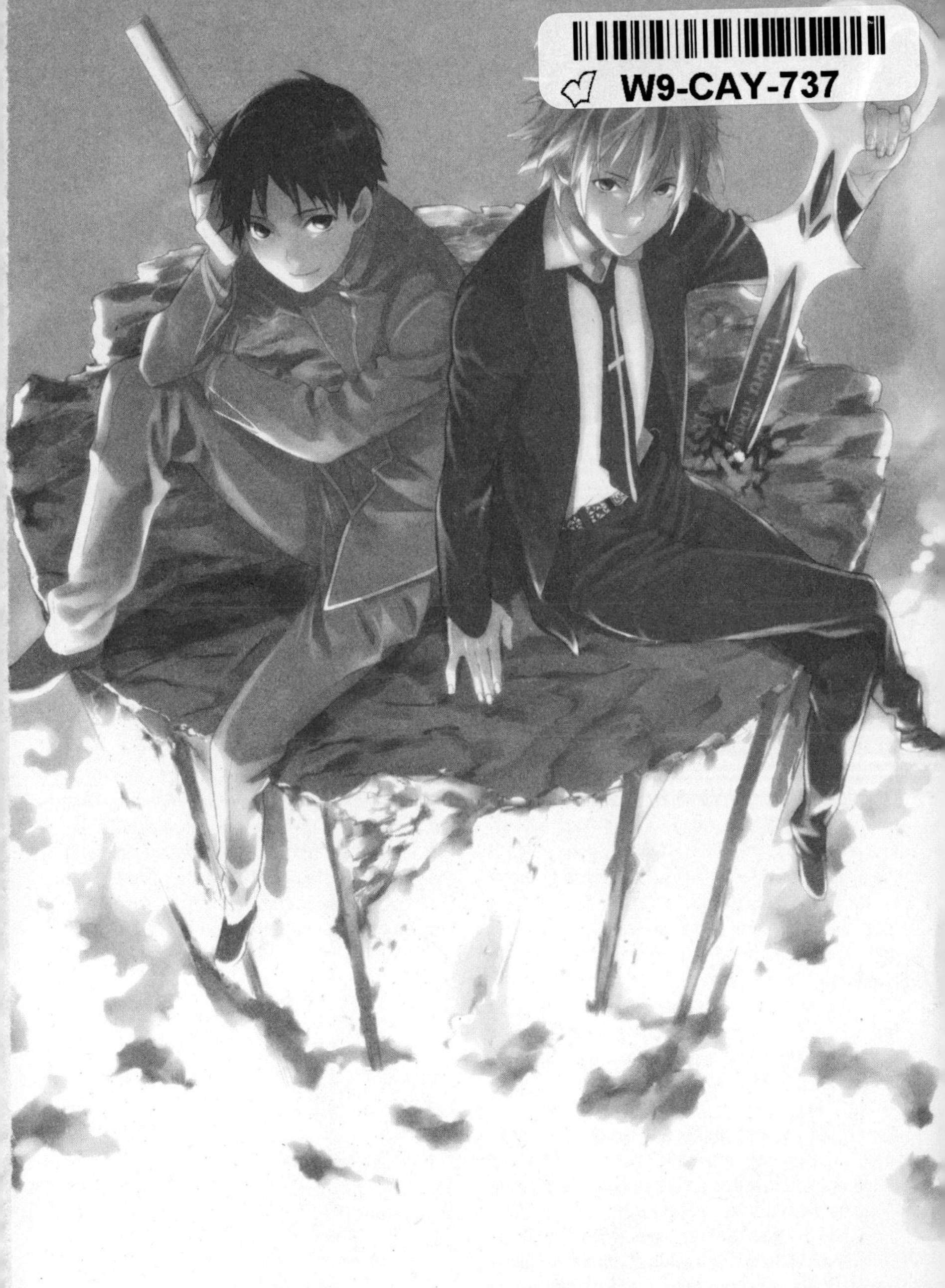